Crossing Aspectual Frontiers

Emergence, Evolution, and Interwoven Semantic Domains in South Conchucos Quechua Discourse

Crossing Aspectual Frontiers

Emergence, Evolution, and Interwoven Semantic
Domains in South Conchucos Quechua Discourse

Daniel J. Hintz

University of California Press
Berkeley • Los Angeles • London

Volume 146

University of California Press, one of the most distinguished university presses in the United States, enriches lives around the world by advancing scholarship in the humanities, social sciences, and natural sciences. Its activities are supported by the UC Press Foundation and philanthropic contributions from individuals and institutions. For more information, visit www.ucpress.edu

University of California Press
Berkeley and Los Angeles, California

University of California Press, Ltd.
London, England

Library of Congress Control Number: 2011929998

ISBN 978-0-520-09885-5 (pbk. : alk. paper)

Manufactured in the United States of America

10 9 8 7 6 5 4 3 2 1

The paper used in this publication meets the minimum requirements of ANSI/NISO Z39.48-1992 (R 1997) (Permanence of Paper).

*To the memory of Mavis
sister, encourager, friend*

Cay pachacta ñócanchic runa caccóna cauçanganchícpac,
tianganchícpac, rurapuárcanchic.

'He made this world so that we human beings could live
and dwell with him.'

—Domingo de Santo Tomás (1560:175)

Contents

PART V – CONCLUSION   273

Tables

Figures

Maps

Acknowledgements

I take great pleasure in recognizing some special people who provided guidance throughout the research and writing process for this book. Marianne Mithun's engaging seminar on tense, aspect, and modality led to the "first emergence" of this research topic. It would be difficult to imagine this undertaking without her exceptional scholarship and contagious enthusiasm. Sandra Thompson inspired confidence in me to articulate ideas as they began to take shape. I thoroughly enjoyed our many conversations on the nature of language and the art of letting the data speak for itself. Bernard Comrie pored over fascinating Quechua data with me and encouraged the investigation of features unique to these languages. W. Randall Garr's insights into aspect in biblical Hebrew helped inform my own research on aspect in Quechua.

Much appreciation goes to Wallace Chafe, Carol Genetti, and Diane Hintz for many animated and congenial discussions. I am also grateful to Willem Adelaar, David Weber, and an anonymous reviewer for insightful feedback on this work. Thanks to Mary Ruth Wise for sharing her editorial skills, and to Larry Hyman and Laura Cerruti for their help in getting this manuscript to press.

For teaching me the beautiful South Conchucos Quechua language, special thanks go to Pedro Carhuapoma, César Cruz, Elías Márquez, Eduardo Mendoza, Tobías Mendoza, Sumer Trujillo, Edilberto Valenzuela, Reida Valenzuela, and the late Niceas Valenzuela. These individuals, along with their families and friends, graciously recorded their speech and helped with the transcriptions. Together with me and other SIL colleagues, they also produced over one hundred titles in their mother tongue, including books of traditional stories, songs, riddles, a health manual, literacy materials, a translation of the novel *Heidi* and a translation of the New Testament. Without taking part in the creation of this body of literature, I could not have begun to grasp the nuances of aspectual meaning described in this book. *Yusulupägi, waugicuna.* For introducing me to Quechua dialectology and the joy of fieldwork, I owe a debt of gratitude to Peter Landerman and David Weber.

The material in this work is based upon research supported by the National Science Foundation under Grant No. BCS-0545334, the University of California, Santa Barbara, and the SIL International Fund for Scholarly Advancement. I also gratefully acknowledge the support and encouragement of many fellow Christians.

Finally, thanks to Marjorie Hintz for her contagious spirit of adventure instilled in me on the wild and wintry North Dakota prairie; to the late John Hintz, a man of integrity, rugged, private, and kind; to Diane for sharing this journey through life and love for Quechua; and to Nate and Joel for embracing life in the Andes.

Abbreviations used in glosses

SOUTH CONCHUCOS QUECHUA

1	*-:/-ni:*	1st person (verbal/nonverbal)
1ᵢ	*-ntsi:/-nintsi:/*	1st/2nd person inclusive (verbal/nonverbal)
	-ntsik/-nintsik	
1OBJ	*-ma:/-ma*	1st person object
2	*-nki*	2nd person verbal
2	*-yki/-ki/-niki*	2nd person nonverbal
2ₚ	*-yki*	2nd person with past
2OBJ	*-shu*	2nd person object
3	*-n/-nin*	3rd person (verbal/nonverbal)
ABL	*-pita*	ablative case
ADV	*-ypa,-pa, -yllapa*	adverbializer
AG	*-q*	agentive nominalizer
ALL	*-man*	allative case
APP	*-chir/-char*	appeal evidential
BEN	*-pa:/-pa/-pu*	benefactive
CAUS	*-tsi*	causative
CAUS.BE	*-tsa*	inchoative
CLASS	*-rikoq*	similitude case, class, kind of
CNJ	*-chi*	conjectural evidential
COM	*-wan*	comitative case
COMPL	*-rpu/-rpa*	completive aspect, downward direction
COND	*-man*	conditional mood
COND1ᵢ	*-shwan*	conditional mood (1st person inclusive, alternate form)
CONT	*-yka:/-yka*	continuous aspect (progressive plus nonprogressive)
DEF	*-kaq*	definite
DES	*-na:/-na*	desiderative, on the verge
DIM.SP	*-:tu*	diminutive from Spanish
DIR	*-m(i)/-mer*	direct evidential
DIR.YET	*-ran*	direct episodic evidential
DISTR.T	*=yan*	distributive, occasions/time (verbal and nonverbal)
DISTR.S	*-paku*	distributive, locations/space (verbal)
DLM	*-lla/-lla:*	delimitative, just, only, courtesy
DS	*-pti*	adverbial, different subject
DUB	*-tsura:*	dubitive evidential
DUR	*-ra:/-ra*	durative aspect
DUR.C	*-rayka:/-rayka*	durative-continuous (stative), habitual (dynamic)
EFFORT	*-chaku*	concerted or persistent effort
EVEN	*-pis/-si*	additive, even, too
FAR	*-mu*	cislocative/translocative, action at a distance/from afar
FUT1	*-sha:*	future, 1st person subject
FUT1ᵢ	*-shun*	future/imperative, 1st/2nd person inclusive subject
FUT1>2	*-shayki*	future, 1st person subject, 2nd person object
FUT3	*-nqa*	future, 3rd person subject
FUT.M	*-pa:*	attaches to future suffixes in conversation, modal function

GEN	*-pa*	genitive
HAVE	*-yoq*	have
HELP	*-:shi*	help, accompany in doing
HUMAN	*-q*	human numeral or quantifier
IMP2	*-y*	imperative, 2nd person
IMP3	*-tsun*	imperative, 3rd person
INCH	*-ya:/-ya*	inchoative, transition of a property to a state, become X
INF	*-y*	infinitive
ITER	*-(y)kacha(:)*	iterative
LIM	*-yaq/-ya:*	limitative case
LOC	*-chu/-cho:*	locative case
MID	*-ku/-ka*	reflexive, middle voice, customary
MID.R	*-kuku*	middle voice, reduplicated form, heightened engagement
MUT	*-cha:*	mutual evidential
NEG	*-tsu*	negative
NEG.APP	*-ra:ku*	dubitive negative with appeal
NEG.EMPH	*-ta:ku*	emphatic negative
NMLZ.I	*-na*	nominalizer, irrealis
NMLZ.R	*-nqa/-sh(q)a*	nominalizer, realis
NMLZ.I1ᵢ	*-na*	nominalizer, irrealis, 1st person inclusive
NOW	*-na*	by now, already
OBJ	*-ta*	accusative case, direct/indirect object
PARTIAL	*-qtu, -tuku*	partial, less than complete, pretend
PASS	*-ka:/-ka*	passive
PFV	*-ski/-ska*	perfective aspect
PFV.F	*-ri:ku/-ri:ka*	perfective, forceful manner, vigorous effort with opposition
PFV.M	*-rku/-rka*	completive-perfective, mutual consent, convergent alignment between stances, upward direction
PFV.O	*-yku/-yka*	completive-perfective, obligation, divergent alignment between stances, inward direction
PL.DIR	*-:ri*	plural verbal with directionals (rare in SCQ)
PL.N	*-kuna*	plural nonverbal
PL.V	*-ya:/-ya*	plural verbal
PL.SP	*-s*	plural nonverbal from Spanish
PRMT	*-q*	purpose complement with motion verb
PRS	*-Ø*	present, habitual
PST	*-ra/-rqa*	past perfective, remote past
PST.H	*-q*	past habitual
PST.N	*-na:*	narrative past, past imperfective in conversation
PST.R	*-ru/-rqu*	past perfective, recent past (from outward), shares paradigm with *-sh/sh(q)a*
PST.R3	*-sh/-sh(q)a*	past perfective, recent past (from perfect), 3rd subject, and 3rd subject > 1st/3rd object
PTCP	*-sh/-sh(q)a*	past participle
PUNC	*-ri/-ra*	punctual, brief duration, limited obligation
PURP	*-pa:*	purposive case
Q.C	*-ta:*	content question
Q.P	*-ku*	polar question (yes/no)
Q.T	*-kush*	tag question

RECP	*-naku*	reciprocal
REDUP	~	reduplicated verb root, e.g., ROOT~ROOT, and compounds
RPT	*-sh(i)*	reportative evidential
SIDE	*-la:*	side
SIM	*-no:/-nuy*	similitude case
SS	*-r*	adverbial, same subject
SURE	*-ri*	surely evidential
TOP	*-qa*	topic
TOTAL	*-ka:ku*	totally, customarily
TYPE	*-la:ya*	type
UNDONE	*-:ni*	avertive participle, left undone
VOC	*-y*	vocative
WARN	*-ta:*	warning, exclamatory
WITH	*-ntin*	with, accompaniment, additive
YET	*-ra:*	yet

OTHER QUECHUAN LANGUAGES AND AYMARA

1	*-ni*	1st person verbal in many non-Central Quechuan languages
1>2	*-yki*	1st person subject, 2nd person object in many non-Central
1OBJ	*-wa*	1st person object in non-Central Quechua
COMP	*imanata*	complementizer in Pastaza Quechua
EMPH	*-táq*	emphatic, contrastive in Cuzco Quechua
IMMINENT	*-sti*	imminent, prospective in Cuzco Quechua
INCH, INGRESSIVE	*-gri*	inchoative, ingressive in Northern Quechua
INCP	*-ka*	incomplete in Aymara
IPFV	*-yka:/-yka*	imperfective in Huamalíes Quechua (cf. CONT in SCQ)
LIM	*-kama*	limitative case in many Quechuan languages
LOC	*-pi*	locative in non-Central Quechua
NOM	*-y*	nominalizer (infinitive) in Pastaza Quechua
NOM.PL	*-shca*	nominalizer, plural in Salasaca Quechua
OUT	*-rqu, -ru*	directional outward in many Quechuan languages
OUT	*-qlu/-q*	eductive (draw out), perfective in Huanca Quechua
PERF	*-shca*	perfect in Salasaca Quechua
PL.V	*-chis*	plural verbal in Cuzco Quechua
PROG	*-chka*	progressive in Ayacucho Quechua
PROG	*-ku/-hu/-u*	progressive in Northern Quechua
PROG	*-sha*	progressive in Cuzco Quechua
PROG	*-ska*	progressive in Aymara (or *-s* + *-ka*)
PRTC	*-du*	participle in Inga Quechua
PST.P	*-sqa*	reportative past or pluperfect in Cuzco Quechua
REFL	*-ri*	reflexive, middle voice in Northern Quechua
REFL	*-s*	reflexive in Aymara
SS	*-shpa*	adverbial, same subject in many Quechuan languages
SUB	*-q*	subordinator in Huallaga Quechua

Abstract

This book presents a comprehensive account of the grammatical expression of aspect and related semantic domains in South Conchucos Quechua, a language of central Peru. Based on a corpus of naturally-occurring speech, the approach applied here integrates the description of the synchronic system in South Conchucos with an investigation of cognitive and communicative forces that have shaped aspect and connected structures across the Quechua language family. Additionally, the South Conchucos aspect system is positioned within a typological framework, supporting certain cross-linguistic tendencies and highlighting properties unique to Quechua.

Discourse-based analysis reveals that aspect in South Conchucos does not constitute a neatly organized system of maximal contrasts. Instead, the aspectual system comprises a network of twenty productive grammatical markers characterized by subtle semantic distinctions and considerable overlap within the perfective and imperfective categories. Aspect in South Conchucos is further enriched by the distribution of individual elements through different areas of morphology. The mode of expression ranges from fully derivational to fully inflectional, with several ambiguous cases in between.

While it is useful to maintain a clear analytic distinction between semantic domains, typically one and the same South Conchucos aspect marker encodes elements of more than one domain. In other words, the aspectual system is not a separately delineated grammatical category. Instead, as in many languages, aspect in South Conchucos is interwoven with tense and with modality. This study also presents a detailed analysis of the less explored grammatical interfaces linking aspect with manner and with middle voice.

Aspect and aspectual interfaces in Quechua provide a particularly rich environment in which to investigate emergent properties of grammar. Even though recurring discourse patterns have crystallized over time into relatively stable linguistic structures, such as aspect markers, their grammatical meanings continue to change. The frequency and distribution of these markers in the South Conchucos corpus suggest trajectories and competing motivations for their ongoing grammaticization, occasionally across semantic domains. In addition, foreign patterns and forms exert an influence (via language contact), and new aspect markers emerge in the form of analytic verbal constructions (via renewal).

Building on cross-linguistic models of the evolution of grammar, this study contributes to the refinement of a methodology that uses synchronic discourse data to study grammatical change. By examining the larger context of constructions in connected speech, complemented by patterns and structures across the language family, we can observe this continually adapting natural language system.

PART I – INTRODUCTION

1 PRELIMINARIES

> I have composed this grammar to help raise awareness of the study of languages,
> so fallen and forgotten; and valued less than conscience, charity or reason
> requires. All the ideas we conceive in Romance languages may be found in the
> [Quechua] Language with the same message in its own words and its own
> elegance.…The primary intent is…to give all the tenses and manners of
> speech…together with the ornate particles…without unduly comparing it to our
> Romance languages, because in some ways theirs is more complete than ours,
> and it is a principal aim of this book to show this.
>
> —Diego González Holguín ([1607] 1842:xii, 5, my translation)

The Jesuit linguist González Holguín entered uncharted linguistic territory in aspiring to
understand "all the tenses and manners of speech" in a radically unfamiliar grammatical system
native to the Andes of South America. Four centuries later, we are still exploring certain vital,
yet enigmatic components of Quechua grammar. According to Parker, for example, the system
of non-final verbal suffixes "constitutes by far the most complex area of Quechua morphology.
[These] systems vary greatly among the modern dialects…and have been relatively poorly
studied" (1969a:136). In a state-of-the-art volume on Andean languages, Adelaar and Muysken
characterize many verbal suffixes as "elusive and difficult to define…often hard to translate"
(2004:231-2). Throughout the Americas, in fact, "the fascination of these languages, so different
from those of Europe, was evident to outsiders early on, but the capacity to appreciate them
could develop only slowly, a development that continues to the present" (Mithun 1999a:2).

In the spirit of discovery and the advancement of linguistic knowledge expressed (above) by
González Holguín, in this work I seek to portray in "its own elegance" the grammatical
expression of aspect through verbal suffixes and analytic constructions in South Conchucos
Quechua (Chapters 1-4). I then explore how the aspectual system is interwoven with related
semantic domains (Chapters 5-8). Finally, I examine South Conchucos and related Quechuan
languages in the light of forces that shape grammatical systems over time (Chapters 9-12).

1.1   Aspect and aspectual interfaces

Most linguists agree that aspect is a semantic domain "based in human cognitive abilities" (Smith 1997:xvii). Essentially, aspect concerns how discourse participants view a situation as a complete entity in time (perfective) or as unfolding over time (imperfective). As such, aspectual categories represent "different ways of viewing the internal temporal constituency" or "temporal contour" of a situation (Comrie 1976:3; Bybee, Perkins, and Pagliuca 1994:317). While aspect reports temporal structure, tense reports temporal location, deictically reckoned in relation to another time (e.g., Comrie 1985:6ff.).

Aspect provides a particularly rich environment in which to investigate a grammatical system in terms of synchrony (what it is like) and diachrony (how it came to be that way). In recent years minority languages have enriched our general theory of aspect, yet vital discoveries have yet to be made through detailed language-specific studies as articulated, for example, by Sasse: "We must now look more deeply into individual languages of different types to see in what way they confirm or modify our picture" (2002:266). A similar appeal for more fine-grained analyses of aspectual systems and their historical development in particular languages is expressed by Binnick (1991:viii, 488), Comrie (1995:1245), Mithun (1998:189; 2004:121), Hooper (2002:308), and many others. In a nutshell:

> ...the aspectual system holds the key to understanding the structure of a language. But aspectual systems are also abstract and notoriously difficult to elucidate. One reason for the difficulty is that the aspectual system of every language tends to be unique at least in some respect, and aspectual systems of genetically unrelated languages are often dramatically different (Li 1991:25).

Quechua in particular, with its wealth of enigmatic forms—many analyzed here as aspect markers—offers an excellent opportunity to deepen our understanding of grammatical systems through the investigation of aspect. I begin by describing the synchronic system in South Conchucos Quechua (henceforth SCQ) using discourse data from original fieldwork, especially spontaneous conversation. Unlike aspect in Romance, Chinese, and many language families, in SCQ there is no clear single perfective marker, nor one clear single imperfective marker. Instead, at least twenty derivational and inflectional aspect markers with more specific meanings subdivide perfective and imperfective semantic space.[1]

---

[1] Semantic distinctions within the domain of aspect can be expressed formally in a language inflectionally, derivationally, and lexically. The lexical expression of aspect is often referred to as *Aktionsart*, that is, aspect-like meanings inherent to certain lexical items (e.g., *wishqa-* 'sneeze' as semelfactive). Since the focus of this study is the grammatical expression of aspect rather than its lexical expression, *Aktionsarten* in that sense will not be discussed further here. Within the Slavic tradition, the term *Aktionsart* has been used more narrowly to refer to

The traditional categories of aspect, tense, and modality are increasingly viewed as a single interwoven grammatical system (e.g., Chung and Timberlake 1985:256; Dahl and Velupillai 2005:266). As in many languages, aspect in SCQ closely interacts with tense and modality. An unusual characteristic of SCQ is the interface linking aspect with other semantic domains, including manner and middle voice. In other words, one grammatical marker may combine aspect and tense in its semantics, another aspect and modality, or aspect and manner, and so forth. As Lyons observes:

> Indeed, it is no exaggeration to say that there is probably no tense, mood or aspect in any language whose sole semantic function is the one that is implied by the name that is conventionally given to it in grammars of the language (1977:682).

In a recent study based on English, Ziegeler (2006:1) affirms the foundational work on aspect presented by Vendler (1967), Comrie (1976), Dowty (1979), Vlach (1981), Dahl (1985), Binnick (1991), Heine (1993), Verkuyl (1993), Bybee et al. (1994), Smith (1997), and many others. At the same time, she observes in the literature on aspectology a significant lack of integration with other areas of grammar. She highlights aspect as a "core conceptual category," arguing that:

> ...verbal aspect is not a category that can be considered in isolation; that its interlocking role in the development of other grammatical categories is of prime importance and helps to provide a deeper understanding of the ways in which speakers build grammar (2006:2).

Many of the empirical findings presented in this investigation of Quechua align with this "grammar-building" view of aspect. Quechuan languages offer a panoramic window through which to view the role of aspect in the development of tense and modality, as well as the relatively unexplored grammatical interfaces linking aspect with manner and with middle voice.

This work also contributes to a body of research that explores how aspectual systems take shape over time. The frequency and distribution of aspect suffixes in SCQ discourse suggest trajectories and motivations for sequences or "pathways" of grammatical development. Aspectual auxiliaries and particles in the earliest stages of development provide evidence for the source material from which aspect suffixes would have emerged and begun their journey along these paths.

---

aspectual distinctions expressed through derivational morphology in lexical items. For SCQ it would not be helpful to distinguish the categories of *"Aktionsart"* in this sense from "aspect" because there is no clear-cut boundary between derivational and inflectional morphology. (A formal analysis is presented in Appendix B.)

In sum, my principal aim is to present a unified discourse-based account of the grammatical expression of aspect in SCQ in terms of synchrony and diachrony, together with its various interfaces with tense, modality, manner, and middle voice. This innovative approach to the study of aspect will enhance the linguistic understanding of Quechua grammar, especially the "elusive and difficult to define" verbal suffixes. More broadly, this study situates the SCQ aspect system within a typological framework, building on cross-linguistic models of the evolution of grammar and contributing to the refinement of a methodology that uses synchronic discourse data to study grammatical change. In the process, I hope to deepen and expand our understanding of the emergent properties of grammatical systems and the cognitive and communicative forces that shape them.

1.2   The study of aspect in Quechua

1.2.1   Previous work

Grammarians in the Quechuanist tradition have produced an impressive array of grammars, dictionaries, monographs, edited volumes, and articles on a wide variety of linguistic topics. The new findings and proposals presented in this work are largely nurtured and developed on the foundation of this substantial body of literature on Quechuan languages. Important observations have been made on individual aspect suffixes, and some studies describe aspectual contrasts. At the same time, I am not aware of a comprehensive discourse-based analysis of the elaboration of aspect as a grammatical system in Quechua.

Most individual grammars illustrate a progressive suffix for the Quechua language under consideration (see §10.2). The relevant form is referred to by various terms, including "progressive," "durative," "continuous," "continuative," or "imperfective." Among the more detailed comments to date are those provided by Adelaar and Muysken who report that "aspect systems are more or less well developed in virtually all Quechua dialects" (2004:231). They refer to various progressive forms and point out that some Central Quechuan varieties have an additional "perfective counterpart." In other words, a single progressive suffix contrasts with a single perfective suffix. When neither of these two markers occurs, "the unmarked forms…have a habitual or general truth value."

While the contrast between the progressive (a subtype of imperfective) and perfective markers is evident, in SCQ the grammatical expression of aspect is much more complex. As detailed in PART II, data from naturally-occurring SCQ speech reveal an aspect system which does not constitute a separate and neatly delineated category of binary oppositions. Instead, a wide assortment of grammatical markers with more specific aspectual meanings cover the range of perfective and imperfective viewpoints.

At this point it may be helpful to summarize ground-breaking works on aspect in Quechua. Adelaar (1977:124) introduces the suffix *-ru* as a perfective and the contrastive suffix *-ya(:)* as a durative in Tarma Quechua. In a subsequent article, Adelaar suggests that the SCQ suffixes *-ski* and *-yka:* may "function within a system similar to that described for Tarma" (1988:39).

In a similar vein, Weber (1989:144ff.) provides a brief section entitled "Aspect" in which he reports: "The most fundamental aspectual distinction in Huallaga Quechua is between *-yku* 'perfective' and *-yka:* 'imperfective'. The second-most fundamental contrast is between *-ri* 'punctual' and *-ra:* 'stative or durative'." The aspect section also provides examples of *-ykacha:* 'iterative' and *-ka:ku* 'complete(ly)'. Outside of the "Aspect" section, Weber discusses 'past habitual' and 'perfect tense'.

In a section labeled "Aspect," Cole (1982:147ff.) identifies four aspect markers in Imbabura Quechua (highland Ecuador), including *-shka* 'perfect', *-j* plus *ka-* 'habitual', *-gri* 'ingressive', and *-riya* 'durative'. According to Cole, "there are no perfective or imperfective aspects." Presumably, this means there is no single general perfective nor imperfective marker, given that habitual and durative would be subtypes of imperfective, as is the progressive-continuous suffix *-ju* illustrated in another section of this work (1982:183).

In an innovative study in Pastaza Quechua (lowland Ecuador), Nuckolls (1996) explores the idea of aspect as grammatically encoded sound symbolism, that is, the productive use of ideophones (onomatopoeic words) to express aspectual notions. This approach is thought-provoking and richly illustrated for Pastaza Quechua. Conversely, sound symbolism in SCQ and neighboring highland Quechuan varieties plays a relatively minor role, similar to English. Ideophones are expressed lexically and have not given rise to grammatical markers.

In addition to these pioneering studies of "aspectual systems" in Quechua, there are also a small number of helpful studies of individual aspect markers. Muysken (1977:107) shows how the suffix *-gri* 'inchoative' derives historically from an auxiliary verb construction in Ecuadorian Quechua. Stewart (1984) proposes that the suffix *-ski* marks perfective aspect in Conchucos. Weber (1987b) analyzes the use of nominal versus verbal person markers with the past markers descended from **-rqa* and **-rqu*. Adelaar (1988) discusses the range of aspectual meanings of *-ru* 'perfective' in Tarma. Landerman (1991:262) compares the 'durative' forms *-ku* in Northern, *-yka* in North Peruvian, *-yka:* in Central, and *-chka* in Southern. Hintz (1992) traces the development of **-rqu* 'out' from aspect to tense in several Central Quechuan varieties, including Corongo and SCQ.[2] Calvo (1993:111ff.) illustrates derivational suffixes in Cuzco. Benson (1996) examines functions of *-ski* and *-yku* in Huamalíes. Floyd (1996) suggests cognitive motivations for extended meanings of former directional suffixes in Huanca. Cerrón-Palomino (2003:145ff.) offers a reconstruction of the Central Quechua progressive **-yka:*. Hintz (2005a; 2005b; 2006a; 2007) examines a variety of perfective and imperfective markers in SCQ. Adelaar (2006) takes a closer look at functional and semantic splits involving former directional suffixes in Tarma.[3]

---

[2] "Hintz" refers to Daniel J. Hintz in this work, contrasting with references to "Diane Hintz."

[3] In keeping with the provisional nature of the treatment of aspect in previous studies, Quechua is not included in most cross-linguistic surveys of aspect (e.g., Comrie 1976, Bybee 1985, Chung and Timberlake 1985, Bybee et al. 1994, Smith 1997). Dahl (1985) includes a variety of Southern Quechua in a questionnaire sample, but only two aspect markers are mentioned in that

1.2.2   Challenges

Binnick compares the study of aspect to "a dark and savage forest full of 'obstacles, pitfalls, and mazes which have trapped most of those who have ventured into this much explored but poorly mapped territory'" (1991:135; inner quote from Macaulay 1978:416ff.). In keeping with this characterization, the study of aspect in Quechuan languages presents a number of challenges as well. Many treatments of Quechua verbal morphology principally depend on elicited monologic data, and do not have access to an extensive corpus of spontaneous everyday speech. Embodied conversational interactions, such as those in the SCQ corpus described in the next section, provide much richer contexts in which to analyze the semantic functions of the relevant markers.

Another issue is the fact that synchronic analyses typically are not well informed by the diachronic dimension. Individual aspect forms have been reconstructed to an earlier stage in the language with varying degrees of success, but the development over time of the aspectual system as a whole has not been previously considered. An understanding of past and ongoing developments can help to explain the patterns and idiosyncrasies of the modern system (Mithun 2000:273).

Perhaps more significantly, advances in the study of aspect in Quechua have been hampered by the inherent complexity of the total system. Aspect in Quechua features a highly elaborated derivational component, combined with inflectional and periphrastic elements. As noted above, the system is further complicated in that one and the same aspect marker may combine tense, modality, or manner in its semantics. No wonder Parker and others consider the analysis of non-final verbal suffixes so problematic.[4]

The need for a thorough investigation of aspect in Quechua is reflected in Adelaar's assessment of the current state of affairs: "Grammatical descriptions of Quechua dialects tend to be frugal in their specification of the functions and meanings of non-final verbal suffixes" (2006:125). Floyd's candid appraisal is especially revealing: "The directional suffixes…also have aspectual meanings whose precise senses are still under investigation. Therefore for the present time I have chosen simply to gloss them as ASP without further distinguishing their semantics" (1999:10). The thought of many Quechuanists is typified in a question posed by

---

study—progressive and perfect. Hopefully, the analysis of aspectual distinctions in Quechua presented in this work will contribute to our understanding of the "considerable variation as to the extent to which derivational aspect is elaborated and used in languages" (Dahl and Velupillai 2005:266).

[4] The system of non-final verbal suffixes has been described as "the most complex area of Quechua morphology" (Parker 1969a:136), "a linguistic puzzle" (Stewart 1984:98), "elusive" (Adelaar 1988:17), "extremely difficult to define" (Landerman 1991:60), "difficult to translate… difficult to arrive at a general definition" (Cerrón-Palomino 2003:281-2, my translation), "elusive and difficult to define … often hard to translate" (Adelaar and Muysken 2004:231-2), and "the richest and most elusive part" (Adelaar 2006:124).

Benson: "Is [aspect] purely a matter of stylistic variation or is there some pattern yet to be discovered?" (1996:24).

Each of the aforementioned studies furthers our knowledge of aspect in Quechua. At the same time, taken as a whole, they demonstrate that much more remains to be discovered. Quechuanists have long called for the comprehensive investigation of aspect as a grammatical system, and it is such an endeavor that I carry out in this book.

1.3   Data resources

1.3.1   The corpus of South Conchucos Quechua speech

The analyses presented here are based primarily on everyday SCQ speech. Naturally-occurring conversation offers an ideal environment for examining the semantics and extended meanings of aspect markers within the contexts in which they are used. Because much language change occurs in the context of spontaneous connected speech, these data also provide a fertile environment for investigating the kinds of grammatical constructions from which the aspect suffixes would have emerged over time.

These data, together with additional oral material, were collected during fieldwork conducted in the South Conchucos region of central Peru between 1987 and 2006. The data were recorded and transcribed by Diane Hintz, myself, and language consultants. When conducting the field research, most of the time I interacted using SCQ with native speakers in their home communities. Interviews were occasionally conducted in both SCQ and Spanish to allow for cross-checking.

The corpus of transcribed SCQ data consists of approximately 9,600 clauses in over five hours (317 minutes) of recordings. It includes 37 speakers between the ages of 13 and 75 (pseudonyms are used throughout this work). MonoConc Pro, a concordance program by Athelstan, has proven to be a useful tool for general navigation and data searches. This software tool especially simplified the comparison of large numbers of examples of a given form or pattern within the larger contexts in which they occur. The SCQ corpus is made up of the following texts:

- 5 conversations
- 11 folktales
- 2 epic legendary narratives
- 7 speeches
- 5 first person narratives of events personally experienced
- 1 third person account of situations believed to be true
- 9 prayers
- 5 interviews
- 6 "Frog" stories
- 5 "Pear" stories
- 2 songs
- 2 riddles

1.3.2   The coded data

32 minutes of conversations and 26 minutes of narratives were selected from the full corpus of transcribed speech to code for a variety of linguistic factors in Microsoft Access. This relational database currently includes 1,452 analyzed verbs. I used the query component to test quantitative hypotheses, resulting in a more fine-grained analysis of aspect markers in SCQ than would have been possible through qualitative methods alone. For example, the tool enabled me to answer questions such as: What percentage of verbs carry each type of aspect suffix? Is the semantic class of the verb root a factor? Which suffixes frequently co-occur in the same verb? What is the correlation between overt aspect suffixes and grammatical zero in the inflectional tense-aspect-mood position?

Throughout this work I refer to this subset of the overall corpus as "the coded data." This data set consists of multiple linked tables. Diane Hintz coded information related to clauses and noun phrases, and I coded verb-level information. Each verb is parsed into a verb root plus a sequence of suffixes and enclitics. Detailed information is specified for the individual morphemes of these polysynthetic verbs. For example, the verb root is categorized by semantic class, etymology, and types of arguments. The verb root may appear with a combination of derivational suffixes that mark aspectual distinctions, voice and valence changes, directional movement, and many other relations. I also coded each verb for person, number, tense, aspect, mood, and grammatical zero, as well as evidential markers, negation, deverbal elements, reduplication, and other factors.

1.3.3   On naturally-occurring speech

As noted above, one reason why aspect in Quechua has not been thoroughly investigated before may have to do with the nature of the data upon which prior studies are based. For example, when presented with a maximally contrastive elicited paradigm, e.g., *rura-n* 'he does' versus *rura-rku-n* 'he does', even the most sophisticated native speaker tends to respond that *-rku* adds "forcefulness" (Swisshelm 1974:495), "special importance" (Parker 1976:126), or simply "upward direction" (Hintz 2000:193). These generic responses may then appear in the grammatical description for *-rku* along with the caveat that the form is "difficult to define." Elicited or written folktales and dramatized conversational scenarios have not fared much better at illuminating the semantics of verbal suffixes which have puzzled linguists for centuries.

In contrast, the contextual cues inherent in colloquial conversation enable us to identify more robust meanings for each aspect marker. In the case of *-rku*, naturally-occurring SCQ speech allows us to specify the aspectual meaning as ranging from completive to perfective (§2.1.2) and the modal sense as an expected outcome realized by mutual consent (§6.2).

In a study of Quechua epistemology, Nuckolls echoes the value and necessity of analyses based on everyday speech:

> What is particularly needed are data which go beyond mythic and legendary genres,
> and include a variety of speech types from everyday contexts (1993:253).

Accordingly, the primary data for this investigation of aspect consist of the spontaneous speech component of the SCQ corpus. Embedded genres arise naturally in conversations among family members in daily interaction, including narratives of personal experience, historical accounts, exhortations, conflict resolution, evening retelling of folktales and legends, and a host of other genres. Conversational participants accommodate their speech to the individuals involved. In order to ensure naturalness, I was not present during the recordings of conversations, and the segments selected for transcription typically occur hours into the recording.[5]

Secondary discourse data in the SCQ corpus include more formal registers of oral communication, such as speeches at community and family events. The corpus also includes two specialized types of elicited narratives. "Frog" stories are based on the wordless picture book *Frog, where are you?* (Mayer 1969). This technique was utilized by Berman and Slobin (1994) for a cross-linguistic study of ways that speakers relate events in narrative. "Pear" stories (Chafe 1980) are based on a wordless video which can be viewed online at www.linguistics.ucsb.edu/ faculty/chafe/pearfilm.htm.

Additional resources for this work include descriptions of various Quechuan languages, ranging from brief grammatical sketches to monographs on particular varieties. Most are from the modern era, but I also cite relevant data from the Spanish colonial era, especially Santo Tomás ([1560] 1995) and González Holguín ([1607] 1842). No colonial document represents an early version of SCQ, as far as I am aware.

1.4   The Quechua language family

The Quechua language family is native to western South America. These languages were "extended and fragmented long before the establishment of the Inca Empire" (Torero 1964:477). According to the Ethnologue (Lewis 2009), 44 varieties of Quechua are currently spoken by nearly 10 million people throughout much of the Andean highlands as well as some Amazonian lowlands. Map 1.1 (overleaf) is adapted from Landerman (1991:37).

---

[5] Transcriptions from two spontaneous conversations in the coded data section of the SCQ corpus appear in Appendix F with interlinear glosses and free translations. The sound recordings are available at www.ucpress.edu/9780520098855. Additional transcriptions from the coded data appear as appendix material in Diane Hintz (2007b:292ff.).

Map 1.1 FOUR QUECHUA DIALECT AREAS

Popular myth holds that Quechua originated in Cuzco, the capital of the Inca empire in southern Peru. In part, this notion stems from Quechua classification as understood during the Spanish colonial era. Two varieties were assumed: *"The Language of the Inca"* (the Southern Quechua lingua franca also known as "Lengua General") and *"Chinchaysuyo."*[6] The colonial linguist Huerta, for example, affirms:

------

[6] Mannheim considers Lengua General "the language of the people who were indigenous to the region of the Inka capital, Cuzco, the language of the ruling elite, and a lingua franca (or *lengua general)"* (1991:33). More recently, Durston (2004:150ff.) argues that Lengua General

> The Quechua language... is divided into two types of speech. The first is very polished and elegant, and is called "the language of the Inca." This language is spoken in Cuzco, Charcas, and other parts of the upper [southern] region known as Incasuyo. In contrast, the other language is called "Chinchaysuyo." This language is corrupt and is not spoken with the polish and elegance with which the Incas speak. ... The Inca language is spoken from Huamanga upward [i.e., southward], while the Chinchaysuyo language is spoken from there downward [i.e., northward] as far as Quito ([1616] 1993:18).

Based on data available in modern times, Torero (1964:446, 477) locates the Quechua homeland along the coast and mountains of central Peru. By far the greatest linguistic diversity is found in this region, with twenty distinct modern varieties, including SCQ. Torero proposes the term "Quechua I" for most of these languages.[7] "Quechua II" encompasses all other varieties extending north and south of the original Quechua I homeland. The dark gray (or red) area in Map 1.1 corresponds to Quechua I, an area roughly 1/5 the size of California (twice the size of Switzerland). The larger light gray (or blue) areas correspond to Quechua II. The distance between Inga Quechua (Colombia) and Santiago del Estero Quechua (Argentina) is approximately 2,160 miles (3,476 kilometers), nearly the distance from Los Angeles to Washington, DC.[8]

Landerman argues convincingly that a strictly genetic classification may be beyond reach given currently available data. He proposes an alternate four-fold classification of Quechua dialects "on the basis of their geographic distribution and certain typological features" (1991:36ff.). I find Landerman's use of mnemonic labels convenient and employ the four terms listed in Table 1.1 throughout the present work. These terms correspond to the four geographic areas in Map 1.1 (and to the Index of Quechuan languages on page 342).

---

was an amalgam of Southern Quechuan varieties instituted by Spanish colonial authorities for religious and administrative purposes. See also Torero (2002:54-5).

[7] According to Adelaar, "Quechua I has enough elements in common to be considered a unity, but it is heavily fragmented from a phonological, morphological and lexical point of view. There is certainly no full mutual intelligibility between the different dialects that make up this group" (2006:121).

[8] Parker (1963) independently proposes the terms "Quechua B" and "Quechua A." These terms are essentially equivalent to Torero's "Quechua I" and "Quechua II," respectively.

Table 1.1 *Quechua classification based on geography and typological features*

Northern Quechua: The varieties spoken in Colombia, Ecuador, and in the Peruvian jungle along northern tributaries of the Amazon River

North Peruvian Quechua: The small and widely separated varieties spoken in Lambayeque, Cajamarca, Chachapoyas, and San Martín

Central Quechua: Twenty varieties spoken in central Peru, including SCQ

Southern Quechua: All varieties spoken south of central Peru

The Quechua language family could be further characterized as four regional dialect continua, with diverse linguistic patterns and structures distributed across a vast geographic expanse. It offers us a panoramic view that "has attracted the attention of scholars, and has been welcomed as an auspicious laboratory in which to test old and new hypotheses formulated on the basis of European languages" (Cerrón-Palomino 2003:41, my translation). As noted above, the primary focus of the present work is aspect and aspectual interfaces in SCQ, the Quechuan language introduced in the next section. The SCQ findings are situated within the larger context of the language family throughout this work.

1.5   South Conchucos Quechua

1.5.1   Language and people

SCQ is spoken by some 250,000 people in eastern Ancash and western Huánuco departments in central Peru. The area is bounded on the west by the Cordillera Blanca mountain range and extends northeastward across the Marañón River into the province of Huacaybamba, as shown in the gray (or green) shaded area in Map 1.2 (adapted from Hintz 2000:25).

Quechua is the language of everyday life for people of all ages in South Conchucos. A small percentage of the population are monolingual Quechua speakers. Most adult men and many women can communicate to varying degrees in the local variety of Spanish. I find that internally-motivated grammatical change is very much in evidence in the SCQ aspectual system, whereas contact-induced developments appear to have played a relatively minor role. Replicated grammatical patterns and forms are discussed when relevant and are summarized in §12.2.

Traditional Andean agricultural practices are the norm in these communities which range in elevation from 9,000 to 13,000 feet. Small fields carved from steep, rugged slopes produce potatoes and other tubers, *quinua*, corn, wheat, and beans. Families typically own one or two cows and donkeys, and raise a few pigs, chickens, and guinea pigs, as well as sheep for wool. The community-based production of alpaca wool sold to the national government is a recent innovation.

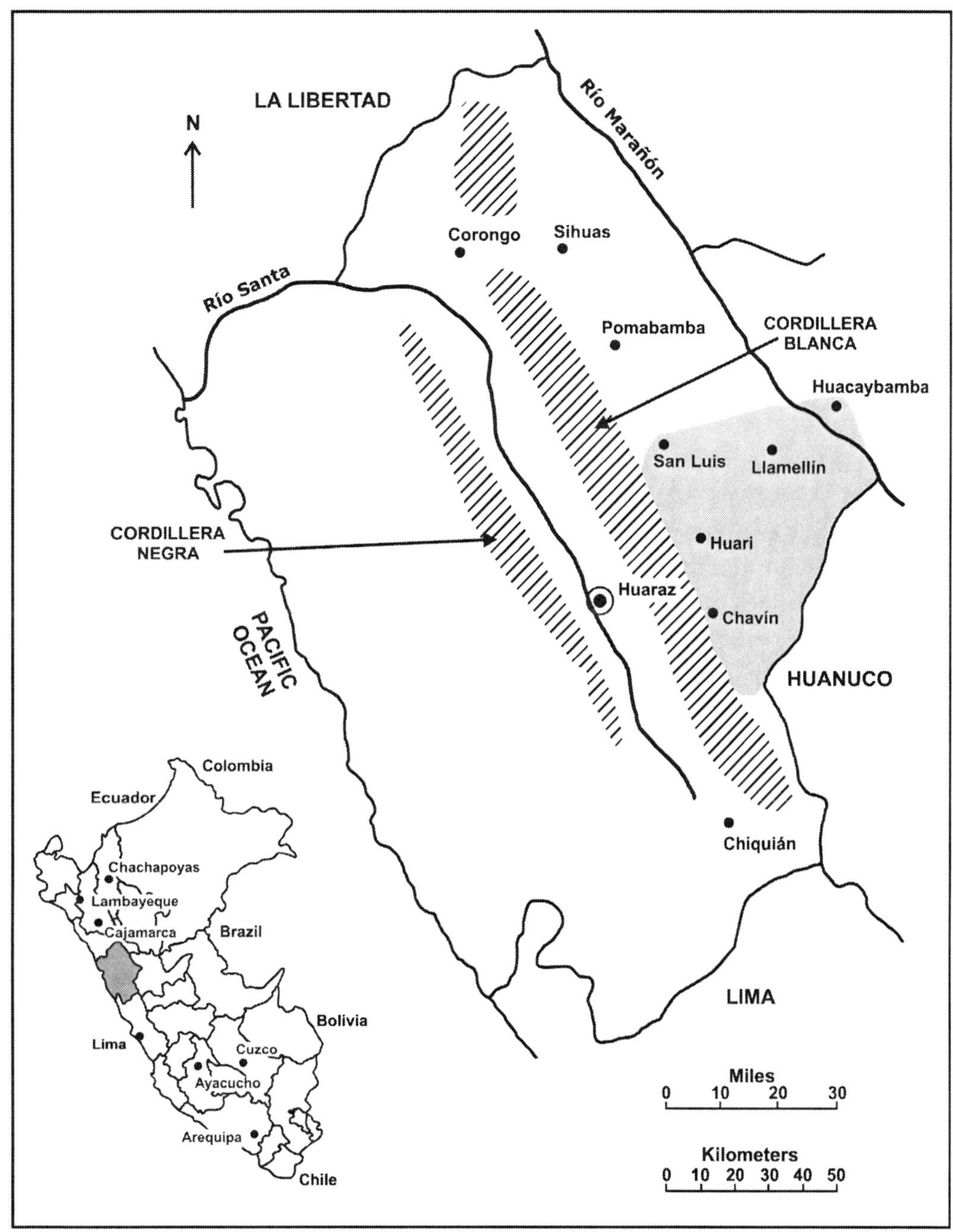

Map 1.2 THE SCQ LANGUAGE AREA

1.5.2   Sketch of verbal morphology

Like other Quechuan languages, SCQ is polysynthetic and agglutinative, non-tonal, and exclusively suffixing. Word order is most frequently SV and OV, with numerous instances of VS and VO motivated by pragmatic factors (Diane Hintz 2003). A nominative-accusative system of grammatical relations is encoded by verbal suffixes and also by case-marked noun phrases, including independent pronouns. The case system distinguishes core arguments and several obliques.

More than 80 productive suffixes appear in SCQ verbs. Normally, a verb must have at least one suffix; marking of the person of the subject is usually obligatory. Subject and tense-aspect or mood are sometimes marked in a single portmanteau suffix, such as *-nqa* 'third person future'. The number of verbal suffixes tends to range from 3 to 6 in a given verb, though 8 to 10 is not uncommon.

Traditionally grammars have organized the discussion of morphology into discrete treatments of inflectional and derivational expression, with an implicit assumption that the distinction is always clear-cut. More recent work, however, such as that by Stephany (1982), Bybee (1985:81ff.), Corbett (1987), Mithun (1999b:41), Haspelmath (2002:71ff.), among others, has demonstrated that at least for many languages, that assumption is unwarranted. Evidence from SCQ suggests that there is instead "a continuum from clear inflection to clear derivation, with ambiguous cases in between" (Haspelmath 1996:47). In other words, certain SCQ aspect markers satisfy some but not all of the traditional criteria for inflectional status. In this work I present such "in between" markers together with the fully derivational markers because they retain some features of derivational expression and do not satisfy certain fundamental criteria for inflection. A formal analysis of the derivational versus inflectional status of SCQ aspect markers, including a fresh approach to the "in between" cases, is presented in Appendix B.[9]

For present purposes, a simplified view of SCQ verb structure is illustrated in Figure 1.1. Suffixes in the DERIVATIONAL position precede the inflectional suffixes. Many Quechua aspect suffixes occur in this non-obligatory position close to the verb root, together with suffixes that perform many other functions, including causative, passive, benefactive, and plural. The INFLECTIONAL positions are obligatory, with the tense-aspect-mood (TAM) marker preceded by the object marker and followed by the subject marker.[10] Optional suffixes and enclitics may

---

[9] The "in between" aspect markers retain derivational features, such as optionality, less regular meaning (some idiosyncrasy), limited applicability, low frequency, relative closeness to the verb root, and openness to further derivation. They lack key inflectional features, such as obligatoriness, and non-occurrence denoting a meaningful zero.

[10] The TAM/DEVERBAL slot is obligatory, with inflectional suffixes in paradigmatic contrast. These include finite TAM markers as well as a set of nonfinite deverbal markers. This verbal position is referred to simply as "the inflectional TAM slot" throughout this work. The formal morphological status of deverbal suffixes is not discussed further. The relevance of deverbal suffixes to the periphrastic expression of aspect is discussed in Chapter 11 and Appendix D.

appear in the INDEPENDENT position, including evidential enclitics and other discourse markers whose scope typically reaches beyond the immediate clause.[11]

Figure 1.1 *General SCQ verb structure*

VERB ROOT	DERIVATIONAL		INFLECTIONAL			INDEPENDENT
			OBJECT	TAM/ DEVERBAL	SUBJECT	

shoqa-	*-ska*	*-tsi*	*-ma*	*-ru*	*-yki*	*-cha:*
comfort	PFV	CAUS	1OBJ	PST.R	2$_\text{P}$	MUT

'You truly made me feel comforted.'

A typical SCQ verb is illustrated in the lower portion of Figure 1.1. The verb root *shoqa-* 'comfort' is followed by one or more suffixes in each position. *-ski* 'perfective' is lowered to *-ska*, a process triggered by *-tsi* 'causative' (see §1.6.2). These two suffixes in the DERIVATIONAL position are followed by the inflectional suffixes *-ma:* 'first person object', *-ru* 'past perfective', and *-yki* 'second person subject (past)'. The final verbal element is the evidential marker *-cha:* 'mutual knowledge'.

The three general verbal suffix positions (DERIVATIONAL, INFLECTIONAL, INDEPENDENT) can be further specified for more detailed internal structure, as shown in Figure 1.2. SET D specifies six derivational positions, SET I specifies four inflectional positions, and SET E specifies two enclitic or independent positions.[12] Suffixes in SLOTS D1-6 appear in a relatively prescribed order, with some exceptions, whereas suffixes in SET I and SET E appear in an invariant order.

---

[11] Grammarians in the Quechuanist tradition use terms such as "independent suffix," "sentential suffix" and "enclitic" for these grammatical morphemes, as noted by Adelaar and Muysken (2004:209). In keeping with conventional terminology, in the present work I refer to this verb-final position as "INDEPENDENT." Both enclitics and suffixes occur in this position in SCQ.

[12] SET E may be properly understood as comprising three INDEPENDENT slots, but I have simplified Figure 1.2 to two slots because the analysis of aspect in SCQ does not depend on a fine-grained account of these markers.

Figure 1.2 *Specific SCQ verbal slots*

VERB ROOT	SLOT SET D						SLOT SET I				SLOT SET E	
	1	2	3	4	5	6	1	2	3	4	1	2

Throughout this work I refer to the individual slots in Figure 1.2. For example, in the verb illustrated in Figure 1.1, the suffix *-ski* [*-ska*] appears in slot D4, *-ma:* in slot I1, *-ru* in slot I2, *-yki* in slot I3, and *-cha:* in slot E2. Most derivational suffixes appear in a fixed slot, but the position of *-tsi* 'causative' varies depending on the other derivational suffixes with which it occurs. A more detailed discussion and chart of the specific positions of 83 suffixes and enclitics in the SCQ verb is provided in Appendix C.

1.6   Conventions

1.6.1   Format

I make extensive use of multi-clause examples from naturally-occurring speech throughout this work. These enriched contexts illustrate the meaning and usage of the relevant aspect marker much better than simply listing the verb in which it occurs. The examples are numbered consecutively throughout this work.[13]

The Quechua data appear in italics with suffixes separated by hyphens. Only proper nouns are capitalized. The relevant morpheme(s), along with the corresponding gloss and translation, are underlined and also appear in boldface type. In the gloss line, lexical roots are not capitalized and suffixes appear in small caps. A list of abbreviations and glosses which follows the Leipzig conventions is located in the front matter.

The Quechua data was initially translated into Spanish, usually with the participation of the original speaker. When the speaker was unavailable, the translation was checked with an SCQ language consultant. Diane Hintz and I then translated the Spanish into English. The intent is to strike a balance between a strictly literal translation, which may sound stilted and make little sense in English, and a somewhat free translation that faithfully renders the sense in Quechua while minimizing the restructuring into English. Occasionally, relevant information from the wider context is included in parentheses.

Throughout the present work, if no language name is specified the example is from SCQ. All examples in PART II are from SCQ. A few examples in PART III are from other Quechuan languages. In those cases the language name appears in small caps on the same line as the

---

[13] As Forsyth observes for the study of aspect in Russian, "the significance of the aspectual opposition only becomes clear in the analysis of whole sentences and ... indeed a much wider context than the sentence is frequently required (1970:357).

example number. PART IV makes extensive use of non-SCQ examples, so the SCQ examples are also labeled explicitly.

1.6.2   Orthography

The native phonemes of SCQ are listed in the first column of Table 1.2. There are seventeen consonants, three short vowels, and three long vowels. Spanish loans introduce four additional consonants /b/, /d/, /g/, and /f/ as well as two vowels /e/ and /o/. Examples in this work follow an orthography used in much of the traditional Quechuanist literature. The second column indicates the five symbols that differ from IPA, including q for the voiced uvular plosive, y for the palatal approximant, and the three digraphs ch, sh, and ll. Some Quechuan languages have preserved the Proto Quechua retroflexed alveopalatal affricate *tʂ. Those examples are represented with the trigraph ch'.

Table 1.2 *Native phonemes of SCQ and orthographic conventions*

IPA CONSONANT	THIS WORK	IPA VOWEL
/p/		/i/
/t/		/i:/
/tʃ/	ch	/a/
/ts/		/a:/
/k/		/u/
/ɢ/	q	/u:/
/s/		
/ʃ/	sh	
/h/		
/m/		
/n/		
/ñ/		
/l/		
/ʎ/	ll	
/r/		
/w/		
/j/	y	

In SCQ, as in most other Quechuan languages, a final high vowel in certain morphemes is realized as a low vowel when followed by one of a small class of "trigger" suffixes, including -*mu* 'cislocative', -*tsi* 'causative', and -*ma:* 'first person object'. For example, punctual -*ri* is realized as -*ra* before the trigger suffix -*mu* (e.g., *rika-ri-n* versus *rika-ra-mu-n*). The trigger suffix need not be adjacent to the affected suffix (e.g., *rika-ri-ya-n* versus *rika-ra-ya:-mu-n*). The convention in this work is to write the lowered vowel.

This morphophonemic lowering process affects many non-final verbal suffixes that end in a high back vowel (*-rpu, -rku, -yku, -ku, -naku, -chaku, -paku, -ka:ku, -ri:ku, -pu*), as well as others that end in a high front vowel (*-ri, -ski*). Some of these suffixes have fused to certain verb roots. The final high vowel in the resulting new lexical form often continues to be susceptible to lowering (e.g., *yayku-n* versus *yayka-tsi-n*), though this trait tends to disappear over time.[14]

The underlying form of many SCQ verb roots and verbal suffixes has a long vowel as the final segment. This includes the suffixes *-ka:, -ma:, -na:, -pa:, -ra:, -rayka:, -ya:, -yka:, and -ykacha:*, and verb roots such as *cha:-* and *tsara:-*. Long vowels are disallowed in closed syllables, resulting in a foreshortened vowel. For example, continuous *-yka:* is realized as *-yka* in closed syllables (e.g., *rika-yka:-mu-n* versus *rika-yka-n*). Foreshortened vowels are frequent in SCQ discourse. The convention in this work is to write a short vowel in closed syllables.

High vowels are lowered to mid vowels due to various phonological processes. A vowel that is invariably pronounced in the mid position (e.g., *noqa* 'I', *reqi-* 'know', etc.) is written as a mid vowel. When lowering occurs due to an attached suffix, however, the high vowel is written. For example, in the southern area of the South Conchucos region (not in the northern area), any suffix that begins with the compensatory lengthening property (e.g., *-:* 'first person') triggers lowering of a preceding high vowel. Thus, /*rika-ku-n*/ is pronounced [*rika-ku-n*], whereas /*rika-ku-:*/ is pronounced [*rika-ko-:*]. Similarly, any suffix that begins with *q* (e.g., *-qa* 'topic') lowers a preceding high vowel. Thus, /*tuku-qa*/ is pronounced [*tuko-qa*]. Because lowering occurs due to an attached suffix in each case, I write the high vowel (e.g., *rika-ku-:, tuku-qa*).

Finally, many SCQ speakers pronounce former *ay* diphthongs as long mid vowel monophthongs in high-frequency lexical items such as *tse:* 'that', *ishke:* 'two', and *e:wa-* 'go'. The convention in this work is to write these as pronounced.

1.7   Organization

1.7.1   Chapters

This book consists of twelve chapters arranged in five parts, plus six appendices. In the present chapter (PART I) I explained the need for a comprehensive discourse-based analysis of the grammatical expression of aspect and aspectual interfaces in Quechua. The corpus of naturally-occurring SCQ speech described here represents an indispensable resource for the realization of this investigation. I also introduced the SCQ language, its verbal morphology, and its place within the Quechua language family.

---

[14] A convention in the traditional Quechuanist literature is to represent a vowel susceptible to morphophonemic lowering with a capital U or I , as in *-ykU* or *-rI*. That convention is not followed in the present work.

In PART II I analyze the grammatical expression of aspect in SCQ. The initial focus is on perfectives in Chapter 2, then imperfectives in Chapter 3, and finally the aspectual system as a whole in Chapter 4. The frequency and distribution of aspect markers in discourse, and recurrent patterns of morpheme combinations provide vital clues for understanding the organization and development of the grammatical system. PART II also serves as a reference grammar of aspect in SCQ.

Typically, a given SCQ aspect marker grammatically encodes elements of more than one semantic domain. Thus, in PART III I examine the interaction of aspect with tense in Chapter 5, modality in Chapter 6, manner in Chapter 7, and middle voice in Chapter 8.

In PART IV I examine the evolution of perfectives in Chapter 9 and the evolution of imperfectives in Chapter 10. In Chapter 11 I illustrate the "first emergence" of aspect markers expressed through developing auxiliaries and particles in SCQ and across the language family. Aspectual systems in Quechua reveal both familiar and unfamiliar patterns of grammatical change. These patterns provide an intriguing scenario for exploring competing forces that shape grammatical systems over time.

In PART V, Chapter 12, I take a bird's-eye view of emergent properties of grammar as illustrated through nineteen distinct mechanisms (fourteen language-internal and five contact-induced) that underlie changes in grammatical structures observed in Quechuan languages. Areal tendencies and a comparison with aspect in Russian are also presented.

1.7.2 Appendices

APPENDIX A provides a set of nine original maps and an inventory of aspectual forms and meanings across the Quechua language family.

APPENDIX B presents an analysis of the formal morphological status of aspect markers in SCQ. The mode of expression ranges from fully derivational to fully inflectional, with cases in between.

APPENDIX C details the relative positions of 83 suffixes and enclitics in the SCQ verb.

APPENDIX D identifies 49 Quechua suffixes with the canonical shape C.CV. Each suffix is analyzed as the historical combination of a deverbal suffix (realized as initial C) plus a second linguistic element (realized as CV).

APPENDIX E presents evidence to support the hypothesis of perfective *-ski* as a former directional suffix.

APPENDIX F presents transcriptions with interlinear glosses and free translations from two spontaneous conversations in the SCQ corpus.

PART II – THE GRAMMATICAL EXPRESSION OF ASPECT IN SOUTH CONCHUCOS QUECHUA

As noted above in §1.1, aspect reports temporal structure while tense reports temporal location. Cross-linguistically, aspectual distinctions are more frequent than tense and "they are often more subtle and complex" (Mithun 1990:62). In Chapters 2-4 I portray the nature of aspect in South Conchucos Quechua (SCQ) using data principally from naturally-occurring speech. At least twenty aspectual distinctions are encoded within the verbal morphology. These grammatical markers constitute a remarkably complex aspectual system with a wide variety of derivational suffixes complemented by inflectional and periphrastic forms.

The derivational and "in between" aspect markers appear in the inner layer of affixation close to the verb root in the non-obligatory slots D1-D4, where D stands for derivation (see §1.5.2). The inflectional aspect markers appear in the outer layer of affixation in obligatory slot I2, adjacent to person markers. In general, obligatory aspectual distinctions (expressed inflectionally) can be further specified by a diverse assortment of optional distinctions (expressed derivationally).

I begin by introducing the individual SCQ aspect markers. Perfective aspect is expressed by nine suffixes with meanings that are more specific than "general perfective." Similarly, imperfective aspect is expressed by eleven markers with meanings more specific than "general imperfective." After characterizing the perfective and imperfective grammatical subsystems in Chapters 2 and 3, respectively, I describe the organization of the aspect system as a whole in Chapter 4. As we will see, this grammatical system is tightly interwoven with tense and modality, and also with the semantic domains of manner and middle voice. Aspect and its interface with each of these semantic domains is the topic of PART III (Chapters 5-8).

2 PERFECTIVES

Before presenting the synchronic meanings of the individual perfective markers, we will first take stock of the characterization of perfectives in the literature on aspectology. Most linguists agree that the notion of perfectivity represents a high-level aspectual opposition, where perfective aspect expresses an external view of a situation (wrapped up as a complete whole) versus imperfective aspect, which expresses an internal view of a situation (unfolded to reveal its inner temporal structure) (e.g., Comrie 1976:3ff.; Chung and Timberlake 1985:219; Smith 1997:93ff.).

Perfectives expressed through derivational morphology differ somewhat from perfectives expressed through inflection. For instance, derivational perfectives have been described as "grammaticized bounders" (Bybee and Dahl 1989:86) and as "highly generalized and elaborated completives" (Bybee et al. 1994:89). These characterizations follow from the observation that completives report a telic situation with an inherent terminal point, e.g., English *eat up* versus *eat*. Completives also express something done "thoroughly and to completion" and can refer to "a totally affected patient" (1994:54). Derivational perfectives appear to retain the completive sense expressed in telic situations, emphasizing "the attainment of a limit" (Dahl 1985:76) and denoting "a complete telic situation" (Comrie 2001:46). Stated succinctly, derivational perfective subsumes completive meaning.

As outlined above, the SCQ data reveal a system of nine perfective suffixes ranging from fully derivational to fully inflectional. These suffixes are listed in Figure 2.1.[15] The first six (*-rpu, -rku, -yku, -ski, -ri, -ri:ku*) fill the non-obligatory derivational slots D3 and D4, and are presented in §2.1. The final three (*-ru, -sha, -ra*) fill the obligatory inflectional slot I2 and are presented in §2.2.[16]

---

[15] Several of the perfective suffixes are former directional suffixes. The geographic distribution of these suffixes is shown in Map A.1 in Appendix A. The grammatical development of these markers is discussed in §2.3, §5.1, and especially Chapter 9.

[16] The absence of a formal marker in the obligatory slot I2 signifies a grammatical zero. Zero in this position of the verbal template is construed as present habitual (see §3.2.2). In contrast, the lack of a formal marker in the non-obligatory slots D3 and D4 is not meaningful, that is, not a grammatical zero.

Figure 2.1 *Perfective suffixes in SCQ (cf. Figure 4.1)*

	DERIVATIONAL						INFLECTIONAL		
PERFECTIVE SUFFIX	*-rpu*	*-rku*	*-yku*	*-ski*	*-ri*	*-ri:ku*	*-ru*	*-sha*	*-ra*
VERBAL SUFFIX SLOT	D4	D4	D4	D4	D3	D4	I2	I2	I2

The discourse data used in this study provide compelling evidence for the morphological productivity of the perfective (and imperfective) suffixes. Each suffix appears with a large number of individual lexical verb roots relative to its token frequency. For example, in the coded data there are 79 tokens of *-ski* distributed over 56 unique lexical items. Even the least productive of the perfective suffixes (*-rpu*) has 21 tokens distributed over 10 lexical items. Moreover, a given verb root can take any perfective suffix; e.g., *punu-* 'sleep' can appear as *punu-rku-, punu-yku-, punu-ski-, punu-ri-*, etc. In general, the lexical items that appear with perfective suffixes are not restricted to any one semantic class, though there are some collocational constraints among the most derivational suffixes, e.g., *-rpu* does not appear with statives. (For more on the frequency and distribution of aspect markers with lexical items, see §4.5).[17]

While the perfective suffixes presented in Figure 2.1 are morphologically productive, some have also become permanently attached to certain verbs, forming an indivisible lexical item. For example, the first three suffixes in Figure 2.1 appear as fused elements in the forms *yarpu-* 'lower', *yarku-* 'climb', and *yayku-* 'enter' (cf. Table 4.9). A productive perfective suffix can subsequently be added to such lexicalized forms, e.g., *sharku-rku-r* in example (6). These and other lexicalized stem combinations are not treated here in the grammatical expression of aspect but in §4.5.3 and §9.1.[18]

---

[17] The morphological productivity of derivational aspect marking in SCQ makes it very different from derivational aspect marking in Russian. According to Forsyth, "the majority of Russian verbs can be grouped in aspectual pairs" (1970:32). In contrast, a given derivational aspect marker in SCQ can appear with nearly any verb root, and the use of any marker is optional. For a head-to-head comparison of aspectual features in Russian and SCQ, see §12.4.

[18] The directional meanings of the Proto Quechua suffixes *-rpu* 'downward', *-rku* 'upward', and *-yku* 'inward' would have contributed their specific meanings to a general verb of movement *ya-*. This initial element *ya-* does not occur synchronically as an independent lexical item.

2.1 Derivational perfectives

The derivational suffixes are down-completive *-rpu,* completive-perfective *-rku,* completive-perfective *-yku,* perfective *-ski,* punctual *-ri,* and perfective *-ri:ku.* Each appears in the inner layer of affixation in the non-obligatory verbal suffix slot D4, except *-ri* which fills slot D3. Although each suffix is productive, in keeping with their derivational status they differ in the degree of productivity. As noted above, they have also fused to a small number of lexical verbs (see §4.5 and §9.1).

2.1.1 *-rpu* 'down-completive'

The derivational suffix *-rpu* (from **-rpu* 'downward') is fully productive as a directional marker with motion verbs. In (1) *-rpu* expresses a literal sense of downward direction to an endpoint in the adverbial clause 'arriving down (the mountain slope) to the road'.[19]

> (1) *tsa   karrete:ra-man   cha-__rpu__-r   ka:rru-ta   shuya-ku-ru-:*
>   then   road-ALL   arrive-__COMPL__-SS   vehicle-OBJ   wait-MID-PST.R-1
>   'Then __arriving down__ (the mountain slope) to the road, I waited for a bus.'

As with other directional suffixes, *-rpu* ends with a high vowel that is lowered to [*a*] when followed by one of a small class of "trigger" suffixes (as described above in §1.6.2). The allomorph *-rpa* is seen in (2), followed by the trigger suffix *-ma:* 'first person object'.

> (2) *kostala-rku-r   ari tsaka-man   chura-yka-ma-y,   tsay-pita   pi-mi*
>   sack-PFV.M-DS   yes bridge-ALL   put-PFV.O-1OBJ-IMP2   that-ABL   who-DIR
>
>   *pi-pis   muna-q-kaq   hayta-__rpa__-ma:-na-n-pa:*
>   who-EVEN   want-AG-DEF   kick-__COMPL__-1OBJ-NMLZ.I-3-PURP
>   'Put me in a sack at the bridge, so that anyone who wants to can __kick me down__ (over the edge to the river below).'

The suffix *-rpu* adds a telic feature or terminal point to the downward motion. In (1) the endpoint is formally expressed by the allative NP *karrete:ra-man* 'to the road'. The endpoint in (2) remains implicit, supplied by the context ('to the river').

In the two previous examples *-rpu* appears in nonfinite clauses. It appears in the coded data with greater frequency in finite clauses, as illustrated in (3)-(5). In (3) the semantics of the verb root *shushu-* 'fall' is inherently imperfective, but the down-completive suffix *-rpu* portrays the motion as telic. Thus, the stem *shushu-rpa-* conveys impact with the ground, translated by native speakers as 'landed hard'. The lowered allomorph *-rpa* is triggered by the following suffix *-mu* 'cislocative'.

---

[19] The suffix *-rpu* is glossed as COMPL for completive.

(3) *ni-ka-sha-n-cho:*   *shushu-**rpa**-mu-sh*   *..tuku laqya-yka-mu-pti-n*
     say-CNT-NMLZ.R-3-LOC fall-**COMPL**-FAR-PST.R3   owl   slap-PFV.O-FAR-DS-3
     'In the midst of its barking (the dog) **landed hard**, while the owl was slapping it.'

While *-rpu* has a literal directional meaning in spatial contexts, this meaning is interpreted as more abstract in contexts outside the domain of space. With non-motion verbs, for example, *-rpu* is interpreted as a completive. In (4) *upa:lla-* 'quiet' is a non-motion verb, and the stem *upa:lla-ku-rpu-* expresses the meaning 'be completely quiet'.[20] The productive middle voice suffix *-ku* (the topic of Chapter 8) intervenes between the verb root and *-rpu*. The occurrence of *-rpu* in this rightward "aspectual" position shows that it has not lexicalized with *upa:lla-*, but rather is productive as a completive suffix.

(4) *tsay-no: ni-pti-n-na-m ...   upa:lla-ku-**rpu**-ya-rqa-n*
     that-SIM   say-DS-3-NOW-DIR   quiet-MID-**COMPL**-PL.V-PST-3
     'After he spoke like that, they were **completely quiet**.'

As detailed above, the 'downward to an endpoint' meaning of *-rpu* is restricted to motion verbs, and this directional meaning has become generalized to completive aspect, especially with non-motion verbs. While the meaning of *-rpu* has become more grammatical, this suffix continues to display lexical restrictions. For instance, *-rpu* does not appear in the coded data with speech-act verbs, stative verbs or verbs of cognition.

While *-rpu* has an abstract grammatical meaning, it is also subject to lexicalization. In keeping with its derivational status, idiosyncratic meanings may result from its combination with the inherent semantics of particular lexical roots. In (5), for example, the verb *qawa-* 'watch' becomes *qawa-rpu-* 'watch intently' or 'stare'.

(5) *"ama **qawa**-nki-tsu" ni-shqa   ari. tsay ni-ka-pti-n   **qawa-rpu**-sha*
     do.not **watch**-2-NEG   say-PST.R3 yes that say-CNT-SS-3   **watch-COMPL**-PST.R3

     tsay   na-n-qa   ... pani-n-qa.
     that   nonce-3-TOP   sister-3-TOP
     ' "Do not **watch**" he (Father God) said. Although that one was prohibiting, she **intently watched**, that other one, the sister.'

In summary, the completive suffix *-rpu* appears with motion verbs, productively expressing the directional meaning 'downward to an endpoint'. When used with non-motion verbs, *-rpu* expresses the more general meaning of something done thoroughly or to completion, i.e., completive aspect. The derivational status of *-rpu* is apparent from its idiosyncratic lexical restrictions, its optionality, and its position close to the verb root prior to inflection. In what

---

[20] The matrix verb in (4) is reminiscent of bipartite English phrasal verbs, as in *they quieted themselves down*.

follows, we will see that many suffixes in the SCQ aspectual system are derivational, but the meanings of these suffixes are typically much more abstract than the illustrations provided here for completive *-rpu*.

2.1.2   *-rku* 'completive-perfective (mutual consent)'

The derivational suffix *-rku* (from **-rku* 'upward') expresses aspectual meanings ranging from completive to perfective aspect.[21] This suffix appears in the coded data more frequently than the down-completive suffix *-rpu* illustrated in the previous section. The higher frequency of *-rku* corresponds to its more grammatical meaning.[22]

In (6) *-rku* occurs twice in the adverbialized form *sharku-rku-r*. The first instance is lexicalized within the verb root *sharku-* 'stand up' and, as such, simply involves a literal directional meaning. The second instance of *-rku* is morphologically productive and corresponds to the completion of the night's sleep, followed immediately by the search for a lost donkey, as planned the night before.

(6)   *tsay-pita-qa*   *tsa:*   *pas*   *maytse:-pa-na*   *Niki:tu-pis*   *sharku-**rku**-r,*
     that-ABL-TOP   then   very   wherever-GEN-NOW   Niko-EVEN   stand.up-**PFV.M**-SS

     ashi-sh   *Wanac-pa*
     seek-PST.R3   Wanac-GEN

     'Then **getting up immediately**, Niko searched all around Wanac.'

(7) is similar to (6) in that the participant Lorenzo completed the act of taking the girl to the community of Chingas. This instance of *-rku* also corresponds to the "totally affected patient" notion of completive meaning detailed by Bybee et al. (1994:57).

---

[21] The suffix *-rku* is glossed as PFV.M for perfective plus the modality of mutual consent (see §6.2).

[22] The Proto Central Quechua directional suffix **-rku* 'upward' may have resulted from the reduction of the historical sequence **-ri* (possibly 'up'; cf. note 30) plus **-ku* 'reflexive'. The Proto Quechua form **-ku* is probably cognate with final *ku* in the SCQ suffixes *-ku* 'middle', *-naku* 'reciprocal', *-paku* 'distributive', *-chaku* 'concerted effort', and *-ka:ku* 'total'. **-ku* is possibly cognate with *-yku* 'inward' as well; a reviewer suggests the Quechua II root *uku* 'inside' as another possible source for **-yku*. The proposal of **-ri* 'up' partially supports Weber's suggested reconstruction of **-rku* 'upward' as resulting from *-ri* 'punctual' (a later meaning of **-ri*) followed by *-yku* 'inward' (1989:125). In light of the propensity for **-ku* to introduce new contrasts through amalgamation with existing grammatical forms, however, the second element is more probably **-ku*, and not the longer form **-yku*. For more on the amalgamation of existing derivational aspect suffixes to yield new categories, see §2.1.6 on *-ri:ku*, §3.1.3 on *-rayka:* and §7.2.2 on *-ka:ku*.

(7) *Wachu-lla-sh   aywa-ku-sha   tsay   chi:na-ta   apa-__rku__-r   Chingas-pa*
Lorenzo-DLM-RPT   go-MID-PST.R3   that   girl-OBJ   take-__PFV.M__-SS   Chingas-GEN
'They say Lorenzo went to Chingas __taking along__ that girl.'

Both (6) and (7) illustrate the completive aspectual meaning of *-rku* with motion verbs. With non-motion verbs *-rku* tends to express a more general bounded or perfective grammatical meaning characterized by "the attainment of a limit," in the sense of Dahl (1985:76). In (8) this limit is made explicit as two consecutive days. Perfective *-rku* here further conveys that the man and his hosts stayed together by mutual consent, not by obligation (cf. §6.2).

(8) *pay-wan-pis   ta:ra:-ya-ru-:   ishke: diya   punu-__rku__-r-yan*
he-COM-EVEN   reside-PL.V-PST.R-1   two   day   sleep-__PFV.M__-SS-DISTR.T
'We provided lodging for him, all of us __sleeping__ here each night for two (consecutive) days.'

In (9) *-rku* expresses perfective aspect, illustrating the sense of "a complete telic situation" (Comrie 2001:46). The compatibility of *-rku* with *ishki-* 'fall' shows that the original sense of **-rku* 'upward' has undergone considerable grammatical development. The lowered allomorph *-rka* is triggered by the translocative suffix *-mu* in the finite verb form.

(9) *ishki-ka-__rka__-mu-shqa   tinyaq-pa   wayi-n-kuna*
fall-MID-__PFV.M__-FAR-PST.R3   bee-GEN   house-3-PL.N
'The hive of the bees __fell__.'

The suffix *-rku* appears on the copula in the complex predicate in (10). As in previous examples, *-rku* here expresses completive aspect and the modality of mutual consent. The original directional meaning of *-rku* 'upward' is sometimes invoked in spatial contexts, such as the locative NP 'on that mountain'.[23]

(10) *tsay   qaqa-chu   ka-ku-__rku__-r   ta:ku-ya-sha   ari*
that   mountain-LOC   be-MID-__PFV.M__-SS   reside-PL.V-PST.R3   yes
'__Being of one accord__ (the bear and the woman) __lived together__ on that mountain.'

Finally, *-rku* also appears with speech-act verbs as in the example below. In such contexts, the focus shifts more heavily to the modal interpretation of mutual consent, that is, convergent alignment between stances.

---

[23] The stem combination *ka-ku-* (copula *ka-* plus middle voice *-ku*) reports an attribute that characterizes the subject over an extended period of time (an aspectual concept). *ka-ku-* also implies the negative evaluation of a behavior outside of usual norms (a modal concept). For more on aspectual and modal functions of *ka-ku-* see §8.5.2.

(11) *ma:*   *porsyaka:su* *tyempu-yki* *ka-pti-n-qa*   *suplika-__rku__-nki*
      let's.see by.chance   time-2   be-DS-3-TOP   request-__PFV.M__-2
      'Let's see if by chance you have time, then __ask__ him.'

This section has shown a number of characteristics of the derivational suffix *-rku*. It can express completive and perfective aspect in the sense of "attainment of a limit." The former directional meaning 'upward' is typically not productive, though it may surface in suitable spatial contexts. Like down-completive *-rpu* presented in the previous section, completive-perfective *-rku* is derivational, but it has fewer lexical constraints. At the same time, *-rku* is more restricted morphosyntactically than *-rpu*, as *-rku* rarely occurs in finite clauses and it does not collocate with past tense markers. Finally, *-rku* does not constitute a neatly delineated aspectual category distinct from modality, but expresses both perfective aspect and mutual consent (cf. §6.2).

2.1.3   *-yku* 'completive-perfective (obligation)'

The suffix *-yku* (from **-yku* 'inward'), like *-rku*, expresses aspectual meanings that span the completive and perfective categories. The completive meaning of *-yku* is illustrated in (12), the denouement of a narrative sequence.[24]

(12) *tsay-ran*   *mantsa-ka-__yku__-ya-ra-:-qa*
      that-DIR.YET   fear-PASS-__PFV.O__-PL.V-PST-1-TOP
      'Until then we were __totally afraid__.'

Perfective aspect is expressed by *-yku* in a wide variety of situations, including events and states.[25] In (13) and (14) the situation is viewed in its totality by virtue of the addition of *-yku*. The lowered allomorph *-yka* in (14) is followed by the trigger suffix *-mu* 'translocative'.[26]

(13) *pay-pis*   *kushi-__yku__-n.*   *seño:ra* *Deona-pis*
      he-EVEN   be.happy-__PFV.O__-3   señora   Deona-EVEN

      kushi-__yku__-ya-n   *llapa-n.*
      be.happy-__PFV.O__-PL.V-3   all-3
      'He __is happy__ too. He and señora Deona __are happy__, all of them.'

---

[24] The suffix *-yku* is glossed as PFV.O for perfective plus the modality of obligation (see §6.2).

[25] Stative verbs, in general, are compatible with the derivational perfective suffixes *-rku*, *-yku*, and *-ski*, and the derivational imperfective suffix *-yka:* (see §3.1.2).

[26] The suffix *-mu* normally expresses movement 'toward' the deictic center (cislocative) with motion verbs such as *shushu-* 'fall' in (3) and *ishki-* 'fall' in (9). With non-motion verbs such as *tari-* 'find' in (14), *-mu* indicates movement 'away from' or 'far from' the deictic center (translocative). Throughout this work *-mu* is simply glossed 'FAR'.

(14) *may-cho:-ta: wawqi   tsay-la:ya   mu:la-ta   qam-qa   tari-__yka__-mu-ru-yki*
where-LOC-Q.C brother   that-TYPE   mule-OBJ   you-TOP   find-**PFV.O**-FAR-PST.R-2ₚ
'Where, brother, **did** you **find** so many mules?'

Completive-perfective *-yku* occurs with all tenses and moods. Past is illustrated above in (14), future in (15), conditional in (16), and imperative in (17).

(15) *ima   alli-ra: ka-__yku__-nqa*
what   good-YET   be-**PFV.O**-FUT3
'What a good person **he will be**.'

(16) *tsay   ebanhelista   ka-ya-sha-n-kaq-kuna-pa-m   mas   alli-qa*
that   evangelist   be-PL.V-NMLZ.R-3-DEF-PL.N-GEN-DIR   more   good-TOP
aywa-__yku__-nki-man-qa
go-**PFV.O**-2-COND-TOP
'Better, you **should go** instead to the places where those evangelicals are.'

(17) *wamra-qa   aywa-ku-sha   tullu-n   apari-sh,   huk-nin-ta   huk-nin-ta*
child-TOP   go-MID-PST.R3   bone-3   carry-PTCP   one-3-OBJ   one-3-OBJ
"paka-__yka__-ma-y"   ni-r
hide-**PFV.O**-1OBJ-IMP2   say-SS
'The child escaped carrying the bones, pleading to each person, "**Hide** me".'

Completive-perfective *-yku* appears in negated clauses, such as (18). In contrast, down-completive *-rpu* and completive-perfective *-rku* do not appear in negated clauses.

(18) *mana-na   tari-__yku__-ya-:-na-tsu*
no-NOW   find-**PFV.O**-PL.V-1-NOW-NEG
'We still do not **find** it (our donkey).'

In summary, the suffix *-yku* expresses a range of meanings from completive to perfective aspect. The former directional meaning of *-yku* 'inward' is no longer productive. Completive-perfective *-yku* is twice as frequent in the coded data as either *-rpu* or *-rku*, expressing perfective aspect in a greater variety of communicative situations. It is more diffused through the lexicon, including stative verbs, and collocates with all tenses and moods, including negation. In addition to perfective aspect, *-yku* also expresses the modality of "obligation." This modal extension of *-yku* presents intriguing contrasts with "mutual consent" expressed by perfective *-rku*, as presented in detail in §6.2.

2.1.4   *-ski* 'perfective'

The suffix *-ski* presents a situation as a complete whole without reference to its inner temporal structure. It is the most general of the perfectives expressed through derivational morphology.[27] In (19) the many travels of the individual are packaged as a single, complete unit of experience.[28]

> (19) *tsa   aywa-__ski__-nqa-yki-kuna-cho: alli-ku   pa:sa-ru-yki*
>   then   go-__PFV__-NMLZ.R-2-PL.N-LOC   good-Q.P   pass-PST-2$_P$
>   'So then **in all your travels** did you have a good time (pass well)?'

-ski is also the most frequent and the most productive of the perfective suffixes. It appears freely with all semantic classes of lexical verbs, and in all inflectional morphosyntactic constructions. For example, perfective *-ski* occurs in the deverbal clauses (19)-(21), and in the finite clauses (22)-(24). (19) is a nominalization marked by locative case, (20) is an adverbial clause with a subject that is coreferential with the matrix clause, and (21) is an adverbial clause with a non-coreferential subject.

> (20) *tsay-chu huk sema:na ka-__ski__-r-qa   chakra-ntsik-kuna-ta-ra:-chir aru-sha:*
>   that-LOC one week   be-__PFV__-SS-TOP   field-1$_1$-PL.N-OBJ-YET-APP   work-FUT1
>   'After a week in that village **is complete**, I will work our fields (here).'

> (21) *ni-__ska__-ma-pti-n-qa   Niki:tu-ta-pis   willa-__ski__-pti-:   Niku-pis   aywa-ra-n*
>   say-__PFV__-1OBJ-DS-3-TOP Niko-OBJ-EVEN   tell-__PFV__-DS-1   Niko-EVEN   go-PST-3
>
>   *Wanac-pa   ashi-q   ari*
>   Wanac-GEN   search-PRMT   yes
>   'When she **told** me (the whole situation), then after I **told** it to Niko, he went to search near Wanac.'

Perfective *-ski* occurs with any mood or tense, whether past as in (22), future as in (23), or conditional as in (24).

---

[27] The suffix *-ski* is glossed as PFV for perfective aspect, an analysis first proposed by Stewart (1984:77ff.).

[28] The perfective suffix *-ski* is not attested in most of the language family, only in SCQ and five neighboring Central Quechuan varieties. The form *-ski* appears in Lambayeque (North Peruvian) as a 'simultaneous progressive' (Torero 1968:297; cf. (15)-(17) in Appendix E). Elsewhere in Central Quechua, perfective aspect is expressed by the suffix *-yku* (from *-yku* 'in') in Huallaga Quechua (Weber 1989:144) and by *-ru* (from *-rqu* 'out') in Tarma Quechua (Adelaar 1977:124). The cognate suffix *-ru* in SCQ has undergone further grammatical development and has become an inflectional past perfective (see §2.2.1). Perfective aspect is not formally marked in Northern Quechuan varieties, such as Imbabura (Cole 1982:149).

(22)   *tsay-mi*   *llantu-ku-q-chir*   *may-pa-pis*   *aywa-__ski__-shqa*
       that-DIR   make.shade-MID-PRMT-CNJ   where-GEN-EVEN   go-**PFV**-PST.R3
       'Therefore, it probably **went** somewhere to shade itself.'

(23)   *ma:*   *chaqcha-tsi-ka-__ska__-mu-sha:-ra:*   *may-pa*   *ashi-q*
       let.see   chew.coca-CAUS-MID-**PFV**-FAR-FUT1-YET   where-GEN   search-PRMT
       aywa-ya:-na-:-pa:-pis
       go-PL.V-NMLZ.I-1-PURP-EVEN
       'I think I will have her **chew coca** (go through the entire divining process) and then return so that we can go and search where she indicates.'

(24)   *runa-qa*   *suwa-__ski__-n-man-ra:ku*   *tsay*   *kinray-lla-chir*
       person-TOP   steal-**PFV**-3-COND-NEG.APP   that   vicinity-DLM-APP
       'A person **would never steal** at that place, right?'

Like completive-perfective *-yku*, perfective *-ski* occurs in negated clauses as in (24) and (25).

(25)   *ni*   *noqa-ntsik-pis*   *yarpa-__ski__-ntsik-tsu*
       nor   I-1₁-EVEN   think-**PFV**-1₁-NEG
       'Not even we ourselves **think at all** (about chores during the fiesta).'

As with other perfectivizing suffixes, the aspectual meaning of *-ski* has modal extensions. In addition to perfective aspect, *-ski* expresses unexpectedness due to limited foreknowledge. An unprepared mind and the subsequent unexpected outcome of an event has been referred to as "(ad)mirative," an epistemic modality (e.g., DeLancey 1997). The semantic domains of aspect and modality are intricately interwoven in SCQ, a topic taken up in Chapter 6.

In the previous three sections the former directional markers **-rpu* 'downward', **-rku* 'upward', and **-yku* 'inward' are shown to have perfective meanings. Like these three suffixes, the final high vowel of *-ski* lowers to *-ska* when followed by the trigger suffixes *-ma:* 'first person object' above in (21) and *-mu* 'translocative' in (23).

Another formal characteristic shared by these four suffixes is that each occurs in the non-obligatory position D4, and can be followed by derivational suffixes prior to the inflectional person and TAM markers in slot I2. Another former directional marker that developed perfective meaning is the suffix *-ru*, discussed in §2.2.1. Unlike the four perfective suffixes presented so far, only *-ru* has continued along a path of grammatical development to become a fully inflectional marker of past tense. Evidence for *-ski* as a former directional suffix is presented in Appendix E.

2.1.5　*-ri* 'punctual'

The suffix *-ri* presents an event as temporally limited, in that its duration is relatively brief.[29] Depending on the context, however, the duration in absolute terms may vary from instantaneous in (26) and (27), to "a short while" in (28) and (29), to twenty years in (30).[30]

(26)　*hukaq　la:du-chu　qeru-man　tuku　rata-**ri**-n*
　　　other　　side-LOC　　tree-ALL　　owl　　land-**PUNC**-3

　　　'On the other side the owl **lands in that instant** on the tree.'

(27)　*tsa　rastru-ta-qa　tari-shqa　ari　washa　tiyu-ntsik　Shanti-pa*
　　　then　track-OBJ-TOP　find-PST.R3　yes　over.there　uncle-1ᵢ　Santiago-GEN

　　　*e:ra-n-kaq-chu　　　qoshpa-**ri**-sha-n-ta　　llapa-n-pis*
　　　threshing.floor-3-DEF-LOC　wallow-**PUNC**-NMLZ.R-3-OBJ　all-3-EVEN

　　　'Then she found its tracks over there in uncle Shanti's threshing floor, right where (the donkey) **rolled over quickly**.'

Under ordinary circumstances the usual or expected duration for dancing at the annual fiesta would be all night. In contrast, the speaker in (28) was under obligation to play in the band and thus could dance with his friends only during a short break.

(28)　*noqa-kuna-pis　ichik　tushu-**ri**-ya-ra-:-ra:*
　　　I-PL.N-EVEN　　small　dance-**PUNC**-PL.V-PST-1-YET

　　　'We also danced a short while.'

The punctual meaning of *-ri* is sensitive not only to the pragmatic context, but also the linguistic context. In both (28) and (29) the verb marked with punctual *-ri* is preceded by the lexical adverb *ichik* 'small', further specifying the relatively short duration of the time period.

---

[29] The suffix *-ri* is glossed as PUNC for punctual aspect. Most linguists view punctual as a type of perfective by virtue of its lack of internal temporal structure (e.g., Comrie 1976:42). Cognates of **-ri* are attested throughout the language family, but its grammatical meaning varies considerably. See Map A.3 in Appendix A.

[30] Several SCQ verb forms that end with *ri* include the notion 'up' in their semantics, e.g., *apari-/apiri-* 'carry on back/shoulder', *ñukiri-* 'look up', *kawari-* 'resurrect, rise up', *pallari-* 'lift up', *pa:ri-* 'fly', *qari-* 'lift partially', *sha:ri-* 'stand up', *shiri-* 'cover'. These forms suggest that the punctual suffix *-ri* may have meant 'up' at a prior stage of development. The meaning 'up' may be related to **ri-* 'go' which has modern reflexes attested in Quechua II varieties).

(29)   *ichik   upu-__ri__-ya-ra-:-mi*   *noqa-kuna-pis   tiyu-ntsi: Florentinu*
     small   drink-**PUNC**-PL.V-PST-1-DIR   I-PL.N-EVEN   uncle-1₁   Florentino

     imbita-ya:-ma-pti-n
     invite-PL.V-1OBJ-DS-3

     'We also **drank a short while** when our uncle Florentino invited us.'

An especially long period of time is presented as punctual in (30). The narrator tells of a man who sold his soul to the devil in exchange for twenty years of a self-gratifying lifestyle. The suffix *-ri* presents the allotted time period as relatively brief, contrasting with the usual perception of twenty years as "a long time."

(30)   *tsa   tsay-pita-qa   benti   a:ñus   mas-na   pa:sa-__ri__-na:*
     then   that-ABL-TOP   twenty   years   more-NOW   pass-**PUNC**-PST.N

     'Then after that the twenty years **quickly passed**.'

In each of the previous examples, the punctual suffix *-ri* presents the duration of an event as relatively brief. *-ri* can also indicate that the lapse of time between successive events is relatively brief, as in (31).

(31)   *noqa-pis   Waroya-pa,   Acorma-pa,   Orqush-pa,   maytse: Cruz-kaq-pa*
     I-EVEN   Waroya-GEN   Acorma-GEN   Orcush-GEN   wherever   Cruz-DEF-GEN

     tuma-__ra__-mu-Ø-:
     turn-**PUNC**-FAR-PR-1

     'I also **hurriedly went around** by Waroya, Acorma, Orgush, everywhere near Cruz (without staying a long time in any one place).'

In addition to perfective aspect, punctual *-ri* shares several other characteristics with the perfectivizing suffixes presented in the previous four sections. First, *-ri* can be followed by other derivational suffixes prior to the inflectional person and tense markers. It appears in the non-obligatory derivational slot D3, slightly closer to the verb root than slot D4. Second, the final high vowel of *-ri* lowers to *-ra* when followed by a trigger suffix, such as *-mu* 'translocative' in *pa:sa-ra-mu-r* in (32).

(32)   *tse:-na   kicha-pa:-ma-n,   pa:sa-__ra__-mu-r   don Donatu-ta-qa*
     that-NOW   open-BEN-1OBJ-3   pass-**PUNC**-FAR-SS   sir   Donato-OBJ-TOP

     tari-__ri__-:
     find-**PUNC**-1

     'Then he opens it for me and **the moment I pass** inside I **immediately find** Donato.'

Third, *-ri* occurs freely in both finite and nonfinite clauses. In (32) the first instance of *-ri* occurs in the adverbial clause marked by *-r* 'SS' and the second instance occurs in the finite verb form *tari-ri-:*. Fourth, the aspectual meaning of *-ri* is also linked to modal meanings. For example, limited time duration has a natural extension via inference to actions of limited consequence, as in (33). Similarly, brief events often happen suddenly, and may be interpreted as unexpected (mirative modality); cf. (179).

(33) *ima-ta-ra:* *rura-ya-nqa-pis* *ichik* *huk* *ishke:* *qelle:-ta*
     what-OBJ-YET do-PL.V-FUT3-EVEN small one two coin-OBJ
     apa-__ra__-tsi-r
     take-**PUNC**-CAUS-SS
     'What will they be able to do, **only contributing** a few small coins?'

The high frequency, extensive lexical distribution, and relatively unrestricted morphosyntactic characteristics of punctual *-ri* are very similar to those associated with perfective *-ski* (see previous section). The semantics of these two suffixes are also similar, but punctual *-ri* presents the event as more brief (aspect), more sudden (manner), and more unexpected (modality) than perfective *-ski*. A detailed examination of *-ri* versus *-ski* is presented in §6.3.[31]

2.1.6 *-ri:ku* 'perfective (forceful)'

The perfective suffix *-ri:ku* is transparently derived historically from the frequent combination of punctual *-ri* followed by completive-perfective *-yku*.[32] This combination occurs about 10% as often as *-ri* alone or *-yku* alone. Whereas *-ri* and *-yku* appear with both transitive and intransitive verbs, perfective *-ri:ku* only appears with transitive verbs, as in the following examples.[33]

(34) *kay-kaq-cho:-na* *wamra-ta* *kay* *tarush* *hita-__ri:ku__-sh*
     this-DEF-LOC-NOW child-OBJ this deer throw-**PFV.F**-PST.R3
     'Now in this one, this deer **hurled** the child (over a cliff).'

(35) *tsa* *tse:-chu* *ka-yka-pti-n-qa* *deskarga-ri-r* *chip* *llapa-n*
     then that-LOC be-CONT-DS-3-TOP shoot-PUNC-SS total all-3
     leyon-kuna-ta *qarqu-__ri:ku__-na:* *na-n-pa* *selba-pa*
     lion-PL.N-OBJ drive.out-**PFV.F**-PST.N nonce-3-GEN jungle-GEN
     'Then while they were there, by shooting he **forcefully drove out** every one of the lions to the jungle.'

---

[31] The suffix *-ski* is not attested in neighboring Huaylas Quechua (except for borrowing at the fringes of the Huaylas-speaking area). When written materials are adapted from SCQ to Huaylas, the *-ski* suffix is almost always replaced with *-ri*, but occasionally with *-yku*.

[32] Bean (1990) argues that the combination of *-ri* plus *-yku* is becoming a single suffix in Dos de Mayo Quechua (Huánuco). The frequent combination of these two suffixes was observed in Huaylas Quechua by Larsen (1976:19).

[33] The suffix *-ri:ku* is glossed as PFV.F for perfective aspect plus forceful manner.

Beyond its aspectual meaning, consummation of an action, *-ri:ku* emphasizes that the action obtains via forceful effort in the face of resistance. The successful outcome tends to exceed typical expectations. Speakers often exploit this effect by using *-ri:ku* in the climax of a narrative.

The sense of forceful effort is compatible with the inherent semantics of the verb roots in (34) 'throw' and (35) 'drive out'. Similarly, *-ri:ku* can report an action completed in the face of a dilemma. This concept of "forcing a tough choice" is seen in (36) where the verb root *haqi-* 'leave' becomes *haqi-ri:ku-* 'abandon'. In (37) the hero, having proven his worth by capturing all the devils, makes the tough choice of releasing them.

(36) *tsa: fyesta-na qalla-pti-n-na bu:rriku ashi-y-ta-pis haqi-__ri:ku__-r ...*
then fiesta-NOW begin-DS-3-NOW donkey seek-INF-OBJ-EVEN leave-**PFV.F**-SS

fyesta-cho:-na warat tushu-ku-ya-rqu-:
fiesta-LOC-NOW all.night dance-MID-PL.V-PST.R-1

'After the fiesta began, **forced to abandon** the search for the donkey...we danced all night at the fiesta.'

(37) *ni-pti-n-shi "ya" ni-r kacha:-__ri:ku__-pti-n-qa*
say-DS-3-RPT yes say-SS loose-**PFV.F**-DS-3-TOP

aywa-ku-ya:-na: chip llapa-n diyablu-kuna total
go-MID-PL.V-PST.N total all-3 devil-PL.N completely

basyu tabake:ra-n-ta deja-ski-r
empty cigar.box-3-OBJ leave-PFV-SS

'After they pleaded, and he said "agreed," **releasing** them (from captivity), all the many devils went away leaving the cigar box completely empty.'

Punctual *-ri* does not occur with past perfective *-ru* in the SCQ corpus. In contrast, the fused suffix *-ri:ku* does, as seen in (38). The lowered allomorph *-ri:ka* is triggered by the following suffix *-tsi* 'causative'.

(38) *kanan si:, papa:, reqi-__ri:ka__-tsi-ma-__ru__-yki maytse: patsa-ta*
now yes dear know-**PFV.F**-CAUS-1OBJ-**PST.R**-2ₚ wherever ground-OBJ

'Now indeed, my dear, you **took me beyond** anything I'd ever known.'

In addition to semantic and distributional evidence for the fusion of *-ri:ku* as a single suffix, there is further evidence from morphosyntax. First, no other suffix can intervene between *-ri* and *-yku*. Second, the initial component *-ri* does not lower to *-ra* when followed by the suffixes that otherwise trigger lowering, as seen in (38). The facts are more fully illustrated in (39) with the verb *yarqu-* 'leave'. Punctual *-ri* lowers to *-ra* before cislocative *-mu* in (39)b, even when a suffix that does not trigger lowering intervenes, such as plural *-ya:* in (39)c. In the same way, completive-perfective *-yku* lowers to *-yka* before *-mu* in (39)e, even when *-ya:* intervenes in (39)f. In contrast, when the combination *-ri:ku* occurs before *-mu*, the result in (39)g is *-ri:ka*, not *-rayka*.

(39) a. *yarqu-ri-sha*   'it left'
     b. *yarqa-ra-mu-sha*   'it left from there'   *-ri* lowers to *-ra* before *-mu*
     c. *yarqa-ra-ya:-mu-sha*   'they left from there'   (even when plural *-ya:* intervenes)

     d. *yarqu-yku-sha*   'it left'
     e. *yarqa-yka-mu-sha*   'it left from there'   *-yku* lowers to *-yka* before *-mu*
     f. *yarqa-yka-ya:-mu-sha*   'they left from there'   (even when plural *-ya:* intervenes)

     g. *yarqa-ri:ka-mu-sha*   'it left from there'   *-ri:ku* does not lower to *-rayka*
                                                         before *-mu* (*i* does not lower)

In summary, the suffix *-ri:ku* combines perfective aspect and forceful manner in its semantics. It is derived historically from the combination of punctual *-ri* followed by completive-perfective *-yku*. In terms of semantics, morphosyntax, and relative frequency, perfective *-ri:ku* is best analyzed as a grammatical construction, a single suffix distinct from either *-ri* or *-yku*. Further discussion on the relationship between the domains of aspect and manner is presented in Chapter 7; additional examples of *-ri:ku* are provided in §7.2.1.[34]

2.2 Inflectional perfectives

In this section I present the inflectional past perfective suffixes *-ru, -sha,* and *-ra.* There are no present perfectives. Each past perfective is fully productive in the outer layer of affixation in the obligatory TAM slot I2. These suffixes often combine with the derivational suffixes presented in the previous section, resulting in more fully specified aspectual distinctions. Inflectional imperfectives (both past and present) are presented below in §3.2.

2.2.1 *-ru* 'past perfective'

The inflectional suffix *-ru* (or *-rqu*) (from **-rqu* 'outward') combines elements of both perfective aspect and past tense in its semantics.[35] In other words, it presents a situation as temporally bounded, but only in the past. For example, in (40) the situation is presented as a complete whole, without regard to internal temporal structure; cf. *-rqu* in *tushu-ku-ya-rqu-:* 'danced' in (36).[36]

---

[34] For more on the amalgamation of existing derivational aspect suffixes to yield new categories in SCQ, see §3.1.3, §8.7, §10.4, and §11.6.

[35] The suffix *-ru* is glossed as PST.R because it reports event sequences that are relatively recent (R) in time, though that may range from earlier the same day to many years ago. The development of past perfective *-ru* from the suffix **-rqu* 'outward' is detailed in Chapter 9.

[36] In most other Quechuan varieties in which a synchronic reflex of **-rqu* is attested, the relevant form appears in a non-obligatory derivational slot, such as D4 in SCQ, not an inflectional slot. A wide array of meanings have been reported for this marker, arranged as

(40) *ima-kuna-ta-ta:*   *tsay-pita-qa*   *yacha-ku-ya-**rqu**-yki*
      what-PL.N-OBJ-Q.C   that-ABL-TOP   learn-MID-PL.V-**PST.R**-2ₚ
      'What things, then, **did** you **learn**?'

In (41) *-ru* emphasizes that a limit has been attained.

(41) *runa-pa*   *abe:na-n-kuna-ta-si*   *qashu-tsi-r*   *usha-**ru**-:*
      person-GEN   oats-3-PL.N-OJB-EVEN   trample-CAUS-SS   finish-**PST.R**-1
      'I **completely trampled** the owner's oat field.'

As seen in (40) and (41), alternate forms are *-ru* and *-rqu*, respectively. The postvelar *q* is softened and then lost through the phonological process of lenition. In the coded data the reduced phonological form *-ru* appears 43 times, *-rqu* only twice. The reduced form is especially frequent in spontaneous speech.

Past perfective *-ru* is not compatible, in general, with imperfective markers (such as continuous *-yka:*) or with stative verbs. In particular, *-ru* is incompatible with the copula *ka-*, and thus does not appear in predicate nominal or predicate locative constructions.[37] The

---

follows by mode of morphological expression. The geographic distribution of **-rqu* is shown in Map A.1 in Appendix A. The range of meanings is illustrated in §9.3.

INFLECTIONAL

Huaraz	CENTRAL	*-rqu*	'perfect'	Swisshelm 1974:505
Huaylas	CENTRAL	*-rqu*	'recent past'	Parker 1976:127
Llamellín	CENTRAL	*-ru*	'recent past'	Snow and Stark 1971:172
Tarma	CENTRAL	*-ru*	'perfective', 'punctual', 'recent past', 'sudden change'	Adelaar 1977:124

DERIVATIONAL

Huallaga	CENTRAL	*-rqu*	'remarkable speed', 'surprisingly', 'immediate'	Weber 1989:127
Ambo-Pasco	CENTRAL	*-ru*	'recent past', 'unexpectedly'	Ralph Toliver, p.c.
Huanca	CENTRAL	*-qlu*	'recent past', 'courtesy', 'urgency'	Cerrón-Palomino 1976:202
Ayacucho	SOUTHERN	*-rqu*	'urgently', 'personal interest' 'recent past'	Parker 1969d:67 Soto 1976a:98-9
Cuzco	SOUTHERN	*-rqu*	'consummation', 'intention', 'suddenly', 'exhortative'	Cusihuamán 1976a:207

[37] Of the 45 past perfective *-ru* exemplars in the coded data, none attaches to the copula and only two (4%) appear with continuous *-yka:*. In contrast, of the 78 past perfective *-ra* exemplars, 9 (11%) attach to the copula and 7 (9%) appear with *-yka:*. Predicate nominal and locative constructions are freely marked by the past perfectives *-ra* and *-sha*, past habitual *-q*, and

incompatibility of past perfective *-ru* with statives and imperfectives is a characteristic it shares with the derivational perfectives presented above (*-rpu, -rku, -yku, -ski, -ri*). At the same time, *-ru* appears only in the obligatory (inflectional) TAM position of finite verbs, while the derivational perfectives appear in non-obligatory positions close to the verb root, whether the form is finite or nonfinite. The elaboration of aspectual categories in SCQ provides a fertile environment in which to examine issues in derivation versus inflection, a topic taken up in Appendix B.

Curiously, past perfective *-ru* obligatorily involves speech-act participant subjects or objects, that is, first person, second person, or first-second person inclusive. The corpus of SCQ speech contains hundreds of examples of *-ru* inflected for speech-act participant subjects. Only two *-ru* exemplars have third person subjects, and both include speech-act participant objects. In contrast, past perfective *-sha* (introduced in the next section) is a portmanteau suffix that refers to third person subjects exclusively. In this way, *-ru* and *-sha* appear in complementary distribution with respect to person, together forming a single "mixed" inflectional past perfective category (cf. Diane Hintz 2007b:24ff.).

2.2.2   *-sha* 'past perfective'

The inflectional suffix *-sha* (from **-shqa* 'past participle, perfect'), like *-ru*, presents a past situation as temporally bounded, but only in the past. In the following examples each situation is presented as an unanalyzable whole, without specification of internal temporal structure. In some communities *-sha* reduces to *-sh* in word final position, as in the verb *ashi-mu-sh* in (43).[38]

> (42)   *apiri-ra-mu-pti-n-qa*   *puri-ya-__sha__*   *tsay*   *wawa-n-wan*
>   carry-PUNC-FAR-DS-3-TOP   walk-PL.V-__PST.R3__   that   child-3-COM
>
> 'After carrying him here, she __walked__ with her child.'

> (43)   *washa*   *Asya-q*   *pukyu*   *kinray-pa*   *Ongup-pa*   *ashi-mu-__sh__.*
>   over.there   Stink-AG   spring   vicinity-GEN   Ongup-GEN   seek-FAR-__PST.R3__
>
> *bu:rru-qa*   *ka-__sha__-tsu.*
> donkey-TOP   be-__PST.R3__-NEG
>
> 'She __searched__ over there by Stinky Spring and in the vicinity of Ongup. But the donkey __wasn't there__.'

As pointed out in the previous section, *-sha* forms a hybrid past perfective category together with the suffix *-ru*. While past perfective *-ru* inflects for speech-act participants (whether subject

---

narrative past *-na:*. Predicate nominals are illustrated with past perfective *-ra* in (48), and with narrative past *-na:* in (144) and (146).

[38] Past perfective *-sha* is glossed as PST.R3 (third person) to concord with past perfective *-ru* PST.R. Like *-ru*, it reports events that are relatively recent in time (cf. note 35).

or object), past perfective *-sha* inflects exclusively for third person subjects. Conversational participants exploit this complementary distribution of *-ru* and *-sha* with respect to person for tracking referents. Even though restricted to third person, *-sha* is the most frequent of all the perfective markers.

Past perfective *-sha* developed from a perfect expressed through periphrasis (see §9.5). This former perfect construction combined the past participle *-shqa* with the copular auxiliary *ka-*. Like its past perfective partner *-ru*, *-sha* typically narrates sequences of mainline events, as illustrated in a conversation in (43) and a legend in (44). This discourse function shows that *-sha* is no longer a perfect in SCQ.

(44)   *tsay-ta   tullu-n   apari-__sha__   wamra-qa.*
        that-OBJ   bone-3   carry-__PST.R3__   child-TOP

        watu-tsa-ku-rku-r   aywa-ku-__sha__   hunish-pa.
        cord-CAUSE.BE-MID-PFV.M-SS   go-MID-__PST.R3__   on.high-GEN

        'The child __carried__ those bones (of her brother). Tieing herself (to the gold cord), she __went__ to heaven.'

Like *-ru*, past perfective *-sha* is incompatible with the continuous (imperfective) suffix *-yka:*. (Of 176 instances of *-sha* in the coded data, it never appears with *-yka:*.) At the same time, *-sha* does not share all of the characteristics observed for past perfective *-ru*. For example, *-ru* does not appear with the copula, but *-sha* does, e.g., *ka-sha-tsu* in (43).

In summary, the suffixes *-ru* and *-sha* comprise a single inflectional past perfective category. *-ru* is used with speech-act participants and *-sha* exclusively marks third person subjects. (For more on the relationship between *-ru* and *-sha*, see §5.1.) This developing category, not found in other Quechuan varieties, offers an excellent opportunity to examine diachronic mechanisms of semantic change and interacting forces that underlie a series of grammatical developments leading to the synchronic perfective system in SCQ. This scenario is examined in detail in Chapter 9 "The evolution of perfectives."

2.2.3   *-ra* 'past perfective'

The inflectional suffix *-ra* (from **-rqa* 'past'), like the past perfective suffixes *-ru* and *-sha*, combines elements of both perfective aspect and past tense in its semantics. It presents a situation as temporally bounded in the past, as in (45) and (46).

(45)   *tsay-pita   raki-ra-mu-pti-:-qa   sha-ka-mu-__ra__-n-cha:*
        that-ABL   divide-PUNC-FAR-DS-1-TOP   come-MID-FAR-__PST__-3-MUT

        'Then after I divided (the cows) they __came__ to me.'

(46)　*noqa-qa　pase:pa　qela-na-yka-r-mi　　　yarqa-mu-**ra**-:.*
　　　 I-top　　 very　　 be.lazy-DES-CONT-SS-DIR　leave-FAR-**PST**-1

　　　 *i　　tsay-pita-na-m　　 tayta　 dyos-nintsik-man　maña-ku-**ra**-:.*
　　　 and　 that-ABL-NOW-DIR　father　god-1ᵢ-ALL　　　　ask-MID-**PST**-1

　　　 'I **left** feeling very lazy. After that I **prayed** to our Father God.'

The previous examples of *-ra* are taken from spontaneous conversations. The unreduced phonological form *-rqa* is sometimes used in more formal storytelling genres, as in (47). In the coded data *-ra* occurs 78 times, *-rqa* only 5 times. The phonological reduction of *-rqa* to *-ra* is parallel to that of past perfective *-rqu* to *-ru*.

(47)　*allqu　yarpa-**rqa**-n　may,　tsay　qepi-na-chu　　　aytsa　ka-nqa-n-ta*
　　　 dog　　think-**PST**-3　maybe　that　wrap-NMLZ.I-LOC　meat　be-NMLZ.R-3-OBJ

　　　 'The dog **thought** maybe there was meat in that package.'

Past perfective *-ra* appears with the copula *ka-* in the following predicate nominal construction.

(48)　*mas　pi:-ta:　ka-ya-**ra**-:*
　　　 more　who-Q.C　be-PL.V-**PST**-1

　　　 'Who else **were we** (in our group)?'

Synchronic reflexes of *-rqa* are found in virtually all Quechuan languages. It is usually described as "simple past tense." According to Bybee et al. (1994:83 ff.) a simple past can signal past time for both perfective and imperfective situations. While *-ra* in SCQ signals past time, it does not report habitual or continuous (imperfective) situations. Thus, *-ra* is referred to here as past perfective.[39]

Although the semantics of *-ra* does not encompass imperfective aspect, one should not assume that a perfective is necessarily incompatible with imperfective situations (Comrie 1976:24). For example, a past imperfective reading of the verb can be derived by adding continuous *-yka:* (cf. §3.1.2). Accordingly, the matrix verbs with *-ra* in (45)-(47) above could be further specified by *-yka:* to cast a continuous (imperfective) viewpoint on the past situation, as in the second lines of (49)a-d.

---

[39] Alternatively, the term "simple past tense" could be understood as contrasting with "compound past tense," that is, past tense expressed via a suffix versus periphrasis. In any case, synchronic reflexes of *-rqa* 'past' report perfective situations, not imperfective situations.

(49) a. *sha-ka-mu-__ra__-n-cha:*   'they came to me'
     sha-ka-__yka:__-mu-__ra__-n-cha: 'they were coming to me'
     sha-ka-mu-__q__-cha: 'they used to come to me'

  b. *yarqa-mu-__ra__-:*   'I left'
     yarqa-__yka:__-mu-__ra__-:   'I was leaving'
     yarqa-mu-__q=ka__-:   'I used to leave'

  c. *maña-ku-__ra__-:*   'I prayed'
     maña-ku-__yka__-__ra__-:   'I was praying'
     maña-ku-__q=ka__-:   'I used to pray'

  d. *yarpa-__rqa__-n*   'the dog thought'
     yarpa-__yka__-__rqa__-n   'the dog was thinking'
     yarpa-__q__   'the dog used to think'

Habitual meaning restricted exclusively to the past is expressed by the inflectional marker *-q* (or *-q=ka*) (cf. §3.2.1), not by combining *-yka:* with *-ra*. Past habitual *-q* is translated in the third lines of (49)a-c as 'used to'.

In summary, the inflectional suffix *-ra* expresses perfective aspect and past tense. It is very frequent and has no lexical restrictions. Past perfective *-ra* is an "older" suffix with cognate forms in virtually all Quechuan languages, in contrast to the developing SCQ past perfectives *ru* and *-sha*. The compatibility of *-ra* with continuous *-yka:* and with stative verbs suggests that *-ra* is closer to a true simple past than the "younger" suffixes *-ru* and *-sha*, which almost never occur with *-yka:*, and *-ru* never occurs with the copula *ka-*. The grammatical interface between aspect and tense is examined in detail in Chapter 5.

2.3 Summary of perfectives

Perfective aspect is expressed in SCQ through a loosely organized grammatical system in which different markers have developed specialized meanings that are more specific than "general perfective." All are morphologically productive and widely distributed over many lexical forms. The diverse assortment of derivational suffixes combines with fully inflectional items to convey a wide array of aspectual distinctions. The perfective suffixes also encode meanings from the domains of tense, modality, and manner.

The perfective markers and their specific aspectual meanings are summarized in Figure 2.2.[40] The synchronic meanings of these nine markers range from directional, to completive and

---

[40] The suffixes above the dashed line in the left column of Figure 2.2 are former directional markers. The form *qa* in the final two markers (*-shqa* and *-rqa*) was probably a demonstrative at a pre-Proto stage of the language, as proposed by Weber (1987a; 1987b:60); see §11.6).

perfective aspect, to past tense.[41] Each individual marker expresses a continuous subset of these meanings that overlap within perfective semantic space. For example, the range of meanings associated with down-completive *-rpu* is represented as a solid bar that spans the directional category, partially extending into the completive category. In turn, the range of meanings associated with completive-perfective *-rku* spans the entire completive category, partially extending into the adjacent directional and perfective categories. The meanings of the other perfective markers are similarly represented. (For convenience, from this point forward I refer to *-rpu* as 'completive', *-rku* as 'perfective', and *-yku* as 'perfective'.)

Figure 2.2 *Synchronic meanings of perfective suffixes in SCQ discourse*

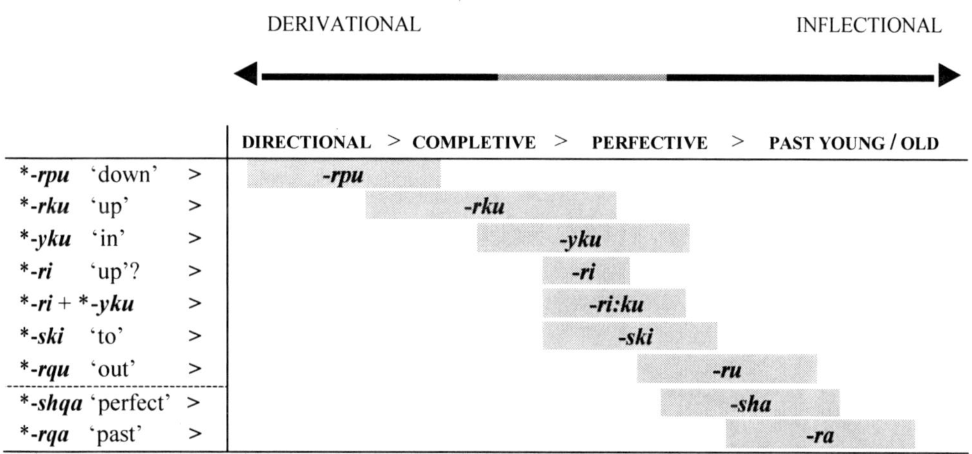

Figure 2.2 previews the diachronic dimension, with Proto Quechua directional suffixes in column 1 (above the dashed line) developing completive, perfective, and past tense meanings over time. We can also visualize in Figure 2.2 the gradual progression of morphological expression from derivation to inflection. The derivational forms at the top left (e.g., *-rpu*) have fused to a small number of lexical items, but they are very productive synchronically. The forms at the lower right (derived from *-rqu*, *-shqa*, and *-rqa*) are clearly inflectional in terms of traditional criteria, that is, these forms appear in an obligatory verbal position far from the verb root in the "outer" morphology, the meanings are semantically general and regular with unlimited applicability, they are very frequent, etc. Intriguingly, the forms in the middle (e.g., *-yku* and *-ski*) share characteristics of both derivation and inflection (represented by the gray area

---

[41] While inflectional *-ru*, *-sha*, and *-ra* represent one kind of perfective category, restricted to the past, the derivational markers in Figure 2.2 represent another kind of perfective, not restricted to the past.

between the arrows in the DERIVATIONAL-INFLECTIONAL scale above the table). Derivational and inflectional morphology as a gradient phenomenon is examined in detail in Appendix B.

Finally, what would account for the semantic and pragmatic utility of so many markers jockeying for position within the confines of an expanding perfective space? This line of inquiry is examined in terms of synchrony in PART III "Aspect and related semantic domains," and in terms of diachrony in PART IV, Chapter 9 "The evolution of perfectives."

3 IMPERFECTIVES

In Chapter 2 we saw that perfective aspect presents a situation as an unanalyzable whole. Imperfective aspect, on the other hand, reveals inner temporal contours. This "internal" view of temporal structure expressed by imperfectives presents a high-level contrast with the "external" view expressed by perfectives.

Comrie (1976:25) outlines a useful taxonomy of aspect (see Figure 3.1) with general perfective meaning in one branch, and imperfective meaning in another. In this framework, general imperfective subsumes habitual plus continuous aspect, and the continuous category is further subdivided into non-progressive and progressive aspect. Bybee et al. add that "an imperfective situation may be one viewed as in progress at a particular reference point, either in the past or present, or one viewed as characteristic of a period of time that includes the reference time, that is, a habitual situation" (1994:125-6). SCQ is especially rich in habituals as well as repetitive distinctions which specify internal temporal structure through recurrence over time.[42]

Figure 3.1 *Classification of aspectual oppositions (Comrie 1976)*

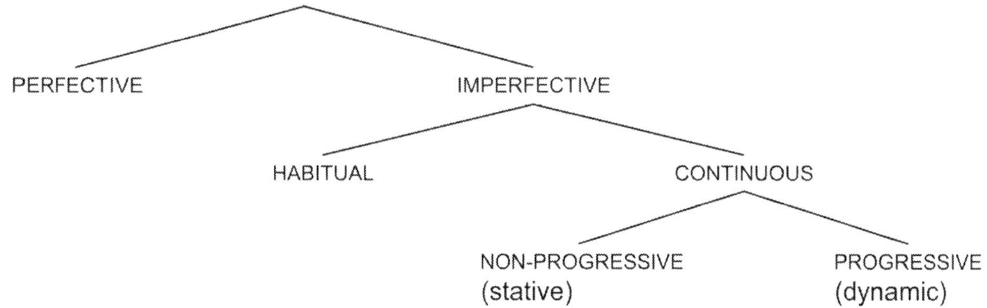

---

[42] Habitual aspect typically reports a "customary" situation, just as completive aspect reports a "telic" situation.

As indicated in Figure 3.1, continuous aspect views both dynamic and stative situations as ongoing at reference time, but it does not include habitual meaning. Bybee et al. find this notion appealing, but point out that no true continuous marker has actually been attested in the aspect literature (1994:139). We will see an excellent example of continuous aspect expressed by the SCQ suffix -*yka:* in §3.1.2.

Just as there is no single general perfective marker, there is no single general imperfective marker. Instead, as shown in Figure 3.2, eleven markers constitute a set of imperfectives in SCQ. They range from fully derivational to fully inflectional. The first five (durative -*ra:*, distributive -*paku*, iterative -*ykacha:*, continuous-durative -*rayka:*, and continuous -*yka:*) fill the non-obligatory derivational slots D1-D4. The two verbal reduplication types are also derivational. Habitual past -*q* and narrative past -*na:* fill the obligatory inflectional slot I2, while the absence of a formal marker in slot I2 (-∅) marks habitual aspect and present tense. In addition, the distributive enclitic =*yan* appears beyond the outer layer of inflectional affixes in slot E1.[43]

Figure 3.2 *Imperfective markers in SCQ (cf. Figure 4.1)*

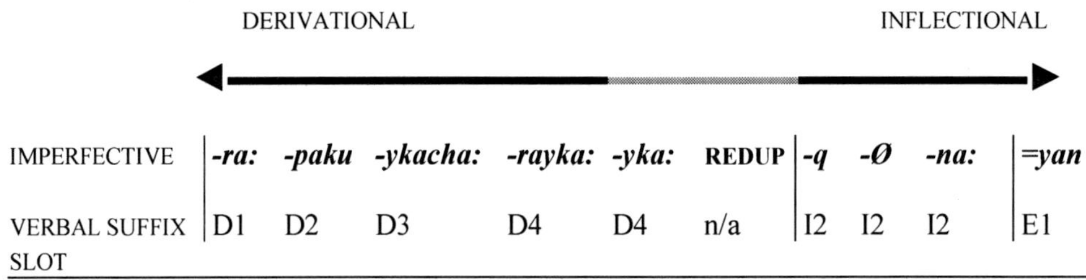

IMPERFECTIVE	-*ra:*	-*paku*	-*ykacha:*	-*rayka:*	-*yka:*	REDUP	-*q*	-*∅*	-*na:*	=*yan*
VERBAL SUFFIX SLOT	D1	D2	D3	D4	D4	n/a	I2	I2	I2	E1

Each imperfective marker in Figure 3.2 is morphologically productive and is not restricted to any one semantic class of lexical verbs. Naturally, the first six markers differ somewhat in the degree of productivity, in keeping with their derivational status. Yet even the most derivational markers appear with a high percentage of individual verb roots relative to token frequency. For example, in the coded data there are 13 tokens of -*ra:* distributed over 10 unique lexical items, and 169 tokens of -*yka:* distributed over 59 lexical items.

---

[43] As compared to naturally-occurring speech, I observed a much higher frequency of imperfectives, especially habituals, in stories elicited using the wordless picture book *Frog, Where are you?* (Mayer 1969). The frog story approach facilitated a more fine-grained analysis of semantic distinctions in SCQ within the imperfective domain. For example, 75% of all verbs in one frog story are marked imperfective, but only 17% are so marked in a conversation text. Presumably, the high frequency of habituals in SCQ frog stories can be attributed to the inherent stativity of illustrations which cannot "move," even though they may represent dynamic actions.

Just as perfective markers have fused to certain verbs, some imperfective markers have also become permanently attached to certain verbs, creating new lexical items. For example, *-ra:* contributes its durative meaning to the verbs *ta:ra:-* 'reside, stay', as above in (8), and *tsara:-* 'hold'. The initial verb element *tsa-* (from pre-Proto **cha-*) does not occur synchronically as an independent lexical item. Lexicalized forms of this type are not treated here, only the productive grammatical aspect forms.

3.1 Derivational imperfectives

In this section I present the derivational imperfective markers, beginning with durative *-ra:*, continuous *-yka:*, and continuous-durative (habitual) *-rayka:*. The suffix *-rayka:* can also specify internal temporal structure through recurrence over time as a continuative. Recurrence is also expressed by iterative *-ykacha:*, distributive *-paku*, the distributive enclitic *=yan*, and by verbal reduplication. Each of the five derivational imperfective suffixes appears close to the verb root in the non-obligatory slots D1-D4.[44]

3.1.1   *-ra:* 'durative'

The derivational suffix *-ra:* (from **-raya* 'action performed in an excessive degree', Parker 1969a:136) presents a situation as temporally extended, that its duration is longer than normal.[45] For example, in (50) the speaker tells his sister that their mother misses her now because the sister spends a long time away from home.

---

[44] Four of the derivational imperfective markers end with a long vowel which is foreshortened in closed syllables, e.g., durative *-ra:* is foreshortened to *-ra* in the verb *hunta-ra-p.ti-ki* in (50). The long vowel may also be foreshortened when the immediately following suffix has a single initial C synchronically, reduced over time from initial **CC* in an earlier stage of the language. For example, *-ra:* is foreshortened to *-ra* in the verb *watqa-ra-sha* look.at-DUR-PST.R3 in (192) because the suffix *-sha* (from **-shqa* 'past participle') began with a consonant cluster in a prior stage.

In addition to CV-initial suffixes such as *-sha* which foreshorten the preceding long vowel, there are a few other suffixes which induce foreshortening even though the initial CV is not transparently derived from initial **CCV*. For example, durative *-ra:* (from **-raya* by most accounts) foreshortens the verb root *yarpa:-* 'think' to *yarpa-* in (52). Other such suffixes include *-chaku* 'EFFORT' in (212) and *-ka:* 'PASS' in Appendix F (line 29), as well as *-ka:ku* 'TOTAL', *-na:* 'DES', and *-pa:* 'BEN'.

[45] Cognates of **-raya* are attested throughout the language family. Its grammatical meaning varies from distributive to durative to habitual. See Map A.5 in Appendix A.

(50) *llullu-no:-na-chir llaki-shu-nki-na   mas   hunta-__ra__-pti-ki*
      baby-SIM-NOW-APP be.sad-2OBJ-2-NOW   more fill-__DUR__-DS-2
      'Like a baby she misses you now because you **spend a long time** (lit. fill your time)
      away.'

In (51) durative *-ra:* indicates that the adults remained standing a long time conversing.

(51) *tsay-no: parla-r   ichi-__ra:__-ya-sha-n-yaq-qa*
      that-SIM   speak-SS   stand.up-__DUR__-PL.V-NMLZ.R-3-LIM-TOP

      ... wamra-kaq-pa heqa-ski-na:
         child-DEF-GEN   go-PFV-PST.N
      'While they were **still standing and conversing a long time** like that, the child
      secretly slipped out to where the other child was.'

Durative *-ra:* appears in an adverbial clause in (50) and in a nominalized clause in (51). It
appears equally in finite clauses, as in (52) and (53). In (52), *-ra:* derives the meaning 'ponder'
from the verb root *yarpa:-* 'think'.

(52) *grasyas   i:ha,   tsay konsehu-ta   yarpa-__ra:__-sha:-lla-m*
      thanks   daughter that advice-OBJ   think-__DUR__-FUT1-DLM-DIR
      'Thank you, daughter, I will **ponder** that advice.'

The longer-than-normal duration of time expressed by *-ra:* can be interpreted as a state when
added to telic verbs. For example, the verb root *warku-* denotes the dynamic action 'hang up'
(note the fused final element *-rku* 'upward'). The addition of durative *-ra:* yields the stative
meaning 'hang, remain suspended' in (53). In terms of syntax, *-ra:* can also function as a
passive.

(53) *huk planta-chu warku-__ra__-n   pepinillu*
      one   tree-LOC   hang.up-__DUR__-3   cucumber
      'A cucumber **hangs** on one of those trees.'

In summary, the derivational suffix *-ra:* expresses durative aspect, that is, it presents the
duration of a situation as relatively extended. Durative *-ra:* contrasts with punctual *-ri* (§2.1.5)
which presents the duration of a situation as relatively brief.[46]
Durative *-ra:* has a relatively low frequency, presumably due to collocational constraints. In
terms of morphosyntax, *-ra:* does not occur with past perfective *-ra* (§2.2.3), nor with

---

[46] The lexicalization of the punctual-durative aspectual contrast is observed in pairs such as
tsari- 'grab' versus *tsara:-* 'hold'. The form *tsa-* does not occur synchronically as an
independent lexical item. Both *tsari-* and *tsara:-* form single lexical units in which no suffix can
intervene.

conditional or imperative moods, nor in negated clauses. In terms of lexical restrictions, *-ra:* generally occurs with dynamic verbs that do not involve motion or cognition (*yarpa:-* 'think' in (52) is exceptional). It does not occur with stative verbs, but can derive a stative from a nonstative, and can also passivize. Finally, durative *-ra:* frequently combines with the continuous suffix *-yka:* yielding *-rayka:*, a suffix with a qualitatively new meaning. The latter two suffixes are treated in the next two sections.

3.1.2   *-yka:* 'continuous'

The suffix *-yka:* presents a situation as ongoing at reference time. It is more general than progressive because it collocates with all predicates, whether dynamic or stative. At the same time, *-yka:* is not a general imperfective because it does not express habitual meaning. In other words, the meaning of *-yka:* corresponds well to the notion of "continuous" aspect offered by Comrie (1976:25ff.), a category rarely attested cross-linguistically (e.g., Bybee et al. 1994:139).[47]

With dynamic predicates, continuous *-yka:* presents an ongoing situation as requiring sustained effort to continue. This progressive meaning of *-yka:* is illustrated in (54) and (55), which are inflected for present and future tense, respectively.

> (54)   *kapas Chi:nu ima-m   qati-__yka:__-mu-n*
> maybe Chino   what-DIR follow-__CONT__-FAR-3
> 'Maybe Chino or someone else **is guiding** her back.'

> (55)   *imayka-ta-pis   rura-__yka:__-ya:-sha:-mi   i   qam-pis   cha:-mu-r*
> all.kinds-OBJ-EVEN do-__CONT__-PL.V-FUT1-DIR   and   you-EVEN arrive-FAR-SS
> *imayka-lla-ta-pis   patsa:-tsi-shun   llapa-ntsik-na-m*
> all.kinds-DLM-OBJ-EVEN agree-CAUS-FUT1$_1$ all-1$_1$-NOW-DIR
> 'We (exclusive) **will be doing** all those things, and when you arrive too we will together do all those things we agreed on.'

With stative predicates *-yka:* presents a situation as ongoing without requiring a constant input of energy. This non-progressive meaning of *-yka:* is illustrated with present tense in (56) and with conditional mood in (57).

---

[47] The suffix *-yka:* is glossed as CONT for continuous aspect, a term that specifically includes progressive meaning, and excludes habitual meaning. Habitual aspect is expressed in SCQ by a variety of markers presented in subsequent sections, including derivational *-rayka:*, inflectional past *-q*, and inflectional present *-Ø*. In neighboring varieties, continuous *-yka:* has taken on additional imperfective functions and is approaching inflectional status (see §5.4). The etymology of *-yka:* is introduced in §10.2 and further elaborated in §11.5. Its geographic distribution is shown in Map A.4 in Appendix A.

(56)   *kanan   o:ra   llaki-__yka__-n   papa:-nin   ima-na-chi*
       now   hour   be.sad-__CONT__-3   father-3   what-NOW-CNJ
       'Perhaps at this time his father **is missing** him.'

(57)   *ohala: kuti-na-:-pa:-pis   llapa-n   yamay-lla*
       hopefully   return-NMLZ.I-1-PURP-EVEN   all-3   fine-DLM
       ka-__yka:__-ya-n-man
       be-__CONT__-PL.V-3-COND
       'Hopefully by the time I return everybody **might be fine**.'

In (54)-(57) continuous *-yka:* is illustrated with finite clauses. It also appears in nonfinite
clauses 27% of the time, as in (58). In contrast, durative *-ra:* appears in nonfinite clauses 54% of
the time, twice as often as *-yka:*. The distribution of these suffixes with respect to finiteness
reflects the fact that continuous *-yka:* is compatible with past perfective *-ra*, conditional mood
and imperative mood, while durative *-ra:* is incompatible with those finite markers.

(58)   *tsay   aswana-chu   yaku   puwa-__yka__-pti-n-qa ...   pani-n-ta-wan*
       that   deep.pot-LOC   water   boil-__CONT__-DS-3-TOP   sister-3-OBJ-COM
       tsay   yaku   puwa-__yka__-q-man   qarpu-rpu-nki
       that   water   boil-__CONT__-AG-ALL push.down-COMPL-2
       'When the water **is boiling** in that pot, you push his sister down into that **boiling**
       water.'[48]

Continuous *-yka:* presents a paradigmatic contrast with the set of derivational perfective
suffixes in the non-obligatory verbal slot D4. Yet this slot goes unfilled by any aspect suffix in
approximately 50% of all predicates. The absence of a formal marker in this position is not
construed as aspectually meaningful.

In similar fashion, *-yka:* is not generally compatible with the younger inflectional past
perfective suffixes *-ru* and *-sha*, presumably because *-ru* was formerly a derivational perfective
(cf. §9.3) and *-sha* developed from a perfect expressed through periphrasis (cf. §9.5). In
contrast, *-yka:* does appear with the older past perfective *-ra*. This past imperfective combination
is illustrated with a dynamic predicate in (59) and with a stative predicate in (60).

(59)   *Upaya:cu-cho:-pis   tuka-__yka:__-ya-__ra__-n   ko:sa*
       Opayaco-LOC-EVEN   play-__CONT__-PL.V-__PST__-3   well
       'Even in Opayaco (the band members) **were playing** well.'

---

[48] The comitative suffix *-wan* stacked on the object suffix *-ta* in the form *pani-n-ta-wan* refers
to the sister plus several jewelry items already tossed into the boiling water.

(60) *tsay o:ra-qa-m   Ninfi-:tu   ari bu:rru-ntsi:-qa pri:ma-ntsi:*
    that hour-TOP-DIR Nymph-DIM.SP yes donkey-1$_1$-TOP cousin-1$_1$
    Dumicha-pa   ka-q   wayi-n-kaq-chu   ka-__yka:__-mu-__rqa__-n
    Domitila-GEN   be-AG   house-3-DEF-LOC   be-__CONT__-FAR-__PST__-3
    'At that time Ninfito, our donkey, __was at__ the house of our cousin Domitila.'

As illustrated above in (56) and (57), with stative predicates continuous *-yka:* presents a situation as ongoing yet non-progressive (without requiring sustained effort to continue). The combination of *-yka:* with the copula *ka-* can also form a predicate locative construction, as in (61), and a predicate attributive/nominative construction, as in (62). Continuous *-yka:* here indicates that the attribute 'frightened' is not an inherent or permanent characteristic of the subject. SCQ-Spanish bilinguals typically translate *ka-yka:-* into Spanish as *estar* and the copula *ka-* (without continuous *-yka:*) as *ser* (cf. Zagona 2002:47-8).

(61) *tronku hana-n-chu:-na   sa:pu-kuna llapa-n   ka-__yka:__-ya-n*
    log   top-3-LOC-NOW   frog-PL.N   all-3   be-__CONT__-PL.V-3
    'All the frogs __are on top__ of the log now.'

(62) *wamra   mantsa-ka-sha   ka-__yka__-n*
    child   fear-PASS-PTCP   be-__CONT__-3
    'The child __is__ frightened.'

As we have seen, continuous *-yka:* with the copula *ka-* ordinarily presents an ongoing situation as non-progressive, while *-ra:* indicates extended duration. This is not the case, however, in the syntactic configuration illustrated in (63) and (64). Here, *-yka:* appears with the copula marked with finite morphology, and durative *-ra:* appears with a dynamic predicate in an adjacent adverbial clause. These two syntactic elements, linked through periphrasis as a single aspectualizing construction, emphasize instead that the ongoing action characterizes the extended time period.[49]

(63) *tsay-ta chupa-ku-q-ta   ta:pa-__ra__-r-mi   may   ka-__yka__-n*
    that-OBJ drink-MID-AG-OBJ   guard-__DUR__-SS-DIR   maybe   be-__CONT__-3
    'She may be __vigilantly guarding__ him from a drinking binge.'

(64) *llapa-n   ka-__yka:__-ya-n   rika-__ra__-r   wamra-ta*
    all-3   be-__CONT__-PL.V-3 see-__DUR__-SS child-OBJ
    'All (together) __are watching__ the child.'

---

[49] "V-SS AUXILIARY", exemplified in (63) and (64), is just one type of analytic verbal construction that expresses an aspectual distinction. Aspectual constructions are the focus of Chapter 11.

While continuous *-yka:* and durative *-ra:* appear on separate syntactic elements in (63) and (64), these two suffixes often combine within the same verb as in (65). The frequent combination of *-ra:* plus *-yka:* gives rise to the suffix *-rayka:*, the topic of the next section.

(65) *tsay puka ratash-nin-ta wallqa-__rayka__-nqa-n-pita   hipi-ska-mu-r-nin-qa,*
     that   red   cloth-3-OBJ   hang-__DUR.C__-NMLZ.R-3-ABL remove-PFV-FAR-SS-3-TOP

     tsay-wan limpiya-ski-r-nin-qa, a:nir wiña-n   kanasta-man
     that-COM   clean-PFV-SS-3-TOP   later put.in-3   basket-ALL

     'Removing that red cloth from where it __customarily hangs__ from his neck, cleaning it with that, he then puts it into the basket.'

This section has shown several characteristics of the suffix *-yka:*. We can formulate the following conclusions. First, *-yka:* expresses continuous aspect, that is, it presents a situation as ongoing but not habitual. With dynamic predicates *-yka:* conveys progressive meaning, and with stative predicates non-progressive meaning. In contrast, durative *-ra:* does not appear with statives but derives statives from dynamic verbs. Second, continuous *-yka:* functions as an imperfective counterpart to the derivational perfective suffixes in the non-obligatory slot D4 (cf. §2.1). It is generally incompatible with the inflectional past perfective suffixes *-ru* and *-sha*, but occurs freely with past perfective *-ra* to derive a past imperfective. Third, continuous *-yka:* collocates with all lexical items. It is thirteen times more frequent in the coded data than durative *-ra:*. Fourth, *-yka:* can be followed by derivational suffixes prior to the inflectional person and TAM markers in slot I2. Finally, the amalgamation of durative *-ra:* followed by continuous *-yka:* yields the more general imperfective suffix *-rayka:*, which is presented in the next section.

3.1.3   *-rayka:* 'continuous-durative (stative), habitual (dynamic)'

The derivational suffix *-rayka:* is transparently derived from the frequent combination of durative *-ra:* and continuous *-yka:*. Semantic, structural, and distributional evidence for the fusion of *-rayka:* as a single suffix is presented in Table 3.1 at the end of this section.[50]

With stative verbs *-rayka:* expresses the compositional meaning continuous-durative, which presents a continuing state over a relatively extended period of time. With dynamic verbs *rayka:* spans a range of connected senses in which an event is presented as repeated continually (continuative), customarily (habitual), or frequently (frequentative). Continuatives and frequentatives are habituals in which the internal temporal structure of recurrence is more fully specified. These noncompositional meanings are more than the sum of the individual durative and continuous elements (from *-ra:* and *-yka:*, respectively). This spectrum of interrelated senses is illustrated below, beginning with dynamic verbs, and followed by stative verbs.

---

[50] The suffix *-rayka:* is glossed as DUR.C for its compositional continuous-durative reading with stative verbs. More frequently, *-rayka:* occurs with dynamic verbs yielding a habitual reading.

The suffix *-rayka:* most frequently appears with dynamic verbs inflected for present, though it does occasionally appear with pasts and futures. Continuative, often translated as 'deliberately continue doing' or 'keep on', is illustrated in (66)-(68). Continuative aspect should not be confused with continuous aspect expressed by *-yka:* alone, which refers more generally to an ongoing situation.

(66) *imayka-ta-pis   mas   puri-__rayka:__-ya:-mu-n   wakin,*
      all.kinds-OBJ-EVEN   more   walk-__DUR.C__-PL.V-FAR-3   some

      peru   wakin   deha-ku-ya-n
      but   some   leave-MID-PL.V-3

      'Some __keep on doing__ (go about) most of their duties, but others abandon them.'

(67) *atoq-qa   puri-sh   ga:latuku-r.   a:nir,   puri-__rayka__-pti-n-qa*
      fox-TOP   walk-PST.R3   show.off-SS   later   walk-__DUR.C__-DS-3-TOP

      "grasyas   tiyu-y ..."   ni-na: ari   sapate:ru-ta-qa
      thank.you   uncle-VOC   say-PST.N   yes   shoemaker-OBJ-TOP

      'The fox walked around showing off. Later, after __parading__ around, he said to the shoemaker, "Thank you, sir ..."

In (68), *-rayka:* is formally expressed in an adverbial clause marked by *-r* 'SS'. The continuative notion is reinforced through periphrasis with the verb *si:gi-* 'continue, keep on' (from Spanish *seguir* 'follow, continue').[51]

(68) *yapay   na:ni-ta-qa   tari-ski-ya-:   hawa   u:ra-chu.*
      again   path-OBJ-TOP   find-PFV-PL.V-1   below   down-LOC

      tsa   __si:gi__-ya-:   aywa-__rayka__-r
      then   __continue__-PL.V-1   go-__DUR.C__-SS

      'Again we find the path far below. Then we __keep on going__.'

The habitual function of *-rayka:* is illustrated with the dynamic predicate in (69). It may be translated as 'customarily' or 'constantly'.

---

[51] The verb *si:gi-* 'continue' is recruited from Spanish to participate in the native aspectual periphrastic construction "V-SS AUXILIARY". Within this construction, the erstwhile "matrix" verb *si:gi-*, illustrated here in (68) and also in (75), is better analyzed as a nascent aspectual auxiliary. Continuative *si:gi-* is comparable to the copular auxiliary *ka-* which appears in the "V-SS AUXILIARY" construction illustrated in (63) and (64). Aspectualizing constructions and auxiliation are treated in detail in Chapter 11.

(69) *osyo:su-kuna   rika-__rayka:__-ya-n   listu-lla-ta   wap tsari-r apa-r*
lazy-PL.N   see-__DUR.C__-PL.V-3   ready-DLM-OBJ fast grab-SS take-SS
rantiku-ri-ya:-na-n-pa:
sell-PUNC-PL.V-NMLZ.I-3-PURP
'Lazy people __customarily watch__ to grab anything and take it to sell.'

Frequentative is illustrated in (70) and (71), and may be translated as 'often' or 'regularly'.

(70) *ari watuka-__rayka__-nki, sino:-qa   llaki-ku-n   mas-cha:*
yes visit-__DUR.C__-2   or.else-TOP be.sad-MID-3 more-MUT
'Yes, you __visit often__, or else she may become too sad.'

(71) *kanta-y-ta   ora-ku-y-ta   llapa-n-ta wamra-kuna ko:sa-na*
sing-INF-OBJ   pray-MID-INF-OBJ all-3-OBJ   child-PL.N   well-NOW
yacha-ku-__rayka__-n
learn-MID-__DUR.C__-3
'The children __regularly learn__ well how to sing, to pray, everything.'

Turning now to stative verbs, *-rayka:* presents a continuing state over a relatively extended period of time. This compositional continuous-durative sense is translated here as 'remain' or 'be'. *-rayka:* can appear in finite stative verbs where the time period is specified as present (72), as past (73), or as future (74).

(72) *ichik imayka-kuna-pis   wayi-cho: falta-__rayka__-n,*
small all.kinds-PL.N-EVEN   house-LOC lack-__DUR.C__-3
imayka   ichik ka-__rayka__-n   problema-kuna
all.kinds small be-__DUR.C__-3 problem
'A few small things in the house __are in short supply__. A few small problems __remain__.'

(73) *tse:pita ishpa-ku-nqa-n-pita   kuti-mu-na-n-pa: bu:rru-n*
then   urinate-MID-NMLZ.R-3-ABL   return-FAR-NMLZ.I-3-PURP donkey-3
ka-na:-tsu,   kolcha-lla-n   qotu-__rayka:__-na:
be-PST.N-NEG saddle-DLM-3 lie.in.heap-__DUR.C__-PST.N
'By the time he returned from urinating, his donkey was gone. Just his saddle __remained lying__ in a heap.'

(74) *wakin wanu-__rayka__-nqa i   mas-mi   keda-__rayka:__-shun*
some   die-__DUR.C__-FUT3 and   more-DIR remain-__DUR.C__-FUT1$_1$
'Some will __die__ (in the coming years) and others of us will __remain__ (alive).'

-rayka: can also appear in nonfinite statives, such as the adverbial clause here in (75), and the nominalized form above in (65).

(75) *tsay qeru-chu si:gi-n pepinu wata-__rayka__-r*
that tree-LOC continue-3 cucumber tie.up-__DUR.C__-SS
'In that tree the cucumber continues to __remain tied up__.'

The dynamic predicates illustrated in (65)-(71) above present semantic evidence for the fusion of *-rayka:* as a single suffix, distinct from the individual suffixes, durative *-ra:* and continuous *-yka:*. The meanings of these three suffixes are listed in row 1 of Table 3.1. The coded data also provide structural and distributional evidence. The facts presented in rows 1-3 of Table 3.1 make a general distinction between *-rayka:* and the two individual forms *-ra:* and *-yka:*. *-rayka:* is differentiated specifically from durative *-ra:* in rows 4-7, and from continuous *-yka:* in rows 8 and 9.[52]

Table 3.1 *Evidence for -rayka: as a single fused suffix*

	-ra: ALONE	*-yka:* ALONE	*-rayka:* COMBINED
-rayka:* versus *-ra:* and *-yka:			
1. Semantics	durative	continuous	continuous-durative (state) habitual (dynamic)
2. Token frequency	13	169	31
3. Suffixes do not intervene	n/a	n/a	✓
-rayka:* versus *-ra:			
4. Verbal suffix slot	D1	D4	D4
5. Present habitual *-Ø*	23%	76%	94%
6. 3rd person	30%	82%	90%
7. Nonfinite clause	46%	16%	3%
-rayka:* versus *-yka:			
8. Copula *ka-*	0%	25%	≈0%
9. Motion verbs	0%	25%	3%

In row 2 the combined form *-rayka:* differs from both durative *-ra:* and continuous *-yka:* in terms of token frequency. *-rayka:* appears more than twice as often as *-ra:* alone (31 versus 13 exemplars), and about 20% as often as *-yka:* alone (31 versus 169 exemplars).

---

[52] The fusion of derivational aspect suffix combinations in SCQ, e.g., *-ri-yku* 'perfective' and *-ra-yka:* 'habitual', is comparable to the process of "amalgamation" described by Mithun and Ali (1996) for Central Alaskan Yup'ik (Eskimoan). This language, like SCQ, is characterized by extensive polysynthesis, with aspect expressed through derivational morphology. Mithun and Ali suggest that these morphological qualities may facilitate "the extensive amalgamation of existing aspectual markers to yield new categories" (ibid.:127).

Row 3 shows that other derivational suffixes ordinarily do not intervene between the two components *-ra:-yka:*, even though two verbal slots present that morphological possibility. For example, durative *-ra:* fills verbal slot D1 in (76), preceding middle voice *-ku* in slot D2. In contrast, the combined form *-rayka:* fills slot D4, following *-ku* in (77).[53]

(76)   *tse: serra:nu-qa   maya-**ra:-ku**-na:*   *upa:lla   katri   siki-n-chu*
       that   hillbilly-TOP   be.alert-**DUR-MID**-PST.N   silent   bed   butt-3-LOC
       'That hillbilly was silently **alert a long time** under the bed.'

(77)   *aywa-:   kuti-**ku-rayka:**-sha:,   tayta-y*
       go-1   return-**MID-DUR.C**-FUT1   father-VOC
       'I am going, I will **continue returning** home, sir.'

In row 4 *-rayka:* fills verbal slot D4, the position of *-yka:*. It does not fill slot D1, the position of *-ra:*. In row 5, we see that 94% of *-rayka:* exemplars occur with present habitual *-Ø*; in contrast, only 23% of *-ra:* exemplars occur with *-Ø*. In row 6, 90% of *-rayka:* exemplars appear with third person; only 30% of *-ra:* exemplars do. In row 7, only 3% of *-rayka:* exemplars appear in nonfinite clauses but half of *-ra:* exemplars do.

The distributional facts presented in rows 8 and 9 distinguish *-rayka:* from *-yka:*. In row 8, *-rayka:* almost never appears with the copula, but 25% of *-yka:* exemplars do. In row 9, only 3% of *-rayka:* exemplars appear with motion verbs, but 25% of *-yka:* exemplars do.

Summarizing, the derivational suffix *-rayka:* marks continuous-durative aspect with stative verbs, and subtypes of habitual aspect with dynamic verbs. *-rayka:* is typically inflected for present. It is derived historically from the combination of durative *-ra:* followed by continuous *-yka:*. Synchronically, in terms of its semantics and also its lexical and morphosyntactic distribution, *-rayka:* is analyzed here as a single suffix, distinct from both *-ra:* and *-yka:*.

With dynamic verbs *-rayka:* spans a range of closely related senses, including continuative (action deliberately continued on one occasion), habitual (action customarily repeated on different occasions), and frequentative (action frequently occurs on various occasions). A common thread which connects these senses is the notion of recurrence. Recurrence is also expressed in SCQ by the iterative suffix *-ykacha:* (subactions repeated on a single occasion), the distributive suffix *-paku* (action repeated at various locations), the distributive enclitic *=yan* (action repeated on various occasions) and by verbal reduplication (a variety of iterative and

---

[53] In the SCQ corpus middle voice *-ku* (discussed in Chapter 8) precedes *-rayka:* in all but one verb, *unchu-**ra:-ku-yka**-n* 'it is sitting still on hind legs'. The verb *unchu-* 'sit' and durative *-ra:* appear to have co-lexicalized, such that *-ku* and *-yka:* are added to the inseparable lexical element *unchura:-* 'sit still'. The fact that *-ku* frequently combines with *-yka:* (8% of *-yka:* exemplars) may also be relevant.

repetitive senses). These repetitive markers are presented in the next four sections, beginning with iterative *-ykacha:*.

3.1.4   *-ykacha:* 'iterative'

The derivational suffix *-ykacha:* (*-kacha:* after *i*) presents a situation with multiple subactions which recur on a single occasion. This is illustrated in (78) where the flowers are not shining steadily, but rather are glittering in the sunlight.[54]

> (78)   *tsay   qaqa-kuna-cho:-qa   imayka-la:ya   lindu   tuktu-q*
>   that   mountain-PL.N-LOC-TOP   all.kinds-TYPE beautiful bloom-AG
>
>   *wayta-kuna-pis   atsikya-__ykacha:__-na:-ra:*
>   flower-PL.N-EVEN   shine-__ITER__-PST.N-YET
>
>   'In those mountains, all kinds of beautiful blooming flowers were **glittering**.'

The recurring subactions marked by iterative *-ykacha:* generally take place at a single location. The location may be interpreted more broadly, however, based on the inherent semantics of the verb. For instance, with motion verb constructions the location includes the entire trajectory. In (79) the sick bull did not just hit an obstacle along the path, but rather was stumbling into things repeatedly.

> (79)   *pasaypa   antsa   ka-r-na-sh   wiru-ka-__ykacha__-r-lla-na   puri-yka:-na:*
>   very   sick   be-SS-NOW-RPT   hit-PASS-__ITER__-SS-DLM-NOW   walk-CONT-PST.N
>
>   'Being very sick now, **repeatedly stumbling**, it was walking into things.'

The derivational nature of iterative *-ykacha:* is evident in the previous examples not only from its occurrence in a non-obligatory position close to the verb root, but also from its interaction with the inherent semantics of particular verbs. This interaction is also seen when iterative *-ykacha:* occurs with cyclical verbs. For example, the verb root *hiruru-* 'spin' involves multiple cycles. When 'spin' is combined with *-ykacha:* in (80), the resultant meaning is 'keep going around', that is, continuative aspect.

> (80)   *allaw-chi   bu:rru-ntsi:-kuna-pis   kuya-pa-ypa   hinan   kinray-lla*
>   pity-CNJ   donkey-1ᵣ-PL.N-EVEN   love-BEN-ADV   same   vicinity-DLM
>
>   *hiruru-__ykacha__-yka:-ya-n-pis*
>   spin-__ITER__-CONT-PL.V-3-EVEN
>
>   'Our poor donkeys pitifully **keep going around** to the same (grassless) places.'

---

[54] The etymology of iterative *-ykacha:* is uncertain. Further discussion is presented following (291) in §10.4.

In (81) the verb root *ko:rri-* 'run' also involves multiple cycles, and results in continuative meaning when combined with *-ykacha:*. In contrast, the semelfactive verb root *tiwya-* 'bounce' specifies a single cycle. When *-ykacha:* is added to 'bounce', the single cycle is realized repeatedly, a true iterative.

(81) *tsay-qa   tiwya-__ykacha__-r-shi   ko:rri-__kacha__-yka-n   uma-n-qa*
      that-TOP   bounce-__ITER__-SS-RPT   run-__ITER__-CONT-3   head-3-TOP
      'That head (of the giant worm) __repeatedly bouncing__, __keeps on rolling__ (downhill).'

Iterative *-ykacha:* is often followed by continuous *-yka:* in multi-cycle verbs, as illustrated by *hiruru-* 'spin' in (80), and by *ko:rri-* 'run' in (81). In this context, the suffix combination *-ykacha:-yka:* communicates that the action repeated at a single location does not involve purposeful, decisive action. In contrast, with habitual *-ra-yka:* (used as a continuative) the unfolding action is deliberate, and the location is not restricted, as illustrated above in (66)-(68). In other words, the aspect suffix combinations *-ykacha:-yka:* and *-rayka:* further distinguish meanings in the semantic domains of modality (intention), manner (subaction), and space (location). Each of these topics is discussed below in PART III.

Just as *-ykacha:* can be followed by an imperfective suffix, it can also be followed by a perfective, such as *-yku* in (82). Here, *-yku* wraps up the entire scene of repeated action (expressed by *-kacha*) as a single whole within the narrative (cf. note 59 on the combination of perfective and imperfective markers).

(82) *wakin-na-sh   wiru-r,   toqi-r,   hayta-r,   samqa-r*
      other-NOW-RPT   whip-SS   spit-SS   kick-SS   stone-SS
      qati-__kacha-yku__-ya:-na:
      follow-__ITER-PFV.O__-PL.V-PST.N
      'Others __kept pursuing it__, whipping, spitting, kicking, and throwing stones at it.'

Finally, speakers may enlarge what they present as a single occasion with multiple subactions. For example, the speaker in (83) gives advice to a couple before their wedding. Here, *-ykacha:* specifies that challenges appear "back and forth" throughout married life.

(83) *huk   familya-ta   taku-ka-ski-r   yunta-no: apa-__ykacha__-naku-n*
      one   family-OBJ   join-MID-PFV-SS   pair.oxen-SIM   carry-__ITER__-RECP-3
      ishka-n-la:-pa:
      two-3-SIDE-PURP
      'Forming a single joined family, like a pair of yoked oxen they __carry__ the load together __shifting back and forth__ between the two sides (throughout life).'

The situation in (84) is similarly construed by the speaker as an iterative sequence on a single extended occasion. A member of the community died as authorities dispersed an organized protest. At the funeral the speaker in (84) admonishes the community to confront the authorities in order to circumvent further injustices repeated "at every opportunity."

(84) *mas-mi   sha:-ya:-mu-nqa.   kushi-ku-r   tapri-**ykacha:**-ma:-shun-mi*
      more-DIR   stand-PL.V-FAR-FUT3   be.happy-MID-SS   knock.over-**ITER**-1OBJ-FUT1ᵢ-DIR
      'They will come again. They will happily **knock us down at every opportunity**.'

As shown in (83) and (84), an iterative sequence may transpire during a single extended occasion spanning months or years, especially when projected into the future. Repeated action during a relatively long time period may easily be understood as a frequentative or a habitual, that is, a situation that is frequently or customarily repeated on separate occasions. Not surprisingly, iteratives are a common source for habitual markers in many languages, with the inference of customary repetition becoming reanalyzed as the central meaning over time (Bybee et al. 1994:172).

In summary, the derivational suffix *-ykacha:* reports a multiplicity of subactions repeated on a single occasion. Generally, the occasion is brief, but the speaker may portray a long sequence of subactions as a single extended occasion. Iterative *-ykacha:* appears in the inner layer of affixation in verbal suffix slot D3 and interacts with the inherent semantics of particular verb roots and classes. For example, *-ykacha:* can convey a continuative interpretation with multi-cycle verbs. Unlike the derivational aspect markers presented so far, iterative *-ykacha:* combines with both perfective and imperfective derivational suffixes. The distributive suffix *-paku*, presented in the next section, also combines with both types of derivational aspect markers.

3.1.5 *-paku* 'spatial distributive'

The derivational suffix *-paku* presents a recurring action distributed over various locations within a circumscribed area. Although the central meaning is not temporal, the notion of duration is conveyed in every instantiation.[55] Typically, the specific locations indicated by *-paku* are not arranged in advance. For example, in (85) an individual is directed to go to a certain vicinity asking each neighbor whether they have seen a lost animal.[56]

(85) *tsay-pa-tsura:-pis   aywa-sh.   ma: aywa-y   tapu-**paku**-r*
      that-GEN-DUB-EVEN   go-PST.R3   lets.see go-IMP2   ask-**DISTR.S**-SS
      'Maybe it went by that area. So go **asking all around**.'

---

[55] The suffix *-paku* is glossed as DISTR.S for spatial distributive. The fact that duration, a secondary aspectual notion, is conveyed by *-paku* 100% of the time suggests that the distinction between semantics and inference is not always clear-cut. Aspect as an extension from recurring action (iterative *-ykacha:*, distributive *-paku*, and verb root reduplication) is discussed in §7.2.2.

[56] The etymology of distributive *-paku* is uncertain. It may have formed over time through the amalgamation of benefactive *-pu* or *-paya* (benefit of others) plus *-ku* 'reflexive/middle voice' (benefit of self). Evidence is presented in §10.4. Cognates of *-paku* are reported throughout the Central Quechua area, in Cuzco, and in Lambayeque. See Map A.8 in Appendix A.

As with the derivational perfective suffixes (cf. §2.1), distributive *-paku* ends with a high vowel that is lowered to *a* when followed by a trigger suffix. The allomorph *-paka* appears in the nominalized subject in (86), triggered by cislocative *-mu*.

(86) *ichik   ka-ra-n-ra: ranti-__paka__-ya:-mu-sha-:*
     small   be-PST-3-YET   buy-__DISTR.S__-PL.V-FAR-NMLZ.R-1

     yapay   kuti-ya:-mu-na-:-pa:
     again   return-PL.V-FAR-NMLZ.I-1-PURP

     'A few things which we __bought here and there__ for the return trip were still left.'

Like iterative *-ykacha:*, distributive *-paku* combines with both perfective and imperfective derivational suffixes (cf. note 59). For example, *-paku* appears frequently with perfective *-yku* and punctual *-ri*, seen here in (87) and (88), respectively.

(87) *ishki-yku-r   hicha-__paku__-__yku__-shqa*
     fall-PFV.O-SS   dump-__DISTR.S__-__PFV.O__-PST.R3

     'Falling to the ground, he __dumped__ them __all over__.'

(88) *tsa   tse:-chu mika-__paku__-__ri__-r-na   pa:sa-ya:-mu-:   tsakay   tsakay-na*
     then   that-LOC eat-__DISTR.S__-__PUNC__-SS-NOW   pass-PL.V-FAR-1   night   night-NOW

     ka:si   Caras-man
     almost   Caraz-ALL

     'Then after __hastily eating some things__ (reaching for different foods) there, we pass through the night to Caraz.'

Distributive *-paku* is the only suffix presented here in §3.1 which co-occurs with perfective *-ski*.[57]

(89) *ichik   dyos-nintsik-mi   makya-ma-ru-ntsik   ka: ichik   huk   ishke:*
     small   god-1-DIR   hand-1OBJ-PST.R-1₁   here   small   one   two

     aru-__paku__-__ski__-na-pa: *ima-pis   faltamyentu-ntsik-pa:*
     work-__DISTR.S__-__PFV__-NMLZ.I₁-PURP   what-EVEN   lack-1₁-PURP

     'Our God has handed us a small job or two __to work here and there__, so that we will not lack anything.'

---

[57] Although *-paku* occurs with the perfectives *-yku*, *-ri*, and *-ski*, it does not occur with the perfectives *-rpu* and *-rku*. David Weber (p.c.) suggests a plausible explanation. To the extent that *-paku* indicates distribution on a two-dimensional "horizontal plane" of daily existence, forms derived from **-rpu* 'down' and **-rku* 'up' would take one off this plane.

Distributive *-paku* occasionally precedes imperfectives as well, such as continuous *-yka:* in (90). The compatibility of *-paku* (in slot D2) with derivational perfectives and imperfectives (in slot D4) reflects the less abstract (more derivational) adverbial semantics of distributed action.

(90) *tsa: sa:badu   hunaq-na   qoya-ya-ru-:*   *tse:-cho: resa-ku-yka-r*
      then   saturday   day-NOW   pass.day-PL.V-PST.R-1   that-LOC   pray-MID-CONT-SS

      libru-kuna-ta   liyi-pa-yka-r ...   tsay-cho: rika-yka-r
      book-PL.N-OBJ   read-BEN-CONT-SS   that-LOC   see-CONT-SS

      musya-__paku__-__yka__-r
      know-DISTR.S-CONT-SS

      'Then on Saturday we passed the day there praying, reading books... **getting to know that area** by looking around.'

We have seen that distributive *-paku* reports an event that is spread over various locations. This "plurality of action" is often distributed over an implied collection of direct objects, e.g., 'ask (the neighbors)' in (85), 'buy (snacks)' in (86), 'dump (produce)' in (87), and 'eat (some things)' in (88). The collection is sometimes expressed by an overt plural object, e.g., 'all kinds of things' in (91), where the fiesta sponsor went from house to house making arrangements for the coming celebration.

(91) *tsa   fyesta   cha:-mu-q-no:-na*   *ka-pti-n-qa   lista-ku-sha,*
      then   fiesta   arrive-FAR-AG-SIM-NOW   be-DS-3-TOP   prepare-MID-PST.R3

      imayka-ta-na   rura-__paku__-sh
      all.kinds-OBJ-NOW   do-**DISTR.S**-PST.R3

      'Then because the time for the fiesta was approaching, he prepared, he **did here and there** all kinds of things.'

Mithun (1999a:90) has shown that distributives are a common source for plural markers in many languages, with the inference of plurality becoming reanalyzed as the central meaning over time. Given this scenario, it is plausible that distributive *-paku* and the verbal plural suffix *-pa:ku* (found in Central Quechuan varieties east and south of SCQ) are cognate. Further evidence for the DISTRIBUTIVE > PLURAL hypothesis is found in the similar SCQ forms, distributive *=yan* and plural *-ya:* (see the final paragraph in the next section).

While distributive *-paku* presents a recurring action spread over multiple locations, the recurring subactions marked by iterative *-ykacha:* are generally realized at a single location or along a single trajectory. Both markers are presented here as subtypes of imperfective aspect because they specify recurrence, which implies internal temporal structure in all cases. As repetitives, however, these suffixes also report adverbial characteristics of an event, that is, how the action is carried out in particular locations. We will take a closer look at the adverbial and spatial meanings associated with these and other markers in Chapter 7 "Aspect and manner."

3.1.6   *=yan* 'temporal distributive'

The distributive enclitic *=yan* appears in verbs and also in nonverbal syntactic elements.[58] With nouns *=yan* presents entities as distributed over space. For example, in (92) the shortcuts are located at various switchbacks on the mountain trail.

(92) *tse:-cho:-pis   chaki na:ni-n-pa=__yan__   noqa   ga:na-mu-: ishka-n-ta pase:pa*
      that-LOC-EVEN foot   path-3-GEN=__DISTR.T__ I   win-FAR-1   two-3-OBJ   very
      'Also, by those **various footpaths** (shortcuts) I arrived far ahead of both of them.'

Distributive *=yan* may also appear with numerals, as in (93), where the full set of sixteen participants is spread over subsets of four each.

(93) *chunka hoqta-ta chura-rqa-n   chusku   chusku=__yan__*
      ten   six-OBJ   put-PST-3   four   four=__DISTR.T__
      troka-pa-pa   kwi:da-ya:-na-n-pa:
      trade-ADV-GEN   watch-PL.V-NMLZ.I-3-PURP
      'They placed sixteen guards in order to watch him by turns **in groups of four**.'

In the preceding examples, *=yan* indicates that the entities are distributed over space. In line with general space to time developments, *=yan* most often marks occasions as distributed over time. In the predicate construction below, the speaker portrays the hunger of a single individual (himself) as recurring on many separate occasions.

(94) *o:ra-ta-qa   mallaq-lla=__yan__-pis   ka-rqu-:-mi*
      hour-ADV-TOP   hunger-DLM=__DISTR.T__-EVEN be-PST.R-1-DIR
      'I was often hungry on various occasions.'

Similarly, in (95) *=yan* appears in a nominalized form of the verb *kicha-* 'open' which functions as an argument of the verb *tari-* 'find'. The meaning of the matrix clause is that they found the door left open on each occasion, that is, each morning when they came downstairs.

---

[58] The enclitic *=yan* is glossed DISTR.T for temporal distributive. Parker describes a suffix *-yan* in Huaylas Quechua as "the only case marker whose analysis remains in doubt" (1976:85). Subsequent research shows that *=yan* is a distributive enclitic in SCQ and Corongo Quechua (Hintz 2000:189). This form is limited to Ancash and western Huánuco departments in central Peru. The etymology is uncertain (see Map A.8 in Appendix A). It may derive from a distributive numeral meaning 'n each', later generalizing to 'each entity', a current meaning with nonverbal elements. The distribution of entities in space would have extended to the distribution of events in time. Distributive *=yan* may be cognate with the verbal plural suffix *-ya:*; a form with which *=yan* does not co-occur. Both forms are attested only in the Central Quechuan varieties of Ancash and western Huánuco.

(95) *empliya:du-n-kuna altus-cho: punu-ya-sha-n-pita,   qoya-kuna-pa*
     servant-3-PL.N   top.floor-LOC   sleep-PL.V-NMLZ.R-3-ABL   morning-PL.N-GEN

     yarpa-mu-r-qa   sawan   punku-ta-na   tari-ya:-na:
     descend-FAR-SS-TOP main.door   doorway-OBJ-NOW find-PL.V-PST.N

     *kicha-rayka-q-ta=**yan***
     open-DUR.C-AG-OBJ=**DISTR.T**

     'When the servants came down in the mornings from where they slept on the top floor, they discovered the main door **left wide open each time**.'

As an enclitic, distributive *=yan* also appears in verbs, where it presents events as distributed over various occasions. In (96) *=yan* indicates that the participants prayed on many separate occasions over time. This meaning is reinforced by the adverb *syempri* (from Spanish *siempre* 'always').

(96) *ashma-pa:-pis   imayka-pa:-pis   tse: maña-ku-ru-ntsik=**yan***   *syempri*
     animal-PURP-EVEN all.kinds-PURP-EVEN   that ask-MID-PST.R-1ᵢ=**DISTR.T**   always

     ari   noqa-ntsik wakin   mana   yarpa-pti-n-pis   tayta   dyos-nintsik-man
     yes   I-1ᵢ   other   no   think-DS-3-EVEN father god-1ᵢ-ALL

     'We always **prayed on each occasion** to our Father God for the animals and for all kinds of things, even though others don't think about this.'

In (97) *=yan* individuates the man's repeated visits in the past.

(97) *tsay-man huk   runa   cha:-na:=**yan***   *enamora:du tuku-r*
     that-ALL one   man   arrive-PST.N=**DISTR.T** in.love   pretend-SS

     ishka-n-man
     two-3-ALL

     'A certain man **would arrive on various occasions** pretending to be in love with both of them.'

Distributive *=yan* appears not only on finite verbs, as in (96) and (97), but also on nonfinite verbs, as in the following examples.

(98) *parla-ku-r   sha-ya:-mu-n   noqa punta-ta haqi-**ski**-r=**yan***   *shuya-:*
     speak-MID-SS come-PL.V-FAR-3 I   first-ADV leave-**PFV**-SS=**DISTR.T** wait-1

     'They come along chitchatting (and) **leaving them each time** to go further ahead, I wait (impatiently).'

Interestingly, in nonfinite verbs *=yan* typically appears together with a derivational perfective suffix, such as *-ski* in (98), once each with *-yku* and *-ri* in (99), and with *-rku* above in

(8). The combination of *=yan* with a perfective suffix results in a "habitual perfective" reading, that is, a continuative composed of a series of bounded actions.[59]

(99)   *nirkur   ashma   oqra-ka-q-ta   kuti-tsi-ya:-mu-ru-:*
       then   animal   lose-PASS-AG-OBJ   return-CAUS-PL.V-FAR-PST.R-1
       maha:da-n-pita ama:las   komisyun-ta   apa-__yku__-r=__yan__
       flock-3-ABL   obligated commission-OBJ take-__PFV.O__-SS=__DISTR.T__
       komisyun-ta   manda-__ri__-r=__yan__
       commission-OBJ   send-__PUNC__-SS=__DISTR.T__
       'Then we made them return the animals that were lost from the flock, obligating them by __taking a posse each time__, by __sending a posse each time__.'

Although distributive *=yan* is similar to distributive *-paku*, it differs in several important respects. First, as we saw above, the enclitic *=yan* can attach to verbal or nonverbal syntactic elements. With nonverbal elements *=yan* presents entities distributed over space. With verbs and with deverbal elements it presents events distributed over time. In contrast, *-paku* is restricted to verbs, where it generally reports a sequence of events spread over various locations.

Second, the enclitic *=yan* appears beyond the outer layer of inflectional affixes in slot E1 (where E stands for enclitic), while *-paku* appears in the inner layer of affixation in slot D2. In terms of the usual morphological criteria, *-paku* is expressed derivationally, while *=yan* shares some characteristics of both derivation and inflection. In terms of derivation, *=yan* has a very low frequency, its verbal position is optional, and lack of a formal marker in this position is not meaningful. In terms of inflection, *=yan* appears far from the verb root, it closes off further derivation, and the meaning 'distributed over occasions' is both abstract and regular.[60]

Finally, distributive *=yan* is spoken only in the southern SCQ subdialect (not in the northern SCQ area) and in a few neighboring Quechuan varieties in Ancash and western Huánuco. As

---

[59] The concept of "habitual perfective" has been described for a variety of languages, including Russian (Comrie 1976:31), Central Pomo (Mithun 2000:274-6), and Dublin English (Hickey 2005:117-8). Grammatical constructions which similarly combine perfective and imperfective include "perfective progressive" in Spanish and in Portuguese, "perfective imperfect" in Georgian, and both "imperfective aorist" and "perfective imperfect" in Bulgarian (Comrie 1976:22ff., 126), as well as "perfective repetitive" and "perfective distributive" in Koyukon Athabaskan (Axelrod 1993:120). The "perfective repetitive/distributive" constructions in particular are reminiscent of the SCQ derivational aspect suffix combinations illustrated here, viz., iterative *-ykacha:* with perfective *-yku* in (82), distributive *-paku* with the perfectives *-yku* in (87), *-ri* in (88), and *-ski* in (89), and distributive *=yan* with the perfectives *-rku* in (8), *-ski* in (98), and once each with *-yku* and *-ri* in (99). SCQ aspect marker combinations are summarized in Table 4.2 (Chapter 4).

[60] For analysis of the derivational and inflectional status of several SCQ aspect markers, see Appendix B.

noted in the previous section, distributives are a common source for plural markers through the grammaticization of the inference of plurality. Intriguingly, distributive *=yan* is attested in the same geographical region as the verbal plural suffix *-ya:*, and these two markers do not co-occur, suggesting that the similarity in form is not incidental. By the same reasoning, distributive *-paku* and plural *-pa:ku* (spoken east and south of SCQ) may be cognate (see §3.1.5). Pathways of grammaticization linking distributive with durative, habitual, and plural meanings are discussed in §10.4 and §10.5.

3.1.7   Verbal reduplication

Imperfective aspect in SCQ is expressed grammatically not only through verbal affixation and enclitics, but also through verbal reduplication. In this section I present various verbal reduplication configurations, each with a specialized imperfective meaning that further specifies internal temporal structure.[61]

Verbal reduplication is iconic in the sense that repetition of the verb may signal repetition of the action described by the verb. Thus, especially with dynamic verbs, reduplication can express iterative, distributive, continuative, or frequentative meanings. Some reduplicated forms yield a habitual reading in which a recurring action characterizes the time period. As with iterative *-ykacha:*, the aspectual meanings associated with reduplication can give rise to semantic extensions into the realms of modality (e.g., intentionality, affect) and manner (e.g., intensity, speed).[62]

Reduplication is derivational in that it is optional (nonreduplication is not aspectually meaningful) and it introduces a new concept relevant to the base meaning. Moreover, this concept may be semantically irregular and its meaning may be influenced by the inherent semantics of the verb and by the pragmatic context. In what follows, I describe six types of verbal reduplication which yield an aspectual interpretation, and an additional type which is non-aspectual.

---

[61] In the conclusion of this section and in subsequent chapters, inflected verbs reduplicated in their entirety (Types 1 and 2) are referred to as REDUP₁. Similarly, reduplications of the verb root alone (Types 3-6) are referred to as REDUP₂.

[62] The reduplication of nonverbal syntactic elements in SCQ often specifies plurality that involves a large number of individuated participants, e.g., *huk-wan huk-wan-pis* one-COM one-COM-EVEN 'with each partner'. Nonverbal reduplication is not discussed further in this work.

TYPE 1: Entire inflected finite verb

An inflected finite verb may be reduplicated in its entirety. This structure typically expresses continuative aspect, presenting an ongoing situation that involves extended intense effort. For example, the reduplicated finite verb in (100) yields the interpretation that the speaker and her family kept searching intensely through the night.

> (100) *llapa-:-kuna tsakay **ashi-ya-:**   **ashi-ya-:**   bu:rru-ta-qa*
> all-1-PL.N   night   search-PL.V-1   search-PL.V-1   donkey-OBJ-TOP
> 'All of us **keep searching** all night long for the donkey.'

In (101) the oats in the field are collectively in the intensive head-forming stage.

> (101) *kanan-kuna-qa **shikshi-n**   **shikshi-n**   pe,*
> now-PL.V-TOP   form.head-3   form.head-3   so
> 'In fact, the current ones (oats) are **in the process of forming heads**.'

Reduplicated finite verbs do not appear in the SCQ corpus with perfective markers, but do appear with imperfective markers, such as continuous *-yka:* in (102). Here, the reduplicated finite verb emphasizes that the speaker and his friend kept going a long time along the unfamiliar mountain trail, and that it was tough going.

> (102) *entons **aywa-yka:-ya-:**   **aywa-yka:-ya-:**, ni ima ka-n-tsu.*
> then   go-CONT-PL.V-1   go-CONT-PL.V-1   not any be-3-NEG
> 'Then we **keep going and going**, there's nothing out there.'

An inflected finite verb may be reduplicated along with an additional clausal element or as part of a reduplicated clause. For example, in (103) not only is the verb reduplicated, but also the following vocative *tiyay*. The children have been stirring the pot all day and impatiently complain that the food never gets done.

> (103) *"**cha-n-ta:ku**   tiya-y,   **cha-n-ta:ku**   tiya-y"*
> arrive-3-NEG.EMPH   aunt-VOC   arrive-3-NEG.EMPH   aunt-VOC
> '**It's still not done, auntie. It's still not done, auntie**.'

In (104) the verb is reduplicated along with the preceding negative morpheme *mana-m*. The speaker is not just impatient, but desperate after a long unsuccessful search for her lost donkey.

> (104) *"**mana-m ka-n-tsu**,   **mana-m ka-n-tsu**"*
> no-DIR   be-3-NEG   no-DIR be-3-NEG
> '**It's gone, it's gone**.'

Negation is formally marked on the reduplicated forms in both (103) and (104). These reduplicated negations, or "frustrative" constructions, communicate failure to achieve the desired outcome (marked by negation) in spite of ongoing, intensive effort (marked by reduplication).

Reduplicated finite verbs tend to be inflected either with present tense, as in (100)-(104), or with imperative mood.[63] Imperatives are directives which typically express the deontic modality of obligation. A reduplicated imperative has the effect of intensifying the obligation. For example, in (105) the doctor urges the child to continue crying intensely so that her heartache will eventually diminish. In (106) the children are worn out from hours of stirring rocks (which they thought were potatoes), but the deceiving witch tells them to continue the intense effort.

(105) *tsay-no: waqa-pti-n-na doktor-qa ni-na:*
      that-SIM cry-DS-3-NOW doctor-TOP say-PST.N

      "***waqa-y-lla***   ***waqa-y-lla***   *llullu, kiki-ki harta-nqa-yki-yaq" ni-r*
      cry-IMP2-DLM   cry-IMP2-DLM   baby self-2 satiate-NMLZ.R-2-LIM say-SS

      'Because she was crying like that, the doctor urged her, "Child, **continue crying** until you yourself are all cried out.'

(106) "***wayku-ya-y*** ***wayku-ya-y***, *may-na-m   may   cha-yka-n-na"*
      stir-PL.V-IMP2 stir-PL.V-IMP2 where-NOW-DIR surely arrive-CONT-3-NOW

      '**Continue stirring**, it's surely almost done now.'

In the previous two reduplicated imperatives, the action of the verb recurs, presumably because each involves a dynamic verb. When the reduplication involves a stative verb, however, only intensification is in focus. For example, in (107) the reduplication of the imperative 'Let's stay together' reflects the eagerness of those extending the invitation, thus intensifying the pressure of the obligation.

(107) "***keda-ku-shun***   ***keda-ku-shun***" *ni-r ama:las keda-yku-ya-:*
      remain-MID-IMP1₁ remain-MID-IMP1₁ say-SS obligated remain-PFV.O-PL.V-1

      'Saying "**Let's stay together**, **let's stay together**", we obligated him to stay.'

In each example presented above, the reduplicated finite verb corresponds to a high level of affect.[64] Not surprisingly, these reduplications all involve speech-act participants. In addition, they often appear in direct speech, a mode in which affect is customarily expressed. Present

---

[63] In the SCQ corpus there are many reduplicated finite verbs inflected with present or imperative, but only one inflected with past.

[64] Following Izard (1977:65) and Ochs and Schieffelin (1989:7), my use of the term "affect" includes emotions and feelings, as well as attitudes associated with people and situations, including stance.

tense forms are reduplicated in direct speech in (103) and (104), and reduplicated imperatives in (105)-(107).

Type 2: Entire inflected nonfinite verb

Just as an inflected *finite* verb form may be reduplicated, an inflected *nonfinite* verb may be reduplicated in its entirety. This structure also expresses a high degree of affect, and presents a situation as ongoing on frequent occasions or an extended occasion. For example, the reduplicated adverbial clause *waqarir waqarir* in (108) yields a frequentative meaning 'cry often', not a continuative meaning 'keep crying'. Recurring action is emphasized by punctual *-ri*.

> (108) *alla:pa kiki-:-ta-na-m*   *ultraha-ma-sha*   *ari...,*
>   very   self-1-OBJ-NOW-DIR   mistreat-OBJ1-PST.R3 yes,
>
> *tsay-no:-si*   *karu-pita*   *ka-r*   ___**waqa-ri-r**___   ___**waqa-ri-r**___
> that-SIM-EVEN   distant-ABL   be-SS   cry-PUNC-SS   cry-PUNC-SS
>
> 'She severely mistreated me, making me **cry often** like that because I was from a distant place.'

The reduplicated adverbial clause *kushinar kushinar* in (109) indicates a gradually increasing feeling of happiness during the span of a single extended occasion, not a recurring feeling of happiness on separate occasions.

> (109) *entonsi*   *"pay-qa*   *musya-ku-n-na-m"*   *ni-r-na*
>   and.so   he-TOP   know-MID-3-NOW-DIR   say-SS-NOW
>
> ___**kushi-na-r**___   ___**kushi-na-r**___   ... *shuya-ku-ru-:*
> be.happy-DES-SS   be.happy-DES-SS   wait-MID-PST.R-1
>
> 'Then saying "He already knows," and **gradually feeling happy** (less sad over time), I waited.'

Type 2 NONFINITE VERB reduplication has a very low frequency in the data. In contrast, Type 1 FINITE VERB reduplication and Type 3 ROOT~ROOT reduplication are both very frequent. Type 3 reduplication is presented next. (The symbol "~" indicates reduplication of the root.)

Type 3: Root~Root (plus inflectional verb morphology)

A third reduplication construction is one in which the bare verb root is reduplicated and this lexical unit is inflected with the usual verbal morphology. Unlike the reduplication of an entire inflected verb (Types 1 and 2), this ROOT~ROOT structure does not correspond to a high intensity of affect, but is more purely aspectual. For example, in (110) the women individually turn toward the old man seated in the back of the church. This iterative action transpires during a relatively limited time span. The reduplication *tikra-tikra* 'turn-turn' also resembles a distributive in that the action is spread over various participants (plural subject).

(110) *warmi-kaq-kuna-na:-qa   ruku   hamara-yka-nqa-n-man*
woman-DEF-PL.N-NOW-TOP old.man   sit-CONT-NMLZ.R-ALL

tikra~tikra-*yku-r-ra: pasaypa   parla-ya:-na:*
turn~turn-PFV.O-SS-YET   very   speak-PL.V-PST.N

'**Turning around individually** toward where the old man was seated, the women spoke excitedly.'

In (111) the action of climbing trees (plural object) is repeated by a single participant on a relatively extended occasion. Here, the reduplication *yarku~yarku* 'climb~climb' resembles an iterative in many respects, but may be best analyzed as a sequential distributive since the action is spread over multiple discrete objects over a relatively extended time span.

(111) *wamra   puklla-yka-n   atska qeru-kuna-man   **yarku~yarku**-rku-r*
child   play-CONT-3   many tree-PL.N-ALL   climb~climb-PFV.M-SS

'The child is playing, **climbing** one tree after another.'

The reduplicated verbs in the previous two examples are further specified aspectually with derivational perfective suffixes, -*yku* in (110) and -*rku* in (111). In fact, there is a strong tendency for this reduplication construction to combine with an aspect marker. In the SCQ corpus this marker is almost always a perfective, but continuous -*yka:* (an imperfective) can also appear in a Type 3 ROOT~ROOT reduplication. For example, in (112) the wind was gusting over an extended period of time. The inflectional morphology is finite here in (112), and nonfinite above in (110) and (111).

(112) *tsay   tuma-yku-na-n-pa:-qa   pasaypa   **byentu~byentu**-yka:-na:*
that   turn-PFV.O-NMLZ.I-3-PURP-TOP   very   wind.blow-wind.blow-CONT-PST.N

'Just as she turned that corner (of the building), strong **gusts were blowing**.'

The illustrations of reduplication in this section call for a more fine-grained analysis of the iterative-distributive distinction. The boundary is not always clear-cut because these notions are based to some extent on scalar criteria from the domains of space and time. For example, an iterative action is normally repeated at a single location, while a distributive is generally spread over various locations. This distinction may be less transparent, however, when the distance is minimal, e.g., the locations of trees in a yard, as in (111), or foods on a table during a meal. Similarly, iterative is usually associated with a single occasion and distributive with multiple occasions. At the same time, either iterative or distributive actions may be realized during a single "relatively extended" occasion, e.g., the iterative gusting wind in (112), and the distributive (sequential) tree-climbing action in (111).

The difference between iteratives and distributives, at least in SCQ, appears to lie in the individuation of multiple patients. The iterative gusting wind in (112) has a single (implied) patient. Similarly, the iterative head-turning action in (110) is spread over various participants, but directed toward a single patient. In contrast, the distributive tree-climbing action in (111) has a single participant, but is spread over various patients. In other words, in SCQ reduplications, iterative gives rise to distributive in contexts involving individuated patients, and this may entail a further extension to multiple locations and/or occasions.

TYPE 4: SOUND~SOUND-Inchoative (plus inflectional verb morphology)

In a variation of Type 3 ROOT~ROOT reduplication, the reduplicated element is not a verb root per se but an ideophone followed by the productive inchoative suffix -*ya:*. This lexicalized onomatopoeic expression is then available for inflection with the usual verbal morphology. For example, the reduplicated ideophone *shiw* in (113) is followed by inchoative -*ya:*, and by finite verbal morphology. *shiw-shiw-ya:-* denotes the recurring sound of the wind blowing through the trees.

> (113) *qenwa-kuna-pa   rapra-n-pis   alla:pa   byentu-pti-n*
> tree-PL.N-GEN   leaf-3-EVEN   very   wind.blow-DS-3
> ***shiw~shiw**-ya-ku-na:-ra:*
> sound~sound-INCH-MID-PST.N-YET
> 'When the leaves of the trees would blow, it **made the sound "*shiw-shiw*".**'

The reduplicated ideophone *shap* in (114) is followed by inchoative -*ya:*, and inflected with nonfinite verbal morphology. *shap-shap-ya:-* represents the recurring sound of people whispering to one another.

> (114) *llapa-n   runa-kuna-pis   ruri   iglesia-cho:-qa   **shap~shap**-ya-yllapa*
> all-3   person-PL.N-EVEN   inside church-LOC-TOP   sound~sound-INCH-ADV
> *parla-r   ni-ya:-na: "..."   ni-r*
> speak-SS   say-PL.V-PST.N   say-SS
> 'All the people inside the church speaking **by whispering**, said "…".'

Nuckolls (1996) explores the notion of aspect as grammatically encoded sound symbolism in Pastaza, a Northern Quechuan language spoken in lowland Ecuador. She shows that the productive use of ideophones (onomatopoeic words) constitutes a principle means for the expression of aspect in this language. Sound symbolism plays a more modest role in SCQ and neighboring highland Quechuan languages. These derived forms are expressed lexically and have not given rise to grammatical markers. Instead, for example, the perfective category in SCQ is elaborated from the set of former directional markers, which are not found in Northern Quechuan varieties.

TYPE 5: ROOT~ROOT (minus inflectional verb morphology)

In a more radical variation of Type 3 ROOT~ROOT reduplication, the bare verb root is reduplicated, but the resulting form does not take verbal morphology; that is, the reduplication is not inflected for person, tense, aspect, or mood. Instead, ROOT~ROOT explicitly marks recurring or ongoing action and reports adverbial notions, such as intensity. For example, the bare verb *ko:rri-* 'run' in (115) is repeated to express an iterative action realized in a rapid manner. (In some instances *ko:rri-* is repeated three or more times, corresponding to greater intensity; cf. (208).)[65]

(115)　*tsay-pita-qa*　　*Cruz-kaq-pa*　**_ko:rri_　_ko:rri_**　*tuma-ski-na-:-pa:-qa*
　　　　that-ABL-TOP　　Cruz-DEF-GEN　run　　　run　　　turn-PFV-NMLZ.I-1-PURP-TOP

　　　　Chi:nu　munta-sh　　witsa-yka:-tsi-mu-na:
　　　　Chino　mount-PTCP　climb-CONT-CAUS-FAR-PST.N

　　　　After that, as I was **running rapidly** right at Cruz, just as I turned the corner, there was Chino mounted (on the donkey) urging it up toward me.'

(116) is like (115), except that the affective suffix *-lla* appears on the second element of the reduplicated verb root *maya-* 'be alert'. Again, the form is not inflected for person, tense, aspect, or mood. Reduplication here conveys that the mouse is intensely vigilant, constantly monitoring for an opportunity to escape.[66]

(116)　*ukush　kushi-ku-na:*　　　　　*patsa-man*　　*chura-yku-pti-n,*
　　　　mouse　be.happy-MID-PST.N　ground-ALL　put-PFV.O-DS-3

　　　　i　　**_maya_　_maya_**-*lla*　　*ka-na:*
　　　　and　be.alert　be.alert-DLM　be-PST.N

　　　　'The mouse was happy when (the cat) put it back on the ground, and then it was **vigilantly alert** (for the opportune moment to escape).'

TYPE 6: ROOT-SS ROOT (plus inflectional verb morphology)

In this reduplication construction, a verb root with a same subject adverbial marker, such as *(y)pa* or *-r-pis* is combined with a second instance of the verb which has the usual inflectional morphology. This construction presents a sustained action or effort, a type of durative with intentionality. For example, in (117) an owl goes flying far away.

(117)　*tsay　qeru-pita　tuku　bwe:la-ri-n,　aywa-yka-n　**pa:ri-pa**　**pa:ri-r***
　　　　that　tree-ABL　owl　fly-PUNC-3　go-CONT-3　fly-ADV　fly-SS

　　　　'An owl suddenly flies from that tree, and he goes **flying far away**.'

---

[65] The SCQ lexicon includes ambivalent forms that take either verbal or nominal morphology. The reduplicated forms illustrated here, however (*ko:rri-* 'run' and *maya-* 'be alert'), do not take nominal morphology and are not clausal arguments.

[66] Other examples of this type include *panta-pantallara:* 'err', *qeshpi-qeshpilla* 'escape', and *wiya-wiyallanam* 'hear'.

The adjacent verbal element can be either nonfinite as in (117) *pa:rir*, or finite, as in (118) *wanuna:*. Here, a man tries to kill his brother who tricked him into killing his mules in order to sell worthless mule skins.

(118) *tsa   cha-yka-mu-r-qa   qechu-na: llapa-n mu:la-n-ta.*
      that   arrive-PFV.O-FAR-SS-TOP   take.force-PST.N all-3   mule-3-OBJ

      wanu-tsi-ypa   wanu-na:
      die-CAUS-ADV die-PST.N

      'Then when he arrived, he took away all of his brother's mules and **tried to kill** him (in any way possible).'

The reduplicated elements can appear in reverse order as in (119), where a worker resolutely continues harvesting fruits through his fatigue on a hot day. The phrase *aqyan aqyaypana* falls under a single intonation contour, that is, there is no pause or pitch reset between the two elements.

(119) ***aqya-n   aqya-ypa-na***   *aru-ku-yka-n   atska fru:ta-ta*
      be.tired-3   be.tired-ADV-NOW work-MID-CONT-3   many fruit-OBJ

      '**Through his ongoing tiredness** he continues working (harvesting) many fruits.'

The reduplication of *qori-* 'gather' in line 2 of (120) communicates that the man would raise the orphan girl as his own child, even if his sick daughter should die. (The auxiliary verb *ima-* in line 1 is discussed in the next section.)

(120) *tsay qeshya-q-ya-shqa   wanu-yku-**pti-n**   **ima-pti-n**-qa*
      that   be.sick-AG-INCH-PTCP die-PFV.O-DS-3   happen-DS-3-TOP

      *tsay runa-qa   wamra-ta **qori-r-pis**   **qori**-ku-nqa-chir*
      that   person-TOP   child-OBJ gather-SS-EVEN gather-MID-FUT3-APP

      'If the sick one dies or whatever else may happen to her, that man would surely **raise the other child** as his own.'

Non-aspectual verbal reduplication. ROOT+morphology₁ *ima*+morphology₁

SCQ has a specialized bipartite construction in which the verbal morphology, not the verb root, is reduplicated. The first element can be any inflected verb. The second element is the auxiliary verb *ima-* 'happen' or 'do' inflected with the same verbal morphology as the first verb. (The nonverbal form *ima* also functions as an indefinite or interrogative pronoun.) This reduplication construction does not express aspect but has the disjunctive meaning 'or something comparable happens'. In the first line of (120), for example, the final suffixes *-pti* 'DS' and *-n* '3' attached to the verb *wanu-* 'die' are reduplicated on the following auxiliary verb *ima-*. The resultant meaning is 'if the sick one dies or whatever else may happen to her'. The reduplicated morphology can be either nonfinite, as in (120), or finite as in (121).

(121) *yana buːrru-pis   wacha-mu-__nqa__   __ima-nqa__-na.*
      black donkey-EVEN give.birth-FAR-FUT3 happen-FUT3-NOW

      peyor ka-nqa   alli-pis-tsu
      worse be-FUT3   good-EVEN-NEG

      'The black donkey will give birth **or something else may happen** now. That would be even worse.'

Summary of verbal reduplication

Verbal reduplication in SCQ is not a homogeneous aspectual category. Instead, there are various configurations, each with a specialized imperfective meaning that further specifies internal temporal structure. The six major verbal reduplication types and their corresponding aspectual functions are summarized in Table 3.2. Each type is associated with a repetitive meaning.

Table 3.2 *Aspect and verbal reduplication types in SCQ*

REDUPLICATION TYPE / **ASPECT**	ITERA-TIVE	DISTRIBU-TIVE	DURA-TIVE	CONTIN-UATIVE	FREQUEN-TATIVE
	NEUTRAL AFFECT			*INTENSE AFFECT*	
REDUP₁					
1. INFLECTED FINITE VERB				✓	
2. INFLECTED NONFINITE VERB					✓
REDUP₂					
3. ROOT~ROOT + VERB MORPH.	✓	✓			
4. SOUND~SOUND + VERB MORPH.	✓				
5. ROOT~ROOT	✓				
6. ROOT-SS ROOT + VERB MORPH.			✓		

Interestingly, the aspectual meanings cluster into two groups, a result that was not anticipated at the outset of the study. In the first group (REDUP₁ in Table 3.2), inflected verbs are reduplicated in their entirety. These express continuative (Type 1 FINITE) or frequentative (Type 2 NONFINITE) meanings. With emotion verbs, Type 2 reduplication may indicate a gradual shift in feeling over a single extended occasion. Type 1 and Type 2 reduplications typically involve speech-act participants and correspond to intense affect.

In the second group (REDUP₂ in Table 3.2), only the verb root is reduplicated. Types 3-6 express iterative, distributive, and durative meanings, without necessarily indicating a high degree of affect. The aspectual meanings associated with all verbal reduplication types give rise to semantic extensions into modality (intentionality, affect) and manner (intensity, speed). (For more on the interfaces linking aspect with modality and manner, see Chapters 6 and 7, respectively.)

The cognitive and historical motivations for the distribution of aspectual meanings in Table 3.2 are not immediately obvious. Bybee et al. assume that "iterative is the earliest aspectual meaning of reduplication" (1994:159). Based on this assumption, it is plausible that Type 1 and Type 2 reduplications could have developed as continuatives and frequentatives without retaining iterative meaning. Types 3-6 would represent earlier aspectual meanings that have not undergone further grammatical development.

In fact, Table 3.2 suggests a different scenario in which Type 1 and Type 2 inflected verb reduplications in SCQ are not former iteratives. Instead, the continuative and frequentative meanings would be more directly motivated by high affect situations in which speech-act participants are involved in long intensive effort. These meanings are conveyed in English reduplications as well, e.g., *we searched and searched (kept searching)*, or *I tried and tried (kept trying) in spite of difficulty*.

Type 3-5 ROOT~ROOT reduplications, on the other hand, do support the hypothesis of iterative as the earliest aspectual meaning, at least for reduplication that does not involve an entire inflected verb. ROOT~ROOT reduplications encode iterative meaning, which yields a distributive reading when the repeated action involves additional patients, or takes place in a wider area over a longer time span. The natural inclination for ROOT~ROOT combinations to co-lexicalize would make them unavailable for further grammaticization. Finally, reduplication Type 6 ROOT-SS ROOT is a specialized construction which reports sustained action or effort (manner), interpreted as durative (aspect) with intentionality (modality). The sense of 'sustained effort' is similar to that of the suffix *-chaku* 'concerted effort', a type of manner with incipient aspectual functions (see §7.2.2).[67]

3.2 Inflectional imperfectives

The inflectional imperfective markers are past habitual *-q* (or *-q=ka*), present habitual *-Ø*, and narrative past *-na:* (or *-na:=ka*). These appear in the obligatory verbal slot I2, in paradigmatic contrast with the past perfectives presented in §2.2, as well as futures and moods. The obligatory imperfective distinctions may be further specified by the addition of derivational aspect suffixes.

---

[67] For examples of reduplication structures in Tarma Quechua see Adelaar (1977:158ff.) and in Huallaga Quechua see Weber (1989:317ff.).

3.2.1   -*q* 'past habitual'

The inflectional marker -*q* (from *-*q* 'nominalizer') combines elements of habitual aspect and past tense in its semantics.[68] This marker presents a situation as customarily repeated in the past or characteristic of a time period restricted to the past. The simple form -*q* marks past habitual with third person subjects, as in (122) and (123).[69]

(122)   *Tayanqocha-pita-qa   pe   sha-ka-ya:-mu-q   kiki-n-kuna-lla*
      Tayancocha-ABL-TOP   then   come-MID-PL.V-FAR-**PST.H**   self-3-PL.N-DLM
      'From Tayancocha (the cows) **used to come** all by themselves.'

(123)   *ni-q-cha,   unay   mama-:-pa   awila-n-kuna*
      say-**PST.H**-MUT   long.ago   mother-1-GEN   grandmother-3-PL.N
      kwenta-ku-ya-q
      tell-MID-PL.V-**PST.H**
      'They **used to say** that, long ago my mother's grandmothers **used to tell** that.'

The longer form -*q=ka* (from *-*q* 'nominalizer' plus copula **ka*-) marks past habitual with speech-act participant subjects. An overt person suffix, usually first person -:, specifies the speech-act participant, as in (124) and (125). Incidentally, 95% of the past habituals in the coded data have third person subjects, while less than 5% have speech-act participant subjects.

(124)   *trabaha-ya-q=ka-:*   *eskwe:la-kuna-cho: wamra-kuna-ta   yachatsi-r*
      work-PL.V-**PST.H=be**-1 school-PL.N-LOC   child-PL.N-OBJ   teach-SS
      'We **used to work** in the schools teaching the children.'

(125)   *estudya-y-pa:-pis   wanu-q=ka-:*
      study-INF-PURP-EVEN   die-**PST.H=be**-1
      'I **was dying** (strong desire) to study.'

For some speakers, an independent final suffix may intervene between the two elements -*q* and =*ka* of the past habitual construction. This discontinuity is illustrated in (126) with the intervention of negative -*tsu*. For other speakers, however, -*q* and =*ka* are inseparable. In (127) negative -*tsu* is attached after both elements and the person marker. This example shows that the adjoining elements -*q* plus the former auxiliary =*ka* are beginning to fuse together, forming a single grammatical morpheme in the past habitual construction.

---

[68] The suffix -*q* is glossed as PST.H for past habitual. As shown in Map A.6 in Appendix A, this form is common throughout the language family.

[69] The simple form of the past habitual is exclusive to third person verbs because the copula is not formally marked with third person, only with speech-act participants, e.g., *ka-:* 'I am', *ka-nki* 'you are' *ka-ntsik* 'we (incl.) are', but Ø 's/he is'.

(126) *po:ku importansya ka-ra-n, i mana maña-ku-__q-tsu ka-:__*
little importance be-PST-3 and no ask-MID-__PST.H-NEG be-1__

tayta dyos-man
father god-ALL

'It had little importance, and __I was not in the habit of praying__ to Father God.'

(127) *riñon-wan sufri-r ... trabaha-y-ta pwe:di-__q=ka-:-tsu__*
kidney-COM suffer-SS work-INF-OBJ be.able-__PST.H-1-NEG__

'During the time I was suffering with a kidney infection __I was not able to work__.'

Summarizing, the inflectional marker *-q* (or *-q=ka*) presents a situation as customarily repeated in the past or characteristic of a time period restricted to the past. It appears in paradigmatic contrast with other inflectional TAM markers in the obligatory slot I2. The simple form *-q* marks third person past habitual, and the less frequent longer form *-q=ka* marks past habitual with speech-act participants. The longer form is inflected with a person marker.

The past habitual was formed by the reduction of a periphrastic construction in which the nominalizer **-q* was followed by the copular auxiliary **ka-* inflected with a past suffix plus a person marker. The past suffix no longer occurs in SCQ, but the past meaning is absorbed by the remaining phonological material *-q/-q=ka* (see §5.3 and §10.6). Auxiliation and the development of aspect suffixes from analytic verbal constructions are treated in detail in Chapter 11.

3.2.2   *-Ø* 'present habitual'

Present habitual is marked inflectionally by grammatical zero (*-Ø*), that is, the meaningful absence of a formal marker in the obligatory suffix slot I2.[70] It presents a situation as customarily repeated or as characteristic of a time period that includes present reference time (usually the moment of speech). Present habitual *-Ø* is not a general present imperfective because it does not mark progressive aspect. Instead, progressive is marked by the continuous aspect suffix *-yka:* (§3.1.2).[71]

Present habitual *-Ø* is the most frequent of all the aspect markers, comprising one third of all the verbs in the coded data (488 of 1,452). In keeping with its inflectional status, this *-Ø* marker is mutually exclusive with the other inflectional TAM markers that have formal expression in slot I2. These include the past perfective suffixes *-ru*, *-sha*, and *-ra* (§2.2), past habitual *-q* (§3.2.1), and narrative past *-na:* (§3.2.3). Present habitual *-Ø* is explicitly marked and glossed as PRS

---

[70] Two languages in the Gramcats database—Kui (Dravidian) and Tucano—have present habituals, and both are expressed by grammatical zeros (Bybee et al. 1994:175).

[71] Continuous *-yka:*, habitual *-rayka:*, and past habitual *-q* all appear to have taken over some of the imperfective functions of *-Ø*. The evolution of imperfective categories is addressed in Chapter 10.

throughout the current section to clarify its analysis. Elsewhere in this work, the lack of a formal marker in the obligatory I2 verbal position should be understood as present habitual by convention.[72]

In most instances of present habitual -Ø, only the habit holds at the present moment, not the action itself. For example, in (128) the habit of crying holds at the moment of speech, not the act of crying. Similarly, in (129) the habit of doing the annual fiesta holds at the moment of speech, not the action of doing the fiesta. In (130) the people are characterized as badly behaved.

(128) *allaw-chi waqa-**Ø**-n feyu-pa   sha-ka-mu-pti-:-pis*
      pity-CNJ   cry-**PRS**-3   much-ADV come-MID-FAR-DS-1-EVEN
      'Such a pity she (our mother) **cries** a lot, even though I come home often.'

(129) *Tsuyu marka-:-cho: fyesta-ta rura-ya-**Ø**-:   tres   de   octubri-m*
      Tsuyo town-1-LOC   fiesta-OBJ do-PL.V-**PRS**-1   third   of   october-DIR
      'In our town Tsuyo we **do** the fiesta (every) third of October.'

(130) *kostumra-sh   tsay-kuna-qa ka-ya-**Ø**-n*
      accustom-PTCP   that-PL.N-TOP   be-PL.V-**PRS**-3
      'Those people **are** always badly behaved.'

Examples (131) and (132) describe a more general habitual scenario in which the participants are less specified than in (128)-(130). This type of habitual has been referred to as generic aspect. Both habitual and generic are referred to here as habitual aspect, since each presents a situation as characteristic of a time period. That is, the difference between habitual versus generic lies in the specificity of the participants. The aspectual meaning of -Ø is the same for both uses.[73]

In (131) small dogs are characterized as understanding Spanish. This characterization incidentally holds at the present moment. Similarly, entering a "second childhood" stage of life is characterized in (132) without necessarily holding at the present moment.

---

[72] The habitual meaning of -Ø in connected SCQ speech is very similar to the "unmarked present" in English. For example, *what do you do? I drink coffee* is necessarily habitual in English. The equivalent expression in SCQ—*imatata: ruranki? kafe:ta upu:*—is habitual as well. By contrast, in conversational Spanish, *qué haces? tomo café* can convey the non-habitual reading 'What are you doing? I'm drinking coffee.' For more on the tense component of present habitual -Ø see §5.4.

[73] For further discussion on habitual versus generic, see Chafe (1970:168-78) and Bybee et al. (1994:152).

(131) *pichi   allqu   mana-ku   ko:sa   kastellanu-ta-shi   entyendi-Ø-n*
       small   dog   no-Q.P   well   spanish-OBJ-RPT   understand-**PRS**-3
       'Small dogs **understand** Spanish very well, right?'

(132) *chakwas-ya-q   ruku-ya-q   llullu-n-man-na-sh   tikra-Ø-n   ari*
       old.woman-INCH-AG   old.man-INCH-AG   baby-3-ALL-NOW-RPT   turn-**PRS**-3   yes
       'When a woman or a man gets old, she or he **becomes** a baby again.'

Typically, when the inflectional habitual meaning of *-Ø* is further specified by the
continuous suffix *-yka:*, the action of the verb holds at the present moment. It is striking that
88% of the exemplars of *-yka:* occur with present habitual *-Ø* and only 12% occur with some
other TAM marker in slot I2. (For more on continuous *-yka:* refer to §3.1.2 and §5.4.)

Above in (128) the verb *waqa-n* 'she cries' refers to the habit of crying. That habitual
meaning contrasts with the verb *waqa-yka-n* 'he is crying' in (133) where the action holds at the
moment of speech. Similarly, the action of chewing holds at the present moment in (134).

(133) *allaw   tiyu-ntsi: waqa-**yka**-**Ø**-n.*
       pity   uncle-1₁   cry-**CONT**-**PRS**-3
       'Such a pity our uncle **is crying**.'

(134) *tayta   dyos-ni: qara-ka-ma-nqa-n-ta-chi*
       father god-1   give-MID-1OBJ-NMLZ.R-3-OBJ-CNJ
       *kapchu-**yka:**-mu-**Ø**-n   ukush*
       chew-**CONT**-FAR-**PRS**-3   mouse
       'A mouse **is chewing** on (the rope up there) that my Father God gave me, I think.'

In rare instances, the action marked by present habitual *-Ø* holds at the moment of speech,
even though continuous *-yka:* does not occur in the verb. In these instances, other linguistic and
pragmatic factors come into play. For example, the action may hold at the moment of speech in
the performative use of the present, that is, a punctual reading in which the beginning and
endpoints are identical. The matrix verbs in the following two examples are performatives.

(135) *hura-**Ø**-:-mi   qara-na-:-pa: ka-q-ta*
       promise-**PRS**-1-DIR   give-NMLZ.I-1-PURP   be-AG-OBJ
       'I **promise** to give it to you.'

(136) *tayta   dyos,   tsay-no:-lla-mi   maña-ka-ra-ya:-mu-**Ø**-:   ari*
       father god   that-SIM-DLM-DIR   ask-MID-PUNC-PL.V-FAR-**PRS**-1   yes
       familya-:-kuna   marka-:-cho: ka-yka-q-pa:
       family-1-PL.N   town-1-LOC   be-CONT-AG-PURP
       'Father God, like that I also **pray** for my family who are in my hometown.'

The "action" also appears to hold at the moment of speech in (137), where the negated cognition verb *yarpa:-* 'remember' is marked by *-Ø*. Negated cognitive processes, however, often receive a habitual interpretation which incidentally includes the present moment. Here, the "present" component of present habitual receives greater focus due to the pragmatics of the specific communicative situation. Moreover, continuous *-yka:* rarely occurs with cognition verbs, which suggests that imperfective aspect may be inherent in the semantics of these verbs.

(137) *yarpa-**Ø**-:-tsu   atska wata-na   ka-pti-n*
      remember-**PRS**-1-NEG many year-NOW be-DS-3

      'I don't **remember** because that was many years ago.'

In many languages a present imperfective—present habitual in SCQ—can also be used to report a past (historical present) or future situation, given a suitable linguistic or pragmatic context. In these cases, the reference time shifts from the moment of speech to a past situation, as in (138), or to a future situation, as in (139). Such time shifts occur in nearly one third of all instances of *-Ø* in the coded data.[74]

(138) *aywa-r shoqa-ya-pti-:   mas-ran   waqa-**Ø**-n-pis*
      go-SS   console-PL.V-DS-1   more-DIR.YET   cry-**PRS**-3-EVEN

      'After we went to him and "consoled" him (in jest), he **cried** all the more.'

(139) *kanan noqa-qa aywa-ku-**Ø** -:, kuti-ku-**Ø**-:-qa   waray   hwe:bis-qa*
      now   I-TOP   go-MID-**PRS**-1   return-MID-**PRS**-1-TOP   tomorrow   thursday-TOP

      'And now I **will go**, I **will return** there tomorrow Thursday.'

The reference time can also shift to the immediate past in certain surprising (mirative) situations, as illustrated in the following example.

(140) *diyablu-pa   wacha-shqa-n,   roqu-ku-ski-**Ø**-:*
      devil-GEN   give.birth-NMLZ.R-3   cut-MID-PFV-**PRS**-1

      'Son of the devil! I **cut** myself!'

---

[74] Present habitual *-Ø* does not express a general future, only a situation that is specifically planned for the immediate future, as in (139). This immediate future use of *-Ø* contrasts with the general future which is formally marked (in all but second person) by a set of portmanteau suffixes. These suffixes combine future tense and person, e.g., *-sha:* 'first person future' and *-nqa* 'third person future'. The contrast between immediate and general future involves both time reference (tense and aspect) and high certainty that the event will be realized (epistemic modality).

In summary, the inflectional present habitual marker -Ø presents a situation as customarily repeated or as characteristic of a time period that includes present reference time (usually the moment of speech). It appears in paradigmatic contrast with other inflectional TAM markers in the obligatory verbal slot I2. Typically, the habit or characterization holds at the present moment, but not the action itself, except in performatives and with a small set of inherently imperfective cognition verbs. To further convey that an action holds at the present moment, the continuous suffix -*yka:* may be added. In certain contexts, the reference time can shift from the moment of speech to the past (historical present), to the immediate past, or to the immediate planned future. In these latter three uses of -Ø the action holds at the non-present reference time.

3.2.3   -*na:* 'narrative past'

The inflectional marker -*na:* is a multifaceted grammatical morpheme in SCQ, combining elements of imperfective aspect and past tense, together with modal and evidential senses in its semantics. I focus here on aspectual attributes of -*na:* in naturally-occurring speech, and on other senses in PART III "Aspect and related semantic domains."[75]

The suffix -*na:* typically presents a situation as in progress in the past (141) or characteristic of a time period restricted to the past (142).

(141) *punta-ta-qa*   *"Ni:ku-m   apa-sh"*   *ni-ya:-***na:***
      first-ADV-TOP   Niko-DIR   take-PST.R3   say-PL.V-**PST.N**
      'At first they **were saying** (to our neighbors), "Niko took it".'

(142) *unay-qa*   *ukush-pis*   *parla-***na:***-shi*
      long.ago-TOP   mouse-EVEN   speak-**PST.N**-RPT
      'Long ago even mice **could speak**, they say.'

The simple form -*na:* is used with third person subjects, and the longer form -*na:=ka* with speech-act participant subjects. An overt person marker specifies the speech-act participant, such as the first person suffix -*:* in (143). The longer form is exceedingly rare, with only one exemplar in the SCQ corpus. In contrast, hundreds of instances of the simple form -*na:* mark third person subjects.[76]

---

[75] In the traditional Quechuanist literature, the category expressed by -*na:* and cognate forms in Central Quechua is often referred to as the "narrative past," glossed here as PST.N. In this section I highlight the propensity of -*na:* to express ongoing past situations in naturally-occurring speech, that is, past imperfective aspect. Cerrón-Palomino's description of the cognate form -*ña-q* in Huanca Quechua—"alludes to a prolonged action in the past" (1976:174, my translation)—could also be interpreted as imperfective aspect.

[76] The longer form of narrative past (-*na:=ka*) results from an earlier stage of development in which the mode of expression was a periphrastic construction involving the copular auxiliary

(143) *ke:-no:　baha:da-qa　kurba　kurba　kurba　kurba　tse:-no:-pa　dere:chu-n-pa*
　　　 this-SIM　descent-TOP　curve　curve　curve　curve　that-SIM-GEN　straight-3-GEN

　　　 pa:sa-ski-ya:-__na:__=__ka__-:　mana　kurba-ta　tuma-ypa
　　　 pass-PFV-PL.V-__PST.N__=__be__-1　no　curve-OBJ　turn-ADV

　　　 'Though the path descended with many curves, we __were going straight__ down without following the switchbacks.'

Narrative past *-na:* has an unusually high correlation with stative verbs and is especially frequent with the copula *ka-*. The form *ka-na:*, illustrated in (144)-(146), appears in 28% of all *-na:* exemplars. In contrast, past perfective *-ru* never appears with the copula, and the set of derivational perfectives rarely do.

(144) *haw　mati-rikoq　ka-__na:__　tsay-si*
　　　 wow　dish-CLASS　be-__PST.N__　that-EVEN

　　　 'Wow, those (eucalyptus seeds) __were__ just like dishes!'

(145) *unay-shi　　ka-ya:-__na:__　ishke:　wawqi-kuna.*
　　　 long.ago-RPT　be-PL.V-__PST.N__　two　　brother-PL.N

　　　 hukaq-kaq-qa ri:ku yarqu-__na:__. hukaq-kaq-qa　pobri　ka-__na:__.
　　　 other-DEF-TOP　rich　leave-__PST.N__　other-DEF-TOP　poor　be-__PST.N__

　　　 'Long ago they say there __were__ two brothers. One of them __turned out__ rich. The other one __was__ poor.'

(146) *a:nir　yarpu-ski-r-nin-qa　　kanasta-kuna　kimsa　ka-__na:__*
　　　 later　lower-PFV-SS-3-TOP　basket-PL.N　　three　be-__PST.N__

　　　 'Later after he descended __there were__ (he had) three baskets.'

Narrative past *-na:* often presents information off the main storyline in narratives, an attribute associated with imperfectives in many languages (e.g., Hopper 1979:216). For example, (145) establishes the setting in a legend, (146) provides relevant information for the continuation

---

ka-. The simple form (*-na:* alone) is exclusive to third person subjects because the copula *ka-* in general does not appear when the subject is third person; it appears only with speech-act participant subjects.

In the Central Quechuan varieties Tarma and Huanca (cf. Map A.7 in Appendix A), the cognate suffix *-ña* (or *-na*) is immediately followed by a person marker. The copula form no longer appears in the narrative past in Tarma, regardless of the subject (Adelaar 1977:95). Huanca speakers use either the longer copula form or the reduced form (Cerrón-Palomino 1976:176). See note 69 on the past habitual forms *-q* and *-q=ka* which arise from a parallel aspectual periphrasis. The development of these and other analytic verbal constructions is discussed in more detail in §5.2, §5.3, §10.6, and §11.2.

of a story, and (147) supplies background information within a spontaneous conversation. In contrast, when *-na:* appears in a clause that advances the action in a story as in (143), or evaluates an outcome as in (144), it marks the outcome as unexpected, an epistemic modality sometimes referred to as "mirative."

(147)   *Damian-wan-shi   huntu   estudya-__na:__*
        Damian-COM-RPT   together   study-__PST.N__
        'He **formerly studied** (attended classes) with Damian, they say.'

Derivational perfective and imperfective suffixes can further specify aspectual distinctions on verbs inflected with narrative past *-na:*. For example, *-na:* appears with continuous *-yka:* in (148), and with perfective *-ski* in (149) as well as in (143).[77]

(148)   *huk   erye:ru-qa   ka-__yka:-na:__   tsay huk ru:ta-pa*
        one   blacksmith-TOP   be-__CONT-PST.N__   that one route-GEN
        'A blacksmith **was there** along that route.'

(149)   *tsay qawa-rpu-pti-n-qa   a: kay pichi allqu-lla   tikra-__ski-na:__*
        that watch-COMPL-DS-3-TOP   yes this small dog-DLM   turn-__PFV-PST.N__
        'After that (girl) looked down, this (boy) **turned into** a small dog.'

Finally, as mentioned above, the examples presented in this section are taken from naturally-occurring speech. Interestingly, when the scope of inquiry is limited to elicited folktales and legends, I find that *-na:* has tense and mirative functions, but does not appear to mark aspect systematically. Instead, the meanings of verbs inflected with *-na:* are often imperfective, but can also receive a neutral aspectual reading in some narrative contexts. Presumably, oral storytelling tradition gives rise to a formulaic or prescriptive mode of expression for these genres in which *-na:* represents an archaic form. Moreover, because folktales and legends are so familiar within the speech community, the formal expression of inflectional aspect, and the communicative function it affords, may be less relevant in this context-rich "parallel world." The traditional Quechuanist term "narrative past" is appropriate for the use of *-na:* within the confines of narrative and legendary genres. On the other hand, as I have shown here, *-na:* tends to mark past imperfective in everyday SCQ conversation.

Summarizing, the inflectional narrative past *-na:* (or *-na:=ka*) typically marks past imperfective in naturally-occurring speech, that is, it presents a situation as in progress in the past or characteristic of a time period restricted to the past. The simple form *-na:* is used with

---

[77] The further specification of aspectual distinctions via derivational morphology in SCQ is similar to processes in other languages through which imperfectives can be perfectivized and vice versa. Examples include Bulgarian and Georgian (Comrie 1976:31-2, 126), Koyukon Athabaskan (Axelrod 1993:111ff.), and Central Pomo (Mithun 2000:274-6).

third person subjects, and the vanishingly rare longer form *-na:=ka* is used with speech-act participant subjects. The suffix *-na:* appears in paradigmatic contrast with other inflectional TAM markers in the obligatory verbal slot 12. The perfective markers *-ru, -ski, -yku,* and *-rku* rarely if ever occur with the copula *ka-*. In contrast, the stative form *ka-na:* is very frequent. Finally, *-na:* often presents background information off the main storyline, a function of imperfectives in many languages.

In addition to imperfective aspect (the focus here in §3.2.3) and past tense (the focus in §5.2), the multi-purpose suffix *-na:* also has modal and evidential functions. Specifically, in some contexts it reports surprise value. More generally, *-na:* presents a situation as outside the experience of interlocutors or outside the experience of participants within the narrative itself. These notions are elaborated in §6.4.

Narrative past *-na:* (and *-na:=ka*) was formed by the reduction of a periphrastic construction in which the form *-ña-q* was followed by the auxiliary *-ka-* inflected with a past suffix plus a person marker. The past suffix no longer occurs in SCQ, but the past meaning remains. The development of aspect suffixes from a wide array of analytic verbal constructions is the topic of Chapter 11.

3.3 Summary of imperfectives

Imperfective aspect is expressed in SCQ through an elaborate grammatical system in which eleven different markers have developed specialized meanings that are more specific than "general imperfective." All are morphologically productive and most are widely distributed over many lexical items. As with perfectives, imperfectives also encode meanings from the domains of tense, modality, and manner (cf. PART III).

The imperfective markers and their specific aspectual meanings are summarized in Figure 3.3. The formal expression of these markers ranges from fully derivational to fully inflectional. The more specific meanings appear on the left, and more general imperfectives on the right. For example, continuous *-yka:* includes progressive and nonprogressive meanings, but it is not a general imperfective because it does not encode habitual meaning. This range of meanings is represented in line 1 as a solid bar within the progressive and continuous categories.

As seen in the middle lines of Figure 3.3, SCQ is particularly rich in habitual distinctions, broadly construed to include various iteratives and repetitives (cf. §10.5). Interestingly, some habituals are expressed inflectionally (e.g., past habitual *-q* and present habitual *-Ø*), while others are derivational. For example, with dynamic verbs the derivational suffix *-rayka:* expresses frequentative and continuative, which are specific habitual categories, and it can also express a more general habitual meaning. This range of meanings is represented in line 3 as a solid bar partially within durative space and extending to habitual space. The meanings of the other imperfective markers are similarly represented.[78]

Figure 3.3 *Synchronic meanings of imperfective suffixes in SCQ discourse*

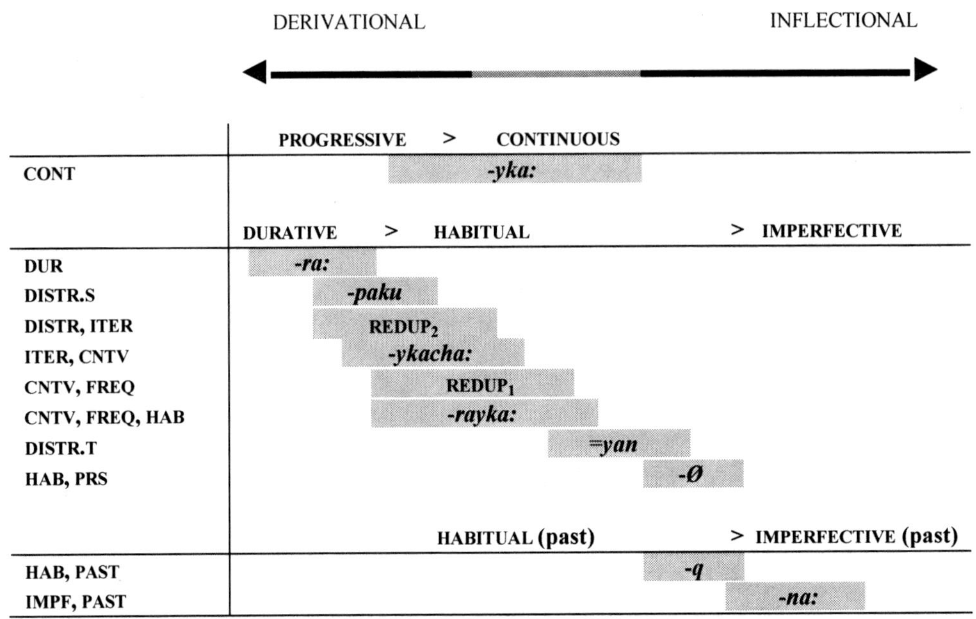

In addition, Figure 3.3 highlights issues in morphology, e.g., continuous *-yka:* shares attributes of both derivation and inflection, represented by the gray area between the arrows in the continuum above the table. (A formal analysis is presented in Appendix B). The synchronic patterns in Figure 3.3 also suggest fruitful directions for the investigation of diachrony. Durative and various repetitive categories (e.g., iterative, frequentative, etc.) appear to develop more general habitual meaning over time, with habitual and progressive-continuous categories further generalizing to imperfective and present tense (see Chapter 10).

---

[78] While inflectional narrative past *-na:*, past habitual *-q*, and present habitual *-Ø* represent one kind of imperfective category, restricted to a particular tense, the derivational markers in Figure 3.3 represent another kind of imperfective, not restricted to a particular tense.

4   THE SCQ ASPECT SYSTEM

SCQ provides an excellent illustration of some kinds of elaboration that may develop in an aspectual system. The grammatical expression of perfective aspect was presented in Chapter 2 and imperfective aspect in Chapter 3. The aim of the present chapter is to examine the organization of the SCQ aspectual system as a whole.

The structure of the perfective category is represented above in Figure 2.2, and the imperfective category in Figure 3.3. As seen in these figures, aspect in SCQ comprises a network of twenty individual markers characterized by subtle semantic distinctions and considerable overlap within the perfective and imperfective domains. The aspectual system is further enriched by the interaction of derivational and inflectional elements.

Each aspect marker is morphologically productive. One should not assume, however, that all possible combinations occur. Nor should it be assumed that perfective and imperfective markers are inherently incompatible (Comrie 1976:24; cf. note 59). Empirical investigation of SCQ discourse reveals patterns in the combinations of aspect markers that speakers actually use, and the distribution of these markers with other linguistic elements.

I begin with a summary of the individual aspect markers and their position within SCQ verb structure in §4.1. Following a brief orientation to aspect systems found in many languages of the world in §4.2, I analyze the derivational and inflectional layers of the SCQ aspectual system in §4.3. This theme is continued in §4.4 with a focus on aspect marker combinations. I examine the distribution of individual aspect markers with lexical elements in §4.5, and with non-aspectual morphosyntactic elements in §4.6. Finally, in §4.7 I assess the SCQ aspect system as a whole and preview connections between aspect and related semantic domains and the development of the grammatical system over time.

4.1   Elements in the grammatical expression of aspect in SCQ

The twenty aspect markers presented in Chapters 2 and 3—nine perfectives and eleven imperfectives—are summarized in Figure 4.1. Each marker is aligned with its verbal slot in the lower part of the figure. As detailed above, derivational aspect suffixes occur in the non-obligatory slots D1-D4 close to the verb root (e.g., *-ra:* 'durative' in slot D1). Derivational aspect is also expressed formally through two principal verbal reduplication types (§3.1.7). The fully inflectional markers occur in paradigmatic contrast in the obligatory slot I2 far from the verb root (e.g., *-ru* 'past perfective').

The enclitic *=yan* 'distributive' appears beyond the outer layer of inflectional affixes in slot E1. The formal status of this marker is ambiguous because it satisfies certain inflectional features but also some derivational features (§3.1.6). Similarly, criteria that traditionally distinguish derivation from inflection would locate several slot D4 suffixes "in between" (see note 9 above). The formal status of these markers is discussed in detail in Appendix B.[79]

Figure 4.1 *The verbal position of SCQ perfective and imperfective markers*

	DERIVATIONAL						INFLECTIONAL				INDEPENDENT	
VERB ROOT	SLOT SET D						SLOT SET I				SLOT SET E	
	1	2	3	4	5	6	1	2	3	4	1	2

IMPERFECTIVES

REDUP₁	-ra:	-paku	-ykacha:	-yka:			-Ø				=yan
REDUP				-rayka:			-q/-q=ka
							(-na:/-na:=ka)

PERFECTIVES

		-ri	-rpu				-ru
			-rku				-sha
			-yku				-ra
			-ski
			-ri:ku

It is interesting to note that each imperfective marker (except *-Ø* and verbal reduplication) has a low vowel (long or short), whereas the perfective forms predominantly have high vowels (short), especially in the derivational set.

---

[79] The difficulty of establishing the formal status of these suffixes is highlighted by Cerrón-Palomino (2003:281, my translation), "... even though the basic function of such suffixes is to form new verb stems, there is no agreement among Quechuanists as to whether all of these [suffixes] really have a derivational status or not; it may be that some of them are in fact inflectional."

4.2   Orientation to aspect systems

Before examining the internal organization of the SCQ aspect system, it will be helpful to review four common aspect system types. These are described in recent studies based on broad cross-linguistic language surveys.[80]

4.2.1   TYPE 1: Bipartite inflectional system

The semantic opposition between perfective and imperfective aspect is expressed grammatically through inflectional morphology in many languages, such as Mandarin Chinese (Smith 1997:263ff.; Xiao and McEnery 2004:2). A formal tense distinction is not relevant in such a system (Comrie 1976:94).

Figure 4.2 *The bipartite inflectional aspect system*

PERFECTIVE 'complete situation'	IMPERFECTIVE

4.2.2   TYPE 2: Tripartite inflectional system

An especially pervasive pattern across languages is the "tripartite aspect system" shown in Figure 4.3 (Dahl 1985:81ff.). As with the Type 1 bipartite system, the mode of expression in the Type 2 tripartite system is characteristically inflectional. The tripartite analysis is based on the observation that perfective aspect is typically restricted to the past, whereas a tense distinction may be relevant only in the imperfective. The tripartite system can be illustrated with Spanish forms such as *viví* 'I lived' (past perfective), *vivía* 'I was living' or 'I used to live' (past imperfective), and *vivo* 'I live' (present imperfective).

Figure 4.3 *The tripartite inflectional aspect system*

PERFECTIVE 'complete situation'	IMPERFECTIVE	
	PRESENT	PAST

---

[80] The aspect system types presented here are those most relevant to the morphological expression of aspect and tense in SCQ. Statives figure more directly in other system types, e.g., Iroquoian (Mithun 2005). Aspect is less frequently interwoven with case marking, e.g., the partitive in Finnish (Bybee and Dahl 1989:89) and the preposition *'et* in biblical Hebrew (Garr 1991).

4.2.3   TYPE 3: Bipartite "Slavic-style" derivational system

A third well-known aspect system has been referred to as "the Slavic-style system" or "the bounder system" (Dahl 1985:84; Bybee and Dahl 1989:87). The Slavic-type system is similar to the Type 1 bipartite aspect system in Figure 4.2 in that the perfective-imperfective opposition is "independent of the category of tense" (1989). There are, however, a number of critical distinctions between these two aspect systems. One difference lies in the formal morphological status of the aspectual categories. According to Dahl, "Slavic Perfective/Imperfective is realized as a derivational rather than as an inflectional category" (1985:189). In keeping with the derivational status of aspect, in some Slavic languages imperfective verbs can be formed from perfective verbs, resulting in an especially large number of "aspectual pairs."

Another difference lies in the precise meaning of the perfective category. For example, it has been observed that Slavic perfectives are restricted to telic situations, a restriction not shared by perfectives in Romance languages. This difference motivates Comrie's proposal to define the Slavic Perfective as denoting "not a complete situation in general, but more specifically a complete telic situation" (2001:46).

Figure 4.4 *The bipartite "Slavic-style" derivational aspect system*

PERFECTIVE 'complete telic situation'	IMPERFECTIVE

We have seen that the three synchronic aspect system types introduced above differ with respect to their semantics, means of expression, and relation to tense. As shown by Bybee and Dahl (1989:83ff.) and Bybee et al. (1994:83ff.), these important differences can be explained by examining their origins, that is, how the aspect systems came to be the way they are today. In general, perfectives in Type 1 and Type 2 aspect systems develop from constructions with an original perfect function. Alternatively, imperfectives may result from extended habitual uses of an original progressive (see the discussion on Central Quechua *-yka:* in §5.4). In contrast, individual perfective elements in the Type 3 Slavic-style system derive historically from morphemes that introduce a boundary or limit. These source morphemes may include verb particles such as *up* in the English phrasal verb *eat up*, or directional suffixes such as Proto Quechua **-yku* 'in' illustrated in §2.1.3.

4.2.4   TYPE 4: Mixed or layered system

The final aspect system type we will consider here is essentially a hybrid, mixing the Type 2 tripartite inflectional system (Figure 4.3) with the Type 3 Slavic-style system (Figure 4.4).

Bybee and Dahl cite Bulgarian (Slavic) and Georgian (Kartvelian) as languages in which "the bounder system coexists with a tripartite tense-aspect system" (1989:87).[81]

It is evident from the preceding discussion that aspect in SCQ is best characterized as a Type 4 mixed or layered system. The two "layers" could be analyzed as 1) a tripartite inflectional system and 2) a Slavic-type derivational system. At the same time, these two components of the SCQ aspect system do not simply coexist. Rather, they are interdependent, both synchronically and diachronically, a theme elaborated throughout this work. In the next section I analyze the inflectional and derivational components, underscoring features that distinguish aspect in SCQ from the general system types described above, especially noting how the two components are integrated into a single aspectual system.[82]

4.3 The layered SCQ aspect system

The SCQ aspectual system shows tremendous complexity in the interaction of elements from different areas of the morphology. In order to better understand the semantic relations that obtain between the aspectual categories, and the organization of the aspectual system as a whole, it may be useful at the outset to consider the structure of the inflectional and derivational layers separately. Interconnections between these two layers are noted in the following discussion, and summarized in §4.7.

When viewed in isolation, the inflectional component could be analyzed as shown in Figure 4.5.[83] The perfective markers are restricted to the past, as in the tripartite system described above (Figure 4.3). Unlike the typical tripartite system, however, a tense distinction is not relevant at the level of "general imperfective," but rather in the habitual category, one level down. Past habitual *-q/-q=ka* is mutually exclusive with present habitual *-Ø*. The continuous category is formally expressed not through inflectional morphology, but through derivational morphology via the suffix *-yka:* (Figure 4.6). The absence of this suffix simply means that continuousness remains unspecified.

The two inflectional habitual markers occur in paradigmatic contrast with the past perfectives in slot I2 (mood markers also contrast in slot I2; see §4.6.2). Rather than a single marker, the past perfective suffixes *-ru*, *-sha*, and *-ra* further distinguish personhood and degrees of remoteness in the tense domain (§5.1).

---

[81] In addition, Dahl (1999:36) finds parallels to this kind of layering in Sorbian (Slavic), as well as Athapaskan.

[82] The characterization of aspect in SCQ as a "mixed system" corresponds to similarities previously noted between SCQ, Bulgarian, and Koyukon Athabaskan in Chapter 3, note 77.

[83] As described in §3.2.3 and §5.2, the aspectual status of the multi-purpose suffix *-na:* ranges from imperfective (in spontaneous conversation) to neutral. Its primary meaning pertains to tense, modality, and evidentiality. In the present discussion I focus on the clearly aspectual elements.

Past perfective *-ru* (from **-rqu* 'out') has shifted over time from the "Slavic-type" derivational layer (its current function in many Quechuan languages) to the "tripartite" inflectional layer. This type of historical connection between these two system types has not been reported outside the Quechua language family. I analyze this unique development in detail in Chapter 9.

Figure 4.5 *The inflectional component of the SCQ aspect system*

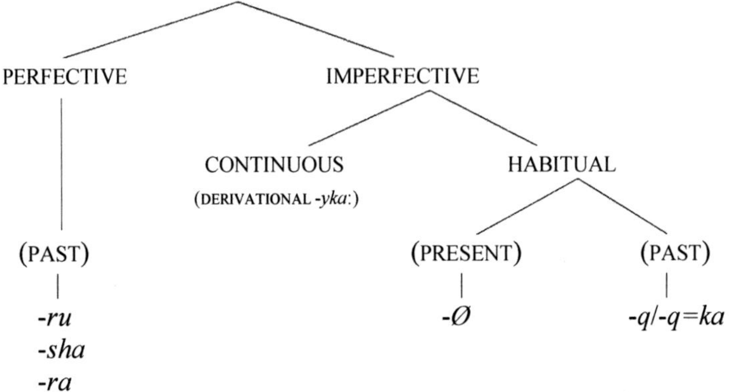

The organization of the derivational component of aspect in SCQ is represented in Figure 4.6. In general, obligatory aspectual distinctions expressed inflectionally can be further articulated by optional distinctions expressed derivationally. Aspect markers in the derivational component are not specified for tense, but the relevance of tense can be seen in patterns of co-occurrence between derivational and inflectional markers (see §4.4.1).

Figure 4.6 *The derivational component of the SCQ aspect system*

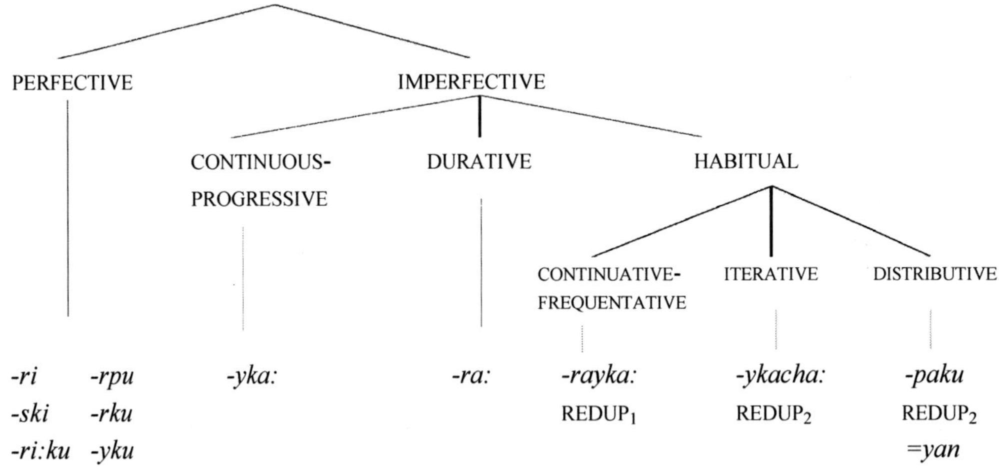

The derivational aspect categories are richly elaborated. Derivational perfectives denote punctual (*-ri*), completive (*-rpu*), and complete telic situations (*-rku, -yku, -ski, -ri:ku*). Many of these suffixes also encode modal distinctions (see Chapter 6).

Derivational imperfectives include the continuous-progressive suffix *-yka:* (which connects to the inflectional layer in Figure 4.5), the durative suffix *-ra:*, and a variety of repetitive types subsumed under the umbrella of habitual, which is interpreted here in the broadest sense of recurrence. Strictly-speaking, iterative subactions occur on a single occasion and not on multiple (habitual) occasions. The line dividing iterative from habitual situations, however, is not always clear-cut in SCQ, as "iterative" *-ykacha:* can also portray a lifetime of recurrent activities (see §3.1.4).

In sum, the grammatical expression of aspect in SCQ could be characterized as "an array of grammaticized and grammaticizing constructions of different ages and sources sharing or competing for overlapping territories" (Bybee et al. 1994:21). In other words, aspect in SCQ does not constitute a tidy structured arrangement of maximal binary contrasts within the perfective and imperfective domains. Instead, a network of twenty productive markers distributed through derivational and inflectional layers of morphology express a wide spectrum of aspectual concepts. Some of these markers co-occur freely, but many combinations do not.[84]

4.4   Aspect marker combinations

While each aspect marker is productive, not all possible configurations are actually attested in the SCQ corpus. Combinations of derivational with inflectional aspect markers are presented in §4.4.1, and derivational markers with other derivational markers in §4.4.2. The fully inflectional markers do not co-occur (by definition) as they are found in paradigmatic contrast in verbal slot I2.

4.4.1   Derivational with inflectional aspect markers

Table 4.1 presents combinations of perfective and imperfective aspect markers in terms of their derivational and inflectional expression. As mentioned above, derivational aspect markers can further specify distinctions conveyed via inflectional markers. The check mark symbol "✓" indicates a valid combination, and the minus symbol "−" an invalid combination (the combination does not occur in the corpus and my language consultants do not consider this collocation valid). Minus followed by a check "− ✓" indicates that the combination is extremely

---

[84] Patterns in the distribution of aspect markers in SCQ discourse are reported in §4.4 (aspect marker combinations), as well as in §4.5 (lexical diffusion) and §4.6 (distribution with non-aspectual elements). I highlight here the most salient patterns. The detailed information provided in these tables also serves as reference material for ongoing research.

rare. In general, the rare combinations in each of the tables in the present chapter provide excellent opportunities for investigating the contexts in which innovation occurs.[85]

Table 4.1 *Combinations of derivational with inflectional aspect markers*

		INFLECTIONAL PERFECTIVES			INFLECTIONAL IMPERFECTIVES		
		-ru	*-sha*	*-ra*	*-Ø*	*-q*	*-na:*
		PST.R	PST.R3	PST	PRS	PST.H	PST.N
DERIVATIONAL PERFECTIVES							
-ri	PUNC	–	✓	✓	✓	– ✓	✓
-rpu	COMPL	–	✓	–	✓	–	✓
-rku	PFV.M	–	–	–	✓	–	–
-yku	PFV.O	✓	✓	✓	✓	–	✓
-ski	PFV	✓	✓	✓	✓	–	✓
-ri:ku	PFV.F	✓	✓	–	✓	–	✓
DERIVATIONAL IMPERFECTIVES							
-ra:	DUR	✓	✓	–	✓	✓	– ✓
-paku	DISTR.S	✓	✓	✓	✓	–	✓
-ykacha:	ITER	–	–	–	✓	–	✓
-yka:	CONT	– ✓	– ✓	✓	✓	–	✓
-rayka:	DUR.C	–	– ✓	–	✓	–	✓
=yan	DISTR.T	✓	–	–	–	✓	–
REDUP₁	FREQ	–	✓	–	✓	–	✓
REDUP₂	ITER	–	–	–	✓	–	✓

Inflectional perfectives

Valid and invalid combinations between the three inflectional past perfectives (*-ru*, *-sha*, and *-ra*) and the derivational aspect markers are highly idiosyncratic. All three occur with the derivational perfectives *-yku* and *-ski*, as well as distributive *-paku*. The shaded cells in the columns for *-ru*, *-sha*, and *-ra* highlight the fact that none occurs with perfective *-rku*, iterative *ykacha:*, nor in verb root reduplications (REDUP₂).

Inflectional *-sha* occurs with five of the six derivational perfectives (not with *-rku*). Inflectional *-ru* occurs with three of the six derivational perfectives, while inflectional *-ra* occurs with a different set of three.

Inflectional *-ra* occurs freely with continuous *-yka:* yet never with durative *-ra:*. In contrast, inflectional *-ru* and *-sha* occur freely with durative *-ra:* but almost never with continuous *-yka:*. (Table 4.2 shows that continuous *-yka:* never occurs with the derivational perfectives.)

---

[85] One example of a rare combination is continuous *-yka:* with past perfective *-sha*. These two suffixes do not combine in any of the 1,452 verbs in the coded data, even though there are 174 instances of *-sha* and 169 of *-yka:*. In the larger 9,600-clause SCQ corpus, however, there is a single example of *-yka:* with *-sha*. Thus, the combination is marked by the symbol "– ✓".

Inflectional imperfectives

The distribution of the three inflectional imperfectives among the derivational aspect markers is somewhat less idiosyncratic. For example, present habitual *-Ø* occurs with all of the derivational markers, except the distributive enclitic *=yan*. Narrative past *-na:* occurs with all of them, except *=yan* and perfective *-rku*. Past habitual *-q*, on the other hand, is incompatible with the derivational aspect markers, except durative *-ra:* and distributive *=yan*.

Inflectional perfectives and imperfectives

Of the six inflectional aspect markers, only present habitual *-Ø* occurs with derivational perfective *-rku*. Likewise, only past perfective *-ru* and past habitual *-q* occur with distributive *=yan*. Past habitual *-q* is the only inflectional aspect marker that does not occur with derivational perfective *-ski* nor with distributive *-paku* (as highlighted in the shaded cells in the column for *-q*).

4.4.2   Derivational with other derivational aspect markers

Table 4.2 shows the derivational aspect markers that co-occur and those that do not, as well as the order of the two elements. Valid combinations are indicated by the check mark symbol "✓", and invalid combinations by the minus symbol "−". An additional symbol "N/A" indicates that the combination is not applicable because 1) the verbal slots for the two markers are out of sequence or 2) the marker cannot follow another instance of itself. For example, punctual *-ri* occurs in slot D3, and perfective *-yku* in slot D4. Thus, the combination *-ri-yku* has a felicitous order, whereas **-yku-ri* does not, and is marked "N/A". The two types of verb reduplication are also marked "N/A" as these structures are mutually exclusive.

Table 4.2 *Combinations of derivational aspect markers*

			2ND ELEMENT													
			PERFECTIVES						IMPERFECTIVES							
			-ri	-rpu	-rku	-yku	-ski	-ri:ku	-ra:	-paku	-ykacha:	-yka:	-rayka:	=yan	REDUP₁	REDUP₂
			D3	D4	D4	D4	D4	D4	D1	D2	D3	D4	D4	E1		
1ST ELEMENT																
PERFECTIVES																
-ri	PUNC	D3	N/A	—	—	✓	—	—	N/A	N/A	—	—	—	✓	✓	—
-rpu	COMPL	D4	N/A	N/A	—	—	—	—	N/A	N/A	N/A	—	—	—	—	—
-rku	PFV.M	D4	N/A	—	N/A	—	—	—	N/A	N/A	N/A	—	—	✓	✓	—
-yku	PFV.O	D4	N/A	—	—	N/A	—	—	N/A	N/A	N/A	—	—	✓	—	—
-ski	PFV	D4	N/A	—	—	—	N/A	—	N/A	N/A	N/A	—	—	✓	—	—
-ri:ku	PFV.F	D4	N/A	—	—	—	—	N/A	N/A	N/A	N/A	—	—	—	—	—
IMPERFECTIVES																
-ra:	DUR	D1	—	—	—	—	—	—	N/A	—	—	✓	—	—	—	—
-paku	DISTR.S	D2	✓	—	—	✓	✓	—	N/A	N/A	—	✓	—	—	—	—
-ykacha:	ITER	D3	—	—	—	✓	—	—	N/A	N/A	N/A	✓	—	—	—	—
-yka:	CONT	D4	N/A	—	—	—	—	—	N/A	N/A	N/A	N/A	—	—	✓	—
-rayka:	DUR.C	D4	N/A	—	—	—	—	—	N/A	N/A	N/A	—	N/A	—	—	—
=yan	DISTR.T	E1	N/A	N/A	N/A	N/A	N/A	N/A	N/A	N/A	N/A	N/A	N/A	N/A	—	—
REDUP₁	FREQ		✓	—	—	—	—	—	—	—	—	✓	—	—	N/A	N/A
REDUP₂	ITER		—	—	✓	✓	—	—	—	—	—	✓	—	—	N/A	N/A

Derivational aspect markers do not reduplicate, at least not as a productive morphological process. For example, the addition of durative *-ra:* to *qaya-* 'shout' yields the stem *qaya-ra:-* 'shout a long time', but **qaya-ra:-ra:-* is ungrammatical. On the other hand, derivational markers have "co-lexicalized" or fused over time with particular verb roots, forming new lexical items. Thus, the fused form *tsara:-* 'hold' can take an additional instance of *-ra:* (e.g., *tsara:-ra:-* 'hold a long time'). Lexicalized perfective forms show similar characteristics.

As can be seen in Table 4.2, derivational perfectives do not co-occur (except the combination of punctual *-ri* plus perfective *-yku* described in §2.1.6). In addition, derivational perfectives cannot be followed by derivational imperfective suffixes, as highlighted by the shaded cells in the upper right quadrant of Table 4.2. The perfective suffixes *-rku* and *-yku* are common in the second element of verb root reduplications (REDUP₂) as illustrated in (110) and (111).

The situation involving derivational imperfectives is more complex. First, the shaded cells in the lower right quadrant highlight the fact that continuous *-yka:* (slot D4) is compatible with most derivational imperfectives in other slots. Specifically, distributive *-paku* and iterative *-ykacha:* can both be followed by continuous *-yka:*, as seen in examples (80) and (90). Likewise, continuous *-yka:* is the only derivational imperfective that occurs in verbal reduplications, as in (102) and (112). In addition, the frequent co-occurrence of durative *-ra:* with continuous *-yka:* has given rise to a new suffix *-rayka:* which has a frequentative meaning with dynamic predicates (see §3.1.3).

Second, the shaded cells in the lower left quadrant of Table 4.2 highlight the fact that durative *-ra:*, continuous *-yka:*, and the amalgamated form *-rayka:* do not occur with any derivational perfective marker. In contrast, distributive *-paku* can be followed by punctual *-ri*, perfective *-yku*, or perfective *-ski*, as illustrated in (87)-(89); cf. note 57. Similarly, iterative *-ykacha:* is followed by perfective *-yku* in (82).

Finally, distributive *=yan* does not occur with any of the derivational imperfectives.

4.5 Lexical diffusion

In this section I present the frequency of grammatical aspect markers, the distribution of these markers among semantic classes of verb roots, and the formation of new lexical items from the frequent combinations of aspect markers with particular verb roots. In order to facilitate consistent comparisons, Tables 4.3 to 4.8 are based solely on the coded data of 1,452 verbs (see §1.3.2). The semantic analyses presented throughout the present work are not limited to the coded data, but rather are based on exemplars found throughout the much larger SCQ corpus.

4.5.1 Frequency and productivity of aspect markers

Tables 4.3 and 4.4 present the number of exemplars of each aspect marker in the coded data, along with the number of unique lexical verb roots that occur with the marker at least once. The morphological productivity of each aspect marker is shown by the large number of unique lexical items relative to the token frequencies of the individual markers. For example, in the first line of Table 4.3 there are 64 exemplars of punctual *-ri* (token frequency) distributed over 41 unique verb roots (type frequency).[86]

Table 4.3 *The frequency and distribution of* PERFECTIVE *markers with verb roots*

		EXEMPLARS	UNIQUE VERB ROOTS
DERIVATIONAL PERFECTIVES			
-ri	PUNC	64	41
-rpu	COMPL	21	10
-rku	PFV.M	24	21
-yku	PFV.O	48	35
-ski	PFV	79	56
-ri:ku	PFV.F	4	4
INFLECTIONAL PERFECTIVES			
-ru	PST.R	45	31
-sha	PST.R3	174	71
-ra	PST	78	39

Table 4.4 *The frequency and distribution of* IMPERFECTIVE *markers with verb roots*

		EXEMPLARS	UNIQUE VERB ROOTS
DERIVATIONAL PERFECTIVES			
-ra:	DUR	13	8
-paku	DISTR.S	2	2
-ykacha:	ITER	6	4
-yka:	CONT	169	59
-rayka:	DUR.C	31	16
=yan	DISTR.T	3	2
REDUP$_1$	FREQ	11	10
REDUP$_2$	ITER	5	4
INFLECTIONAL IMPERFECTIVES			
-∅	PRS	488	137
-q	PST.H	22	14
-na:	PST.N	58	29

---

[86] Aspect suffixes have "co-lexicalized" or fused over time with particular verb roots, forming new indivisible lexical items, e.g., *yayku-* 'enter', *tsara:-* 'hold', etc. Such forms are specifically excluded from these tables. Lexicalized forms are treated in §4.5.3 and §9.1.

4.5.2 Distribution with semantic classes of verb roots

Although the focus of this work is the grammatical expression of aspect in SCQ, I also address the lexical influence of particular verb roots on each aspect marker presented in Chapters 2 and 3. In this section we consider the intersection between the meanings of aspect markers and the semantic type of the verb root. Lyons finds that often "one and the same aspect will be interpreted differently according to the character of the verb" (1977:713). A connection between aspect and the semantic classes "dynamic versus stative" is observed by Comrie (1976:82), Chung and Timberlake (1985:214ff.), Dahl (1985:28ff.), Binnick (1991:83ff.), Mithun (2000:266ff.), and many others.

Tables 4.5 and 4.6 present the distribution of perfective markers among five semantic classes of lexical verb roots. I find that these semantic classes show a preference or dispreference for a given aspect marker. This fine-grained approach allows us to ascertain the degree of generality in the meaning of a given aspect marker by examining its spread through the lexicon.

Table 4.5 *The distribution of* PERFECTIVE *markers with semantic classes of verb roots*

SEMANTIC CLASS		MOTION	OTHER DYNAMIC	STATIVE	SPEECH	COGNITION
DERIVATIONAL PERFECTIVES						
-rpu	COMPL	✓	✓	–	–	–
-rku	PFV.M	✓	✓	– ✓	– ✓	–
-yku	PFV.O	✓	✓	– ✓	– ✓	– ✓
-ski	PFV	✓	✓	✓	– ✓	– ✓
-ri	PUNC	✓	✓	– ✓	–	– ✓
-ri:ku	PFV.F	–	✓	✓	–	– ✓
INFLECTIONAL PERFECTIVES						
-ru	PST.R	✓	✓	– ✓	– ✓	– ✓
-sha	PST.R3	✓	✓	– ✓	– ✓	✓
-ra	PST	– ✓	✓	✓	✓	– ✓

For example, the set of nine perfective markers (including many former directionals) in Figure 2.2 (§2.3) express a continuous subset of meanings that overlap within perfective semantic space. These meanings extend from more specific to more general (abstract), viz., from directional, to completive, to perfective, to past tense. The distribution of these markers among the five semantic classes in Table 4.5 corresponds to their increasingly general meanings. The more specific the meaning, the more limited its co-occurrences. The more general the meaning, the wider its collocational range.

This is illustrated by the shaded area in Table 4.5. Completive *-rpu* is restricted to motion and other dynamic verbs. Perfective *-rku* collocates not only with dynamic verbs, but also occasionally occurs with stative verbs and speech verbs. Perfective *-yku* is compatible with all semantic classes, corresponding to its more general meaning. Finally, perfective *-ski* collocates with all semantic classes and furthermore occurs with stative verbs more frequently than *-yku.*

Table 4.6 summarizes the distribution of imperfective markers among the same semantic classes. Unlike the inflectional perfectives in Table 4.5, the inflectional imperfectives tend to occur freely not only with motion and other dynamic verbs, but also with stative verbs and speech verbs (see the shaded area in Table 4.6). The preference or dispreference of a given semantic class for a particular derivational imperfective marker appears to be highly idiosyncratic.

Table 4.6 *The distribution of* IMPERFECTIVE *markers with semantic classes of verb roots*

SEMANTIC CLASS		MOTION	OTHER DYNAMIC	STATIVE	SPEECH	COGNITION
DERIVATIONAL IMPERFECTIVES						
-ra:	DUR	—	✓	— ✓	— ✓	—
-paku	DISTR.S	—	✓	— ✓	✓	✓
-ykacha:	ITER	✓	✓	—	—	—
-yka:	CONT	✓	✓	✓	— ✓	—
-rayka:	DUR.C	— ✓	✓	—	— ✓	— ✓
=yan	DISTR.T	✓	✓	—	✓	—
REDUP$_1$	FREQ	✓	✓	✓	—	—
REDUP$_2$	ITER	✓	— ✓	—	—	—
INFLECTIONAL IMPERFECTIVES						
-Ø	PRS	✓	✓	✓	✓	✓
-q	PST.H	✓	✓	✓	✓	—
-na:	PST.N	✓	✓	✓	✓	— ✓

The distribution of perfective markers with the copula *ka-*, a prototypical representative of statives, is shown in Table 4.7. Interestingly, all of the former directional suffixes (now perfectives) show a dispreference for the copula *ka-*, presumably because copulas have more to do with existence and statehood (durativity) than with space. In fact, the most general former directional—past perfective *-ru*—never occurs with *ka-*. In spite of its synchronic inflectional status, *-ru* patterns with the derivational perfective set from which it emerged. Past perfective *-sha*, on the other hand, is quite compatible with *ka-* (13%), presumably because it developed from an inflectional perfect.

Table 4.7 *The distribution of* PERFECTIVE *markers with the copula ka-*

		COPULA *ka-*	TOKEN FREQUENCY	WITH *ka-*	PERCENTAGE
DERIVATIONAL PERFECTIVES					
-ri	PUNC	—	64	0	0 %
-rpu	COMPL	—	21	0	0 %
-rku	PFV.M	— ✓	24	1	4 %
-yku	PFV.O	— ✓	48	2	4 %
-ski	PFV	— ✓	79	1	1 %
-ri:ku	PFV.F	—	4	0	0 %
INFLECTIONAL PERFECTIVES					
-ru	PST.R	—	45	0	0 %
-sha	PST.R3	✓	174	23	13 %
-ra	PST	✓	78	9	11 %

Table 4.8 shows that most of the derivational imperfectives, like their derivational perfective counterparts, are incompatible with the copula *ka-*. Continuous *-yka:* is marked by "✓+" to highlight its exceptional preference for *ka-* (26%). As discussed in §5.4, *-yka:* is developing characteristics of a more general imperfective in Central Quechuan varieties.

Narrative past *-na:* (also marked by "✓+") has a comparable preference for the copula *ka-* (28%). In other words, speakers often use the combination *ka-na:* to describe the way things were. This combination constitutes one type of evidence for the past imperfective sense of *-na:*. According to Bybee (1994:244), perfective aspect and past tense tend to narrate what happened, not to tell how things were. The latter function would be reserved for a specially-marked past imperfective, such as *-na:*.

Table 4.8 *The distribution of* IMPERFECTIVE *markers with the copula ka-*

		COPULA *ka-*	TOKEN FREQUENCY	WITH *ka-*	PERCENTAGE
DERIVATIONAL IMPERFECTIVES					
-ra:	DUR	—	13	0	0 %
-paku	DISTR.S	—	2	0	0 %
-ykacha:	ITER	—	6	0	0 %
-yka:	CONT	✓+	169	44	26 %
-rayka:	DUR.C	—	31	0	0 %
=yan	DISTR.T	—	3	0	0 %
REDUP$_1$	FREQ	—	5	0	0 %
REDUP$_2$	ITER	— ✓	15	1	7 %
INFLECTIONAL IMPERFECTIVES					
-Ø	PRS	✓	488	59	12 %
-q	PST.H	— ✓	22	2	9 %
-na:	PST.N	✓+	58	16	28 %

4.5.3   Lexicalized forms

Table 4.9 is a compilation of lexical items in SCQ composed of a former directional suffix or related form fused to a particular verb root. In keeping with the derivational status of the suffix at the time of lexicalization, the meanings of the fused forms are not entirely predictable. In addition, the distribution is idiosyncratic as reflected by the gaps in the table. Rows with at least two lexicalized forms are shaded. The root forms **hu-*, **qa-*, **ta-*, **wa-*, and **ya-* do not occur as independent lexical items in SCQ, nor in other modern Quechuan languages, as far as I am aware.[87]

There are important differences between productive aspect suffixes and those that have "co-lexicalized" or fused with particular verb roots. As shown above in Table 4.2, for example, perfective *-yku* does not combine synchronically with perfective *-ski* nor with continuous *-yka:*. In contrast, fused verb roots in the column labeled **-yku* 'in' in Table 4.9 can and frequently do combine with *-ski* and *-yka:*, e.g., *yayku-ski-n* 'she enters (complete situation)', *yayku-yka-n* 'she is entering'.

In addition, the verb roots in Table 4.9 are indivisible, such that no morpheme can intervene between the erstwhile suffix and the lexical item to which it is now permanently attached. [88]

---

[87] Nouns with shapes similar to the verb forms in Table 4.8 include *hirka* 'hill/mountain', *hirqa* 'blanket', *iski* 'nit', *kurku* 'hump', *qorpa* 'guest', *ruri* 'inside', *turqu* 'roof pole', *urku* 'forehead', *urpu* 'deep jug', and *urqu* 'male'. Not all of the verb roots with *-ri* as the final element easily fit in Table 4.8. Additional forms include *awri-* 'unravel yarn', *haqiri-* 'abandon', *kamari-* 'prepare', *pallari-* 'lift', *qonquri-* 'kneel', *shinri-* 'tie up', *shiri-* 'cover/mate hen', *tapri-* 'knock over', *toqri-* 'poke', and *yuri-* 'be born'.

[88] **-rqa* 'past perfective' is not a former directional, but three verb roots ending in *rqa* add to the overall lexicalization picture: *marqa-* 'hold in arms', *pirqa-* 'build wall', and *warqa-* 'belabored speech'.

Table 4.9 *Lexicalization of former directional suffixes and related forms in SCQ*

-rpu 'down'	*-rku* 'up'	*-yku* 'in'	*-ski* 'to'	*-ri* 'go?, up?, middle?'	*-rqu* 'out'
—	—	—	alliski- 'heal'	—	—
—	—	—	—	apari- 'carry on back'	—
—	arku- 'harvest corn'	—	—	—	—
—	—	—	chaski- 'receive'	—	—
—	churku- 'put on to cook'	—	—	—	—
hirpu- 'make drink'	—	—	—	—	—
—	hurku- '2nd cultivate'	—	—	—	hurqu- 'remove'
—	—	—	—	kawari- 'resurrect'	—
—	—	—	—	—	—
—	—	—	muski- 'sniff'	—	—
—	nirkur 'in addition'	—	—	—	—
—	—	—	—	pa:ri- 'fly'	—
—	—	—	—	—	—
—	—	—	—	puri- 'walk'	—
qarpu- 'push down' qarpa- 'irrigate'	qarku- 'herd'	qayku- 'enclose'	—	qari- 'lift part'	qarqu- 'expel'
—	sharku- 'stand'	—	—	sha:ri- 'get up'	—
tarpu- 'plant'	—	—	—	tari- 'find'	—
—	—	—	—	tsari- 'grab'	—
—	warku- 'hang up'	wayku- 'stir, stoke'	—	—	—
yarpa:- 'think'	—	—	—	—	—
yarpu- 'lower'	yarku- 'climb'	yayku- 'enter'	—	—	yarqu- 'leave'

4.6   The distribution of aspect markers with non-aspectual elements

In this section I present the frequency and distribution of SCQ aspect markers with non-aspectual morphosyntactic elements.

4.6.1   Finite versus nonfinite form

Table 4.10 shows that SCQ derivational aspect markers, in general, occur more frequently in finite forms than in nonfinite (nominalized and adverbialized) forms. This asymmetry corresponds with the fact that inflectional aspect is expressed only in finite verbs and a primary use of derivational aspect markers is to further specify those inflectional distinctions. (The inflectional aspect markers are not listed in Table 4.10 because they occur in finite verbs 100% of the time.)

The derivational aspect markers show a more interesting distribution. First, the derivational perfectives prefer finite forms, except for *-rku* which prefers nonfinite forms 71% of the time. The difference is associated with the modal meaning of *-rku*, as discussed in §6.2. Second, the derivational imperfectives show more mixed preferences. On the one hand, durative-continuous *-rayka:* (97%) and continuous *-yka:* (84%) strongly prefer finite forms. In contrast, the two distributive markers *-paku* and *=yan* prefer nonfinite forms (67% each), as does REDUP₁ verb root reduplication (80%).

Table 4.10 *The distribution of derivational aspect markers according to finiteness*

FINITENESS		FINITE FORM	NONFINITE FORM
DERIVATIONAL PERFECTIVES			
-ri	PUNC	79 %	21 %
-rpu	COMPL	74 %	26 %
-rku	PFV.M	29 %	71 %
-yku	PFV.O	76 %	24 %
-ski	PFV	63 %	37 %
-ri:ku	PFV.F	50 %	50 %
DERIVATIONAL IMPERFECTIVES			
-ra:	DUR	54 %	46 %
-paku	DISTR.S	33 %	67 %
-ykacha:	ITER	67 %	33 %
-yka:	CONT	84 %	16 %
-rayka:	DUR.C	97 %	3 %
=yan	DISTR.T	33 %	67 %
REDUP₁	FREQ	82 %	18 %
REDUP₂	ITER	20 %	80 %

The finite forms in Table 4.10 are examined in more detail in the next section.[89]

---

[89] Most of the nonfinite forms in the second column of Table 4.10 are adverbial clauses formed with either the 'same subject' suffix *-r*, or the 'different subject' suffix *-pti*. All of the

4.6.2 Distribution with finite types

SCQ has five finite verb types, represented by the tense-aspect-mood columns in Table 4.11. We have already seen above in Table 4.1 the distribution of derivational aspect markers with the three perfectives restricted to the past (*-ru*, *-sha*, and *-ra*) and the two imperfectives restricted to the past (*-q* and *-na:*). These five slot I2 markers are combined in the 'PAST' column in Table 4.11. The "PRESENT" column" equates with present habitual *-Ø* in slot I2. The "FUTURE" column combines the four portmanteau suffixes which mark future tense as well as the person of the subject in slot I2. Imperative mood is similarly marked by portmanteau suffixes in slot I2. Conditional mood is marked by the person of the subject in slot I3 and the suffix *-man* in slot I4.

Table 4.11 *The distribution of derivational aspect markers with finite verb types*

		PAST	PRESENT	FUTURE	IMPERATIVE	CONDITIONAL
DERIVATIONAL PERFECTIVES						
-ri	PUNC	✓	✓	✓	✓	—
-rpu	COMPL	— ✓	✓	—	— ✓	—
-rku	PFV.M	—	✓	✓	—	—
-yku	PFV.O	✓	✓	✓	✓	✓
-ski	PFV	✓	✓	✓	—	✓
-ri:ku	PFV.F	✓	✓	—	—	—
DERIVATIONAL IMPERFECTIVES						
-ra:	DUR	✓	✓	—	—	—
-paku	DISTR.S	✓	✓	—	—	— ✓
-ykacha:	ITER	—	✓	—	—	—
-yka:	CONT	✓	✓+	— ✓	—	—
-rayka:	DUR.C	— ✓	✓+	—	—	—
=yan	DISTR.T	— ✓	✓	—	—	—
REDUP₁	FREQ	— ✓	✓	— ✓	— ✓	—
REDUP₂	ITER	—	—	—	—	—

In finite clauses, the derivational perfective suffix *-rku* does not occur in the corpus with any of the inflectional past markers nor with mood markers. Similarly, the completive suffix *-rpu* does not occur with future nor conditional markers, and only rarely occurs with the inflectional past markers. Punctual *-ri* occurs with all finite types except conditional mood, and perfective *-ski* occurs with all except imperative mood. Perfective *-yku* occurs with all finite types (though not specifically with past habitual *-q*, as shown in Table 4.1).

---

derivational perfectives in adverbial clauses occur with same subject *-r* at least 67% of the time, and *-rku* nearly 100% of the time. Among the derivational imperfectives in adverbial clauses, *-yka:* shows an opposite preference for different subject *-pti* (60%).

The derivational imperfectives are almost completely restricted to past or present, the first two columns in Table 4.11. The present is strongly preferred by continuous *-yka:* (89%) and durative-continuous *-rayka:* (97%).

4.6.3   Non-aspectual derivational suffixes

SCQ has many derivational suffixes that do not mark aspect. Ten of the most common are listed in the first row of Tables 4.12 and 4.13. Those that combine freely with aspect in the SCQ corpus are marked with "✓", those that rarely combine are marked with "– ✓", and those that do not combine are marked with "–". The leftmost columns represent the most common combinations and the rightmost columns the least common.

Table 4.12 *The distribution of PERFECTIVES with non-aspectual derivational suffixes*

		-ya: PL.V	*-ku* MID	*-tsi* CAUS	*-mu* FAR	*-pa:* BEN	*-ka:* PASS	*-na:* DES	*-naku* RECP	*-lla:* DLM	*-pu* BEN
DERIVATIONAL PERFECTIVES											
-ri	PUNC	✓	✓	✓	✓	– ✓	✓	–	✓	– ✓	–
-rpu	COMPL	–	– ✓	– ✓	✓	✓	–	–	–	–	–
-rku	PFV.M	✓	✓	✓	✓	✓	–	✓	–	– ✓	–
-yku	PFV.O	✓	✓	✓	✓	✓	✓	–	– ✓	✓	–
-ski	PFV	– ✓	✓	✓	✓	✓	✓	✓	– ✓	–	✓
-ri:ku	PFV.F	–	– ✓	– ✓	– ✓	–	–	–	– ✓	–	–
INFLECTIONAL PERFECTIVES											
-ru	PST.R	✓+	✓	✓	✓	– ✓	–	–	– ✓	– ✓	–
-sha	PST.R3	✓	✓	✓	✓	✓	✓	–	– ✓	– ✓	✓
-ra	PST	✓	✓	✓	✓	✓	✓	– ✓	– ✓	– ✓	–

Table 4.13 *The distribution of IMPERFECTIVES with non-aspectual derivational suffixes*

		-ya: PL.V	*-ku* MID	*-tsi* CAUS	*-mu* FAR	*-pa:* BEN	*-ka:* PASS	*-na:* DES	*-naku* RECP	*-lla:* DLM	*-pu* BEN
DERIVATIONAL IMPERFECTIVES											
-ra:	DUR	✓	✓	✓	✓	–	–	–	–	–	–
-paku	DISTR.S	✓	–	–	– ✓	–	–	–	–	–	–
-ykacha:	ITER	✓	–	–	–	–	– ✓	–	– ✓	–	–
-yka:	CONT	✓	✓	✓	✓	✓	–	✓	✓	– ✓	–
-rayka:	DUR.C	✓	✓	– ✓	✓	–	–	–	–	–	–
=yan	DISTR.T	–	✓	✓	– ✓	–	–	–	–	– ✓	–
REDUP₁	FREQ	✓	✓	✓	–	–	–	✓	–	–	–
REDUP₂	ITER	–	– ✓	–	–	–	–	– ✓	–	– ✓	–
INFLECTIONAL IMPERFECTIVES											
-Ø	PRS	✓	✓	✓	✓	✓	✓	✓	✓	– ✓	✓
-q	PST.H	✓+	✓	– ✓	✓	–	✓	–	✓	–	–
-na:	PST.N	✓	✓	✓	✓	✓	✓	–	– ✓	– ✓	✓

A few brief comments are in order. First, the verbal plural suffix *-ya:* (column 1) can combine with most of the aspect markers. Notably, plural *-ya:* occurs twice as often with past perfective *-ru* (56%) and past habitual *-q* (50%) than with the other inflectional aspect markers. This is indicated by the shaded cells with the symbol "✓+". At the opposite extreme, plural *-ya:* rarely occurs with perfective *-ski* (4%) and never occurs with completive *-rpu*, perfective *-ri:ku*, nor distributive *=yan*.

All of the perfectives in Table 4.12 can combine with middle *-ku*, causative *-tsi*, and cislocative-translocative *-mu*, and many of these combinations are very frequent in the SCQ corpus. The former directional suffixes (from most specific to most abstract: *-rpu*, *-rku*, *-yku*, *-ski*) show the same pattern as the shaded area in Table 4.5 (above), illustrating that semantic specificity restricts collocational range. *-rpu* occurs with only four of the ten suffixes in Table 4.12, *-rku* with seven, *-yku* with eight, and *-ski* with nine. The inflectional past perfective suffix *-ru* has the most abstract meaning of the former directionals. Surprisingly, *-ru* does not occur with passive *-ka:*, desiderative *-na:*, nor benefactive *-pu*, possibly attributable to its restriction to speech-act participants.

The imperfectives in Table 4.13 appear to be less compatible with most of the non-aspectual derivational suffixes. On the other hand, they have a greater tendency to combine with plural *-ya:*. Present habitual *-Ø* can combine with any of the ten derivational suffixes. Continuous *-yka:* can combine with any except passive *-ka:* and benefactive *-pu*. None of the derivational imperfectives occurs with benefactive *-pu*, and only iterative *-ykacha:* occurs with passive *-ka:*.[90]

4.7 Conclusions: The SCQ aspect system

Chapters 2 and 3 focused on the grammatical expression of perfective and imperfective aspect through twenty individual markers. The concern in the present chapter was to examine the organization of the SCQ aspectual system as a whole. We observed that aspect consists of interdependent layers of derivational and inflectional elements which express aspectual distinctions more specific than "general perfective" and "general imperfective." Succinctly stated, "successive layers of grammaticization along similar paths produce grams [grammatical morphemes] with similar meanings rather than grams participating in maximal contrasts" (Bybee et al. 1994:22).

---

[90] Aspect and negation: Completive *-rpu* and perfective *-rku* cannot occur with negative *-tsu*, and punctual *-ri* rarely does. Among imperfectives, durative *-ra:* and continuous *-yka:* rarely occur with negative *-tsu*. Adelaar (2006:134) makes a similar observation in that perfective *-ru* and progressive *-ya(:)* are not allowed in the main verb of a negative sentence in Tarma Quechua. Presumably, if an event or situation did not happen, then aspectual details are of little concern. It remains a mystery, then, why all of the inflectional aspect markers in SCQ, plus the derivational perfectives *-yku* and *-ski*, do occur freely with negative *-tsu*, while the aspect markers mentioned above do not.

In the inflectional component, perfective markers are restricted to the past. Unlike the typical "tripartite" system (Figure 4.3), in SCQ a present-past tense distinction is relevant in the habitual category, not at the level of "general imperfective" (Figure 4.5). The habitual markers (*-Ø* and *-q/-q=ka*) occur in paradigmatic contrast with narrative past (*-na:*) and the past perfective suffixes (*-ru, -sha,* and *-ra*). The latter suffixes further distinguish personhood and degrees of remoteness in the tense domain (see §5.1).

Aspectual distinctions expressed in the inflectional component can be further specified by distinctions expressed in the derivational component (Figure 4.6). Derivational aspect categories are not specified for tense, but richly articulate additional semantic distinctions in the domains of aspect and modality. Derivational perfectives report punctual (*-ri*), completive (*-rpu*), and complete telic situations (*-rku, -yku, -ski, -ri:ku*). Derivational imperfectives report continuous (*-yka:*) and durative (*-ra:*) situations, as well as a variety of repetitive situations.

The derivational "Slavic-type" system and the inflectional "tripartite" system do not simply co-exist. They are highly interdependent in SCQ. For example, the general imperfective category is usually understood to subsume habitual plus continuous aspect. In SCQ, present and past habitual (*-Ø* and *-q*) are expressed inflectionally, whereas continuous (*-yka:*) is expressed derivationally. In addition, markers have gradually "shifted" over time from the derivational component to the inflectional component (*-ru*), paving the way for similar developments by other markers. It is not a coincidence that the formal status of several markers is difficult to determine (*-ski, -yku, -yka:*). These markers may be better understood as midway along a scale ranging from clear derivation to clear inflection (A formal analysis of the "in between" cases is presented in Appendix B). Each of these features of aspect in SCQ yields a degree of fusion between the two layers which increasingly function as a single interdependent grammatical system.

We continued the investigation of the derivational and inflectional layers by examining patterns of co-occurrence among the aspect markers and their distribution with other linguistic elements. While each aspect marker is productive, not all combinations are possible. Instead, SCQ speakers regularly use only a small subset of preferred combinations. Frequent combinations with particular lexical items lead to lexicalization, that is, enrichment of aspectual or *Aktionsart* distinctions in the lexicon. The frequent combination of two aspect markers may lead to amalgamation, that is, the development of a new suffix with a non-compositional meaning (e.g., *-ri:ku, -rayka:*).

Aspect markers of the same category (e.g., past perfective *-ru* versus past perfective *-ra*) may be interpreted as indicating an additional tense or modal distinction. When routinized and strengthened over time, such non-aspectual inferences can grammaticize as an additional semantic component of the marker. The grammatical interfaces linking aspect with related semantic domains are examined in PART III (Chapters 5-8). The shifting internal organization of the aspect system over time is treated in PART IV (Chapters 9-12).

PART III – ASPECT AND RELATED SEMANTIC DOMAINS

5   ASPECT AND TENSE

The aim of the present chapter is to examine the grammatical interface between the semantic domains of aspect and tense. While aspect reports "the temporal contour of a situation" (Bybee et al. 1994:317), tense reports "location in time," a deictic relation that holds between a situation time and a reference time, such as the present moment (Comrie 1985:9). The situation time may be located prior to reference time (past), concurrent with reference time (present), or subsequent to reference time (future). In many languages aspect and tense are not expressed as separate grammatical categories, but rather are interwoven in the grammatical system due to the conceptual affinity between these two time-related notions (Dahl and Velupillai 2005:266).

In keeping with this cross-linguistic portrayal of grammaticized temporal concepts, aspect in SCQ does not constitute a separately delineated category. Instead, individual inflectional forms combine elements of aspect and tense in their semantics, including the past perfectives *-ru*, *-sha*, and *-ra*, narrative past *-na:*, past habitual *-q*, and present habitual *-Ø*. The inflectional tense-aspect markers often combine with particular derivational markers that convey more specific aspectual distinctions (e.g., perfective *-ski*, continuous *-yka:*, etc.). In general, the derivational aspect markers are not temporally restricted, freely appearing with past, present, and future tense markers.[91]

In this chapter I examine the tense component of each inflectional tense-aspect marker, beginning with perfectives and then imperfectives. The interaction of aspect with tense gives rise to distinctive patterns in the grammatical system. Together, the individual inflectional elements comprise a highly articulated tense-aspect network (see Figure 5.4 in §5.5). A detailed account of tense as a later grammaticization of prior aspectual meanings is presented in Part IV "The evolution of aspect in Quechua."

---

[91] The six inflectional markers which code tense and aspect functions in SCQ are fully productive in the outer layer of affixation in the obligatory verbal slot I2. They appear in paradigmatic contrast with future tense and mood markers, as well as various deverbal (nonfinite) markers. The derivational markers which code aspect and modal functions (but not tense) are fully productive in the inner layer of affixation in the non-obligatory verbal slots D1-D4. The aspectual functions of these derivational markers are treated above in Chapters 2-4, and their modal and manner functions are treated below in Chapters 6 and 7.

5.1 Past perfectives *-ru*, *-sha*, and *-ra*

The inflectional past perfective suffixes *-ru*, *-sha*, and *-ra* (cf. §2.2) span the semantic domains of aspect and tense. Each presents a situation as temporally bounded, but only in the past. In contrast, the derivational perfective suffixes *-rku*, *-yku*, *-ski*, and *-ri* (cf. §2.1) represent another type of perfective, not confined to the past.

Many languages have a "simple" past tense which "is semantically more general [than a past perfective] since it can also be used to signal past time for situations viewed imperfectively" (Bybee et al. 1994:84). The SCQ suffixes *-ru*, *-sha*, and *-ra*, however, do not present a habitual or ongoing (imperfective) view of the past situation, only a temporally bounded (perfective) view. At the same time, the high compatibility of past perfective *-ra* with continuous *-yka:* and with stative verbs shows that the grammatical meaning of *-ra* is more general than the newly developing past perfectives *-ru* and *-sha*, which almost never occur with *-yka:* (and *-ru* never occurs with the copula *ka-*).

As past perfective markers, *-ru*, *-sha*, and *-ra* naturally contrast with the past imperfectives, as well as with markers that do not report past meanings (e.g., present, future, imperative).[92] In addition, they distinguish person and tense contrasts within the past perfective category itself. First, *-sha* is a portmanteau suffix that combines past perfective with third person subject. *-sha* appears only when there is also a first or third person object, or no object (intransitive). Past perfective *-ru* is used for all other person inflections, that is, *-ru* appears with speech-act participant subjects (regardless of the object), as well as third person subjects (provided there is also a first inclusive or second person object). In this way, *-ru* and *-sha* appear in complementary distribution with respect to person, together forming a single "hybrid" past perfective category. Both are illustrated in the following excerpt from a conversation.[93]

(150) *"tsa   wara:-mu-nqa-na-chi"*   *ni-ya-__ru__-:.*   *tsa waray-nin qoyaq*
     then   be.dawn-FAR-FUT3-NOW-CNJ say-PL-__PST.R__-1 then tomorrow-3 morning

     mama-ntsi:-qa ari tsakaq-lla-na   ashi-q   sharku-__sh__.
     mother-1₁-TOP   yes   darkness-DLM-NOW search-PRMT stand.up-__PST.R3__

     'We __said__ (*-ru*) "Then maybe it will appear at dawn." Then the next morning when it was still dark our mother __got up__ (*-sh*) to search.'

---

[92] The past imperfective category is expressed inflectionally in SCQ by narrative past *-na:* (§5.2) and by past habitual *-q* (§5.3). Past imperfective meaning is expressed derivationally by the further specification of continuous *-yka:* or durative *-ra:* combined with an inflectional past marker, as illustrated above in (59) and (60) (§3.1.2) and below in (159)d (§5.4).

[93] Past perfective *-ru* appears with speech-act participant subjects in the coded data 96% of the time. In contrast, as a portmanteau suffix, past perfective *-sha* marks third person subject 100% of the time (though never with a first inclusive or second person object).

Second, while each past perfective expresses past tense, a situation marked by either *-ru* or *-sha* is typically more recent than a situation marked by *-ra*. In other words, the past perfective markers encode a remoteness distinction in the past, as represented in Figure 5.1. Although *-ru* and *-sha* report event sequences that are relatively recent, the time reference may range from earlier the same day to many years ago.[94]

Figure 5.1 *Time reference of past perfectives -ru, -sha, and -ra*

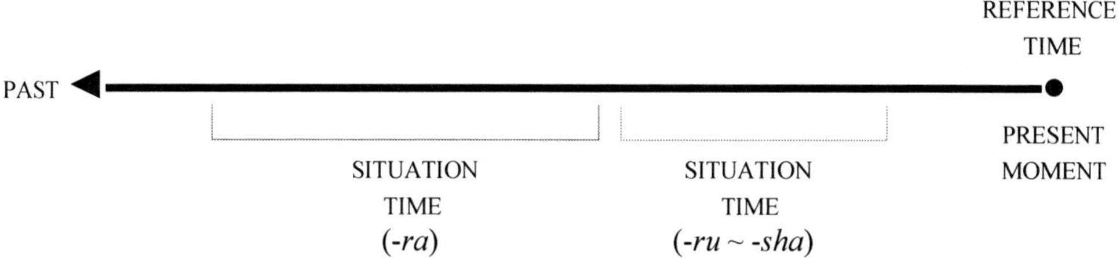

The grammatical marking of relative distance in time is illustrated in (151), where the event marked by *-ra* ('Juan came') is specified as prior to the event marked by *-ru* 'we provided lodging'; cf. the sequence of finite verbs with *-ra* followed by *-ru* in (178).

(151) *shamu-__ra__-n*   *pri:mu-ntsi:*   *Juan-pis.*   *pay-wan-pis*
      come-**PST**-3   cousin-1₁   Juan-EVEN   he-COM-EVEN

      ta:ra:-ya-__ru__-:   *ishke:*   *diya*   *punu-rku-r-yan*
      reside-PL.V-**PST.R**-1   two   day   sleep-PFV.M-SS-DISTR.T

      'Our cousin Juan **came** (*-ra*) too. We **provided lodging** (*-ru*) for him, all of us sleeping here each night for two (consecutive) days.'

Typically, the past perfectives are used in connected speech to narrate foregrounded event sequences, with the series of events marked by *-ra* prior in time to events marked by *-ru ~ -sha*. The narrative situation may have occurred recently or years prior to the moment of speech. For example, the sequence of events in (151) took place weeks before the conversation. Since *-ru* and *-sha* are not restricted to recent situations, the "recent past" glosses PST.R and PST.R3 could be potentially misleading, though they are historically accurate, since both forms result from the grammaticization of the inference of recent completion. In order to avoid terminological

---

[94] Diane Hintz (2007b:247-53) observes that the distinction between (recent) past *-ru ~ -sha* versus (remote) past *-ra* may be as much a matter of "involvement with or detachment from the situation" as of chronological time, with *-ru ~ -sha* corresponding to events in which the speaker may have a personal stake.

confusion, in Table 5.1 and elsewhere I refer to innovative *-ru* and *-sha* as "young" past perfectives, and to *-ra* as the "old" past perfective.[95]

Table 5.1 summarizes the person and remoteness distinctions expressed within the SCQ past perfective category. Although this hybrid category may seem synchronically unusual, it makes perfect sense when we consider how it acquired these functions. Briefly, *-ra* is an "old" past perfective (from *-*rqa* 'past') with cognate forms in virtually all modern Quechuan languages. This past suffix would have acquired perfective meaning via contrast with the past imperfective category. The synchronic form *-ra* is now construed as a "remote" past perfective in SCQ (column 3) due to the innovation of the newly developing past perfectives *-ru* (for speech-act participants) and *-sha* (for third person) which report more recent events (column 2).

Table 5.1 *The past perfective category in SCQ*

	"YOUNG" PAST PERFECTIVE (SUBSEQUENT SITUATION)		"OLD" PAST PERFECTIVE (PRIOR SITUATION)	
SPEECH-ACT	*punu-**ru**-:*	'I slept'	*punu-**ra**-:*	'I slept'
PARTICIPANTS	*punu-**ru**-ntsik*	'we (incl.) slept'	*punu-**ra**-ntsik*	'we (incl.) slept'
	*punu-**ru**-yki*	'you slept'	*punu-**ra**-yki*	'you slept'
3ᴿᴰ PERSON	*punu-**sha***	's/he slept'	*punu-**ra**-n*	's/he slept'

At a prior stage of development, *-ru* (from *-*rqu* 'outward') was a derivational perfective (the synchronic aspectual function of *-ski* and *-yku*). At the same time, *-sha* (from *-*shqa* 'past participle') was used in a periphrastically expressed perfect construction. These two meanings— derivational perfective and perfect—are reported for cognate forms in other modern Quechuan languages (see Adelaar 1986:23; Weber 1989:107; Hintz 2000:233; among others).

The reanalysis of perfects to recent past is well documented cross-linguistically (cf. §9.5). Once this reanalysis took place in SCQ, the emerging past perfective *-sha* was inflected exclusively in third person, presumably due to the non-occurrence of the auxiliary in third person. In SCQ, *-sha* has developed further to report non-recent past events as well.[96]

While the path of development from perfect meaning to past perfective/tense is now familiar, the reanalysis of a derivational perfective, such as *-ru*, to an inflectional past marker has not been

---

[95] The past perfectives *-ru* and *-sha* are glossed PST.R and PST.R3, respectively, to indicate that the situation time is prior to the moment of speech, and (usually) more recent than the time reference for past perfective *-ra*, glossed PST. I reserve the gloss PFV for perfectives which are not restricted to the past, that is, the derivational perfectives *-rku*, *-yku*, and *-ski*.

[96] As Comrie (1976:52-61) and others explain, perfect refers to the "continuing present relevance of a past event," and an event that occurs recently tends to be one that is currently relevant. As the current relevance component of meaning erodes, what remains is an event conceptualized as recent past.

described previously in the literature on the development of tense-aspect systems (e.g., Comrie 1976, Dahl 1985, Bybee et al. 1994). Although movement of a grammatical marker along this particular path is cross-linguistically rare, it is not unmotivated. As we will see in Chapter 9, the developing past perfective category in SCQ offers an excellent opportunity to examine mechanisms of semantic change that shape the emerging system over time.

Finally, the past perfective suffixes *-ru*, *-sha*, and *-ra* express a subset of general past tense meaning, with imperfective functions of past tense expressed by narrative past *-na:* and past habitual *-q*, the topics of the next two sections.

5.2 Narrative past *-na:*

The multi-dimensional inflectional marker *-na:* was introduced in §3.2.3 to highlight its propensity to function as an imperfective in naturally-occurring speech, as well as to preview its role as a past tense marker. Narrative past *-na:* presents a situation as in progress in the past or characteristic of a time period restricted to the past. Beyond aspect and tense, the central meaning of *-na:* appears to be evidential, as elaborated below in §6.4.

In terms of tense, narrative past *-na:* invokes a relative reference time (supplied by the context) situated prior to an absolute reference time (the present moment). The situation formally marked by *-na:* may be concurrent with, prior to, or subsequent to the time of that past reference point, which often corresponds to a main storyline event (see Figure 5.2). In other words, the absolute location in time is always prior to the present moment (past tense), but the location in time relative to the past reference time is a function of the pragmatic context.

Figure 5.2 *Time reference associated with narrative past -na:*

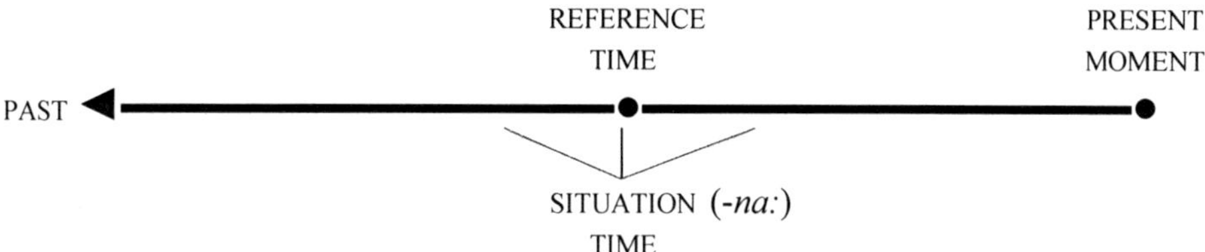

In the following example, the past reference time is indicated in the first sentence with past perfective *-ra*, and the situation marked by *-na:* in the following sentence is *concurrent with* it. Concurrence also holds in (192), where the sentence with past perfective *-sha* is followed by a sentence marked with *-na:*.

(152) *Niku-pis   aywa-__ra__-n Wanac-pa   ashi-q   ari.   mama-ntsi:-qa   tsa*
       Niko-EVEN   go-__PST__-3   Wanac-GEN   search-PRMT   yes   mother-1ᵢ-TOP   then

       hina-lla-pis   ari   mundongu-ta-qa   hichka-ku-yka:-__na:__
       same-DLM-EVEN   yes   tripe-OBJ-TOP   scrape-MID-CONT-__PST.N__

       mantsa-ka-sha-lla-pis
       fear-PASS-PTCP-DLM-EVEN

       'Niko also __went__ (*-ra*) to search near Wanac. Meanwhile, our mother __was continuing to scrape__ (*-na:*) tripe just as if the situation were normal, even though she was afraid.'

In (153) the time of the situation marked by *-na:* is *prior to* the past reference time (marked by past perfective *-sha*), similar to the English pluperfect or "past within the past." Unlike a typical pluperfect, *-na:* appears on consecutive sentences in (189) below in §6.4.

(153) *Tayanqocha-la:-pa   ari,   qeshpi-pa:-ma-__sha__-qa   Huamparan-pita*
       Tayancocha-SIDE-GEN   yes   escape-BEN-1OBJ-__PST.R3__-TOP   Huamparán-ABL

       Kachitsinan-la:-pa.   tsay-la:-chu:-na-sh   punta-ta-si   tari-ya:-__na:__.
       Kachitsinan-SIDE-GEN   that-SIDE-LOC-NOW-RPT   first-OBJ-EVEN   find-PL.V-__PST.N__

       'It __escaped__ (*-sha*) from me near Huamparán heading toward Tayancocha and Kachitsinan. Reportedly, in the latter area they __had found__ (*-na:*) them on previous occasions.'

As we have just seen, the situation marked by *-na:* can be *prior to* the past reference time, as in (153) and (189), or *concurrent with* it, as in (152) and (192). In the following more extended conversational excerpt in (154), the situation time is *subsequent to* the past reference time, continuing the narrative sequence. In other words, *-na:* can occasionally be used to advance the main storyline.

Each verb in (154) that advances the storyline is indicated by an arrow to the left of the translation line. Initially, the narrative moves forward with a sequence of verbs marked with past perfective *-sh*. It continues with two verbs marked with narrative past *-na:*. The motivation for the shift from *-sh* to *-na:* in this narrative sequence is based on factors other than placement in time. Evidential and modal functions of *-na:* are discussed below in §6.4.[97]

---

[97] For a thorough treatment of discourse motivations underlying the elaborate tense shifts among all of the past time reference markers in SCQ, see Diane Hintz (2007b).

(154) R: *tsay-na   aywa-**sh**   tsay-man,   ... tsa   papa:-nin-ta   willa-pti-n-qa,*
　　　　that-NOW   go-**PST.R3**   that-ALL   then   father-3-OBJ   inform-DS-3-TOP

→　　'After he told his dad, he (his dad) **went** (*-sh*) over there.

　　　　*tsay ..a   Ernesto Garay-qa   aywa-**sh**   don Benito-man-qa   ari ni-q-nin,*
　　　　that   um Ernesto Garay-TOP   go-**PST.R3**   sir   Benito-ALL-TOP   yes say-PRMT-3

→　　So Ernesto Garay **went** (*-sh*) to Benito's to say to him,

　　　　　　*"wamra-yki   suwa-pa-**sh**   wamra-:-pa ro:pa-n-kuna-ta.*
　　　　　　child-2   steal-BEN-**PST.R3**   child-1-GEN   clothes-3-PL.N-OBJ

　　　　　　"Your son <u>stole</u> (*-sh*) my son's clothes.

　　　　　　... tsay-rikoq-ta   wamra-ta   ashma-Ø-nki",
　　　　　　　that-CLASS-OBJ   child-OBJ   raise-PRS-2

　　　　　　Is this the way you <u>raise</u> (*-Ø*) your son?"

　　　　*ni-pti-n-qa   qeru-wan   ka:si   wiru-ska-mu-**na:**   na-qa.*
　　　　say-DS-3-TOP   wood-COM   almost   hit-PFV-FAR-**PST.N**   thing-TOP

→　　When he (Ernesto) said this, so-and-so (Benito) almost **hit** (*-na:*) him with a stick.

　　　　　　"noqa   tsay-no:-ta-ku   ashma-Ø-:   wamra-:-ta   ima-m,
　　　　　　I   that-SIM-OBJ-Q.P   raise-PRS-1   child-1-OBJ   what-DIR

　　　　　　"As if I <u>raise</u> (*-Ø*) my son like this,

　　　　　　o   noqa-ku   manda-<u>ra</u>-:",   ... ni-r,
　　　　　　or   I-Q.P   send-PST-1   say-SS

　　　　　　or I <u>sent</u> (*-ra*) him (to do it)," saying.

　　　　tsay-na   doña   Ado:ra-qa   ari,   um   "kay-cho:-cha: ka-yka-Ø-n.
　　　　that-NOW   mrs.   Adora-TOP   yes   um   this-LOC-MUT   be-CONT-PRS-3

　　　　Then Mrs. Adora, "Here it <u>is</u> (*-Ø*).

　　　　ama-ri   pi-ta-pis   willa-ku-yku-ya-<u>y</u>-tsu."   ni-r-nin,
　　　　no-SURE   who-OBJ-EVEN   inform-MID-PFV.C-PL.V-**IMP2**-NEG   say-SS-3

　　　　Don't you dare <u>tell</u> (*-y*) anybody," saying,

　　　　*... hipi-mu-**na:**   chachak   qepi-sha-ta   tsay-chu   Walter-pa*
　　　　take.out-FAR-**PST.N**   very.tight   wrap.up-PTCP-OBJ   that-LOC   Walter-GEN

　　　　sapatu-n-ta-pis.
　　　　shoe-3-OBJ-EVEN

→　　she **took out** (*-na:*) a tightly tied bundle with Walter's shoes inside too.'

Finally, sequences of *-na:* can also be used for past situations, even when an additional past reference point is implied but not specified. The reference time may be remote, as when establishing the setting of a story, but the remote sense is not necessarily temporal, as in the retelling of a dream. The following example is from a legendary tale embedded in a conversation. The speaker begins with *-na:* to indicate a past orientation for this situation which is outside of normal experience. Subsequently, she switches from *-na:* to the historical present and to the past perfective *-sha* to advance the action of the story.[98]

(155) *kay-no: pobri-sh   ka-ya:-**na:***   *ari.*   *mama-n-kuna   wamra-n-kuna*
        this-SIM   poor-RPT   be-PL.V-**PST.N**   yes   mother-3-PL.N   child-3-PL.N

        *atska   ka-**na:**.   tsay   ashi-ku-q*   *aywa-ya:-**na:***   *mama-n-kuna-qa.*
        many   be-**PST.N**   that   search-MID-PRMT   go-PL.V-**PST.N**   mother-3-PL.N-TOP

        'They **were** extremely poor. There **were** many parents and their children. Those parents **would go** to search (for food).'

Summarizing, the multifaceted narrative past marker *-na:* appears in paradigmatic contrast with other inflectional TAM markers in the obligatory verbal slot I2. It typically reports a situation in progress in the past or characteristic of a time period restricted to the past. Specifically, it presents a situation as located concurrent with, prior to, or subsequent to a reference point that is itself located in the past. That past reference point (supplied by the context) often corresponds to a main storyline event.

Narrative past *-na:* can also serve discourse functions in which an additional past reference point is not specified, e.g., establishing the setting of a story or retelling a dream. In addition to aspect and tense, *-na:* also has modal and evidential functions, as discussed in §6.4.

5.3 Past habitual *-q*

The inflectional marker *-q* (or *-q=ka* with speech-act participants) was introduced above in §3.2.1 as a past habitual, that is, a grammatical morpheme that presents a situation as customarily repeated in the past or as characteristic of a time period restricted to the past.

A closer inspection of the past tense component of *-q* reveals that it is located wholly within the past without including the absolute reference time, i.e., the present moment. As illustrated in Figure 5.3, the meaning of *-q* entails an additional reference point (supplied by the context) intervening between the habitual situation marked by *-q* and the present moment. After that past reference point, the situation no longer holds.[99]

---

[98] For a complete transcription of this portion of the Achikay legend in SCQ, see Diane Hintz (2007b:325ff.).

[99] Comrie (1976:28ff.) examines past habitual forms in English and Russian and the (putative) implication that the past situation no longer holds. He argues convincingly that this meaning is not in fact implied in the strict sense, because "the putative implication can be canceled by an

Figure 5.3 *Time reference of past habitual -q/-q=ka*

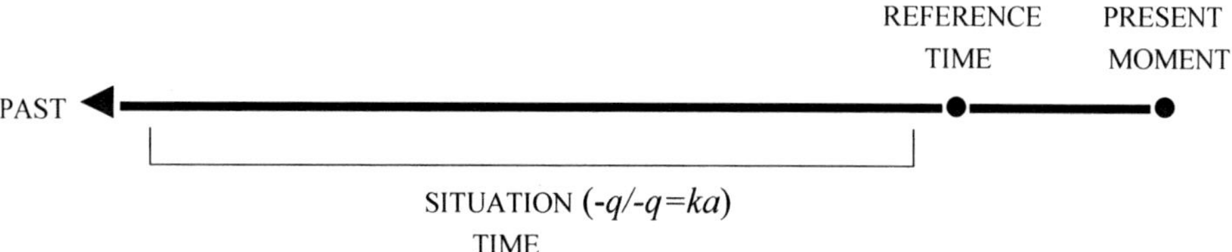

The time reference of past habitual *-q/-q=ka*, as represented in Figure 5.3, is illustrated by the examples presented above in §3.2.1. Two additional examples are presented here. Past habitual *-q* in (156) reports a period of time in which Father Juan regularly came from San Marcos to Chavín to celebrate Mass. It further indicates that, at the moment of speech, he was no longer coming to Chavín. This additional implication cannot be canceled by its explicit denial, e.g., it would be a contradiction to add **tsayno:lla kananyaq shamun* 'and he still does that'. In order to avoid the exclusion of the present moment, one would enlist other grammatical resources, e.g., the derivational continuous marker *-yka:* combined with an inflectional past perfective. (As noted in §3.1.2, *-yka:* can imply a habitual situation in past contexts.)

(156) *padri Juan-na shamu-**q**   San Marcus-pita   mi:sa selebra-q   pay-lla*
      father Juan-NOW come-**PST.H** San Marcos-ABL   mass celebrate-PRMT he-DLM
      'Only Father Juan **used to come** here from San Marcos to celebrate Mass.'

In (157) *lamun kuru* (a giant worm) made the villagers tie up a child each day for it to eat. Past habitual *-q* indicates that this practice continued for a period of time, but stopped at some point in the past. The exact reference point is specified later in the story when the hero cuts off the head of the giant worm.

(157) *kay-no: to:ka-**q**   kada tardi-pa-shi   wawa-n-kuna-ta*
      this-SIM   have.turn-**PST.H** each afternoon-GEN-RPT child-3-PL.N-OBJ
      wata-pu-ya:-na-n-pa: *lamun kuru*
      tie.up-BEN-PL.V-NMLZ.I-3-PURP   lamun kuru
      'Lamun kuru (a giant worm) **took turns** like this to tie up one of their children every afternoon.'

Bybee (1994:251) observes that the overt expression of past habitual meaning is common cross-linguistically. Since perfective is the default aspectual interpretation for dynamic verbs in past tense, she argues, a "special linguistic signal" is required for habitual or ongoing situations

---

explicit denial of it." In contrast to English and Russian, the inflectional past habitual suffix *-q* in SCQ does imply in the strict sense that the past situation no longer holds.

in the past. This signal, or a reduction of it, may eventually grammaticize as an overt past habitual marker.

This scenario aptly characterizes the development of past habitual *-q/-q=ka* in SCQ. At an earlier stage, habitual meaning could be expressed in some contexts by a periphrastic construction in which the nominalizer **-q* was followed by the copular auxiliary **ka-*. In order to further specify this habitual for past situations, the copula was inflected with a past suffix, as currently attested in Huanca Quechua (Cerrón-Palomino 1976:176), Imbabura Quechua (Cole 1982:149), and Lambayeque Quechua (Shaver 1987:31).[100] The past suffix no longer occurs in SCQ, but the past meaning was absorbed by the remaining phonological material, i.e., the former nominalizer *-q* (for further details, see Chapter 11).[101]

In SCQ, habitual meaning is inflectionally marked not only in the past (*-q*), but also in the present (*-Ø*). Present habitual *-Ø* is treated in the next section.

5.4   Present habitual *-Ø*

In previous sections of this chapter we examined the conceptual interface between aspect and past tense, focusing on inflectional markers which report a perfective or imperfective view of a situation prior to the present moment. We now turn to imperfective aspect and present tense. While a subset of imperfective functions are expressed by present tense, perfective functions are not so expressed in general because a situation concurrent with the present moment would not be viewed as bounded (unless the beginning and endpoints are identical, as in the performative use of present).

The SCQ imperfective markers discussed above (past habitual *-q* and narrative past *-na:*) are restricted to past tense. The sole imperfective marker that includes present tense in its semantics is present habitual *-Ø*. As introduced in §3.2.2, this zero marker presents a situation as customarily repeated or as characteristic of a time period that includes the present moment. In keeping with its inflectional status, present habitual *-Ø* appears in paradigmatic contrast with other inflectional TAM markers, as sketched in (158) for the verb *tushu-* 'dance' (*-n* marks third person).

---

[100] A past suffix is optional in this past habitual construction in Cuzco (Cusihuamán 1976a:172), Ayacucho (Soto 1976a:100), and Cajamarca (Quesada 1976:117).

[101] In fact, **-q* has split into distinct productive morphemes in SCQ, realized synchronically as the nominalizing suffix *-q* and the innovative past habitual *-q*. The participation of **-q* in additional syntactic configurations has given rise to further (usage-based) bifurcations, e.g., the purpose suffix *-q* in the "purpose-motion" construction (see the auxiliaries *ri-* and *aywa-* in §11.3).

(158) *tushu - **Ø** - n*   PRESENT HABITUAL   'she dances'

       *tushu - **q***   PAST HABITUAL   'she used to dance'

       *tushu - **na:***   NARRATIVE PAST   'she was dancing (in general)'

       *tushu - **ra** - n*   PAST PERFECTIVE   'she danced'

       *tushu - **nqa***   FUTURE   'she will dance'

       *tushu - **tsun***   IMPERATIVE   'may she dance!'

Present habitual *-Ø* is not a general imperfective because it does not mark continuous aspect (nor the more specific progressive meaning). Instead, continuous meaning is expressed by *-yka:*, a derivational suffix not specified for tense (§3.1.2). The following illustrates the combination of *-yka:* with present habitual *-Ø* and with past perfective *-ra*.[102]

(159) a. *tushu -   - **Ø** - n*   PRESENT HABITUAL *-Ø*   'she dances (customarily)'

      b. *tushu - **yka** - **Ø** - n*   PRESENT HABITUAL *-Ø*   'she is dancing'
                                      with CONTINUOUS *-yka:*

      c. *tushu -   - **ra** - n*   PAST PERFECTIVE *-ra*   'she danced'

      d. *tushu - **yka** - **ra** - n*   PAST PEFECTIVE *-ra*   'she was dancing'
                                      with CONTINUOUS *-yka:*

In the vast majority of *-Ø* exemplars, as noted above, the habit or characterization holds at the present moment, but not the action itself. Instances in which the action does hold at the present moment (illustrated in §3.2.2) include performatives (e.g., (135) and (136)) and a small set of inherently imperfective cognition verbs (e.g., *yarpa:-* 'remember'). In addition, the action of a dynamic verb may be further specified as holding at the present moment by adding (derivational) continuous *-yka:* to the (inflectional) present habitual *-Ø*, as in (159)b (*tushu-yka-Ø-n* 'she is dancing').[103]

Dialect variation in the meaning of the combination of these two imperfective markers—one specified for present tense (*-Ø*), the other unspecified for tense (*-yka:*)—can illuminate the interaction between present tense and imperfective aspect. SCQ and Huamalíes, for instance, are geographic neighbors in the Central Quechua dialect continuum. A comparison of natural

---

[102] The combination of continuous *-yka:* with a past marker often implies past habitual meaning, especially in contexts with a well-defined, yet limited time span (see §3.1.2). For example, the verb *tushu-yka-ra-n* in (159)d appears in a conversation about a week-long fiesta. It means 'she was dancing/performing on multiple occasions during this time span)'.

[103] In certain contexts, the reference time shifts from the moment of speech to a past moment ("historical present" use of *-Ø*). The reference time can also shift to an immediate future moment for specifically planned situations. This latter "imminent future" use *-Ø* combines tense and epistemic modality, that is, high certainty that the event will be realized. In these two uses of *-Ø*, the action holds at the non-present reference time (see examples (138)-(140) above in §3.2.2).

conversations in these two dialects reveals that the cognate suffix *-yka:* is used nearly twice as often in Huamalíes. Likewise, when adapting written texts from Huamalíes, SCQ speakers remove nearly 50% of the *-yka:* suffixes, because this form (which has progressive-continuous meaning in SCQ) is taking on additional imperfective functions in Huamalíes, especially in the context of stative verbs in present tense.

The following two examples of *-yka:* are from Huamalíes. In (160) Howard-Malverde (1990:35) translates the Huamalíes verb *ta-yka:-mu-Ø-n* as '(it) still stands'. In this context SCQ speakers render the verb as *ta:-mu-Ø-n* (without *-yka:*).

(160) Huamalíes Quechua
　　　kay-nu:　　*kallash-chu:-mi*　*ta-__yka:__-mu-Ø-n*　　　　*pullan-chu:*　*kundur*
　　　this-SIM　　gully-LOC-DIR　　sit.stand-__IPFV__-FAR-PRS-3　middle-LOC　　condor
　　　'And over there in the middle of the gully the condor (rock formation) __still stands__.'

Similarly, the use of *-yka:* in the Huamalíes verb *ka-yka-:* 'I am' is anomalous in SCQ, as the appropriate form in this context is simply *ka-:*. Although the form *ka-yka-:* is grammatically acceptable in SCQ, its use here would indicate the pragmatically marked sense 'I continue to be Raul's son'.

(161) Huamalíes Quechua
　　　noqa-qa　*ka-__yka__-Ø-:*　　*Raul-pa*　*suri-n-mi*
　　　I-TOP　　　be-__IPFV__-PRS-1　Raul-GEN　son-3-DIR
　　　'I __am__ Raul's son.'

In general, when adapting Huamalíes texts, SCQ speakers remove *-yka:* when the verb presents a permanent or characteristic state (as opposed to a transient condition) or when the context calls for present habitual *-Ø* without further specification. Only in contexts where the expected meaning is continuous (or progressive) do SCQ speakers consider *-yka:* an appropriate marker.

As the previous examples show, the suffix *-yka:* in Huamalíes is no longer restricted to progressive-continuous aspect, but is becoming a more general imperfective by taking on durative and present meanings as well.[104] In addition, *-yka:* is approaching inflectional status in

---

[104] Languages in which a progressive has become an imperfective by acquiring habitual meaning include Yoruba (Niger-Congo) and Scots Gaelic (Celtic) (Comrie 1976:101), Turkish (Underhill 1976:145ff.), Punjabi and Hindi-Urdu (Indo-Iranian), and Armenian (Dahl 1985:93), as cited by Bybee et al. (1994:141). In Central Pomo, a derivational durative suffix has evolved into a general imperfective (Mithun 2000:273).

Huamalíes as it acquires imperfective functions formerly expressed by present habitual -Ø, which is now relegated to a reduced grammatical role.[105]

These grammatical developments in Huamalíes represent the latest step in the ongoing evolution of *-yka:* and *-Ø* in particular, and the tense-aspect system in general. In the larger historical picture, the zero marker presumably arose as a present imperfective in paradigmatic contrast with past perfective (*-rqa*), as the latter attained inflectional status in the now obligatory TAM slot I2 (see §10.1 and §11.6). As in many languages (Bybee et al. 1994:151), the subsequent innovation of a progressive marker (*-yka:* in Central Quechuan varieties) would have reduced the semantic territory of present imperfective *-Ø* to present habitual, the current meaning of *-Ø* in SCQ.[106]

While present habitual is expressed by zero (*-Ø*), recall that past habitual receives overt expression (*-q*) (§3.2.1 and §5.3). These two modes of expression in SCQ correspond to the cross-linguistic sample in Bybee et al. (1994:153-5) in which two languages have a present habitual, each marked by grammatical zero, and ten other languages have a past habitual, each formally (overtly) marked. Given perfective function as the default interpretation of past tense dynamic verbs (e.g., Dahl 1985:116ff.), Bybee et al. maintain that habitual situations in the past require a "special linguistic signal" which may eventually grammaticize as an overt past habitual marker. Conversely, habitual appears to be the default function of present tense, and thus no overt linguistic signal grammaticizes. (The grammatical development of present habitual *-Ø*, past habitual *-q*, and continuous *-yka:* are treated in detail in Chapter 10 "The evolution of imperfectives.")

5.5 Conclusions: Aspect and tense

Previous chapters described the remarkably complex aspectual system in SCQ. Here, we have examined the grammatical interface between aspect and tense, where tense reports the temporal location of a situation (past, present, future). In accord with the inherent associations linking these time-related domains, aspect and tense are not expressed as separate categories in SCQ, but are interwoven in the grammatical system by inflectional forms that integrate features of aspect and tense in their semantics.

---

[105] In present contexts, that is, in combination with grammatical zero, *-yka:* often appears adjacent to *-Ø* with no marker intervening, e.g., the verb *ka-yka-Ø-:* in (161). Since *-Ø* has no phonological material of its own, this combination is an ideal environment for the reanalysis of derivational *-yka:* as occupying the inflectional TAM slot I2, in terms of verb structure as well as the semantics of the present tense/imperfective category.

[106] As discussed in §10.2, there is semantic and structural evidence that "progressive" suffixes in some other Quechuan varieties have advanced even farther along the path of development from progressive to general imperfective. These forms include *-y(k)a:* in Huanca, *-chka* in Ayacucho, and *-hu/-u* in Ecuadorian Pastaza. For more on *-hu/-u*, see §8.6.

The inflectional perfective markers *-ru*, *-sha*, and *-ra* are restricted to past tense. Past situations marked by *-ru* (first or second person) or *-sha* (third person) are typically more recent than those marked by *-ra*. The suffix *-ra* is an older past perfective with cognate forms attested throughout the language family. *-ru* and *-sha* developed past perfective meaning more recently, each from a different source. *-ru* (from *-*rqu* 'outward') was a derivational perfective and *-sha* (from *-*shqa* 'past participle') was used in a periphrastically expressed perfect construction. The past perfective meaning of each form arose through strengthening the inference of recent completion.

The inflectional imperfective markers *-na:* and *-q* are also restricted to past tense. Narrative past *-na:* presents a situation as prior to, subsequent to, or simultaneous with a reference point that is itself located in the past. The context supplies the past reference point as well as the location of situation time relative to that point. Like *-na:*, past habitual *-q* invokes a reference point supplied by the context. That reference point intervenes between the habitual situation marked by *-q* and the present moment. The situation no longer holds after the past reference point. Both narrative past *-na:* and past habitual *-q* were formerly expressed by periphrastic constructions in which a suffix was followed by the copular auxiliary *ka-* (i.e., *-*ña-q ka-* and *-*q ka-*, respectively).

Just as *-q* expresses past habitual meaning, the primary grammatical meaning of *-Ø* is present habitual. Typically, the habit or characterization holds at the present moment, but not the action itself. To further specify that the action holds at the present moment, the derivational progressive-continuous suffix *-yka:* may be combined with *-Ø*. In contrast, the combination of *-yka:* with a past marker may be interpreted as a past habitual.

The close connections between aspect and tense reveal intricate patterns of organization within the emerging grammatical system. The network of semantic relations linking aspectual and tense functions in SCQ is presented as a "tense-aspect interface map" in Figure 5.4. We have identified two types of inflectional imperfectives in SCQ: One restricted to present tense (present habitual *-Ø*), and the other restricted to past tense (narrative past *-na:* and past habitual *-q*). The fact that there are both present and past imperfectives (and no present perfectives) shows that present tense is a subset of imperfective aspect, as represented in the right-hand box in Figure 5.4.

Figure 5.4 *The interface between tense and aspect in SCQ*

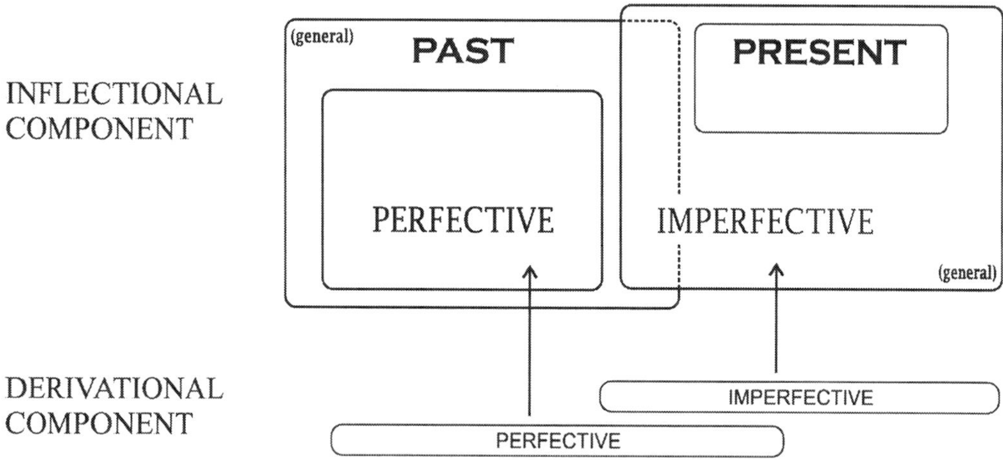

The inflectional perfectives, on the other hand, are restricted to past tense (past perfectives *-ru*, *-sha*, and *-ra*). The fact that there are both past perfectives and past imperfectives (and no present perfectives) shows that inflectional perfective is a subset of past tense. This is represented in the left-hand box in Figure 5.4.[107]

In addition to the six inflectional tense-aspect markers discussed in this chapter, derivational perfectives and imperfectives remain outside the semantic domain of tense, as represented by the narrow boxes below the tense-aspect boxes in Figure 5.4. Some of these aspectual meanings (expressed derivationally) develop tense meanings (expressed inflectionally) with the inference of past or present time reference becoming reanalyzed as a central meaning over time. For example, *-ru* is a derivational perfective marker in Ambo-Pasco Quechua, but has become an inflectional past perfective in SCQ (see §9.3). Likewise, *-yka:* is a derivational continuous marker in SCQ, but is on a path leading to inflectional present tense/imperfective in neighboring Huamalíes Quechua (see §5.4).

In the remaining chapters of Part III we will consider the close interaction between aspect and semantic domains that have received less attention in the scholarly literature, beginning with aspect and modality.

---

[107] In Figure 5.4, the area in the PAST box labeled "(general)" represents general past, which can signal past times for situations viewed perfectively or imperfectively. The area in the IMPERFECTIVE box labeled "(general)" represents general imperfective, which is not temporally restricted.

6 ASPECT AND MODALITY

In the previous chapter we observed how the SCQ aspect system is connected with tense. The aim of the present chapter is to examine the grammatical interface linking aspect and modality, a topic that Sasse characterizes as "hopelessly under-investigated" (2002:266). While aspect reports temporal structure, and tense reports temporal location, modality specifies how speakers or participants relate to the situation itself and to each other in terms of obligation (deontic modality) and knowledge and belief (epistemic modality) (see, e.g., Palmer 2001).

The set of twenty highly specialized perfective and imperfective markers in SCQ provides a fertile environment for even more abstract semantic extensions into the domains of tense and modality. Just as tense is a later grammaticization of aspectual categories, modality appears to emerge as an "inferential byproduct" of aspectual nuances. The resulting modal senses span a wide spectrum of fine-grained distinctions. For example, SCQ aspect markers further distinguish whether an outcome is expected or unexpected, whether the stances of interlocutors converge or diverge, and whether a situation is deemed outside the experience of discourse participants.

This chapter begins with a brief overview of recurrent modal themes expressed through derivational morphology across the Quechua language family. I then focus specifically on aspect markers in SCQ, illustrating expected outcomes marked by the perfective suffixes *-rku* and *-yku*, unexpected outcomes marked by perfective *-ski* and punctual *-ri*, and situations presented as outside the experience of discourse participants by narrative past *-na:*. I conclude by assessing the role of aspect within the domain of modality.

6.1 Aspect and modality in Quechuan languages

Grammarians in the Quechuanist tradition have utilized a rich set of subjective and modal adverbs to characterize markers which are cognate with many of the SCQ aspect markers presented above in Part II. As seen in the list of glosses in column 2 of Table 6.1, these markers exhibit much semantic variation and idiosyncrasy across the language family.[108] The locations of the Quechuan varieties in column 3 are shown in Map 6.1.

---

[108] In addition to the modal terms listed in Table 6.1, these suffixes are also described in the Quechuanist literature using adverbs I would identify as "aspect-like" (e.g., 'completely',

Table 6.1 *Aspectual suffixes described with modal adverbs in the Quechuanist literature*

PROTO SUFFIX	MODAL THEME/GLOSS	QUECHUAN VARIETY	SOURCE
-rpu	'intentional'	Cuzco	Cusihuamán 1976a:201
-rku	'unresisted, special importance'	Huaylas	Parker 1976:126
	'unexpected, definite'	Huaraz	Swisshelm 1974:494
	'means to end'	Llamellín	Snow 1972:17ff
	'unexpected, polite'	Huallaga	Weber 1989:123
	'social act, polite'	Tarma	Adelaar 1977:145
	'social interest'	Pacaraos	Adelaar 1986:38
	'actor indifferent'	Huanca	Cerrón-Palomino 1976:199
-yku	'severity, unexpected, urgency, contrast two extremes'	Huaraz	Swisshelm 1974:499ff
	'special attention, polite'	Huaylas	Parker 1976:129
	'special attention'	Llamellín	Snow and Stark 1971:199
	'personal affect'	Cuzco	Cusihuamán 1976a:206
	'non-resistance, polite'	Huanca	Cerrón-Palomino 1976:201
	'polite, unexpected'	Ayacucho	Soto 1976a:106
	'special reaction, forceful'	Huallaga	Weber 1989:128
	'special attention, polite'	Tarma	Adelaar 1977:145
	'goal-directed, careful'	Pacaraos	Adelaar 1986:38
-ski	'resisted, less sociability, urgency, unexpected, often not translated'	Conchucos	Parker 1976:127
	'unexpected, urgency'	Conchucos	Stewart 1984:90 ,91
	'unexpected, unusual, affective affective'	Llamellín	Snow and Stark 1971:187; Snow 1972:17
	'goal-oriented'	Huánuco	Solá 1958
-ri	'diminutive, little importance'	Huaylas	Parker 1976:125
	'polite'	Llamellín	Snow and Stark 1971:208
	'small action'	Huanca	Cerrón-Palomino 1976:198
	'diminutive, casual'	Tarma	Adelaar 1977:143
	'exhort to action'	Cuzco	Cusihuamán 1976a:210
	'little importance, polite, routine'	Ayacucho	Soto 1976a:105
-rqu	'unexpected, polite'	Cuzco	Cusihuamán 1976a:207
	'unexpected'	Huallaga	Weber 1989:127
	'courtesy, urgency, social act'	Huanca	Cerrón-Palomino 1976:202,205

'briefly', 'initially'), "manner-like" (e.g., 'suddenly', 'dynamically', 'forcefully', 'rapidly', 'intensely'), and "tense-like" (e.g., 'recently', 'immediately'). For more on adverbial qualities of the aspect suffixes, see Chapter 7 "Aspect and manner."

Map 6.1 QUECHUAN VARIETIES ILLUSTRATED IN TABLES 6.1, 6.2 AND 7.1 (DIRECTIONALS) *

---

* "Huaraz" and "Llamellín" are towns within the Huaylas Quechua and SCQ areas, respectively. "Conchucos" includes the North Conchucos and SCQ areas. "Huánuco" primarily corresponds to Huallaga Quechua, but includes other varieties in the department of Huánuco.

When viewed together, the glosses presented in Table 6.1 reflect modal themes across the language family, including such notions as intentionality, (un)expectedness, degree of urgency, and a variety of interpersonal effects. These modal themes are summarized below in Table 6.2.

Table 6.2 *Recurrent modal themes expressed by aspectual suffixes in Quechua*

MODAL THEME/GLOSS	PROTO SUFFIX	QUECHUAN VARIETY
'INTENTIONALITY, GOAL-ORIENTED'	*-rpu*	Cuzco
	-rku	Llamellín
	-yku	Pacaraos
	-ski	Huánuco
'(UN)EXPECTEDNESS'	*-rku*	Huaylas, Huallaga
	-yku	Huaraz, Ayacucho
	-ski	Conchucos, Llamellín
	-rqu	Huallaga, Cuzco
'URGENCY'	*-yku*	Huaraz
	-ski	Conchucos
	-rqu	Huanca
'POLITENESS, AFFECT'	*-rku*	Huallaga, Tarma
	-yku	Huaylas, Tarma, Huanca, Ayacucho, Cuzco
	-ski	Llamellín
	-ri	Ayacucho
	-rqu	Cuzco, Huanca
'SOCIAL ACT/REACTION'	*-rku*	Tarma, Pacaraos
	-yku	Huallaga, Huaylas
	-rqu	Huanca

Interestingly, all five of the modal themes listed in Table 6.2 are attributed to some modern reflex of *-yku* 'inward'. For example, cognate forms of *-yku* are glossed as 'goal-directed' in Pacaraos, 'unexpected' in Huaraz and Ayacucho, 'urgent' in Huaraz, 'polite' in Huaylas, Tarma, Huanca, Ayacucho, and Cuzco, and 'social act' in Huallaga and Huaylas. Likewise, cognate forms of *-rqu* 'outward' are glossed as 'unexpected' in Huallaga and Cuzco, and 'urgent', 'polite', and 'social act' in Huanca. The modal themes attributed to *-rku* 'outward' and *-ski* 'toward' are similarly distributed across Quechuan varieties.

The cross-dialectal picture that emerges from these data is far from clear. We can conclude, however, that a limited inventory of aspectual forms and structures gives rise to a class of similar modal meanings. To better understand the underlying polysemy between aspect and modality, what is needed is a detailed discourse-based investigation of these markers within a particular Quechuan variety, paying particular attention to aspectual and modal nuances. In what follows, I present such an analysis for SCQ.

6.2 Expected outcome: Perfectives *-rku* and *-yku*

The derivational perfective suffixes *-rku* and *-yku* were introduced in Chapter 2. In terms of subjectivity, these markers also involve intentionality (volition) expressed as a planned or expected outcome. This notion of expected outcome appears to be a natural extension of the "attainment of a limit" meaning that Dahl (1985:76) associates with derivationally expressed perfectives.

The primary contrast expressed by these two suffixes involves courses of action that are either complementary (*-rku*) or competing (*-yku*). For example, in (162) the speaker facilitates a divining procedure by bringing coca leaves to her cousin. *-rku* indicates that the consecutive actions (bring coca leaves, then perform the divining procedure) are complementary and carried out according to a mutual plan.

(162) *noqa-pis   mana-na   may-cho:-pis   tari-r-na   mantsa-ka-r-na*
I-even   no-NOW   where-LOC-EVEN   find-SS-NOW   fear-PASS-SS-NOW

prima-ntsi: Dumicha-kaq-pa   aywa-ra-:
cousin-1₁   Domitila-DEF-GEN   go-PST-1

*kuka-ta   apa-**rku**-r   chaqcha-tsi-ku-q*
coca-OBJ   take-**PFV.M**-SS   chew.coca-CAUS-MID-PRMT

'Also, when I didn't find it anywhere, being afraid, I went to our cousin Domitila **taking** coca leaves for her to divine (by chewing).'

In contrast, *-yku* indicates that a competing or rival course of action prevails, usually through the modality of general obligation. The obligation need not be a deontic modality expressed through a directive, such as an imperative or permissive. Instead, the speaker most often simply reports a course of action s/he interprets as imposed on the discourse participants in a given situation. For example, the suffix *-yku* in (163) conveys that the speaker would prefer to stay home after arriving there, but is under legal obligation to appear (before a judge) in Huari.[109]

(163) *byernis-pa-m   notifika-ya:-ma-ra-n.   tsay-no:-pa-m.   i   kanan*
friday-GEN-DIR   summon-PL.V-1OBJ-PST-3   that-SIM-GEN-DIR   and   now

*cha-**yku**-r-qa   tse:-pa-ra:-chi   aywa-sha: wara-ntin-qa*
arrive-**PFV.O**-SS-TOP   that-GEN-YET-CNJ   go-FUT1   tomorrow-WITH-TOP

Huari-pa-ra:.
Huari-GEN-YET

'They summoned me for Friday. Like that. And now after I **arrive** home, I'll have to go to Huari the day after tomorrow.'

---

[109] Perfective aspect has been linked to epistemic modality, and imperfective aspect to deontic modality (e.g., Fleischman 1995). Interestingly, perfective *-yku* in SCQ expresses deontic modality (obligation), and also epistemic modality (expected outcome).

In terms of intersubjectivity, interlocutors use the contrast between *-rku* and *-yku* to display careful convergent or divergent linguistic alignment with respect to each others' stances.[110] With *-rku* the speaker expresses an evaluation that the positions of both parties are held in common, a convergence of alignment between stances. For example, in (164) the speaker uses *-rku* to communicate that her family's guest willingly stayed with them over the course of two days by mutual consent.[111]

(164) *pay-wan-pis   ta:ra:-ya-ru-:   ishke: diya punu-__rku__-r-yan*
     he-COM-EVEN   reside-PL.V-PST.R-1   two   day   sleep-__PFV.M__-SS-DISTR.T
     'We provided lodging for him, all of us __sleeping__ here each night for two (consecutive) days.'

In contrast, *-yku* indicates that the positions are in conflict, a divergent alignment between stances. In (165) the speaker reports with *-yku* (lowered allomorph *-yka*) that Maria obliged her children to sleep, even though they would have preferred to stay up each night during the annual fiesta. In (166) the visitor had other plans, but was obligated to stay. Here, the sense of obligation expressed by *-yku* is reinforced with the adverb *ama:las* 'obligated', a loan from the Spanish phrase *a la mala* 'by force'.

(165) *Maria-pis   shinqiru-ta-m   ishke: tsakay rantiku-sh*
     Maria-EVEN   hot.drink-OBJ-DIR   two   night   sell-PST.R3
     wamra-n-kuna-ta punu-__yka__-tsi-r-yan
     child-3-PL.N-OBJ   sleep-__PFV.O__-CAUS-SS-DISTR.T
     'Maria also sold hot drinks for two nights, after __putting__ her children __to sleep__ each night.'

(166) *"keda-ku-shun   keda-ku-shun"   nir   ama:las   keda-__yku__-ya-:*
     remain- MID-IMP1₁   remain-MID-IMP1₁   say-SS obligated remain-__PFV.O__-PL.V-1
     'Saying "Let's stay together, let's stay together," we __obligated__ him __to stay__.'

As perfectives, the suffixes *-rku* and *-yku* express the attainment of a limit and consummation of an action. The combination of this aspectual meaning with the notion of expected outcome results (via inference) in a further modal extension to "fulfilled intention." In this way, these two

---

[110] For excellent treatments of stance taking, see Haddington (2005) and Du Bois (2007).

[111] The grammatical encoding of "mutual consent" by *-rku* in the aspect-modality interface is echoed in the evidential system of SCQ, where the enclitic *=cha:* expresses "mutual knowledge" (Hintz 2006b). Ethnographic studies have long recognized mutuality and consensus as fundamental values within traditional Quechua communities, as recently mentioned, e.g., by Howard (2002) and Zoomers (2006:1033). The grammatical categories presented here provide linguistic support for these ethnographic observations.

suffixes distinguish not only convergent versus divergent stance alignment, but also which party's intentions are fulfilled. The fulfilled intention may pertain to both parties (as marked by *-rku*), or it may pertain only to the party who "forces the issue," maintaining their position at the expense of the other party's position (as marked by *-yku*).

The fulfilled intention of all parties marked by *-rku* is illustrated in (167). Here the girl is willing to go with Lorenzo to the village of Chingas, and *-rku* further specifies that their mutual intention is fulfilled. Similarly, in (168) *-rku* conveys that Niko fulfilled the intention of waking up especially early to search for a lost donkey, according to a mutually agreed upon plan from the night before.

(167) *Wachu-lla-sh   aywa-ku-sha   tsay chi:na-ta   apa-**rku**-r   Chingas-pa*
      Lorenzo-DLM-RPT go-MID-PST.R3   that girl-OBJ   take-**PFV.M**-SS   Chingas-GEN

'They say Lorenzo went to Chingas **taking along** that girl.'

(168) *tsay-pita-qa   tsa: pas maytse:-pa-na   Niki:tu-pis   sharku-**rku**-r,*
      that-ABL-TOP then very wherever-GEN-NOW Niko-EVEN   stand.up-**PFV.M**-SS
      ashi-sh   Wanac-pa
      seek-PST.R3   Wanac-GEN

'Then **getting up immediately**, Niko searched all around Wanac.'

In contrast, *-yku* expresses the fulfilled intention of the party that forces the issue. This naturally entails the unfulfilled or frustrated intention of the other party. For example, in (169) the speaker is praying prior to a long and difficult journey he believes *Tayta Dyos* wants him to make. *-yku* communicates not only that the speaker prefers not to make this journey (frustrated intention), but also that he will do what *Tayta Dyos* wants (fulfilled intention).

(169) *tayta   dyos, qam-mi   musya-**yku**-nki,*
      father   god   you-DIR   know-**PFV.O**-2
      *qam dispo:ni-**yku**-y   ima-no:-pis   ka-na-:-pa:*
      you   arrange-**PFV.O**-IMP2   what-SIM-EVEN   be-NMLZ.I-1-PURP
'Father God, you **know** (what's best). **Arrange** how I should be.'

Sometimes a frustrated intention is not due to an intersubjective obligation as in (169), but due to the demands of an external obligation as above in (163), or simply due to immediate circumstances. In keeping with the notion of frustrated intention, perfective *-yku* is compatible with negation, as in (170), while perfective *-rku* is not.[112]

---

[112] In Tarma Quechua, perfective *-ru* (from **-rqu*) does not occur in the negated verb of a matrix clause (Adelaar 2006:134).

(170) *pase:pa-cha: ashi-r   kay o:ra-yaq   tari-**yku**-ya-:-na-ta:ku*
      very-MUT   search-SS this hour-LIM   find-**PFV.O**-PL.V-1-NOW-NEG.EMPH
      'Although we completely searched until now, we still do not **find** it.'

The semantics of divergent alignment expressed by *-yku* also corresponds with the traditional notion of deontic modality expressed by directives. Directives are speech acts that elicit an action, such as imperative, optative, or prohibitive. In (171) the divergent stance alignment of *-yku* corresponds with the prohibitive directive.

(171) *ama-ri   pi-ta-pis   willa-ku-**yku**-ya-y-tsu*
      do.not-SURE   who-OBJ-EVEN   tell-MID-**PFV.O**-PL.V-IMP2-NEG
      'Don't **tell** anybody.'

Consistent with the notion of mutual consent, *-rku* appears in directives only when they include the speaker, as in (172).

(172) *ma:,   gasyo:sa-ta-ra: upu-**rku**-shun*
      let's.see   soda-OBJ-YET   drink-**PFV.M**-IMP1₁
      'Let's see, **let's drink** a soda.'

Finally, the semantics of convergent versus divergent stance alignment expressed by the perfective suffixes *-rku* versus *-yku* correspond to additional modal nuances and rhetorical effects. First, speakers use *-rku* to imply the related notions of solidarity, teamwork, and the facilitation of a joint course of action. In (173) *-rku* highlights the sharing of resources (potatoes) and in (174) the sharing of labor or teamwork.

(173) *"ka: tullpa-pis   llanta-pis."   a:nir papa-n-kuna-ta   apa-**rku**-r*
      here hearth-EVEN   firewood-EVEN   later potato-3-PL.N-OBJ   take-**PFV.M**-SS
      aywa-ya-sha
      go-PL.V-PST.R3
      '"Here is a hearth and firewood," (she said). Later, they went to her **sharing** their potatoes.'

(174) *ayuda-**rka**-mu-shun   kompañeru-ntsik-ta*
      help-**PFV.M**-FAR-IMP1₁ comrade-1₁-OBJ
      'Let's go **help** our comrade.'

-rku may also imply the relative ease with which an action is realized or facilitated. In (175) *-rku* emphasizes that it will be easy for the children Chino and Josue to follow (guide) the animals to greener pastures, because the animals are more than willing (due to a severe drought).

(175) *Chi:nu-wan   Josue-lla-pis   qati-__rku__-ya-nqa-chir*
Chino-COM   Josue-DLM-EVEN follow-**PFV.M**-PL.V-FUT3-APP

qati-na-lla-n-ta-qa
follow-NMLZ.I-DLM-3-OBJ-TOP

'Also, Chino and Josue **will easily guide** those that need to be guided.'

On the other hand, the divergent stance alignment expressed by *-yku* corresponds to the related notions of negotiation and altruism. Negotiation essentially refers to getting what one wants. For example, prior to (176) the children had asked Sparrow to save them from a steep cliff, but his legs were too weak. Now in (176) their request to Condor is mitigated by the NP 'only as far as the yellowed potato plants'. What the children want to accomplish through this negotiation is that Condor rescue them. What is at stake for Condor is his sterling reputation as a powerful and commanding force for good.[113]

(176) *qarwa-ra-q   papa-lla-man   hipi-__yka__-lla:-ma-y*
be.yellow-DUR-AG   potato-DLM-ALL   remove-**PFV.O**-DLM-1OBJ-IMP2

'**Take us** from here only as far as the yellowed potato plants.'

Altruism means to opt for personal sacrifice in the face of a worthwhile course of action. In (177) the speaker gave a teacher one of the books he was otherwise responsible for selling, purposely choosing a course of action which entails a level of personal sacrifice (loss of monetary compensation) for the greater good of the children in the school.

(177) *"mas-ta-pis   qara-ma-y"   ni-ma-pti-n-pis   qara-__yka__-mu-ra-:-lla.*
more-OBJ-EVEN   give-1OBJ-IMP2   say-1OBJ-DS-3-EVEN   give-**PFV.O**-FAR-PST-1-DLM

'Because she said to me "Give me another (book)," I **gave** it away.'

The major non-aspectual contrasts expressed by the perfective suffixes *-rku* and *-yku* are summarized in Table 6.3 in terms of intentionality, modality, and subjectivity.

---

[113] Such requests have been referred to as "politeness," a vague term that has remained undefined in the Quechuanist literature (see Table 6.2, line 4). I prefer the terms "obligation" and "negotiation" which entail an insistence on one's position, while recognizing the other party's point of view. In this sense, "polite" is more akin to diplomacy, and refers to getting what one wants without resulting in a broken relationship or aroused hostilities (see, e.g., Brown and Levinson 1987).

Table 6.3 *Intentionality, subjectivity, and modality expressed by -rku and -yku*

PERFECTIVE SUFFIX	*-rku*	*-yku*
INTENTIONALITY		
Outcome	expected	expected
Courses of action	complementary	competing
Intention fulfilled	both parties	obligating party
Intention unfulfilled	none	other party
MODALITY		
Deontic	mutual consent	general obligation
Directive	speaker included	imperative, prohibitive
Negation	not compatible	compatible
SUBJECTIVITY		
Points of view	solidarity, harmony	negotiation, conflict
Stance alignment	convergence	divergence

Table 6.4 presents the distribution of *-rku* and *-yku* with other morphosyntactic elements in SCQ discourse. These patterns of co-occurrence correspond to the modal and subjective uses illustrated above and outlined in Table 6.3. For example, *-rku* often appears in the coded data with a first person inclusive subject ('you and I'), while *-yku* never does. This feature is listed in row 1a. Similarly, in row 1b *-yku* appears with first person objects (all imperatives, e.g., 'listen to me'), while *-rku* does not. In row 1c *-rku* appears with plural marking only in third person, presumably because speech-act participants are referred to using inclusive person marking.

Table 6.4 *The distribution of perfective -rku and -yku with other morphosyntactic elements*

PERFECTIVE SUFFIX	*-rku* (MUTUAL CONSENT)	*-yku* (GENERAL OBLIGATION)
1. PERSON AND NUMBER		
a. 1st person inclusive subject	yes	none
b. 1st person exclusive object	none	yes (imperatives)
c. Plural	3rd person only	1st, 2nd, and 3rd person
2. MOOD AND TENSE		
a. Imperative	0 (frequencies)	8 (5 1st person object)
b. Conditional	0	2
c. Future	0	4
d. Past tense	0	8
3. OTHER		
a. Finiteness	71% SS adverbial clauses	76% finite clauses
b. Other morphosyntactic constraints	highly constrained	unconstrained

In row 2 *-yku* appears with imperatives, conditionals, futures, and pasts, while *-rku* does not. In row 3 *-yku* is most frequent in finite clauses (76%), while *-rku* is most frequent in adverbial clauses linked to a matrix clause via a shared subject within the same or a concurrent/complementary event.

The interpersonal marking of speech-act participants reported in row 1 and the marking of mood, tense, and finiteness reported in rows 2 and 3 concord with the notions of complementary versus competing courses of action, consensual agreement versus obligation, and convergent versus divergent stance alignment.

6.3 Unexpected outcome: Perfective *-ski* and punctual *-ri*

The aspectual qualities of perfective *-ski* and punctual *-ri* were presented in Chapter 2. Each of these derivational suffixes also reports an outcome that is not anticipated by the affected participants. An unprepared mind and the subsequent unexpected outcome of an event has been referred to as "(ad)mirative," an epistemic modality (e.g., DeLancey 1997).

The primary modal contrast expressed by *-ski* versus *-ri* involves two different types of unprepared mind. Perfective *-ski* indicates that a prior expectation held by discourse participants does not turn out accordingly. In other words, the mind is prepared in some way, but not for the specific eventuality that materializes. Punctual *-ri*, on the other hand, reports that a completely unanticipated situation transpires.

These two types of unprepared mind are contrasted below with the verb root *cha:-* 'arrive'. In (178) the speaker expected to arrive but had no idea how long it would take. Perfective *-ski* (lowered allomorph *-ska*) reports the endpoint of the journey and further implies that the arrival was faster than anticipated.

(178) *mikru-wan-na-m ...*   *shamu-ra-:*   *Ca:tac-pita-qa.*   *tse:-pita*
      small.bus-COM-NOW-DIR   come-PST-1   Catac-ABL-TOP   that-ABL
      cha-__ska__-mu-ru-:
      arrive-**PFV**-FAR-PST.R-1
      'Next I came from Catac on a small bus. From there I **arrived** here **faster than I anticipated**.'

In contrast, *-ri* (lowered allomorph *-ra*) in (179) indicates that the foreigner and his child arrived totally unannounced, precipitating a situation outside the experience of the discourse participants. Neither the foreigner nor the local residents could have anticipated what to expect in this situation. Here punctual *-ri* reports the instant of arrival and the completely unprepared minds of the affected participants.

(179) *pay-mer*   *cha:-__ra__-ya:-mu-ra-n*   *ñi:ñu-wan*   *hana-man-pis*   *ari*
      he-DIR   arrive-**PUNC**-PL.V-FAR-PST-3 cute.kid-COM above-ALL-EVEN yes
      'He **arrived totally unannounced** to the high place with his adorable child.'

A similar contrast is seen with the verb root *apa-* 'take'. In (180) the agent (a presumed thief) formulated a general plan to take something of value while an unsuspecting victim was celebrating the fiesta. Perfective *-ski* reports that the thief took this particular donkey when the opportunity presented itself, that is, when the owners neglected to put it into the corral as usual.

(180) *bu:rru-:-kuna-ta,   pri:ma,   runa-ku   apa-**ski**-sh   o   ima-m*
     donkey-1-PL.N-OBJ   cousin   person-Q.P   take-**PFV**-PST.R3   or   what-DIR
     'Cousin, did someone **take** our donkey or what?'

In contrast, punctual *-ri* in (181) emphasizes that the captive girl did not plan or even think before grabbing her brother's bones and making her escape.

(181) *wamra-qa   aywa-ku-sha   tullu-n   apa-**ri**-sh*
     child-TOP   go-MID-PST.R3   bone-3   take-**PUNC**-PTCP
     'The girl escaped **carrying** the bones (of her brother).'

Speakers use the marking of unexpected outcomes by perfective *-ski* and punctual *-ri* for a variety of rhetorical effects. For example, under ordinary circumstances it may be appropriate to console someone who is crying. In (182), however, the speaker and her friends conspire to tease their uncle with an exaggerated act of "comfort" that will be both unexpected and unwelcome. As both parties know, the uncle was not really crying. Instead, he was feeling sorry for himself and complaining quite vocally about the behavior of his children who are friends of the speaker.

(182) *allaw tiyu-ntsi: waqa-yka-n.   aku   shoqa-**ska**-mu-shun-ra:*
     pity   uncle-1$_1$ cry-CONT-3   let's.go   console-**PFV**-FAR-IMP1$_1$-YET
     'Such a pity our uncle is crying. Let's go there and **cheer** him up.'

In (183) the hired hands locked the cattle gate with a different padlock without thinking through the possible consequences. In terms of speaker subjectivity, the boy responsible for the animals uses *-ri* in (183) to shift responsibility to them for the cow that was subsequently lost when his key would not open the gate.

(183) *llabi-ta-pis   llabi-**ri**-ya-shqa   huk-wan-na   tsay-si*
     padlock-OBJ-EVEN   lock-**PUNC**-PST.R3   one-INST-NOW   that-EVEN
     'Those guys even **locked it** (without thinking) with another padlock.'

If *-ri* is replaced by *-ski*, the participants are credited with some valid reason for unexpectedly changing the padlock.

The preceding examples show that the aspect markers *-ski* and *-ri* also report mirative meanings. This suggests a conceptual relationship between aspect and mirativity. As we saw in Chapter 2, perfective *-ski* is essentially a highly generalized completive. It is not uncommon cross-linguistically for completive aspect to express the additional semantic nuance of "surprise value" (e.g., Bybee et al. 1994:57). The surprise value is now systematically expressed by *-ski* as the unprepared mind of affected participants, that is, the inference of an unexpected outcome has been reanalyzed as part of the grammatical meaning of *-ski*.

Mirative meaning is also a natural extension of the aspectual meaning of punctual *-ri*. Actions that are brief (aspect) often occur suddenly (manner), and sudden actions are often performed without forethought (unprepared mind). An action without forethought may be surprising to participants (mirative), and may lead to further unexpected consequences. This was illustrated above in (183) where the boy uses *-ri* to place responsibility for the lost cow on the hired hands.

Unlike perfective *-ski*, mirative meaning is not systematically expressed by punctual *-ri*. Examples in which *-ri* does not express this meaning were presented in §2.1.5. The inference of surprise, conditioned by pragmatics (as in the case of *-ri*), has been referred to as a "mirative strategy" (e.g., Aikhenvald 2004:195ff.).

6.3.1   Further examples of perfective *-ski* as unexpected outcome

In (184) the individual is eating lunch with other travelers in a restaurant at a crossroads as he waits to flag down any bus bound for the capital.[114] There is no bus schedule, and one could pass by unannounced at any time. Perfective *-ski* here refers to the complete period of eating with others in the restaurant. In addition, *-ski* communicates a sense of hurriedness and that circumstances limit his preparedness to flag down a bus.

(184) *Catac-cho: almorsa-__ski__-r-na,*   *pa:sa-mu-ra-:*   *ke:-pa*
　　　　Catac-LOC   social.lunch-__PFV__-SS-NOW   pass-FAR-PST-1   this-GEN
　　　　'After hurriedly __eating lunch__ in Catac, I traveled here.'

If *-ski* is replaced by *-ri*, this would indicate that the individual was so absorbed with eating that he was unprepared to flag down a bus at the first opportunity.

In (185) the participants had decided it was too early to round up the animals before they became wrapped up in the activities of the fiesta. They totally forgot about the animals and one of the donkeys got lost, an outcome that was neither intended nor expected.

(185) *tsay-chu   pas   kushi-sh*   *ka-ku-ya-sha-:-yaq*   *oqra-ka-__ski__-na:*
　　　　that-LOC   very   be.happy-PTCP   be-MID-PL.V-NMLZ.R-1-LIM   lose-PASS-__PFV__-PST.N
　　　　'During the time that we were happily occupied there (at the fiesta), it __got lost__
　　　　(wandered off).'

In (186) the participant was involved in a comprehensive plan to search for the lost donkey, but she did not know in advance that she would encounter the donkey in this particular location or under these circumstances.

---

[114] The verb *almorsa-* refers to a midday meal that involves social interaction.

(186) *tsay-pita-qa   Cruz-kaq-pa   ko:rri   ko:ri   tuma-**ski**-na-:-pa:-qa*
      that-ABL-TOP   Cruz-DEF-GEN   run   run   turn-**PFV**-NMLZ.I-1-PURP-TOP
      Chi:nu munta-sh   witsa-yka:-tsi-mu-na:
      Chino mount-PTCP   climb-CONT-CAUS-FAR-PST.N
      'After that, as I was running rapidly right at Cruz, just as I **turned** the corner, there
      was Chino mounted (on the donkey) urging it up toward me.'

As summarized in Table 6.5, the derivational perfective suffix *-ski* has acquired extended
meanings along a path of grammatical development from space to aspect, manner, and modality.
At an early stage, the meaning of *-ski* would have spread from the domain of space to
completive and then perfective aspect.[115] The derivational perfective sense 'attainment of a limit'
received an adverbial reading of rapid action in some contexts. This manner meaning continues
in some situations (see §7.2.1.2). Finally, the grammaticization of the inference of surprise
yields mirative meaning, that is, an unprepared mind and the subsequent unexpected outcome of
an event. The synchronic grammatical meaning of *-ski* is tightly intertwined with the domains of
aspect and mirativity.

Table 6.5 *Manner and modal extensions to perfective -ski*

SEMANTIC DOMAIN	SPACE >	PERFECTIVE ASPECT >	MANNER >	EPISTEMIC MODALITY >	MIRATIVE
MEANING	'toward'	'attainment of a limit'	'rapid action'	'low surprise value'	'unprepared mind (not as anticipated), unexpected outcome'

6.3.2   Punctual *-ri* and subjective evaluation

As discussed above, some punctual events are especially brief and may be perceived as a sudden
occurrence. Sudden events are often unanticipated and may lead to unexpected outcomes. The
examples of punctual *-ri* presented here illustrate unexpected outcomes with an additional
evaluative or subjective connotation on the part of the speaker.

The verb *troka-* 'trade' refers to a public decision to sponsor a music and dance ensemble for
the annual fiesta. This decision entails a major commitment of time and financial resources.
Punctual *-ri* in (187) indicates that Mauro and his sister, carried away by the moment, voiced
their decision "in that instant." An additional, evaluative component of meaning is inferred from

---

[115] Evidence for perfective *-ski* as a former directional suffix 'toward' is presented in
Appendix E.

the pragmatic context, namely, they gave insufficient forethought to the decision and this action will result in further unanticipated consequences for those responsible.

(187) *nirkur Mauru pani-n-wan macha-sh-shi   tse: troka-**ri**-ya-n*
       then   Mauro sister-3-COM drunk-PTCP-RPT that trade-**PUNC**-PL.V-3
       'Then Mauro and his sister, being drunk, **traded in that instant**.'

Just as *-ri* may ascribe consequence or obligation to discourse participants deemed responsible for an unexpected outcome, *-ri* may also imply limited or no obligation on the part of those with limited or no responsibility. We have already seen one example of this above in (183), where the boy uses *-ri* to cast himself as having limited responsibility for the lost cow because of the limited forethought of the ranch workers who changed the lock (*llabi-ri-ya-shqa*).

In other contexts, evaluative inferences of this sort appear to be expressed through the semantics of the marker itself. Above in (187) Mauro and his sister "traded in an instant" in an ill-conceived decision to sponsor next year's fiesta. According to the speaker in (188), their family members will send only a limited or token amount of financial support, reflecting the evaluation of limited obligation for those with limited responsibility (e.g., the family members).

(188) *ima-ta-ra: rura-ya-nqa-pis   ichik huk ishke: qelle:-ta*
       what-OBJ-YET do-PL.V-FUT3-EVEN little one two   coin-OBJ
       *apa-**ra**-tsi-r*
       take-**PUNC**-CAUS-SS
       'What will they be able to do, **only contributing** a few small coins?'

In the previous example, the action does not involve brief duration (aspect). Indeed, they will send the money at the usual time and in no particular hurry. Thus, *-ri* in (188) is not aspectual. Instead, it is beginning to acquire new senses through the grammaticization of the inference of the evaluation of limited responsibility. In fact, this use of *-ri* is reminiscent of the delimitative suffix *-lla* in the sense of 'just, only'.

As summarized in Table 6.6, the derivational punctual suffix *-ri* has acquired extended meanings along a path of grammatical development from space to aspect, with synchronic inferences in the realms of manner and modality. At an early stage, the meaning of *-ri* would have spread from the domain of space to punctual aspect. An action of brief or limited duration often occurs in a sudden manner (see §7.2.1.1). Sudden events may have a high surprise value, along with the inference of a completely unprepared mind. In some situations, speakers also use *-ri* to mark subjective evaluations of consequence and responsibility.

Table 6.6 *Manner and modal extensions to punctual -ri*

SEMANTIC DOMAIN	SPACE >	PUNCTUAL > ASPECT	MANNER >	EPISTEMIC > MODALITY	MIRATIVE >	GENERAL MODALITY
MEANING	go	limited duration	sudden action	high surprise value	unprepared mind (not anticipated) unexpected outcome	conse-quence, respon-sibility

6.4   Outside experience: Narrative past *-na:*

The imperfective function of narrative past *-na:* was illustrated in §3.2.3 and its past tense or "anterior" function in §5.2. This multifaceted inflectional marker also combines modal and evidential senses in its semantics. In general terms, *-na:* presents a past situation as relevant to another past situation in terms of its consequences within the larger discourse context. For a relevant event already completed or in progress, the supplied information marked by *-na:* serves as an explanatory comment. It can also serve as an anticipatory device for events that will soon transpire. In either case, *-na:* presents this information as outside the experience or expectation of discourse participants, whether interlocutors in a conversation or participants within the narrative itself.

In (189) the speaker narrates an event from the previous week. The storyline concerns a nighttime robbery and the subsequent search for the thief. Past perfective *-sh* moves the storyline forward ('the man searched for him'). In the next two bracketed sentences the speaker switches to narrative past *-na:* to provide additional information about the young man's qualifications for leading the search ('he knew him', 'he formerly studied with him'). The mainline narrative sequence then resumes its progress with several instances of past perfective *-sh* ('he recognized his voice', 'they went to his house', 'they told his father', etc.).[116]

(189) *ari ashi-__sh__*   *runa-qa.*   *[reqi-__na:__*   *tsay* *cho:lu.*
      yes search-**PST.R3**   person-TOP   know-**PST.N**   that young.man

      Damian-wan-shi   *huntu*   *estudya-__na:__.]*   *tse:* *reqi-__sh__*   *bos-nin-ta ...*
      Damian-COM-RPT   together   study-**PST.N**   that know-**PST.R3**   voice-3-OBJ

      'Yes, the man **searched** (*-sh*) for him. [That young man **knew** (*-na:*) him. He **formerly studied** (*-na:*) (attended classes) with Damian, they say.] He **recognized** (*-sh*) his voice ...'

---

[116] In keeping with its non-firsthand or indirect reporting function, *-na:* sometimes occurs with the reportative evidential marker *-shi* which further specifies that the source of information is someone other than the interlocutors. Reportative *-shi* appears with *-na:* in the second lines of both (189) and (190).

-na: is also used in legendary genres. In (190) the narrator uses the historical present to advance the storyline ('the mouse says'). In the next bracketed sentence she switches to *-na:* to provide a side comment that it was normal in those days for mice to speak. The narrative sequence then resumes with the usual past tense marking.

(190) *"noqa-qa   a: awilu   rupa~simita   qara-ka-ma-nqa-n-ta-cha:*
       I-top   yes grandfather toasted~wheat   give-MID-1OBJ-NMLZ.R-3-OBJ-MUT

      miku-ku-:"   ni-n.   [unay-qa   ukush-pis   parla-__na:__-shi.]
      eat-MID-1   say-3   long.ago-TOP   mouse-EVEN   speak-__PST.N__-RPT

      '(The mouse) says, "I like to eat the toasted wheat that grandfather gives me." [Long ago even mice **could speak**, they say.]'

In both (189) and (190) *-na:* marks explanatory information that is semantically relevant, but *off the main storyline*. In other examples, *-na:* marks a past situation *within the main storyline*. That is, the information marked by *-na:* falls within the chronological scope of the current narrative sequence.

This use of *-na:* is illustrated in (191). The storyline concerns two lost donkeys. The speaker has already mentioned that her donkey became lost because she got distracted by the annual fiesta celebration. Here, past perfective *-ra* advances the storyline ('yours was lost, too'). In the next sentence the prior situation marked with *-na:* explains how that happened ('they weren't watching your donkey either').

(191) *i   qam-pa-pis   ka-ra-n.   bu:rru-yki-ta   ka:su-ya:-__na:__-tsu*
       and you-GEN-EVEN   be-PST-3   donkey-2-OBJ   obey-PL.V-__PST.N__-NEG

      'And yours <u>was (lost)</u>, too. They **weren't watching** your donkey either.'

In each of the preceding examples a narrative sequence is already in progress when the narrator introduces a prior situation marked by *-na:* to explain something recently mentioned in the main storyline. In those cases, *-na:* functions much like a pluperfect or "past within the past." That interpretation of *-na:* is merely incidental, however, because *-na:* can also present relevant information that anticipates mainline events about to unfold. For example, *-na:* may present information that establishes the setting for a story, often in combination with the past habitual *-q*.

This discourse function of narrative past *-na:* is illustrated in (192). Mrs. Fox and Mrs. Goose, the main characters, are placed on stage in the first sentence using *-na:*. The unsavory character of Mrs. Fox is established in the second sentence with the past habitual *-q*. The action of the story subsequently advances primarily through the use of past perfective *-sha* and the historical present.

(192) *karu   hirka-cho:-shi   ta:-ya:-__na:__   serka pura-lla   doña atoq i*
distant   mountain-LOC-RPT   sit-PL.V-**PST.N** near together-DLM   mrs. fox and

doña wachwa mana alli bi:da-ta   pa:sa-r. alla:pa llulla i   yaqa-kaq
mrs.   goose   no   good life-OBJ   pass-SS   very   lie   and nasty-DEF

doña atoq doña wachwa-ta chiki-__q__   wawa-n-kuna-pa: raykur. huk hunaq
mrs.   fox   mrs. goose-OBJ hate-**PST.H** child-3-PL.N-PURP sake   one day

doña atoq watqa-ra-__sha__   wachwa-pa chipsa-n-kuna-ta suwa-pa-y-ta
mrs.   fox   look.at-DUR-**PST.R3** goose-GEN chick-3-PL.N-OBJ steal-BEN-INF-OBJ

muna-r   miku-rku-na-n-pa:.
want-SS   eat-PFV.M-NMLZ.I-3-PURP

'On a distant mountain __sat__ (-*na:*) close together Mrs. Fox and Mrs. Goose, living a
difficult existence. The very dishonest and nasty Mrs. Fox __hated__ (-*q*) (was jealous of)
Mrs. Goose on account of her children. One day Mrs. Fox __looked intently__ (-*sha*) at
the goslings wanting to steal them so she could eat them up.'

In the previous example, -*na:* appears at the beginning of a story (off the main storyline) in
anticipation of the coming narrative sequence. Once the storyline is in progress, the speaker may
use -*na:* to indicate cataphorically that a dramatic "reversal of fortune" may be imminent. This
rhetorical effect is illustrated in (193). First, the witch instructs her son (marked by past
perfective -*sha*) how to push the girl into a boiling pot at an opportune moment. The switch to
-*na:* in the next sentence ('the girl was secretly listening') corresponds with the heightened sense
of suspense in anticipation of the ensuing drama. As the story unfolds, the girl pushes the
witch's son into the boiling pot, the reverse of what the witch had planned.

(193) *"... pani-n-ta-wan   tsay yaku puwa-yka-q-man   qarpu-rpu-nki"*
sister-3-OBJ-COM   that water boil-CONT-AG-ALL push.down-COMPL-FUT2

ni-r   yacha-tsi-sha.   i   wamra-qa wiya-__na:__   yacha-tsi-nqa-n-ta.
say-SS learn-CAUS-PST.R3   and   child-TOP hear-**PST.N**   learn-CAUS-NMLZ.R-3-OBJ

'She instructed him by saying, "Then push his sister down into that boiling water." But
the girl __was listening__ (in secret) to her instructions.'

Each situation marked by -*na:* above in (189)-(192) is outside the speaker's experience. In
contrast, the situation marked by -*na:* in (193) is outside the experience of a participant within
the narrative itself. The witch did not realize that the girl had been listening in secret, but
surmised that only after suffering the consequences.

Table 6.7 summarizes the four discourse functions of narrative past -*na:* presented above.
When the situation marked by -*na:* is mentioned *after* the relevant situation (consequence), as in
(189)-(191), it serves an EXPLANATORY ROLE (as in the first column). The information may
simply be a side comment off the main storyline, or it may be a central point on the main
storyline.

On the other hand, when the situation marked by -*na:* is mentioned *before* the relevant
situation (consequence), as in (192) and (193), it serves an ANTICIPATORY ROLE (as in the right-
hand column). The information may comprise the setting for a story (off the storyline), or it may

serve as a rhetorical device alerting the listener to a parallel development and the imminent drama soon to unfold.

Table 6.7 *Discourse functions of narrative past -na:*

DISCOURSE FUNCTION	SITUATION MARKED BY -*na:*	
	MENTIONED AFTER CONSEQUENCE	MENTIONED BEFORE CONSEQUENCE
	EXPLANATION	ANTICIPATION
OFF STORYLINE (*no surprise value*)	[SIDE COMMENT] 'He formerly studied with Damian' (how he could identify him)	[SETTING] 'They were extremely poor'
ON STORYLINE (*surprise value*)	[CENTRAL COMMENT] 'They weren't watching your donkey' (how it got lost)	[IMMINENT DRAMA] 'The girl was listening in secret'

Finally, information marked by -*na:* that is on the main storyline has an additional surprise or mirative value. In these instances, the information is not merely outside the experience of discourse participants, as in a side comment or in the setting for a story (as in the middle row). Instead, -*na:* systematically marks mainline events as outside the "normal" experience of participants, either explaining or anticipating an unexpected outcome (as in the bottom row).

For example, the information presented in (191) ('they weren't watching your donkey either') is not anticipated by the speech-act participants because donkeys are usually corralled at night. This information also explains the unexpected outcome in which the donkeys actually got lost. Similarly, in (193) the witch did not realize that the girl had secretly overheard the instructions for her son to kill her. Here, -*na:* marks the situation as unanticipated by the witch, a narrative participant. This information also foreshadows the unexpected outcome in which the girl kills the witch's son.

Summarizing, the inflectional narrative past marker -*na:* presents a past situation as relevant to another past situation in terms of its consequences. In terms of evidentiality, -*na:* presents a situation as outside the experience of conversational participants or participants within the narrative itself.

Narrative past -*na:* also serves an array of discourse functions. The rhetorical effect varies based on whether or not the supplied information is part of the main storyline, and whether or not the relevant situation has already been mentioned. Essentially, the information marked by -*na:* either serves as an explanatory comment or as an anticipatory device, as summarized above in Table 6.7. When used in the mainline of a story, -*na:* directly reports surprise value and indirectly points to a subsequent unexpected outcome. It does not have these mirative functions when used off the main storyline, as in side comments and narrative settings.

6.5 Conclusions: Aspect and modality

We have examined the complex grammatical interface connecting aspect and modality in SCQ. Just as aspectual categories take on more abstract tense meanings through the strengthening of temporal inferences (e.g., complete events tend to occur prior to the moment of speaking), they can also give rise to more abstract modal meanings via the grammaticization of nontemporal inferences.

As a case in point, the derivational perfective markers in SCQ distinguish whether an outcome is expected or unexpected—notions which pertain to an epistemic modality sometimes referred to as mirativity. Expected outcomes are marked by *-rku* and *-yku*, and these two suffixes further distinguish the more fine-grained deontic nuances of "mutual consent" versus "obligation." Unexpected outcomes, on the other hand, are marked by perfective *-ski* and punctual *-ri*. These latter suffixes distinguish types of "unprepared mind" along with additional deontic modal senses.[117]

Fleischman (1989) discusses extra-grammatical uses of tense due to metaphorical extension. These uses arise from modal (epistemic and deontic) and interpersonal (affect, politeness, subjectivity) inferences. As shown throughout this chapter, Quechua speakers exploit the aspectual meanings of derivational perfectives (derived from former directional markers) to convey precisely these types of intersubjectivities. Whereas Fleischman's analysis assumes a well-behaved inflectional tense system from which pragmatic extensions arise, the Quechua data presented here suggest a scenario in which modal and interpersonal meanings are present in aspect markers to begin with. When these aspect markers later evolve into tense markers (e.g., **-rqu* 'out' > 'derivational perfective' > 'inflectional past tense') the original meanings are carried over into the tense system as they grammaticize. In other words, the "metaphorical extensions" of tense markers are explainable, at least in some languages, due to original meanings at a prior stage in the domains of perfective aspect and modality.[118]

The semantics of imperfective markers may be internally complex as well. In addition to tense and aspect functions, the inflectional narrative past marker *-na:* presents a situation as outside the experience of discourse participants—an evidential function. This marker can also report unexpected outcomes, but only when it appears in the mainline of a story, not when it inserts a side comment or introduces setting information. In other words, the inference of surprise value has not generalized to all contexts in which *-na:* appears.

In terms of semantic domains, we have seen thus far that the twenty grammatical aspect markers in SCQ encode abstract perfective and imperfective notions, along with more abstract

---

[117] Smith (1997:309) observes a connection between Russian perfectives and the notion of intentionality. This use of derivational perfectives in Russian parallels the SCQ perfectives *-rku* and *-yku* described in §6.2. On the other hand, as we have seen in §6.3, perfective *-ski* (and punctual *-ri*) typically refer to unintended or unexpected situations.

[118] Extra-grammatical functions of tense in SCQ are described by Diane Hintz (2007b).

semantic extensions to tense and modality. The inferential path from aspect to the epistemic modality of unexpectedness, however, is not usually direct, but rather may be mediated by additional inferences in the realms of subjectivity (e.g., an evaluation as outside of some norm) and manner (e.g., an event carried out suddenly). In the next chapter I will examine the grammatical interface between aspect and the less well studied semantic domain of manner, an essential component of the larger grammatical system.

7 ASPECT AND MANNER

Just as one and the same grammatical marker may combine aspect and modality in its semantics, a grammatical marker may combine aspect and manner. While aspect reports temporal qualities of an event, manner reports nontemporal (adverbial) qualities of an event, that is, how the action is carried out. Modality, in turn, shifts the spotlight from qualities of the event to the way participants relate to the event and to each other.

As we observed in the previous chapter, the path from aspect to modal interpretation is often mediated by the inference of adverbial notions. For example, an event of limited duration (punctual aspect) may be construed as unanticipated (mirative modality) when the event is realized suddenly (manner). In addition to aspect markers with semantic extensions to secondary manner meanings (MANNER₂), other markers in SCQ express manner as their primary meaning (MANNER₁). The MANNER₁ adverbial suffixes do not necessarily encode aspect directly, but aspectual meanings tend to emerge from the implication of the time period in which the situation is realized.

(194) MANNER₁ > ASPECT > MANNER₂ > MODALITY

The aim of this chapter, then, is to investigate the grammatical interface between aspect and manner. I begin by examining forms glossed with English/Spanish adverbials in the traditional Quechuanist literature. I then focus specifically on SCQ, illustrating MANNER₂ as a semantic extension of aspect, and MANNER₁ as a grammatical category in its own right, with a tendency toward aspectual interpretation. After briefly considering adverbial glosses associated with aspect markers cross-linguistically, I conclude by assessing the semantic connections linking aspect, manner, and modality.

7.1 Aspect and manner in Quechuan languages

Careful perusal of the Quechuanist literature can unearth a wealth of manner adverbs used to characterize suffixes that are etymologically related to those presented in Part II as aspect markers. These manner adverbs are generally not distinguished from the modal adverbs summarized above in §6.1. Reading down the list of glosses in column 2 of Table 7.1, one finds a wide range of adverbial notions expressed by modern reflexes of the various Proto Quechua suffixes.[119] Although there is much semantic variation and idiosyncrasy, we can observe certain recurrent adverbial themes, including 'suddenly' (*-rku* in Huallaga, *-ski* in Conchucos, *-rqu* in Cuzco and Tarma), 'dynamically' (*-rku* in Caraz, *-yku* in Huanca), 'forcefully' (*-rku* in Huaraz, *-yku* in Huallaga), 'rapidly' (*-rku* in Huaraz, *-ski* in Conchucos, *-rqu* in Huallaga), and 'intensely' (*-yku* in Huaraz and Cuzco, *-ski* in Conchucos).[120]

Table 7.1 *Aspectual suffixes described with manner adverbs in the Quechuanist literature*

PROTO SUFFIX	ADVERB THEME/GLOSS	QUECHUAN VARIETY	SOURCE
-rpu	'abruptly', 'brusquely'	Cuzco	Cusihuamán 1976a:201
-rku	'dynamically'	Caraz	Escribens and Proulx 1970:43
	'forcefully', 'rapidly'	Huaraz	Swisshelm 1974:494
	'suddenly'	Huallaga	Weber 1989:123
-yku	'intensely', 'with difficulty'	Huaraz	Swisshelm 1974:499ff
	'intense manner'	Cuzco	Cusihuamán 1976a:206
	'dynamically'	Huanca	Cerrón-Palomino 1976:201
	'abnormally', 'distinctly'	Ayacucho	Soto 1976a:106
	'forcefully'	Huallaga	Weber 1989:128
	'carefully'	Tarma	Adelaar 1977:145
-ski	'rapidly', 'suddenly', 'intensely'	Conchucos	Stewart 1984:79,90,91
-ri	'partially'	Huanca	Cerrón-Palomino 1976:198
	'provisionally'	Pacaraos	Adelaar 1986:41
-rqu	'sudden outcome'	Cuzco	Cusihuamán 1976a:207
	'sudden change'	Tarma	Adelaar 1977:131
	'rapidly'	Huallaga	Weber 1989:127

The range of adverbial notions attributed to a particular suffix can vary a great deal across the spectrum of Quechuan languages. For instance, cognate forms of *-yku* are characterized adverbially as 'intense' manner in Huaraz and Cuzco, 'dynamic' or 'enthusiastic' manner in

---

[119] The locations of the Quechuan varieties in Table 7.1 are shown in Map 6.1 in §6.1. "Huaraz" and "Caraz" are towns within the Huaylas Quechua area.

[120] In addition to the adverbs of "manner" listed in Table 7.1, these suffixes are also described in the Quechuanist literature using adverbs I would identify as "aspect-like" (e.g., 'completely', 'briefly', 'initially'), "modal-like" (e.g., 'intentionally', 'unexpectedly', 'urgently', 'politely'), and "tense-like" (e.g., 'recently', 'immediately'). For more on modal qualities of the aspect suffixes, see Chapter 6.

Huanca, 'distinct' or 'abnormal' manner in Ayacucho, 'forceful' manner in Huallaga, and 'careful' manner in Tarma. While *-yku* and the other suffixes in Table 7.1 express adverbial (manner) notions, they also combine aspect and modality in their semantics. For example, in SCQ the suffix *-yku* expresses completive-perfective aspect (§2.1.3) and the modality of an obliged course of action (§6.1).[121]

7.2   The interface of aspect with manner in SCQ

In SCQ we find two classes of grammatical markers that combine aspect and manner. The first includes the derivational perfective suffixes (presented in Chapter 2) whose *Grundbedeutung* is aspect, with manner as an extension from aspectual meaning (MANNER₂). A representative sample of these slot D4 suffixes is presented in §7.2.1. The second class, presented in §7.2.2, is comprised of derivational markers that express manner as their primary grammatical meaning, with aspect as an extension from adverbial meaning (MANNER₁). These latter markers are further subdivided into those that report recurring situations and those that report non-recurring situations. They appear in slot D2, closer to the verb root than the derivational perfective suffixes in slot D4.

7.2.1   Aspect primary, manner secondary (MANNER₂ in slot D4)

I present here the derivational suffixes punctual *-ri*, perfective *-ski*, perfective *-yku*, perfective *-ri:ku*, and completive *-rpu*. The primary meaning of each suffix is aspectual, but the suffix can also convey an adverbial notion such as 'suddenly', 'rapidly', 'intensely', 'forcefully', or 'energetically'. These concepts are similar to the adverbial glosses presented above in Table 7.1 for other Quechuan varieties.

-ri 'punctual aspect', 'sudden manner'

In addition to its central meaning of brief duration (punctual aspect), *-ri* can also report that the action is realized in a sudden manner. For example, there is an illustration in the wordless picture book *Frog, where are you?* (Mayer 1969) in which an owl suddenly pops out of its hole in a tree, surprising the boy who was peering inside. The speaker expresses this part of the story in (195) using *-ri* (lowered allomorph *-ra*). The child's surprise is a natural modal extension from this action realized suddenly.

> (195) *tuku yarqa-__ra__-mu-n   tsay uchku puklla-yka-nqa-n-pita*
> owl   leave-**PUNC**-FAR-3 that hole   play-CONT-NMLZ.R-3-ABL
> 'An owl **suddenly comes out** of that hole where he (the boy) was playing.'

---

[121] Perfective aspect has also been attributed to *-ski* in Conchucos (Stewart 1984), *-yku* in Huallaga (Weber 1989:144ff.), and *-ru* in Tarma (Adelaar 1977:130).

-ski 'perfective aspect', 'rapid manner'

Perfective *-ski* can further specify an action realized in a rapid manner. In (196) the condor rescues the children from the cliff by rapidly flying them on its shoulders to a field far below. In (197) the speaker walks with haste to a neighboring village. In each case, according to my language consultants, the rapid arrival is faster than a discourse participant had anticipated, a type of modal extension.

(196) *tsay-shi   kondor-kush   ima-shi   hipi-__ski__-n   qarwa-ra-q   papa-man*
      that-RPT   condor-Q.T   what-RPT   remove-__PFV__-3   be.yellow-DUR-AG   potato-ALL
      'Then the condor or something __rapidly takes__ them to the yellowed potato plants.'

(197) *noqa-qa   heqa-__ski__-ra-:   Acopa:ra-pa*
      I-top   go.up-__PFV__-PST-1   Acopara-GEN
      'I __hurried up__ to Acopara (town).'

-yku 'perfective aspect', 'intense manner'

Perfective *-yku* can function as an adverbial intensifier as in (198).

(198) *ruku   chip chip setenta a:ñu-s   i   yapay ho:tu-n-ta*
      old.man very very seventy year-PL.SP and again photo-3-OBJ
      rika-__yku__-na: benti   sinku a:ñu-s-yoq   ka-nqa-n-ta
      see-__PFV.O__-PST.N twenty five   year-PL.SP-HAVE be-NMLZ.R-3-OBJ
      'The very old man of seventy years again __looked intently__ at the photo in which he was twenty-five years old.'

When *-yku* is used as an intensifier, the verb in which it appears is often modified by a lexical intensifier. In (199) the verb *ashi-yku-ya-:* is accompanied by the adverb *pas* 'very', a reduced form of *pasaypa* (from Spanish *pasa-* 'pass, happen' plus the adverbial suffix *-ypa*).

(199) *washa   tsay Shayan Tuna kinray   pas   ashi-__yku__-ya-:*
      over.there that Shayan Tuna vicinity very search-__PFV.O__-PL.V-1
      'Over there in the vicinity of Shayan Tuna we __searched intensely__ for it.

-ri:ku 'perfective aspect', 'forceful manner'

Perfective *-ri:ku* further specifies an event that involves forceful effort, as in (200) and (201); cf. §2.1.6.

(200) *wap boltiya-__ri:ku__-: noqa-qa mantsa-ka-sha*
fast turn-__PFV.F__-1 I-TOP fear-PASS-PCTP
'Rapidly I __turn to confront__ it (an evil spirit), frightened.'

(201) *tsa miti-ku-rku-pti-n-qa   warmi-qa atoq-pa rani-n-ta*
then copulate-MID-PFV.M-DS-3-TOP woman-TOP fox-GEN penis-3-OBJ
roqu-__ri:ku__-na:
cut-__PFV.F__-PST.N
'Then after they had intercourse, the woman __severed__ the penis of the fox.'

-rpu 'completive aspect', 'energetic manner'

As described above in §2.1.1, completive *-rpu* continues to be productive as a directional marker with motion verbs, expressing a literal sense of downward direction to an endpoint. In some contexts, *-rpu* also reports an action that is realized in a vigorous or energetic manner. In (202) the giant worm (which has just been beheaded) violently shakes the ground as it descends into the earth.

(202) *ruri-cho:-qa   patsa-pis   i:hu kuyu-pti-n-ra:-shi*
inside-LOC-TOP ground-EVEN very move-DS-3-YET-RPT
kuti-__rpu__-n   kuru   ka-nqa-n
return-__COMPL__-3 worm be-NMLZ.R-3
'As the inner ground shakes violently, the (giant beheaded) worm __vigorously descends__ as just a worm again (its former nature).'

Similarly, in (203) the girl asks Father Emmanuel to cast down from heaven his golden chain so she can climb it to escape the witch.

(203) *tayta-y   Mañuko, qori karina-yki-ta kacha-__rpa__-mu-y*
father-VOC Manuel, gold chain-2-OBJ send-__COMPL__-FAR-IMP2
'Father Emmanuel, __cast down__ here your golden chain.'

In summary, the derivational aspect suffixes presented above can communicate a variety of adverbial notions that characterize how the action is realized. The attributes 'suddenly', 'rapidly', 'intensely', 'forcefully', and 'energetically' are similar to the glosses presented above in Table 7.1 for other Quechuan varieties. They do not represent the central meaning of these suffixes, but rather each reports an extension from aspect to manner via inference.

As noted in Chapter 2, at a prior stage of development these aspect suffixes had directional meanings (e.g., perfective *-yku* is from **-yku* 'inward'). This suggests a series of stages in the development of these grammatical markers. In this scenario, directional suffixes (space-oriented manner) give rise to aspectual meanings, and these in turn report adverbial notions which are not directional (quality-oriented manner). Finally, these adverbial extensions give rise to the modal distinctions presented above in Chapter 6. This discussion is continued in the conclusion to this chapter, after the presentation of grammatical markers in which manner is the central meaning.

7.2.2   Manner primary, aspect secondary (MANNER₁ in slot D2)

In addition to suffixes that express manner as an extension to aspectual meaning (MANNER₂ in slot D4), other grammatical markers in SCQ express manner as their primary grammatical meaning (MANNER₁ in slot D2). Each manner marker presented here is highly derivational with specific adverbial semantics, along with incipient aspectual functions. In this way, these slot D2 markers are comparable to the Slavic-type "procedurals" or *Aktionsarten*, that is, "the lexicalisation of the [aspectual] distinction provided that the lexicalisation is by means of derivational morphology" (Comrie 1976:7).[122]

I illustrate here two types of markers in which manner is primary. The first type presents repeated actions or subactions through which specific imperfective meanings are implied, but not necessarily expressed directly. These include distributive *-paku*, iterative *-ykacha:*, and iterative-distributive meanings expressed through the reduplication of verb roots (REDUP₂). The second type presents attributes of actions that do not necessarily recur, but nonetheless imply duration and, in some cases, customary activities. These include concerted effort *-chaku* and total (customary) *-ka:ku*. Each MANNER₁ suffix appears in slot D2, closer to the verb root than the more productive derivational aspect suffixes which appear in slot D4 (illustrated in the previous section and in Chapter 2).[123]

Recurring action (distributive and iterative meanings)

Distributive *-paku*, iterative *-ykacha:*, and verb root reduplications with similar meanings were presented in Chapter 3 "Imperfectives" because they specify recurrence over time, thus implying internal temporal structure. As noted there, these markers also report adverbial characteristics of an event, that is, how the action is carried out in space and time. I provide here a few illustrations of manner for each of these markers.

First, distributive *-paku* presents a recurring action generally spread over various locations. In (204) various food items were purchased from different street vendors. In (205) improvements were made and items were put away throughout the house. In these illustrations *-paku* specifies distribution in space. The aspectual implication results from the pragmatics of the situation, that is, actions realized at different locations by the same participant(s) ordinarily require a relatively extended duration.

---

[122] In contrast, the slot D4 derivational aspect markers presented above in Part II (and in §7.2.1) are very productive and tend to occur with all verbs, unlike the Slavic-type *Aktionsarten* which tend to depend heavily on the meaning of the verb (Bybee and Dahl 1989:86).

[123] The second element of ROOT~ROOT reduplications may be considered analogous to a derivational slot D1 or D2 suffix.

(204) *fiyambri-kuna-ta   ranti-__paku__-ya-ru-:*   las   *o:chu i   medya-na-m*
     snack-PL.N-OBJ   buy-__DISTR.S__-PL.V-PST.R-1 o'clock   eight and half-NOW-DIR

     'We **bought** snacks **here and there** by eight thirty.'

(205) *tsay-cho: ta:ra-q-no:-na   allitsa-__paku__-r   chura-__paku__-r*
     that-LOC   reside-AG-SIM-NOW   improve-__DISTR.S__-SS   put-__DISTR.S__-SS

     kushi-sha   ka-ya:-na: tsay alala-y   tiempu-kuna
     be.happy-PTCP   be-PL.V-PST.N   that be.cold-INF   time-PL.N

     'As temporary residents now, **improving things here and there** and **putting things away**, they were happy during that winter season.'

Second, iterative *-ykacha:* (*-kacha:* after *i*) presents an event with multiple subactions which recur on a single occasion. While the recurring action marked by distributive *-paku* is realized at multiple locations, the recurring subactions marked by iterative *-ykacha:* generally occur at a single location or along a single trajectory. For example, in (206) the verb *ko:rri-* denotes a generic 'run' movement, and the addition of *-kacha:* narrows the focus to the inherent repeated subactions of running, presumably leg and arm movement. In terms of manner, iterative *-kacha:* not only specifies how running is realized but also implies that this instance of running is particularly fast.

(206) *ni-pti-n-qa   pase:pa ko:rri-__kacha__-r   aywa-yka-ru-:*   *Cruz-pa-na   ari*
     say-DS-3-TOP   very   run-__ITER__-SS   go-CONT-PST.R-1   Cruz-GEN-NOW yes

     'After she spoke, **running rapidly** I was going by Cruz.'

The single occasion with iterative subactions may be relatively brief, as in (206), or it may be presented as an enlarged occasion as illustrated above in §3.1.4. For convenience, (83) is reproduced here as (207). In each of these examples, *-ykacha:* specifies a sequence of subactions which entails the passage of time for their realization.

(207) *huk   familya-ta taku-ka-ski-r   yunta-no: apa-__ykacha__-naku-n*
     one   family-OBJ join-MID-PFV-SS   pair.oxen-SIM   carry-__ITER__-RECP-3

     ishka-n-la:-pa:
     two-3-SIDE-PURP

     'Forming a single joined family, like a pair of yoked oxen they **carry** the load together **shifting back and forth** between the two sides (throughout life).'

Third, both iterative and distributive meanings may be expressed by the reduplication of a bare verb root (REDUP₂). The resulting ROOT~ROOT unit may remain uninflected, as in (208), or it may be inflected with verbal morphology, as in (209) and (210). Such verbal reduplications typically express adverbial concepts such as rapidly or intensely. For example, in (208) the verb root *ko:rri-* 'run' is repeated three times to express a cyclic action realized in a very rapid manner. The meaning here is similar to that expressed by the iterative suffix *-ykacha:* in (206), but reduplication does not further specify the arm and leg movement associated with running.

(208) *i   ..__ko:rri__   __ko:rri__   __ko:rri__   punta   cha:-mu-sh*
      and   run   run   run   first   arrive-FAR-PST.R3
      na:ni-ta   ichik   yaqa-q-ta   witsaypa   tari-ski-r-qa
      path-OBJ   little   fork-AG-OBJ   there   find-PFV-SS-TOP
      'Then **running rapidly**, it arrived first, finding a little fork in the path there.'

The reduplicated verb root *ñuki-* 'look up' in (209) expresses an iterative action realized intensely. Here the reduplicated form appears in an adverbial clause. The shepherd boy was looking up to glare periodically at the young visitor from the city because he was jealous of all the attention she was receiving.

(209) *o:ra~o:ra-ta-qa   shumaq   rika-pa-y-ta   muna-r*
      hour~hour-OBJ-TOP   beautiful   see-BEN-INF-OBJ   want-SS
      __ñuki~ñuki__-rku-r-ra: Lisarda-ta-qa   rika-ra:-na:
      look.up~look.up-PFV.M-SS-EVEN   Lisarda-OBJ-TOP   see-DUR-PST.N
      'Every so often giving her a good looking over, he would **look up** periodically and stare at Lisarda.'

When multiple patients are involved, the reduplicated form may express distributive meaning, that is, an action spread over various locations. In (210) the reduplicated verb root *yarku-* 'climb' presents the action of climbing as spread over various trees.

(210) *wamra puklla-yka-n   atska   qeru-kuna-man   __yarku~yarku__-rku-r*
      child   play-CONT-3   many   tree-PL.N-ALL   **climb~climb**-PFV.M-SS
      'The child is playing, **climbing** one tree after another.'

Each marker illustrated above involves recurring actions or subactions and reports adverbial qualities of an event, that is, how the action is realized. In addition to nontemporal manner, they also imply inner temporal structure, i.e., imperfective aspect (as treated in Chapter 3). The markers presented in the next section express manner and imply duration, but do not necessarily involve recurrence.

Non-recurring action

I introduce here concerted effort *-chaku* and total (customary) *-ka:ku*. These suffixes present attributes of an action that does not necessarily recur, but the manner in which the action transpires gives rise to incipient durative and habitual functions.

-chaku 'concerted effort'

The derivational suffix *-chaku* presents an event as characterized by concerted or persistent effort. This effort usually extends over a period of time. For example, in (211) the verb *qapa-*

means 'shout' and the modified stem *qapa-chaku-* means 'shout with concerted effort' or 'scream'.[124]

(211) *atoq-qa   karambas   allaw tsay qapa-__chaku__-r   wanu-ku-na:*
       fox-TOP good.grief pity   that shout-__EFFORT__-SS die-MID-PST.N

       tsay sapatu-n-kuna-wan
       that   shoe-3-PL.N-INST

       'The fox, what a pity, he died __screaming__ with those (shrinking) boots on.'

Similarly, the verb *yarpa:-* 'think' becomes *yarpa-chaku-* 'think with concerted effort' (to resolve a dilemma), as illustrated in (212).[125]

(212) *tronku   hana-n-chu:-na ka-yka:-ya-n   ishkan, allqu-n-wan yarpa-__chaku__-r*
       log   top-3-LOC-NOW be-CONT-PL.V-3 two   dog-3-COM   think-__EFFORT__-SS

       "kanan-qa ima-nuy-ra: yarqu-yku-shun"   ni-r
       now-TOP   what-SIM-YET leave-PFV.O-FUT1₁ say-SS

       'The two of them (the boy) with his dog are now on top of the log, __thinking hard__ and saying "Now how will we get down?".'

The verb *rika-* means 'see' and *rika-chaku-* in (213) means 'look or search with concerted effort'.

(213) *kay-cho   rika-__chaku__-__yka__-n.   allqu-n-ta*
       this-LOC   see-__EFFORT__-__CONT__-3 dog-3-OBJ

       'Here (in this picture) he __is looking with concerted effort__ for his dog.'

Like distributive *-paku* and iterative *-ykacha:*, concerted effort *-chaku* can be followed by an imperfective suffix, such as *-yka:* in (213), or a perfective suffix, such as *-yku* in (214). The

---

[124] A possible etymology for *-chaku* is the verb **ch'aya-* 'arrive' plus the suffix **-ku*. Within the Quechuan family, however, it is not generally possible to recover the lexical sources of suffixes with certainty. The form *ku* is probably cognate with the final element in distributive *-paku*, total *-ka:ku*, and the perfectives *-rku* and *-yku*.

[125] The verb stems *yarpa-chaku-* in (212) and *yarpa-ra:* 'ponder' (above in (52) in §3.1.1) present an interesting contrast between temporal (aspect) and nontemporal (manner) meanings. While the durative aspect suffix *-ra:* directly specifies an extended duration, the manner suffix *-chaku* specifies concerted effort, which often requires an extended duration. At a certain point the inference of aspect may be reanalyzed as the central meaning of such forms. The role of inference in the grammaticization of aspect, modal, and tense markers is a topic presented in Part IV "The emergence of aspect in Quechua."

compatibility of *-chaku* (in slot D2) with derivational perfectives and imperfectives (in slot D4) reflects the less abstract, adverbial semantics that characterizes slot D2 suffixes.

(214) *noqa feyu-pa-m   yarpa-**chaku**-**yku**-rqo-:   qam wayi-:-man*
        I   very-GEN-DIR   think-**EFFORT**-**PFV.O**-PST.R-1 you house-1-ALL
        cha-yka-mu-r   imayka-kuna-ta-pis
        arrive-CONT-FAR-SS all.kinds-PL.N-OBJ-EVEN
        parla-pa:-ma-nqa-yki-kuna-pa:
        speak-BEN-OBJ1-NMLZ.R-2-PL.N-PURP
        'I **thought** very **deeply** about all the things you told me when you were visiting at my house.'

In summary, the derivational suffix *-chaku* grammatically encodes the adverbial notion of concerted or persistent effort. It is highly lexicalized and occurs in the SCQ corpus with the cognition and sensing verbs *yarpa:-* 'think', *rika-* 'see', and *maya-* 'be alert', and the speech-act verb *qapa-* 'shout'. The notion of concerted effort suggests a semantic affinity with durative aspect, but the limited productivity of *-chaku* would tend to preclude its ongoing development as a durative aspect marker.

-ka:ku 'totally, customarily'

The derivational suffix *-ka:ku* presents a nonagentive situation as realized to a very high or excessive degree. This notion is illustrated in (215) with the stative verb *mantsa-* 'fear'.[126]

(215) *tsay-no: Erika ka-yka-pti-n-pis   tsay wayi-cho:-qa*
        that-SIM Erika be-CONT-DS-3-EVEN that house-LOC-TOP
        *mantsa-**ka:ku**-y-pa: huk-na   rura-ka-r   qalla-yku-na:*
        fear-**TOTAL**-INF-PURP one-NOW do-PASS-SS begin-PFV.O-PST.N
        'While Erica was (depressed) like that, something else **totally frightening** began happening in the house.'

As an anticausative, that is, a type of middle voice indicating a change of state with no implied agent, *-ka:ku* readily applies to unintended actions, as in (216).

(216) *ishki-ski-shqa   washaqan-cho:-qa, pe:ra-qa chip mashta-**ka:ku**-sha*
        fall-PFV-PST.R3   nearby-LOC-TOP   pear-TOP very spread-**TOTAL**-PST.R3
        llapa-n
        all-3
        'He fell nearby and all the pears **got totally scattered**.'

---

[126] Because *-ka:ku* is often translated as 'totally' or 'completely', it is glossed here as TOTAL, though it can also refer to customary activities.

Although completive *-rpu* (§2.1.1) and total *-ka:ku* can both be translated as 'completely', their aspectual values are quite different. Completive *-rpu* (a subtype of perfective) is intrinsically telic, that is, it introduces a terminal point regardless of the inherent semantics of the verb. In contrast, total *-ka:ku* is atelic (aspectually neutral or related to imperfective aspect). At the same time, *-ka:ku* is compatible with inherently telic verbs, such as *usha-* 'finish' in (217). Here, the derived stem combination indicates that the action of the verb is carried out thoroughly or to an absolute extreme (total consummation).

(217) *kada tardi   peru wamra-n-kuna usha-__ka:ku__-n-man-chir   ka-ra-n*
      every afternoon but   child-3-PL.N   finish-__TOTAL__-3-COND-APP be-PST-3
      'Every afternoon, otherwise, their children would have been __completely destroyed__.'

With certain activity verbs, total *-ka:ku* introduces an interpretation in which the situation is characterized as recurring on a regular or customary basis. This incipient habitual meaning of *-ka:ku* is illustrated in (218) and (219). In the first example, the verb *qori-* 'gather (things)' becomes *qori-ka:ku-* 'customarily meet or assemble'. In the second example, the verb *taku-* 'join or mix' becomes *taku-ka:ku-* 'regularly join together'.

(218) *runa-kuna   qori-__ka:ku__-ya:-na-n-pita   qaracha-shqa*
      person-PL.N gather-__TOTAL__-PL.V-NMLZ.I-3-ABL drag-PTCP
      waqta-man hipi-ya:-mu-rqa-n
      back-ALL   take.out-PL.V-FAR-PST-3
      'Dragging him from where people __customarily meet__, they took him out to the back.'

(219) *maha-n-wan-na   taku-__ka:ku__-ya-n*
      mate-3-COM-NOW join-__TOTAL__-PL.V-3
      'They __are regularly joined__ together with their mate now.'

Finally, total *-ka:ku* appears to be derived historically from the amalgamation of two derivational suffixes which are attested synchronically—i.e., passive *-ka:* followed by middle voice *-ku*.[127] No other suffix can intervene between these two fused elements in verbal slot D2. The non-compositional meanings 'totally' and 'regularly' further indicate that *-ka:ku* has become a single suffix. It is much more productive than concerted effort *-chaku*, the suffix presented in the previous section, but it has also co-lexicalized or fused with certain verbs. The

---

[127] The combination of passive *-ka:* plus middle voice *-ku* presents a semantic contradiction. Presumably, passive *-ka:* first became lexicalized or fused with certain verb roots (e.g., *mantsa-* 'fear', *mantsaka:-* 'be afraid'). These passive forms could then take the middle suffix *-ku* (e.g., *mantsaka:-ku-* 'be totally afraid'). The innovative meaning ('totally') was not attributed to *-ku* alone, but rather to the combination of final *-ka:* plus *-ku*, now reanalyzed as the grammatical suffix *-ka:ku*.

role of amalgamation accompanied by lexicalization in the rise of new grammatical categories is treated in Part IV.

Summarizing, the derivational suffix *-ka:ku* grammatically encodes the adverbial notion of a thoroughly realized nonagentive situation. *-ka:ku* is semantically atelic and thus does not express completive (perfective) aspect, but when combined with telic verb roots the situation may be interpreted as reaching an absolute extreme. This low frequency suffix can also report an activity that recurs customarily, suggesting a semantic affinity with habitual (imperfective) aspect (cf. §8.5). While total *-ka:ku* is relatively infrequent, the final element of this form (*-ku*) is very frequent and extremely productive as a middle voice marker, both synchronically and diachronically.

7.3   Aspect and manner in other languages

The semantic connection between aspect and manner in grammatical morphemes is not unique to Quechua but is characteristic of many languages. For example, the formal aspects listed by Streitberg (1891) for Germanic include not only the familiar categories imperfective, resultative, durative, and iterative, but also *intensive* (indicating intensity of action) (Binnick 1991:145). Similarly, Geniušienė and Nedjalkov refer to the aspect-oriented polysemy of various markers in Eastern Nilotic and Austronesian with the related meanings "iterative, durative, *intensive*, inceptive" (2001:57, italics added). In Quechuan languages as well, the perfective suffix *-yku* has been described as an adverbial *intensifier* (see Table 7.1). In other words, from Streitberg to the present time linguists have noticed a tendency for some forms that mark aspect to also have adverbial meanings such as 'intense manner'.

'Intense manner' is not the only adverbial function associated with aspect markers in other languages. For example, the overlap between aspect and grammatical manner in Quechua is reminiscent of "procedurals" in Russian. As Forsyth explains (1970:21-4), the Russian prefix *po-* expresses not only durative aspect, but also *attenuative* manner, as in (220). Similarly, in (221) the prefix *za-* expresses inceptive aspect, and the combination of *za-* with the reflexive suffix *-sja/-s'* yields a non-compositional meaning called *absorptive* manner. The translation of the Russian verb *za-govorili-s'* in (221)b 'became absorbed in conversation' is much like the translation of the Quechua verb in (184) *almorsa-ri-r-na* 'absorbed in eating lunch', which is marked by punctual *-ri*. A detailed comparison of aspect in SCQ and Russian is presented in §12.4. (For more on Russian procedurals, see Forsyth 1970:20ff., 356.)

(220) a. *spal*   'slept'
          po-spal   'had a (little) sleep'   DURATIVE ASPECT

      b. *el*   'ate'
          po-el   'have something to eat'   ATTENUATIVE MANNER

(221) a. *plakal*   'wept'
          za-plakal   'burst into tears'   INCEPTIVE ASPECT

      b. *govorili*   'spoke'
          za-govorili-s'   'became absorbed in conversation'   ABSORPTIVE MANNER

According to Binnick, meanings such as intensive, attenuative, and absorptive tell us "in some sense how something happened, [but] do not quite tell us how they happened, aspectually speaking" (1991:145). The Quechua data presented here show us that these and other adverbial concepts are a natural extension from aspectual meanings. These data also support the idea that the path from aspect to modal interpretation may be mediated by the inference of manner.

7.4 Conclusions: Aspect and manner

Previous chapters presented the grammatical expression of aspect in SCQ. We then observed how the aspect system is interwoven with tense and with modality. Here, we have examined the grammatical interface of aspectual functions with adverbial (manner) functions. In keeping with the diversity of adverbial concepts in general, it comes as no surprise that manner is not a homogeneous category. At the same time, emerging structure can be observed within this grammatical component which, like tense and modality, is interconnected with aspect.

The SCQ data reveal two distinct classes of manner. The first we might call an "adverbial strategy" in which the path from aspect to modal interpretation is mediated by the inference of adverbial notions. In other words, manner may arise as a semantic extension of grammatical aspect. A second set of markers systematically express manner as their primary grammatical meaning. The elaboration of a class of markers that directly encode adverbial notions suggests that manner (how an event happens) may constitute a semantic domain in its own right, distinct from aspect (temporal qualities of an event) and modality (subjective relations between speakers, participants, and events).

These two classes of manner correspond to two distinct positions within the SCQ verb. Markers that encode manner as their primary grammatical meaning appear in the derivational slot D2 (see the column labeled MANNER1 in Table 7.2 (overleaf); small caps indicate primary synchronic meanings). Secondary aspectual meanings emerge from the implication of the time period in which these recurring and non-recurring situations are realized. For example, distributive *-paku* reports an event spread over various locations. This spatial meaning generalizes to events spread over various occasions, which in turn may imply a habitual or characteristically recurring situation.

Markers in the derivational slot D4 encode aspect as their primary grammatical meaning (ASPECT column). These aspect markers secondarily report how an action is realized. For example, an event marked by punctual *-ri* may be realized suddenly (MANNER2 column), which in turn may be construed as surprising (MODALITY column). The markers in slot D2 (which imply internal temporal structure) readily combine with the perfective aspect markers in slot D4, yielding an imperfective reading of an otherwise perfective situation.

Table 7.2 *The semantic domains of manner, aspect, and modality*

SEMANTIC DOMAIN	**MANNER 1** (SPACE, RECURRENCE) SLOT D2	**> ASPECT** SLOT D4	**> MANNER 2** (QUALITY)	**> MODALITY**
UNBOUNDED **ATELIC** from SPACE and MIDDLE VOICE	distributive *-paku* iterative *-ykacha:* concerted *-chaku* customary *-ka:ku*	habitual continuative durative/habitual habitual		— — careful excessive
BOUNDED **TELIC** from SPACE (proto directionals)	downward **-rpu* upward **-rku* inward **-yku* toward **-ski* go **-ri*	completive *-rpu* perfective *-rku* perfective *-yku* perfective *-ski* punctual *-ri*	energetic easily intensely rapidly suddenly	enthusiasm mutual consent obligation unanticipated surprise, lack of obligation

The left-to-right arrangement of columns in Table 7.2 reflects the observation that the aspect markers in slot D4 (ASPECT column) give rise to secondary manner meanings (MANNER2 column) leading to modal interpretation (MODALITY column). In contrast, manner markers that appear in slot D2 (MANNER1 column) do not mediate between aspectual and modal interpretation.

We can also visualize in Table 7.2 how manner meanings give rise to aspectual meanings over time. In the case of the former directional markers, the inference "attainment of a limit" has grammaticized as perfective aspect. The MANNER1 markers appear to be on a similar path of development toward imperfective aspect.[128]

In conclusion, a great deal of research has led to a general theory for aspect, for tense, and for modality, and various works consider aspect-tense-modality as a single, interwoven

---

[128] The path of development for the proto directional suffix **-rqu* 'outward' led first to perfective aspect, which later acquired an inflectional past tense function as past perfective *-ru* in SCQ.

grammatical system (e.g., Dahl and Velupillai 2005:266). The interface between aspect and manner, however, has received relatively little attention. Presumably, we lack a general theory of manner because the boundary between temporal and nontemporal meanings can be difficult to delineate. Furthermore, the internal structure of manner may be obscured by the vast array of adverbial concepts expressed cross-linguistically. To further complicate matters, aspect is linked not only to nontemporal manner meanings, but also to nontemporal modal meanings.

For SCQ, at least, we have identified particular pragmatic and semantic connections between manner and tense-aspect-modality, and the aspect-manner interface provides an indispensable key to understanding this grammatical system. The investigation of the aspect-manner interface also revealed a semantic connection between valence-reducing morphology and incipient habitual functions in the form *-ka:ku* (from the combination of passive *-ka:* with reflexive-middle voice *-ku*). The form *-ku* is also the final element in other MANNER1 suffixes in Table 7.2 (viz., *-paku* and *-chaku*). In the next chapter, we will consider connections linking aspect and middle voice in greater detail.

8   ASPECT AND MIDDLE VOICE

The grammatical interface between aspect and tense, as described in Chapter 5, is well documented cross-linguistically. Connections between aspect and modality (Chapter 6) have also been discussed in the literature on aspect. Links between aspect and manner (Chapter 7) have been noted less frequently. A final type of connection, that between aspect and middle voice, has been described little if at all.

Quechuan languages present a unique opportunity for investigating the role of middle voice in the development of aspect. In what follows, I examine middle voice situation types marked by the derivational suffix *-ku* in SCQ and show how this highly productive suffix acquires modal and habitual functions in the context of generalized activities. I conclude by considering Northern Quechuan varieties in which progressive aspect has become the primary meaning of the cognate forms *-ku/-hu/-u*, accompanied by the innovation of reflexive/middle meaning from punctual *-ri*. The Quechua data presented here reveal the mechanisms that underlie a previously undescribed path of development linking perfective aspect, middle voice, and imperfective aspect.

8.1   Middle voice *-ku* in the Quechuanist tradition

Grammarians in the Quechuanist tradition have made important observations on the suffix *-ku*, which are referenced at various locations in this chapter. At the same time, I am not aware of a thorough treatment of reflexive and middle voice in Quechua, nor on the suffix *-ku* in particular.[129] Probably the most detailed sketch to date is provided by Swisshelm (1974:478-81) on *-ku* in Huaraz Quechua, which is spoken to the west of SCQ in central Peru. The following summarizes Swisshelm's observations on *-ku*, which is referred to as "mediopassive or reflexive":[130]

---

[129] Most if not all Quechuanists agree that the Proto Quechua form *-ku* was associated with reflexive and middle voice meanings. For example, Parker (1969a:137) posits "*-kU* Reflexive-Mediopassive." See also Cerrón-Palomino (2003:190), among others.

[130] Forms that are cognate with *-ku* are traditionally glossed as REFL for 'reflexive'. Throughout the present work, *-ku* is glossed as MID for 'middle voice', which is more general than reflexive

- The subject does something to himself
- The subject does something for his own benefit, pleasure, advantage, or for his disadvantage or detriment
- If the subject is possessed by someone, it refers to the benefit or detriment to the person
- The subject is involved in producing the action in a special manner
- With the copula *ka-*, a common, permanent, perennial, or constant state is expressed

While the connection to middle voice is relatively straightforward in the first three points, the more intriguing final points remain somewhat vague. For example, the notion of "special manner" could refer to virtually any derivational suffix in Quechua, whether its primary meaning is centered within the conceptual domain of voice, aspect, modality, or manner itself, as discussed above in Chapter 7.

The concern in the present chapter, then, is to first situate the suffix *-ku* within the sphere of reflexive and middle voice meanings in order to subsequently expand the investigation into its more abstract aspectual and modal functions. These latter functions in particular can deepen our understanding of the interface between aspect and middle voice.

8.2   Middle voice functions of *-ku*

Middle voice characteristically presents a situation in which the subject (or his or her interests) are affected in some way by the action of the verb (Lyons 1969:373). Typical middle constructions reduce transitivity by merging the semantic agent and patient roles into a single argument (Mithun 2006:223). Just as semantic roles are less differentiated, subevents in the situation are also less differentiated (Kemmer 1993:208). As a result, observes Kemmer, middle voice can be situated as a semantic category "intermediate in transitivity between one-participant and two-participant events" (1993:3). Hopper and Thompson make a similar point with respect to reflexives (1980:277).[131]

---

meaning. Instances of *-ku* literally expressing a reflexive are possible but rare, and are not in fact attested among the 143 exemplars of *-ku* in the coded section of the SCQ corpus. The term "mediopassive" (both middle voice and passive voice) would be misleading in SCQ because *-ku* does not express passive voice. Instead, passive is expressed by the suffix *-ka:*.

[131] Kemmer subsumes the reduced distinguishability of participants and events under a single umbrella referred to as the "relative elaboration of events," that is, "the degree to which the facets in a particular situation, i.e., participants and conceivable component subevents in the situation, are distinguished" (1993:208). In other words, middles are characterized by low elaboration of both participants and events.

The derivational suffix *-ku* (lowered allomorph *-ka*) serves a wide range of semantic functions pertaining to reflexive and middle voice. These two conceptual domains are expressed as a single formal category in SCQ. Any lexical verb root can appear with or without this extremely productive, high frequency suffix.[132]

Reflexives typically mark situations in which a single referent fills the semantic roles of both the agent and the patient, with a clear conceptual distinction maintained between these two roles (Kemmer 1993:94). As in other nominative-accusative systems, in SCQ the agent of a reflexive situation corresponds to the subject, and the patient to the coreferential direct object, e.g., 'don't cut yourself' in (222) and 'I burned myself' in (223). This direct reflexive sense of *-ku* continues to be well understood in SCQ, but the contexts for its use are relatively rare.[133]

(222)   *shuma:-lla   roqu-__ku__-ski-nki-man-ta:*
        beautiful-DLM   cut-__MID__-PFV-2-COND-WARN
        'Be careful, don't __cut yourself__.' (*roqu-nki* 'you cut it')

(223)   *diyablu-pa   wacha-shqa-n,   rupa-__ku__-ski-:*
        devil-GEN   give.birth-NMLZ.R-3   burn-__MID__-PFV-1
        'Son of the devil, I __burned myself__.' (*rupa-:* 'I burn it')

Direct reflexive meaning has spread to contexts in which the action has a less direct effect on the coreferential participants. Following Kemmer (1993:74-7), I refer to the former as direct reflexives, and the latter as indirect reflexives. In indirect reflexive situations, a single referent fills the semantic roles of both the agent and the recipient/beneficiary or patient, interpreted by context. This includes the grooming verbs, as illustrated in (224) with the verbs *awi-* 'rinse' and *naqtsa-* 'comb'.

---

[132] The existence of *miku-* 'eat', etymologically consisting of the root *mi-* and the middle suffix *-ku*, might seem a counterexample, since the simple root *mi-* does not occur in SCQ. However, in this example lexicalization has taken place diachronically, so that synchronically in SCQ the root 'eat' is *miku-* and the corresponding middle is *miku-ku-* 'eat for oneself'. Note, however, that *miku-* does still retain one feature of its historical origin, namely the fact that the final *u* is lowered to *a* when followed by a "trigger" suffix, just as happens to the middle suffix *ku*, e.g., *mika-ma-nki-tsu* 'don't eat me'.

[133] A verb marked with *-ku*, such as *rupa-ku-ski-:*, can be interpreted as a reflexive 'I burned myself' or as a middle 'I burned it for myself'. The reflexive pronoun form *kiki* (obligatorily inflected for person and case) can appear optionally as the direct object to further specify that the intended meaning is reflexive, e.g., *kiki-:-ta rupa-ku-ski-:* 'I burned *myself* (not 'I burned it for myself'). Note that *kiki* places special emphasis on the referent.

(224) *hamara-yka-mu-y   silla-:-cho:.   awi-**ka**-ra-mu-sha:*
rest-PFV.O-FAR-IMP2   chair-1-LOC   rinse-**MID**-PUNC-FAR-1FUT

*naqtsa-**ka**-ra-mu-sha:-ra:*
comb-**MID**-PUNC-FAR-1FUT-YET

'Rest here in my chair. I will **wash myself** and **comb myself** over there and return quickly.' (*awi-sha:* 'I will wash it', *naqtsa-sha:* 'I will comb it')

As more and more verb stems were derived with *-ku*, the original direct and indirect reflexive meanings were applied to more abstract contexts in which the subject is more indirectly affected by the action. Currently, middle voice *-ku* subsumes the reflexive category from which it developed. A wide variety of middle voice situation types marked by *-ku* are illustrated in the remainder of this section. Most of these are identified by Kemmer (1993).[134]

Direct and indirect reflexive situations, such as those illustrated in (222)-(224), are distinguished from most middles in SCQ in that the entity which is coreferential with the semantic agent is never the semantic patient but invariably fills another semantic role, such as (self)-beneficiary. This self-benefactive sense is the most prevalent middle voice function of *-ku* in SCQ. For example, in (225) the 'other devil' (agent) was helping himself to 'the figs' (patient), formally expressed as a direct object. Similarly, in (226) the speaker (agent) is waiting for a bus (patient) for himself.

(225) *hukaq   diyablu-qa   yarku-rku-r   altu-chu   miku-**ku**-na: ari*
other   devil-TOP   climb-PFV.M-SS   high-LOC   eat-**MID**-PST.N   yes

i:gus-ta-qa   kushi-sh
fig-OBJ-TOP   be.happy-PTCP

'The other devil climbing above **was** happily **eating** (helping himself to) the figs.'

(226) *tsa   karrete:ra-man   cha-rpu-r   ka:rru-ta   shuya-**ku**-ru-:*
that   road-ALL   arrive-COMPL-SS   vehicle-OBJ   wait-**MID**-PST.R-1

'Then arriving down to the road, I **waited** for a bus (for myself).'

Each lexical verb root in examples (222)-(226) specifies a canonical two-participant event. Middle *-ku* also appears with one-participant verb roots. The following three middle situations involve the body: posture (non-translational motion) in (227), change of location (translational motion) in (228), and change of state in (229).

---

[134] The related categories of passive and reciprocal are marked in SCQ by the suffixes *-ka:* and *-naku*, respectively. Those are beyond the scope of the present discussion of aspect and middle voice.

(227) *waray-nin-qa   sha:ri-**ka**-ra-mu-n*
       tomorrow-3-TOP   stand.up-**MID**-PUNC-FAR-3
       'The next day she **gets herself up**.' (*sha:ri-ra-mu-n* 'she stands up')

(228) *kuti-**ku**-ya:-sha: ke: Huaraz-pita pani-:   Rita-wan   Erwin-wan-pis*
       return-**MID**-PL.V-FUT1   this Huaraz-ABL sister-1 Rita-COM   Erwin-COM-EVEN
       'We **ourselves will return** home from here in Huaraz with my sister Rita and also
       with Erwin.' (*kuti-ya:-sha:* 'we will return')

(229) *tsay-chu-chir achikay wanu-**ku**-ra-n*
       that-LOC-APP   witch   die-**MID**-PST-3
       'The witch **died** there.'

Middle *-ku* also appears with verbs of emotion and cognition. For example, in (230) *-ku*
conveys the subject's internal state of fear, and in (231) *-ku* reports personal knowledge
available to the subject. See also *llaki-ku-n* 'feel sad' above in (70).

(230) *tsay wa:ray-pa ima-ta-ta: mantsa-**ku**-n-man-pis*
       that   dawn-GEN   what-OBJ-WARN   fear-**MID**-3-COND-EVEN
       'That early no one would **feel fear** about that.'

(231) *pay-kuna musya-**ku**-n   ima-no: ka-ku-na-n-pa: ka-q-ta-pis*
       s/he-PL.N know-**MID**-3 what-SIM be-MID-NMLZ.I-3-PURP be-AG-OBJ-EVEN
       'They **themselves know** how they should behave (but they don't behave
       accordingly).'

In some contexts the situation marked by middle *-ku* has an even more indirect effect on the
subject or the subject's interests. For example, in (232) 'our marriage certificate' is the
inanimate subject of the verb 'remained'. In this case, *-ku* appears to evoke the semantic role of
possessor, which is formally marked as first person in the subject 'our marriage certificate'. The
semantic connection linking the subject with a possessor would involve metonymy, that is, *-ku*
presents the possessor and the possessed item as coreferential based on their association in a
broad sense.

(232) *sigu:ru parti:da.de.matrimoniyu-: ke:da-**ku**-ra-n   ke: Huari-cho:*
       surely   marriage.certificate-1   remain-**MID**-PST-3 this Huari-LOC
       'Surely our marriage certificate **remained permanently** (for us) here in Huari.'

In other contexts the subject of a verb derived with *-ku* is not coreferential with another
participant at all. For example, middle meaning extends to spontaneous events which have an
inanimate patient as the subject and no implied agent, as in (233). Note that 'sun' may be
animate.

(233) *rupay-na-m   tsaka:-__ku__-ski-rqa-n*
     sun-NOW-DIR be.dark-__MID__-PFV-PST-3
     'Now the sun __itself became dark__.'

8.3 Self-benefactive middle *-ku*

As illustrated above in (224)-(226), middle voice *-ku* can report an action performed for one's own personal benefit. Self-benefactive is the most frequent middle voice function of *-ku* in SCQ.[135]

The self-benefactive use of *-ku* contrasts with the benefactive suffix *-pa:*, which indicates a beneficiary other than self. The following two examples are from a short stretch of narrative discourse. In (234) the speaker uses 'self-benefactive' *-ku* to denote that the boy is whistling to/for himself. Later in the story, the boy signals for his dog using 'other-benefactive' *-pa:* in (235). The unmarked form *silba-yka-n* 'he is whistling' does not evoke a beneficiary.

(234) *kay-chu:-na   wamra   silba-__ku__-yka-n   hirka-man   aywa-yku-r*
     this-LOC-NOW child   whistle-__MID__-CONT-3 mountain-ALL go-PFV.O-SS
     'Here now the child is __whistling to/for himself__ going along to the mountain.'

(235) *allqu-n-ta silba-__pa__-yka-n   tsay   tronku hana-n-man*
     dog-3-OBJ whistle-__BEN__-CONT-3 that   log   over-3-ALL

     aywa-ya:-na-n-pa:
     go-PL.V-MNLZ.I-3-PURP

     'He's __whistling for his dog__ in order to go on top of that log.'

Middle *-ku* does not function as an applicative in its self-benefactive use, that is, *-ku* does not promote the oblique to a core argument of the verb, as in (234) and (236). In contrast, benefactive *-pa:* does function (rarely) as an applicative, e.g., *-pa:* promotes 'dog' to direct object status in (235).[136]

---

[135] The self-benefactive function of *-ku* has been observed for other Central Quechuan varieties, such as Llamellín (Snow and Stark 1971:186), Huaraz (Swisshelm 1974:478), Huaylas (Parker 1976:117), Tarma (Adelaar 1977:133), and Huallaga (Weber 1989:167). Weber also notes the contrast between self-benefactive *-ku* and benefactive *-pa:* in Huallaga Quechua.

[136] In most instances, *-pa:* does not pull a beneficiary into the clause, whether as an oblique or a core constituent. For example, in (247) the verb *parla-pa:-ya:-shu-ru-yki* means 'they told you (for your benefit)', whereas *parla-ya:-shu-ru-yki* (without benefactive *-pa:*) simply means 'they told you'. Similar examples include (90), (154), (192), (209), (214), and (248). Occasionally, an explicit beneficiary appears as an oblique, e.g., 'eye' and 'witch' in (237). Examples in which

(236) *mana   ima-ta-si   maya-r-nin   ishpa-__ku__-q   aywa-ku-na:*
     no   what-OBJ-EVEN   aware-SS-3   urinate-__MID__-PRMT   go-MID-PST.N

     huk   ..eski:na-pa   tuma-ri-r
     one   corner-GEN   turn-PUNC-SS

     'Not being aware of anything, he was going around the corner to **relieve himself**.'

(237) *añas-pis   ñawi-n-man-shi   ishpa-__pa__-ski-n   achikay-man*
     skunk-EVEN   eye-3-ALL-PRT   urinate-__BEN__-PFV-3   witch-ALL

     'Also, the skunk **sprayed the witch in the eyes**.'

While middle *-ku* (self-benefactive) can appear with any lexical verb root, benefactive *-pa:* appears to be restricted to dynamic verbs. Other examples of the contrast between stems ending with *-ku* and stems ending with *-pa:* are listed in (238).

(238)

SCQ VERB ROOT		SELF-BENEFACTIVE *-ku*		OTHER BENEFACTIVE *-pa:*	
rura-	'do'	*rura-ku-*	'do for self'	*rura-pa:-*	'do for other'
suwa-	'steal'	*suwa-ku-*	'steal for own gain'	*suwa-pa:-*	'steal at other's expense'
asi-	'laugh'	*asi-ku-*	'laugh with'	*asi-pa:-*	'laugh at other'
kuya-	'love'	*kuya-ku-*	'feel love'	*kuya-pa:-*	'feel/act with compassion'
hati-	'put inside'	*hati-ku-*	'dress self'	*hati-pa:-*	'dress other'
qati-	'follow'	*qati-ku-*	'herd'	*qati-pa:-*	'chase'
qaya-	'shout'	*qaya-ku-*	'call'	*qaya-pa:-*	'yell at'
qeshpi-	'escape'	*qeshpi-ku-*	'escape by self'	*qeshpi-pa:-*	'escape by other'
tapu-	'ask'	*tapu-ku-*	'ask for advice'	*tapu-pa:-*	'interrogate'

8.4 Modal senses of *-ku*

We have seen that *-ku* expresses a class of closely related meanings pertaining to reflexive and middle voice. The indirect reflexive and self-benefactive uses of middle *-ku* give rise to modal readings in which the subject is portrayed as willfully engaged in the situation. This volitional sense characterizes a majority of *-ku* exemplars in the SCQ database; most verbs in which *-ku* does not appear lack this sense.[137]

While middle voice reduces transitivity by merging semantic roles into a single participant, modality highlights the relationship between the participant and the situation itself. The modal

---

the beneficiary is promoted to the clause core, such as 'dog' in (235), are exceedingly rare in the SCQ corpus. As such, benefactive *-pa:* could be considered a nascent applicative.

[137] Cerrón-Palomino defines *-ku* in Huanca Quechua (referred to as pseudo-reflexive) as an action "realized with the emotional and active participation of the actor" (1976:188, my translation). Active participation (though not affect) aligns with the notions of volition and engagement presented here as a modal interpretation of middle voice *-ku* in SCQ.

interpretation of volition may be most clearly visualized in the difference between direct (agent=patient) and indirect (agent=beneficiary) reflexive situations, e.g., 'I have cut myself' (accidental) versus 'I have washed myself' (intentional). The less direct volitional sense has spread to a wide variety of contexts that involve the willful participation of the subject. Many of these contexts, such as those illustrated above in (224)-(228), are typical of middle marking in many languages. The following examples of -*ku* in §8.4.1, and the reduplicated form -*kuku* in §8.4.2, were selected to illustrate less typical middle situation types in which modal senses appear to play a larger role.[138]

8.4.1   Volition and engagement reported by -*ku*

In (239) -*ku* conveys that the subject (the semantic agent) specially prepared holiday foods (the semantic patient) in anticipation of festive activities. The patient is formally expressed as the direct object 'spiced guinea pig and meat soup'. If there had been no -*ku* (*yanu-ya-ra-:*), this would imply that they prepared food in the usual everyday fashion. The modal sense of intention is echoed by the use of middle -*ku* in the direct quote *imbita-ku-na-pa:* 'so we can invite someone over'.

(239) *haka   pikanti-ta   aytsa   so:pa-ta-m   yanu-**ku**-ya-ra-:*
      guinea.pig   spiced-OBJ   meat   soup-OBJ-DIR   cook-**MID**-PL.V-PST-1

      *"pi-lla-ta-pis   imbita-**ku**-na-pa:"*   *ni-r-mi*
      who-DLM-OBJ-EVEN   invite-**MID**-NMLZ.I1ᵣ-PURP   say-SS-DIR

      'We **cooked** spiced guinea pig and meat soup, saying "So we can **invite** someone over".' (*yanu-ya:-ra-:* 'we cooked it')

As in previous self-benefactive examples, middle -*ku* in the verb *yanu-ku-ya-ra-:* evokes a beneficiary that is coreferential with the semantic agent. (239) could be more freely translated as 'we specially prepared these foods for the pleasure of serving our guests'.

---

[138] David Weber (p.c.) observes that some instances of -*ku* in this section appear to be antipassives, that is, the object role is not identified in a single argument with the subject, but is simply "de-emphasized." That may be a valid interpretation for some of these examples. Within the SCQ corpus, however, in a large number of verbs with the productive -*ku* suffix, P is expressed by an overt NP marked with -*ta* 'object'. Also, in many verbs with -*ku*, P is overtly marked by -*ma:* '1ˢᵗ object' or -*shu* '2ⁿᵈ object' (because '3ʳᵈ object' is marked by -*Ø*, those instances are often ambiguous). Following Payne (1997:219), -*ku* would not be antipassive in any of those examples. "1 The P argument is omitted or appears in an oblique case, often the INSTRUMENTAL CASE. 2 The verb or verb phrase contains some overt marker of intransitivity (e.g., it may ... inflect like an intransitive verb)." In addition, it is very common in SCQ for a canonical transitive verb to appear without an overt NP object. Most such verbs do not have the suffix -*ku*.

In (240) the speaker uses *-ku* to emphasize that the subject (agent) should meet with his child (patient), actively engaging her in joint activities instead of simply leaving her on her own in the pasture every day. The verb form *qori-nki-man* (without *-ku*) would simply communicate that the father should get his child.

(240) *peru wamra-yki-ta-qa   qori-**ku**-nki-man*
      but   child-2-OBJ-TOP   gather-**MID**-2-COND
      'But **you yourself** should **meet with** your child.' (*qori-nki-man* 'you
      should get her')

The active engagement sense is also seen in (241), but with a twist. Middle *-ku* appears in a series of directives which express a deontic modality. Thus, the subject (agent) is engaged in the activities, but the speaker himself is cast as the beneficiary. In other words, each semantic role in (241) has a different referent, whereas in (239) and (240) the agent and beneficiary are coreferential. We might think of this use of middle *-ku* as an indirect self-benefactive, that is, '*I tell you to get everything ready for me*'.[139]

(241) *kuti-mu-na-:-pa: tsay o:ra-qa   lista-**ku**-y.   yana u:sha-ta*
      return-FAR-NMLZ.I-1-PURP that hour-TOP   prepare-**MID**-IMP2   black sheep-OBJ

      *pishta-nki,   aswa-**ku**-nki,   masa-**ku**-nki   awi-**ku**-nki*
      slaughter-2   make.beer-**MID**-FUT2   make.dough-**MID**-FUT2   rinse-**MID**-FUT2

      'By the time I return, **get** everything **ready** (for me). Slaughter the black sheep, **make**
      beer, **make** fresh bread, and **wash it all up**.'

8.4.2 Heightened volition and engagement reported by reduplicated *-kuku*

Occasionally, the reduplicated form *-kuku* appears in place of *-ku*. In keeping with the function of reduplications in general, *-kuku* presents a contrast with the non-reduplicated form. Here, *-kuku* intensifies the modal sense from "volition" to "heightened volition" in the action of the verb.[140]

For example, in (242) a father uses *-kuku* when admonishing his daughter to 'be especially on guard' in the dangerous situations she will face in the city. By contrast, a single instance of *-ku* as *kwi:da-ku-nki* would indicate the standard middle meaning 'look after yourself'.

---

[139] In (241) the final verb *awi-ku-nki* has the nonreflexive meaning 'wash it up' (not 'wash yourself up'), even though the stem combination *awi-ku-* is identical in form to the indirect reflexive equivalent in (224). The specific interpretation of *-ku* in a given instance can be greatly influenced by the pragmatic context.

[140] The reduplicated form *-kuku* bears some resemblance in form and meaning to the suffix *-ka:ku* 'totally, customarily' presented above in §7.2.2. *-ka:ku* was formed from the combination of passive *-ka:* (as the final element in lexicalized verb roots) plus middle *-ku*.

(242) *rate:ru-pis   ime:ka-pis   tse:-cho:-qa   peligru-m,*
thief-EVEN   all.kinds-EVEN   that-LOC-TOP   danger-DIR

i ...   ka:lli-pa   yarqu-r-qa   kwi:da-__kuku__-nki
and   street-GEN   leave-SS-TOP   look.after-__MID.R__-FUT2

'All kinds of dangerous thieves are there, and so when you go out on the street, **be especially on guard** (maintain constant vigilance).' (*kwi:da-nki* 'look after it')

In (243) the subject participants are so engaged (absorbed) in concurrent shouted prayers that they do not notice the leader standing in front of them (the speaker of the utterance). The heightened sense of volition in this activity is marked by the reduplicated form *-kuku*. The more usual form *maña-ku-ya-n* (with a single instance of *-ku*) simply means 'they pray'.

(243) *llapa-n-kuna   maña-__kuku__-ya-n   qaya-ra-ypa   ima-ta-pis,*
all-3-PL.N   pray-__MID.R__-PL.V-3   shout-DUR-ADV   what-OBJ-EVEN

dirhi-q-kaq-pa-ta-qa   henti   maya-ya-n-tsu
lead-AG-DEF-GEN-OBJ-TOP   no.one   be.alert-PL.V-3-NEG

'Everyone **prays** by shouting things. No one pays attention to the leader.'

(*maña-ya-n* 'they lend it')

Verb stems with the reduplicated form *-kuku* are infrequent in the SCQ corpus. In the first five stems in (244), this suffix productively expresses a heightened sense of volition and engagement. The final two stems only appear in derived nominalized forms that refer to items exclusively dedicated to a particular activity, e.g., *yacha-kuku-ya:-na-n wayi* 'building dedicated to learning', or *arma-kuku-na* 'place dedicated to washing'.

(244)

SCQ VERB ROOT		MIDDLE VOICE *-ku*		REDUPLICATED FORM *-kuku*	
kwi:da-	'look after'	*kwi:da-ku-*	'look after self'	*kwi:da-kuku-*	'maintain vigilance'
maña-	'lend'	*maña-ku-*	'pray, ask for'	*maña-kuku-*	'absorbed in prayer'
patsa:-	'have room'	*patsa:-ku-*	'stay in room'	*patsa:-kuku-*	'go to bed'
tapu-	'ask'	*tapu-ku-*	'ask for advice'	*tapu-kuku-*	'query for details'
willa-	'tell'	*willa-ku-*	'inform, explain'	*willa-kuku-*	'dedicated to inform'
yacha-	'know'	*yacha-ku-*	'learn'	*yacha-kuku-*	'dedicated to learning'
arma-	'bathe'	*arma-ku-*	'bathe self'	*arma-kuku-*	'dedicated to washing'

8.5   Aspectual senses of *-ku* in SCQ

So far in this chapter we have observed that middle voice *-ku* typically affects the argument structure of derived verb stems by reducing the differentiation of participants as arguments. In addition, as Kemmer observes, the merging of semantic roles (detransitivization) is accompanied by the reduced differentiation of events (1993:208). These two characteristics of middle voice—reducing the distinguishability of participants and events—can have the corresponding effect of reducing telicity, especially in canonical two-participant situations. The examples presented in the next two sections show that SCQ speakers exploit the inference of low telicity by specifically using middle *-ku* in the context of ongoing and customary activities, leading to imperfective (durative and habitual) readings.

8.5.1 Habitual readings of *-ku* with dynamic verbs

The incipient habitual meaning of middle *-ku* can be seen in the following nominalized forms that appear with and without *-ku*. Most exemplars of the verb roots *yachatsi-* 'teach', *ka:su-* 'obey', and *kawa-* 'live' (more than 90%) do not appear with *-ku*. Those that do appear with *-ku* carry the additional sense of a characteristic or habitual activity, usually translated as 'customary' or 'always'.[141]

(245) SOME SCQ MIDDLE FORMS WITH INCIPIENT HABITUAL (AND DURATIVE) MEANING

*yachatsi-**ku**-q*	'one who <u>customarily</u> teaches'	*yachatsi-q*	'one who teaches'
*ka:su-**ku**-q*	'one who <u>customarily</u> obeys'	*ka:su-q*	'one who obeys'
*kawa-**ku**-q*	'one who participates in the <u>customary</u> activities of life'	*kawa-q*	'one who is alive'

In addition, the combination of middle *-ku* with the nominalizer *-q* portrays a participant as a "specialist," that is, someone with special knowledge, ability, or experience for whom the activity has become routine. For example, in the first line of (245) the form *yachatsi-ku-q* characterizes a professional teacher. Similarly, the subjects in both (239) and (241) are indirectly depicted as specialists in holiday food preparation, even without the nominalizer *-q*.[142]

The three middle stem forms in (245) are illustrated below from the database of naturally-occurring SCQ speech. In each example, middle *-ku* characterizes a habituated behavior of the subject. The verb *yacha-tsi-ku-n* in (246) indicates that the professor 'always teaches' in the specified manner ('patiently').

(246) *profesor-ni:-pis   mana   aha-na-yllapa-m   yacha-tsi-**ku**-n*
     professor-1-EVEN no   be.impatient-DES-ADV-DIR know-CAUS-**MID**-3
     'My professor **always teaches** without being the least bit impatient.'

In keeping with the incipient habitual sense of *-ku*, the subject in (247) is predisposed to ignore any appeal to enroll his child in school. The negated statement indicates that he 'always disregarded' those requests.

---

[141] Adelaar (2006:125) provides a similar illustration of *-ku* in Tarma Quechua: *yanaba(:)-* 'to help' versus *yanaba:-ku-* 'to always help, to be inclined to help'.

[142] An interesting parallel in Koyukon Athabaskan is that imperfective (durative) forms can refer to "activities performed as a general means of employment" (Axelrod 1993:62).

(247) *atska   kuti-na-m   parla-pa:-ya:-shu-ru-yki*
     many   time-NOW-DIR   speak-BEN-PL.V-2OBJ-PST.R-2$_\mathrm{P}$

     eskue:la-man   chura-na-yki-pa:,   peru qam mana-m ka:su-__ku__-nki-tsu
     school-ALL   put-NMLZ.I-2-PURP   but you no-DIR   obey-**MID**-2-NEG

     'Many times they told you to put her in school. But you **always disregarded them**.'

Finally, the context in (248) involves the routine of everyday life activities.

(248) *tsa   deha-pa-yku-pti-n   kushi-sh   kawa-__ku__-ya:-na: ami:gu-n-wan*
     then leave-BEN-PFV.O-DS-3 be.happy-PTCP live-**MID**-PL.V-PST.N friend-3-COM

     'Then after (the ghost) left, they **lived** (**customary** life activities) happily, he with his friend.'

To sum up, middle voice typically reduces the distinguishability of participants and events. In examples (245)-(248), however, there is little evidence for the merging of participant arguments. Instead, events are simply presented as customary activities. In other words, in the context of generalized activities, *-ku* appears to function less in the realm of middle voice than of aspect, specifically, as an incipient habitual aspect marker.

8.5.2   Durative and habitual readings of *-ku* with the copula *ka-*

Middle *-ku* often combines with the copula *ka-*. The stem combination *ka-ku-* reports an attribute or habituated activity that characterizes the subject over an extended period of time. The characteristic itself is not specified by the copula stem *ka-ku-*, but by some other element within the larger grammatical construction. For example, in (249) the *ka-ku-* construction characterizes the subject as promiscuous, a behavior specified by the oblique *huk-wan huk-wan* 'with one man after another'.

(249) *tsay-cho:-qa   tsa   allaw warmi-qa huk-wan huk-wan __ka-ku__-na:*
     that-LOC-TOP   then pity   woman-TOP one-COM   one-COM   **be-MID**-PST.N

     'In that place then, the shameful woman **customarily slept** with one man after another.'

The customary behavior can be minimally specified with a generic adverb, such as the derived form *ima-no:* 'how' in (250).

(250) *pay-kuna musya-ku-n ima-no: __ka-ku__-na-n-pa: ka-q-ta-pis*
     s/he-PL.N know-MID-3 what-SIM **be-MID**-NMLZ.I-3-PURP be-AG-OBJ-EVEN

     'They themselves know how they should **behave**.'

In (251) the customary behavior of eating children is interpreted as habitual during the relevant time frame, that is, until the giant worm returned to normal size.

(251) *ima-no: kuru-ra: tsay **ka-ku**-ra-n-si*
     what-SIM worm-YET   that   **be-MID**-PST-3-EVEN
     'How horrible that worm **behaved** (during the time it was a giant and ate one child every day)!'

In (249)-(251), the *ka-ku-* construction portrays *customary activities* of the subject as outside the usual norms, a negative evaluation that involves a subjective conceptualization by the speaker and interlocutors. Alternatively, the stem combination *ka-ku-* can portray an *attribute* that is outside of normal expectations. For example, a child was offered a brand new hat, but she rejects the offer in (252) by saying *ka-ka-pa-ma-n-mi* 'my hat suits me' (*-ku* is lowered to *-ka* by *-ma:*). *ka-pa-ma-n-mi* (without *-ku*) simply means 'the hat belongs to me'. (See (232) for another *ku*-verb in which the subject is a possessed item.)[143]

(252) *noqa-pa-qa   tsuku-:   ka-**ka**-pa-ma-n-mi*
     I-GEN-TOP   hat-1   be-**MID**-BEN-1OBJ-3-DIR
     'My hat **suits me** (I am accustomed to my hat).'

The use of the *ka-ku-* construction in (253) also characterizes an attribute of the subject participants, specified as 'happily occupied'; their activities remain implied. As in the previous examples (249)-(252), *ka-ku-* in (253) implies a negative (sarcastic) evaluation, namely, that they should have been taking care of the donkey during the relevant time period (the fiesta activities).

(253) *tsay-chu pas   kushi-sh   **ka-ku**-ya-sha-:-yaq   oqra-ka-ski-na:*
     that-LOC   very   be.happy-PTCP   **be-MID**-PL.V-NMLZ.R-1-LIM   lose-PASS-PFV-PST.N
     'During the time that we were happily **occupied** there (at the fiesta), it got lost (wandered off).'

In summary, the *ka-ku-* construction involves the stem combination of copula *ka-* plus middle *-ku*. This construction reports an attribute or habituated activity, portrayed as outside of normal expectations, that characterizes the subject throughout the relevant time period. The situations in (249)-(251) involve recurrence over time, resulting in a habitual reading. Those in (252) and (253) do not necessarily involve recurrence, yielding a durative reading. Unlike

---

[143] The suffix *-pa* 'BEN' in (252) is the lowered form of benefactive *-pu*. The difference between the two benefactives *-pu* and *-pa:* in SCQ is similar to the difference Weber describes for Huallaga, viz., "speakers readily recognize *-pU* 'benefactive' but rarely use it. It seems to be nearly synonymous with *-pa:* 'benefactive' " (1989:158). Compare *wata-pu-ya:-na-n-pa:* 'tie.up-BEN-PL.V-NMLZ.I-3-PURP' above in (157); see also note 136 which describes *-pa:* as a nascent applicative.

typical middle voice constructions, *ka-ku-* does not affect semantic roles or transitivity, shifting prominence instead to aspectual (imperfective) functions of the situation.

8.6 Progressive *-ku* and reflexive/middle *-ri* in Northern Quechua

In the previous section we examined a variety of contexts in SCQ connected speech in which middle voice *-ku* is developing durative and habitual meanings. While middle *-ku* functions as an incipient habitual marker in SCQ, the primary grammatical meaning of the cognate forms in Northern Quechuan languages is progressive aspect (an imperfective complement to habitual; see Map A.4 in Appendix A). These forms include *-ku* in Inga (Levinsohn 1976:117), *-hu* in Imbabura (Cole 1982:150), and *-hu/-u* in Ecuadorian Pastaza (Nuckolls 1996:49). Middle *-ku* in SCQ occurs in the derivational slot D2 close to the verb root. The Northern Quechua forms occur adjacent to the inflectional TAM slot (comparable to slot I2 in SCQ), following the object marker (at least in all the examples I have seen).[144]

(254) INGA QUECHUA
 *suya-**ku**-yki*
 await-**PROG**-1>2
 'I am waiting for you.'

(255) IMBABURA QUECHUA
 *shamu-**hu**-ni*
 come-**PROG**-1
 'I am coming.'

(256) PASTAZA QUECHUA
 *wañu-**u**-ra-shi*
 die-**PROG**-PST-RPT
 'He was dying.'

The rise of imperfective meanings (habitual and progressive) from middle voice is not a common development from a cross-linguistic perspective, though it is not without precedent. In Norwegian, for example, the fossilized middle marker *-s* "has undergone a reinterpretation in function, or reanalysis, to a habitual middle passive marker" (Kemmer 1993:191). Presumably,

---

[144] In Inga, the singular form for progressive (continuous) is *-ku*, and the plural form is *-naku* Levinsohn (1976:97). (In SCQ *-naku* is a reciprocal marker.) While some examples of *-ku* and *-naku* in Inga express progressive-continuous meaning, others appear to express habitual (e.g., *chaya-mu-naku-rka-si* 'they used to come') and iterative meanings (e.g., *miti-kú kuti* 'they ran away again') (ibid.:117). These and other examples suggest that *-ku* and *-naku* in Inga have become more general imperfective markers that include both progressive and habitual meanings.

-ku is taking on habitual meaning in SCQ (and not progressive as in Northern Quechua), at least in part, because progressive-continuous semantic space is already staked out by *-yka:* in the existing SCQ aspectual system (see §3.1.2 and Figure 4.6 in §4.3). In contrast, no prior progressive marker is attested in Northern Quechuan languages, and *-ku* (or *-hu/-u*) is the only progressive suffix in those languages.

The shift in the grammatical meaning of *-ku* from reflexive/middle voice to progressive aspect in Northern Quechua may have precipitated the rise of a new reflexive/middle marker *-ri*. This reflexive/middle *-ri* suffix in Northern Quechua is cognate with punctual *-ri* in SCQ (cf. §2.1.5) and other Central and Southern Quechuan languages (see Map A.3 in Appendix A). For example, Cole characterizes *-ri* in Imbabura (referred to as reflexive and reciprocal) as "semantically regular and productive" (1982:185). In other words, the former punctual meaning of *-ri* is no longer available to Imbabura speakers.

> (257) IMBABURA QUECHUA
> *riku-**ri**-nchi*
> see-**REFL**-1PLURAL
> 'We see ourselves/each other.' (*riku-nchi* 'we see it')

The shift in the meaning of *-ri* from punctual aspect to reflexive/middle voice may not be as fully developed in Pastaza. Nuckolls observes that *-ri* in Pastaza continues to function as a punctual in some situations, e.g., *riku-ri-* 'appear' versus *riku-* 'see'. At the same time, "the reflexivizing function of *-ri* is one of its most productive" (1996:44-7). Contrasting pairs include *tiya-ri-* 'sit down' versus *tiya-* 'settle, be in a place', *aspi-ri-* 'scratch own skin' versus *aspi-* 'scrape any surface', and *piña-ri-* 'be angry' versus *piña-* 'speak/act angrily toward someone else'. The modern contrast between reflexive/middle *-ri* (from *-ri* 'punctual') and progressive *-u* (from *-ku* 'middle') is seen in the following example from a longer stretch of Pastaza connected speech (1996:85).

> (258) PASTAZA QUECHUA
> *piña-**ri**-**u**-ni,*   ... *ñuka*
> be.angry-**REFL**-**PROG**-1   I
> 'I'm feeling angry.' (*piña-u-ni* 'I'm speaking/acting angrily toward someone else.')

The middle voice meaning of *-ri* appears to be more fully developed in Salasaca than in other Northern Quechuan varieties. Waskosky (1992:23) provides examples such as (259).

> (259) SALASACA QUECHUA
> *yacu-ga*   *chaqui-**ri**-shca-mi*
> water-TOP   dry-**REFL**-PERF-DIR
> 'The water **dried up**.'

The historical scenario for these voice and aspect shifts with *-ku* and *-ri* has to do with specific contexts of use in which speakers recognize a shared component of meaning which becomes salient in particular constructions, such as those illustrated for SCQ in §8.5. The current meanings of *-ku* (progressive) and *-ri* (middle voice), as attested in Northern Quechuan languages, would have resulted from strengthening of the inferences available within the bridging contexts summarized in the following three points:

In direct reflexive contexts, such as 'Don't cut yourself' in (222) and 'I burned myself' in (223), *-ku* can take on a punctual reading due to the sudden, accidental manner in which the action is realized.

Middle *-ku* in SCQ has a punctual reading in additional telic contexts. For example, *-ku* can report a "moment of change" with verbs such as *aywa-* 'go' in (260).

(260) *ni-ka-sha-n-ta-qa*   *qeshya-na-r-shi*   *aywa-**ku**-na:*
       say-CONT-NMLZ.R-3-OBJ-TOP be.sick-DES-SS-RPT go-**MID**-PST.N
       'Being disgusted by what they were saying, he **left**.'

Just as middle *-ku* can report attributes or behaviors that are outside of normal expectations (§8.5.2), punctual *-ri* can also report unexpectedness via the inference of sudden manner (see Chapter 7).

Because *-ku* and *-ri* receive nearly synonymous readings in telic contexts, speakers can specifically use *-ri* when thinking of direct reflexive actions in which the semantic agent and patient are coreferential. This reflexive reading of punctual *-ri* would have subsequently spread to indirect reflexive and middle voice functions formerly marked by *-ku*, especially as *-ku* was increasingly used in the context of ongoing/progressive contexts in Northern Quechua.[145]

As summarized in Figure 8.1, the primary meaning of *-ri* in SCQ is perfective (punctual) aspect (row 1, column 2), while *-ku* is centered in the unified reflexive/middle voice category (column 3). The direct reflexive meaning of *-ku* continues to be available, but such contexts are infrequent. The use of *-ku* in generalized activities yields imperfective (habitual) readings in which middle voice is less prominent (column 4).

By contrast, the meanings of the cognate suffixes in Northern Quechuan languages are shifted rightward in Figure 8.1, corresponding to shifts in their grammatical meanings. The primary meaning of *-ri* has become reflexive/middle voice (row 2, column 3), though the former punctual meaning persists in lexicalized stems (column 2). The primary meaning of *-ku* (or *-hu/-u*) has become imperfective (progressive) aspect, though the former middle voice meaning is evident in some lexicalized stems.

---

[145] As Maldonado (1999:390-4) observes, middle voice in Spanish can have a punctual reading in telic situations, e.g., *me subí*, 'I went up'. The analysis of middle *-ku* in SCQ as reporting activities and attributes that are outside of normal expectation (an epistemic modality) corresponds to Maldonado's observation that "normal" situations tend to resist the Spanish middle form *se* (and inflectional variants).

Figure 8.1 *Semantic shifts between aspect and middle voice markers in Quechua*

SEMANTIC DOMAIN		PERFECTIVE ASPECT	> REFLEXIVE >	MIDDLE VOICE	>	IMPERFECTIVE ASPECT
GRAM CATEGORY	**SCQ**	PUNCTUAL *-ri*	REFLEXIVE/MIDDLE { *-ku* ⟶			HABITUAL (*-ku*) }
	NORTHERN QUECHUA	PUNCTUAL { (*-ri*) ⟶	REFLEXIVE/MIDDLE *-ri* } { (*-ku*) ⟶			PROGRESSIVE *-ku-/hu/-u* }

These developments in Quechuan languages can be represented as a cline, as in the top row of Figure 8.1. An evolutionary pathway of grammaticization leads from punctual (perfective aspect) to reflexive/middle (voice), to habitual and progressive (imperfective aspect). Although not represented in Figure 8.1, modal interpretations of volition, engagement, total involvement, exclusive dedication, and unexpectedness also branch off at certain points along the path.

Finally, the evolution of imperfective meanings (habitual and progressive) from middle voice is easy to understand once the semantic connection linking aspect and transitivity has been identified. As discussed above, middles evoke two participant roles, but reduce transitivity in that a single argument fills both roles. This detransitivizing effect of middles is consistent with Hopper and Thompson's observation that high transitivity corresponds to perfective readings and low transitivity to imperfective readings (1980:277ff.).

8.7 Conclusions: Aspect and middle voice

In previous chapters we examined connections linking the semantic domains of aspect, tense, modality, and manner within the SCQ grammatical system. The concern in the present chapter was to focus on the less commonly investigated interface between aspect and middle voice, which proves to be another fruitful area for research in Quechuan languages.

The derivational suffix *-ku* was first situated within the sphere of reflexive and middle voice meanings in order to examine subsequently its more abstract aspectual and modal functions. *-ku* is extremely productive, displaying a wide range of core reflexive and middle voice functions expressed as a single formal category. Self-benefactive, the most prevalent middle function of *-ku*, contrasts with the "other-oriented" benefactive suffix *-pa:*.

Middle voice typically reduces transitivity by merging semantic roles. The reduced differentiation of participants and their activities can have the corresponding effect of reducing telicity. SCQ speakers exploit the inference of low telicity by specifically using middle *-ku* in the context of ongoing and customary activities, leading to durative and habitual readings. In some of these constructions, semantic roles are not affected and the aspectual functions are especially prominent.

While middle *-ku* functions as an incipient habitual marker in SCQ and other Central Quechuan languages, the primary grammatical meaning of the cognate forms in Northern Quechuan languages (*-ku/-hu/-u*) is progressive aspect (an imperfective complement to habitual). The grammaticization of *-ku* from middle voice to imperfective aspect in Northern varieties would have precipitated the recruitment of punctual *-ri* as a reflexive/middle marker. The direct reflexive sense of *-ku* is nearly synonymous with punctual *-ri* in telic contexts, providing initial motivation for this latter development.

Regular shifts in the meanings of *-ku* and *-ri* (summarized in Figure 8.1) illuminate an evolutionary pathway of grammaticization leading from punctual (perfective aspect) to reflexive/middle (voice), to habitual/progressive (imperfective aspect). In addition, various modal interpretations of *-ku* branch off at certain points along this path, including the notions of volition, engagement, exclusive dedication, and unexpectedness.

Finally, *-ku* has a propensity for introducing new contrasts through amalgamation with existing grammatical forms (referred to in §11.6 as the STEM–SUFFIX$_1$-SUFFIX$_2$ construction). For example, *-ku* is the final element in several aspect, voice, and manner suffixes, including perfective *-rku*, *-yku*, and *-ri:ku*, customary *-ka:ku*, distributive *-paku*, concerted effort *-chaku*, and reciprocal *-naku*. In each of these suffixes (and in the roots listed below), the final vowel /u/ is lowered to [a] when followed by one of a small class of "trigger" suffixes. The suffix *-ku* has also fused with many lexical verb roots, such as *hatiku-* 'get dressed', *maqaku-* 'thunder', *rantiku-* 'sell', *ta:ku-* 'reside', and *yachaku-* 'learn', enriching the lexicon with middle voice stems in which the final element *-ku* is no longer productive.

PART IV – THE EVOLUTION OF ASPECT IN QUECHUA

9   THE EVOLUTION OF PERFECTIVES

As presented in Chapter 2, perfective aspect is expressed in SCQ through a set of nine suffixes
with meanings that are more specific than general perfective. Markers within the derivational
component combine with inflectional items to more fully denote a wide variety of aspectual
distinctions. I now examine how this grammatical system has taken shape over time, focusing
especially on the trajectory leading from directional meaning, to derivational completive and
perfective aspect, and finally to inflectional past perfective/tense.

Directional markers (with meanings such as 'in', 'out', 'up', 'down') give rise to completive
aspectual meaning in language after language. The resulting markers generalize as derivational
perfectives in only a few languages (Bybee and Dahl 1989:86). SCQ offers the opportunity to
examine an additional line of development from derivational perfective to inflectional past
perfective/tense. This theoretically significant final stage of grammaticization is not documented
outside of the Quechua language family, to the best of my knowledge.[146]

Developments in the emerging grammatical system are demonstrated through an innovative
reconstruction methodology based on synchronic SCQ discourse data. In addition, a fine-grained
analysis of the relevant markers in neighboring Quechuan varieties reveals a patterned sequence
of very small semantic and structural changes along the path from derivational to inflectional
meaning.

The chapter begins by re-introducing the relevant set of former directional suffixes in §9.1.
While each suffix has fused with certain lexical verbs, all have grammaticized as perfective
markers to varying degrees. The rise of completive and perfective meanings is motivated in §9.2.
In §9.3 and §9.4 I examine in detail the unique final stage of development from derivational
perfective to inflectional past perfective and tense. §9.5 shows how past perfective *-ru* (a former
directional) converges with past perfective *-sha* (a former perfect). After situating these Quechua
findings within a cross-linguistic framework for the development of perfective and pasts in §9.6,
in §9.7 I propose a more articulated model of diachronic forces that move grammatical

---

[146] Languages in which derivational perfectives are attested include the Slavic family, Margi
(Chadic), Kusaeian and Mokilese (Oceanic), Latvian and Lithuanian (Baltic), Hungarian (Finno-
Ugric), and Georgian (Kartvelian), as noted by Bybee and Dahl (1989:86). Derivational
perfectives have not become inflectional past tense markers in any of these languages.

morphemes along these evolutionary pathways of grammaticization. I conclude in §9.8 by assessing the status of the emerging perfective system shaped by these forces.

9.1 Lexicalization of the directional suffixes

Most of the perfective suffixes introduced in Chapter 2 developed from a set of suffixes that derive verbs for situations involving directional motion. These include the suffixes **-rpu* 'down', **-rku* 'up', **-yku* 'in', and **-rqu* 'out'. The geographic distribution of Quechua directional suffixes is illustrated in Map 9.1.[147]

---

[147] Synchronic reflexes of the directional suffixes meaning 'in', 'out', 'up', and 'down' are not attested in Northern and North Peruvian Quechua. See, for example, Levinsohn (1976), Coombs et al. (1976), Quesada (1976), Taylor (1979), Cole (1982), and Nuckolls (1996). Suffixes derived from 'down' and 'up' are generally restricted to Central Quechua.

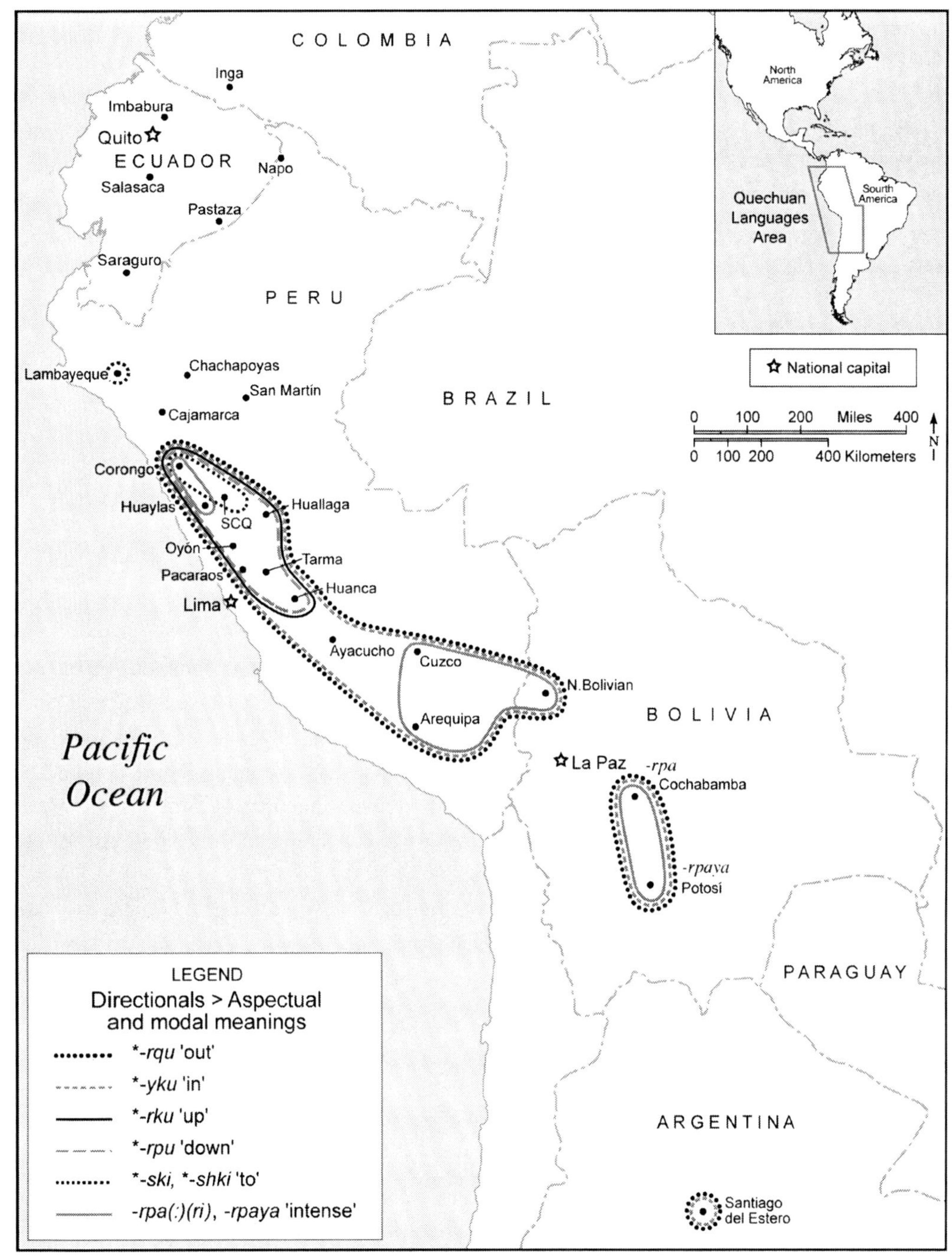

Map 9.1 DIRECTIONAL SUFFIXES > ASPECTUAL AND MODAL MEANINGS

The combination of a directional suffix with particular verb roots can form a close semantic bond, resulting in an indivisible (fused) lexical element in which the directional suffix is no longer productive. The lexicalized verb stems presented in Table 9.1 demonstrate the specific directional sense of each marker at a prior stage in its grammatical development. The proto directional suffixes in the left column would have contributed their specific meanings to a general morpheme of movement *ya* in the middle column, and to a general morpheme of force *qa* in the right column.[148] The pre-Proto forms *ya* and *qa* do not appear synchronically as independent lexical items.[149]

Table 9.1 *Some SCQ verb stems with lexicalized directional suffixes as the final element*

DIRECTIONAL SUFFIX		LEXICALIZED VERB STEM			
		ya 'movement'		*qa* 'force'	
-rpu	'down'	yarpu-	'lower'	qarpu-	'push down'
-rku	'up'	yarku-	'climb'	qarku-	'mound dirt'
-yku	'in'	yayku-	'enter'	qayku-	'enclose'
-rqu	'out'	yarqu-	'leave'	qarqu-	'expel'

The lexicalization of directional suffixes with particular verb roots is common throughout Central and Southern Quechuan varieties. At the same time, these suffixes have developed more abstract grammatical meanings within the domains of aspect, modality, and tense. As more and more verb stems were derived with these suffixes, and their meanings shifted from the conceptual domain of space to aspect, the original directional functions became less apparent. For example, the vertical senses of 'down' and 'up' are still available in some contexts, but the literal senses of 'in' and 'out' are no longer productive in SCQ.

As a case in point, cognate forms of *-rqu* 'out' appear twice in the verb *yarqu-ya-ru-:* 'we left' in (261). The first occurrence is fused in the verb root *yarqu-* 'leave, go out', and the second is the reduced form of past perfective *-ru* in the inflectional verbal slot I2 (see §2.2.1 and §5.1).

---

[148] The final high vowel in each lexicalized form in Table 9.1 lowers to [a] when followed by a "trigger" suffix, just as with the productive perfective suffixes, e.g., *yayku-n* 'he enters there', *yayka-mu-n* 'he enters here'.

[149] The former directional markers appear idiosyncratically in other lexicalized forms, as detailed in §4.5.3. For example, *-rku* appears in *warku-* 'hang up' and *-yku* in *wayku-* 'stir, stoke', but neither *warpu-* nor *warqu-* are attested in SCQ. Similarly, *-rqu* appears in *hurqu-* 'take out', but *hurpu-*, *hurku-*, and *huyku-* are not attested.

(261) SCQ
> *laso:chu   i   medya-na-m   Pamparomas-man   ya__rqu__-ya-__ru__-:*
> 8.o'clock and   half-NOW-DIR   Pamparomás-ALL   go.__out__-PL.V-__PST.R__-1
>
> *huk   kamyune:ta-wan*
> one   small.truck-COM
>
> 'Then at 8:30 __we left__ for Pamparomás on a small truck'.

The two forms derived from **-rqu* 'out' in (261) correspond to the initial and final stages along a path of grammatical development. §9.2 presents evidence from the set of former directional markers that motivates the reconstruction of intermediate stages along this evolutionary pathway of grammaticization.

9.2 Grammaticization of the directional suffixes

Hopper and Traugott (2003:160), among others, have articulated a reconstruction methodology that uses discourse data to demonstrate trajectories and motivations for the grammaticization of isolated forms in different languages. In the present study, I extend this methodology by examining the synchronic range of meanings of related forms in naturally-occurring SCQ speech to motivate the reconstruction of the perfective system as a whole.[150]

Chapter 2 reported the results of an investigation of former directional suffixes in SCQ discourse in which I determined the frequency, distribution, and range of meanings associated with each marker. The synchronic meanings of the individual markers range from directional, to completive and perfective aspect, to past tense. The distribution of the set of directional markers in SCQ discourse allows us to surmise the sequence of stages in the grammatical development of each marker. This pathway of grammaticization, as presented below, is supported by independent evidence, including dialect geography, discourse patterns in related Quechuan varieties, as well as similar developments observed in other languages.

As shown in Figure 9.1 (cf. Figure 2.2), each former directional suffix is used with a different subset of (overlapping) grammatical meanings that can be placed along a cline. The range of meanings of each suffix in the left column is mapped along a path of development in stages leading from directional meaning, to derivational completive and perfective aspect, and finally to inflectional past tense. While each directional suffix has traversed at least part of this trajectory, only past perfective *-ru* (from **-rqu* 'out') has made the "final leap" from derivational

---

[150] The Quechuan languages do not have a written history prior to the colonial era in the 16th to 19th centuries. There are relatively few documents from that era, and none represents an early version of SCQ or its immediate neighbors in north central Peru. Most documents have been associated with "Lengua General," an amalgam of Southern Quechuan varieties instituted by Spanish colonial authorities for religious and administrative purposes (Durston 2004:150-6); cf. note 6 in Chapter 1. Due to these and other limitations, the colonial documents play a relatively minor role in this chapter.

to inflectional meaning. The mechanisms for the rightward migration of *-ru* to the inflectional tense-aspect-mood slot I2 in the verbal template are presented in §9.3 and §9.7.

Figure 9.1 *Overlapping synchronic meanings of former directional suffixes in SCQ discourse*

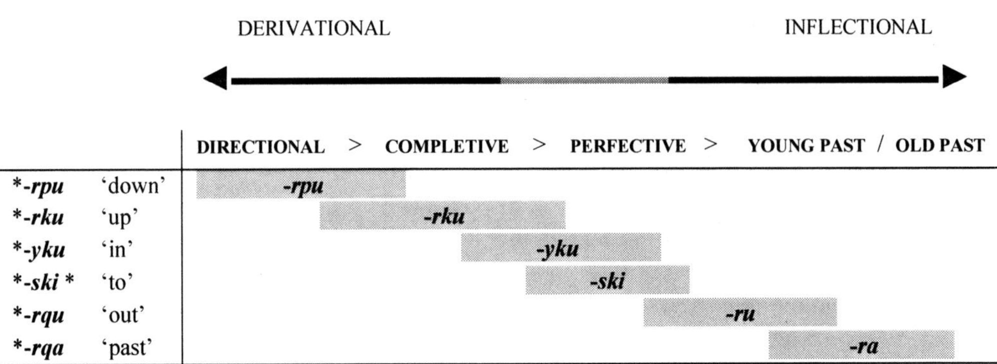

Derivational perfectives were portrayed in Chapter 2 as "highly generalized and elaborated completives" (Bybee et al. 1994:89). In keeping with this characterization, the Figure 9.1 suffixes *-rpu, -rku, -yku,* and *-ski* each expresses at least some element of derivational completive or perfective meaning. The lack of a clear criterial boundary between these categories is attributable to the minimal semantic distinctions that arise from the nature of derivational processes.[151]

---

* The derivational perfective suffix *-ski* is presented above in §2.1.4. This form occurs with similar aspectual meaning only in the neighboring Central Quechuan varieties of North Conchucos, Sihuas, and Corongo in Ancash Department, as well as Huamalíes and Dos de Mayo Provinces in Huánuco Department. These are exactly the dialects in which the derivational perfective suffix *-rqu* (or *-ru*) was reanalyzed as inflectional. As a result, there is no modern variety in which *-ski* and *-rqu* are both derivational perfectives. Evidence for *-ski* as a directional suffix meaning 'toward' is presented in Appendix E.

[151] The original directional suffixes are themselves grammatical morphemes. The *-CCV shape may result from a former deverbal suffix (*-r, *-y, or *-sh) fused to a CV particle (cf. §11.6 and Appendix D). At the same time, their meanings are more specific, more lexical, than the meanings associated with completive and perfective aspect and past tense. This reflects the gradient nature of the lexical-grammatical distinction articulated by Kuryłowicz (1965:69): "Grammaticalisation consists in the increase of the range of a morpheme advancing from a lexical to a grammatical or from a less grammatical to a more grammatical status, e.g. from a derivative formant to an inflectional one." See also detailed cross-linguistic research by Bybee (1985:81-99) on grammaticization advancing from more specific to more abstract meanings. The

First, a directional marker (space) initially develops completive readings (aspect) in telic contexts, that is, in situations bounded by an endpoint. As the directional marker becomes routinely used in such contexts, speakers begin to associate the completive sense with the directional marker itself. We might say the marker "absorbs" completive meaning from the telic contexts in which it is routinely used.

The subsequent path from derivational completive to perfective meaning can be characterized as a gradual, idiosyncratic, item-by-item advance through the lexicon. As completive markers become less lexically restricted over time, they can increase in frequency and become more widely distributed. This process of semantic generalization of derivational markers is parallel in some ways to a sound change that begins with a few lexical items and subsequently works its way through the entire lexicon (Sturtevant 1917; Wang 1969; among others).

While all of the former directional suffixes are morphologically productive (as observed in Chapter 2), *-rpu* and *-rku* display certain lexical and morphosyntactic restrictions. In contrast, *-yku* and *-ski* appear with all types of verb stems regardless of the specific lexical semantics. In other words, the derivational perfective meanings of the latter two suffixes have acquired more inflectional features (e.g., more abstract, higher frequency, more applicable) than *-rpu* or *-rku*, yet they have not attained full inflectional status. Only past perfective *-ru* has advanced through this final stage of development from a derivational to a fully inflectional category. (A formal analysis of the morphological status of these suffixes is presented in Appendix B.)

Finally, as seen in the final line of Figure 9.1, the innovation of *-ru* as a past perfective introduced a remoteness distinction in contrast with the pre-existing past suffix *-ra* (from **-rqa*). For discussion see §9.4.

In sum, the overlapping synchronic meanings of the former directional markers in Figure 9.1 suggest a scenario in which each marker would have passed through the directional to completive path of development at some point in its history. **-yku* and **-ski* generalized further as derivational perfectives. **-rqu* would have passed through each of these prior stages en route to its current status as an inflectional perfective restricted to past tense. The final stage of development leading to past perfective *-ru* involves innovations in grammatical meaning and morphological expression, as well as verbal position.

The final stage of development from derivational perfective to inflectional past tense is not documented outside of the Quechuan language family, nor has it been discussed previously in the literature on tense-aspect systems. In the next section I discuss mechanisms and motivations that underlie this unique set of innovations and shape the emerging perfective system over time.

---

set of directionals would have emerged prior to the Spanish colonial era, during which the **-CCV* shape is already attested (e.g., González Holguín ([1607] 1842:246-52).

9.3   From derivational perfective to inflectional past perfective *-ru*

In the previous section I used a synchronic reconstruction methodology based on SCQ discourse data (presented in Chapter 2) to sketch the path of grammatical development from directional meaning, to derivational completive and perfective aspect, and finally to inflectional past perfective/tense (see Figure 9.1 above and Figure 9.2 below). In this section I introduce data from other modern Quechuan languages to support the reconstruction of the intermediate aspectual stages, and especially to examine in detail the final segment from derivational perfective to inflectional past tense.[152]

Figure 9.2 *Pathway of grammaticization from directional markers to inflectional past tense*

DIRECTIONAL	>	DERIVATIONAL COMPLETIVE	>	**DERIVATIONAL PERFECTIVE**	>	**INFLECTIONAL PAST TENSE**

First, the intermediate aspectual stages in the grammatical development of directional markers is attested in reflexes of *-*rqu* in modern Quechuan varieties. For example, in most Southern Quechuan languages, such as Cuzco, the form *-ru* is a derivational completive (Cusihuamán 1976a:207). In several Central Quechuan varieties, such as Ambo-Pasco (Ralph Toliver, p.c.), *-ru* is a derivational perfective. The forms in Cuzco and Ambo-Pasco correspond to the intermediate aspectual stages along the path from directional meaning to inflectional past tense in Figure 9.2.

Past perfective *-ru* in SCQ contrasts in significant ways in both meaning and morphological structure from the cognate suffixes in Cuzco and Ambo-Pasco, and most other Quechuan languages. The most significant of these differences are summarized in Table 9.2 (Further details on variations in the form, meaning, and mode of expression of this suffix across the language family are presented in note 36 in §2.2.1).

---

[152] Inflectional past perfective/tense from a directional suffix (specifically *-*rqu* 'out') is found only in the Central Quechuan varieties spoken in a contiguous area of north central Peru, including SCQ, Corongo, Sihuas, North Conchucos, Huaylas, and Chiquián in Ancash Department, as well as Huamalíes and Margos-Yarowilca-Lauricocha in Huánuco Department. Pieces of this mosaic have been documented by Torero (1964), Parker (1969a, 1969c), Weber (1987b:62-5), Hintz (2000:62-70), among others.

Table 9.2 *Semantic and structural contrasts in modern reflexes of Quechua *-rqu 'out'*

**-rqu* 'out'	MOST QUECHUAN LANGUAGES	SCQ
1. CATEGORY	Completive/perfective, tenseless	Past perfective, past tense
2. MODE OF EXPRESSION	Derivational	Inflectional
3. VERBAL POSITION	Prior to TAM slot I2 (close to root)	In TAM slot I2 (far from root)
4. CO-OCCUR WITH INFLECTIONAL TAM	Yes	No
5. 2ND PERSON SUBJECT	*-rqu-nki*	*-rqu-yki* (by analogy with *-rqa-yki* -PST-2)

What motivations precipitated this major shift in grammatical meaning and morphological expression from derivational perfective to inflectional past tense *-ru* in SCQ (lines 1 and 2)? And what mechanisms operationalized the rightward migration of a derivational aspect suffix to the inflectional slot I2 in the verbal template (lines 3 and 4)? Naturally, these innovations in meaning and structure did not happen all at once in a single, giant "macro-reanalysis," but rather the path from derivational to inflectional meaning involves a series of intermediate "micro-stages." We can identify the motivations and mechanisms that facilitated these innovations through an examination of these micro-stages in neighboring Quechuan languages, as detailed below.[153]

9.3.1   MICRO-STAGE 1 (Derivational completive)

In Huallaga Quechua the suffix *-rqu* "has lost virtually all directional meaning" and has now assumed aspectual (completive) meaning. Weber attributes perfective aspect only to the former directional suffix *-yku* (1989:127-8, 144).

Cusihuamán similarly characterizes the completive aspectual function of the cognate form *-ru* in Cuzco Quechua as "consummation of the action" (1976a:207). In these two languages, *-rqu* (or *-ru*) appears in the derivational position of the verb, not the inflectional position. In keeping with its derivational status, this suffix can co-occur with an inflectional tense marker, as in Huallaga example (262) and Cuzco example (263).

---

[153] Weber (1987b:62-5) first described a sequence of semantic and structural changes associated with *-rqu* in various Central Quechuan varieties. Further details are elaborated by Hintz (2000:62-70). Neither Weber nor Hintz accounts for these innovations in terms of diachronic mechanisms that move grammatical markers along pathways of grammaticization.

(262) HUALLAGA QUECHUA
    *i   chay-man-qa   tiya-n-ta   puñu-**rqa**-chi-**naq**   chay   sonso*
    and that-GOAL-TOP aunt-3-OBJ   sleep-**OUT**-CAUS-**PST.N** that   stooge
    'And the stooge **made** his aunt **sleep** there!' (where she would be killed
    instead of himself)

(263) CUZCO QUECHUA
    *papa   chakra-ta-qa   chikchi-**ru**-sha-**sqa**-táq*
    potato   field-OBJ-TOP   hail-**OUT**-PROG-**PST.P**-EMPH
    'It **had been hailing** on the potato field!'

9.3.2   MICRO-STAGE 2 (Derivational perfective)

As noted above, *-ru* is a perfective in Ambo-Pasco Quechua. This non-final verbal suffix occurs close to the verb root, preceding the inflectional OBJECT-TAM-SUBJECT complex. As such, perfective *-ru* does not co-occur with the progressive suffix *-yka:*. According to Toliver (p.c.), the Ambo-Pasco verb in (264) can mean either 'you unexpectedly help me' (present time reference) or 'you recently helped me' (past time reference), depending on the context. The past reading is not expected because the lack of a formal marker in the inflectional TAM slot I2 (grammatical zero *-Ø*) ordinarily indexes present habitual situations.

(264) AMBO-PASCO QUECHUA
    *yanapa-**ru**-ma-Ø-nki*
    help-**PFV**-1OBJ-PRS-2
    'You **unexpectedly** help me.' or
    'You **recently** help**ed** me.'

When the direct object is third person (or when the verb is intransitive), no formal marker appears in the object slot I1. This is shown in (265) 'you recently helped him/her', and in (266) 'you recently walked'.

(265) AMBO-PASCO QUECHUA
    *yanapa-**ru**-Ø-nki*
    help-**PFV**-PRS-2
    'You **unexpectedly** help him/her.' or
    'You **recently** help**ed** him/her.'

(266) AMBO-PASCO QUECHUA
    *puri-**ru**-Ø-nki*
    walk-**PFV**-PRS-2
    'You **unexpectedly** walk.' or
    'You **recently** walk**ed**.'

Although the suffix *-ru* occurs close to the verb root in a derivational slot (as in (267)a), the lack of a formal marker intervening between *-ru* and the subject marker, coupled with the recent past reading, presents a situation ripe for the reanalysis of *-ru* as a past tense marker in the inflectional TAM position as in (267)b. This situation, essentially motivated by analogy with other tense markers, constitutes a mechanism by which *-ru* could "migrate" from the derivational position in the verb to the inflectional position. Language users have frequent opportunities to reanalyze *-ru* as appearing in paradigmatic contrast with other tense markers because intransitive verbs are more frequent in discourse than transitive verbs, and because third person objects are more frequent than other objects.

	ROOT	DERIV	TAM	SUBJECT	
(267) a.	*puri*	*-ru*	*-Ø*	*-nki*	AMBO-PASCO QUECHUA
	walk	-PFV	-PRS	-2	
b.	*puri*		*-ru*	*-nki*	HUAYLAS QUECHUA
	walk		-PST	-2	

'You **recently** walk**ed**.'

9.3.3 MICRO-STAGE 3 (Inflectional past perfective: recent)

While (267)a is the current state of affairs in Ambo-Pasco Quechua, the reanalysis represented in (267)b has already taken place in Huaylas Quechua. Unlike Ambo-Pasco example (264) in which *-ru* precedes the object marker (*-ma*) in the derivational position, the Huaylas example in (268) shows that *-rqu* follows the object marker in the inflectional TAM slot I2 (Pantoja, Ripkens, and Swisshelm 1974:94). This is the same slot in which all other tense markers appear in paradigmatic contrast. In other words, in Huaylas the suffix *-rqu* has become an inflectional recent past tense suffix (Parker 1976:108).[154]

---

[154] There is evidence for an additional step we might refer to as "MICRO-STAGE 2A" in which the derivational perfective suffix *-ru* (illustrated for Ambo-Pasco) takes on inflectional features prior to its rightward movement to the tense slot (illustrated for Huaylas). According to Adelaar, for example, the cognate form *-ru* in Tarma belongs to an "inflectional" non-final class intermediate between the "truly derivational" non-final suffixes which occur close to the verb root, and the inflectional final suffixes which occur far from the verb root. Adelaar describes the division between the derivational and inflectional classes of non-final verbal suffixes as "not clear-cut" (2006:126-8). Additional evidence for "MICRO-STAGE 2A" is seen in the SCQ perfective suffixes *-yku* and *-ski* which satisfy some but not all of the traditional criteria for inflection. For details, see Appendix B.

(268) HUAYLAS QUECHUA
    *ima-ta   apa-mu-**rqu**-nki   ranti-pa-q*
    what-OBJ   carry-FAR-**PST.R**-2   buy-BEN-PRMT
    'What **did** you **bring** to sell (or for me to buy)?'

9.3.4   MICRO-STAGE 4 (Inflectional past perfective: non-recent)

Returning now to SCQ, the development of past perfective *-ru* has proceeded two stages further than in Huaylas in terms of both semantics and formal expression. First, *-ru* is no longer restricted to recent situations. For example, in (269) 'you completely trampled' refers to an event that happened months earlier. In addition, the second person suffix used with present tense (*-nki*) has been replaced by the second person suffix *-yki*, presumably by analogy with the older past perfective/tense suffix *-ra* which also uses *-yki* in second person.

(269) SCQ
    *runa-pa   abe:na-n-kuna-ta-si   qashu-tsi-r   usha-**ru**-**yki***
    person-GEN   oats-3-PL.N-OBJ-EVEN   trample-CAUS-SS   finish-**PST.R**-**2**$_p$
    '**You completely trampled** the owner's oat field.'

9.3.5   Summary of MICRO-STAGES (Derivation to inflection)

I have traced the grammatical development of *-ru* (from **-rqu* 'out') from derivational perfective aspect to inflectional past tense in SCQ by examining the synchronic status of cognates in other Quechuan languages. This study suggests that the path from derivation to inflection was not realized in a single giant leap, but rather the relevant marker passed through a series of smaller steps, summarized as the micro-stages in Table 9.3.

The former directional suffix **-rqu* 'out' marks completive aspect early in its development, corresponding to MICRO-STAGE 1 (Cuzco, Huallaga). Completive meaning generalizes to perfective meaning, though the mode of expression continues to be derivational. At MICRO-STAGE 2 (Ambo-Pasco) speakers use this derivational perfective suffix in situations that were recently completed. The suffix attains several features of inflection at MICRO-STAGE 2A (Tarma). Full inflectional status is evident at MICRO-STAGE 3 (Huaylas), though vestiges of its former non-inflectional status are still in evidence. For example, it appears with second person subject *-nki*, an inflectional suffix otherwise reserved for present situations, not past situations (otherwise inflected with *-yki*). Finally, at MICRO-STAGE 4 (SCQ), *-ru* is no longer restricted to recent past situations, and it inflects for second person subjects with *-yki*.[155]

---

[155] In fact, there is more to the story than the five micro-stages presented here. Cognates of the former directional suffix **-rqu* 'out' have developed even further in other Central Quechuan varieties. For example, in SCQ past perfective *-ru* is restricted to speech-act participants

Table 9.3 *From derivation to inflection: Modern reflexes of *-rqu 'out' in Quechua*

MICRO-STAGE	QUECHUAN VARIETY	CATEGORY	MODE OF EXPRESSION	OVERT TAM CO-OCCURS	2nd PERSON SUBJECT
1	Cuzco, Huallaga (and all non-Central)	Completive (some recent situations)	Derivational	Yes	*-nki* (present)
2	Ambo-Pasco	Perfective (many recent situations)	Derivational	Yes	*-nki* (present)
2A	Tarma (cf. note 154)	Perfective (purely aspectual)	Inflectional (but not obligatory)	Yes	*-nki* (present)
3	Huaylas	Recent past	Inflectional	No	*-nki* (present)
4	SCQ	Not restricted to recent past	Inflectional	No	*-yki* (past)

The migration of derivational perfective *-ru* to the inflectional TAM verbal slot I2 is easy to understand once we identify the semantic and structural bridges connecting these categories. In terms of semantics, speakers increasingly used derivational perfective *-ru* in situations that occurred recently. Strengthening of the inference of recent completion yielded recent past tense, that is, the perfective meaning of *-ru* became restricted to past situations. Subsequently, the tense component of past perfective *-ru* generalized further to include non-recent past situations.

In terms of morphological structure, present tense verbs in Quechuan languages are typically marked by grammatical zero in the inflectional TAM slot, and derivational perfective *-ru* appears adjacent to that slot. This situation facilitated the reanalysis of *-ru* as filling the inflectional TAM slot. In effect, the suffix itself did not "move," but the boundary between derivation and inflection would have shifted to the left of the suffix. It is this mechanism of grammatical change which underlies Weber's observation that "Aspectual suffixes tend rightward as though they were trying to reach the position of a tense marker" (1989:80). A similar situation holds for transitive verbs with zero-marked third person objects in present tense. As a result, past perfective *-ru* in SCQ appears in paradigmatic contrast with the other markers in the inflectional TAM verbal slot I2.[156]

(Diane Hintz 2007b:24ff.), but in North Conchucos *-rqu* has generalized to mark third person as well, e.g., *yanapa-n* 'she helps him', *yanapa-rqu-n* 'she recently helped him'. Presumably, *-rqu* in North Conchucos has taken over functions of the third person past perfective portmanteau suffix *-sha* via analogical leveling. Further north in Corongo Quechua, the past function of *-:xu* (from *-rqu*) has generalized to the point at which it has merged with the older past suffix *-:xa* (from *-rqa*). Currently, these two suffixes are nearly synonymous, in effect, neutralizing the recent-remote past distinction (Hintz 2000:62-70; 2008:72).

[156] For a similar shift in status from derivational to inflectional in Cherokee (Iroquoian) infinitives, see Mithun (1999a:251).

9.4   From past to remote past *-ra*

Synchronic reflexes of Proto Quechua *-rqa* 'past' appear in the inflectional TAM verbal slot in virtually all Quechuan languages. This past suffix would have acquired perfective meaning via contrast with the past imperfective category (cf. §10.1). As suggested above in the final line of Figure 9.1, the synchronic SCQ form *-ra* is now construed as a "remote" past due to the innovation of past perfective *-ru* which typically reports more recent situations (cf. Figure 5.1 in §5.1). SCQ speakers use this remoteness distinction as a grammatical resource for the expression of not only degrees of pastness but also of involvement with or detachment from the situation (Diane Hintz 2007b:247-53).

9.5   From periphrastic perfect to inflectional past perfective *-sha*

Before moving on to a cross-linguistic view of the evolution of perfectives, this section presents a brief recap of past perfective *-sha*. As discussed above in §2.2.2 and §5.1, *-sha* is a portmanteau suffix that combines past perfective with third person subject. It developed from a perfect expressed through periphrasis. This perfect construction combined the past participle *-shqa* followed by the copular auxiliary *ka-*, obligatorily inflected from the set of person suffixes. For example, the form for second person perfect would have been *-shqa ka-nki*. In general, however, the copula *ka-* does not formally appear in third person. Thus, the form for third person perfect was simply *-shqa* (see Map A.2 in Appendix A).

The perfect construction is no longer productive in SCQ.[157] Instead, third person perfect became third person recent past, a development that is well documented cross-linguistically.[158] As Comrie and others explain, perfect refers to the "continuing present relevance of a past event," and an event that occurs recently tends to be one that is currently relevant (1976:52-61). As the "current relevance" component of meaning erodes, what remains is an event conceptualized as recent past. In SCQ, the reduced form *-sha* (or *-sh*) has developed a stage further to report non-recent past events as well. The fact that *-sha* contrasts with past imperfectives shows that it is a past perfective and not simply past tense.[159]

---

[157] While finite perfect forms are no longer productive in SCQ, *-shqa* plus *ka-* combinations continue to appear in adverbial clauses. The function of these combinations is to present event sequences in discourse.

[158] According to Dahl, "..historically, it is not uncommon for a perfect to develop into a perfective" or past category (1985:139). In this regard, Comrie (1976:53) mentions spoken forms of French, Italian, Romanian, and southern varieties of German. Bybee and Dahl refer to Swahili (Bantu) (1989:74, citing Heine and Reh 1984:130).

[159] Bybee et al. (1994:85) hypothesize that perfects will generalize to perfectives (and not simple past tense) if past imperfective already exists prior to that development. As we have seen in Chapters 3 and 5, the past imperfective category in SCQ is expressed inflectionally by

While the path of development from perfect meaning to inflectional past is well documented, the converging path from derivational perfective to inflectional past is not attested outside of the Quechuan language family, nor has it been discussed previously in the literature on tense-aspect systems. In the next section I situate these language-specific findings within a cross-linguistic framework for the development of perfects, perfectives, and pasts.

9.6 A cross-linguistic perspective on the evolution of perfectives

In previous sections I described the sequence of developments leading from directional markers to completive and perfective aspect and past tense in Quechua. This evolutionary pathway of grammaticization is represented above with the relevant Quechua markers in Figure 9.1 and, in more schematic form, Figure 9.2. We can situate these findings within the framework set forth by Bybee et al. (1994:105), as illustrated below in Figure 9.3. The intent here is to build on this cross-linguistically well-documented model in which universals are viewed as the evolutionary paths of grammaticization that converge (rightward) on increasingly general categories.

The solid lines in Figure 9.3 represent the principal paths of development leading to inflectional perfective and past tense. In many languages, verbs such as 'be', 'have', 'come', and 'finish' give rise to auxiliaries that combine with nonfinite verb forms to produce resultatives and completives. Over time these categories tend to converge on perfect meaning. A perfect may subsequently become an inflectional perfective or past tense marker. The SCQ past perfective suffix *-sha* provides an ideal illustration for this trajectory. At the same time, perfect is the only aspectual category that leads directly to past tense within this model.

Figure 9.3 *Unidirectional paths of development leading to perfective and past*
(dotted arrow represents the new path brought to light by Quechua data)

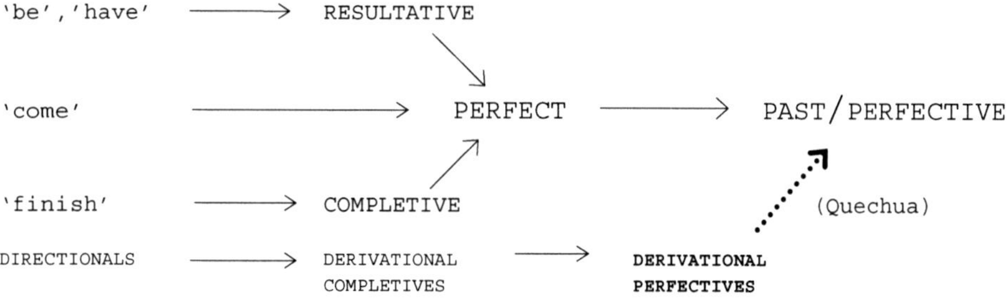

narrative past *-na:* and past habitual *-q*, and derivationally by the combination of continuous *-yka:* with past markers.

The bottom line of Figure 9.3 represents the line of development by which directional markers give rise to derivational completives and perfectives. Previously, it was thought that derivational perfectives do not undergo further grammatical development but rather become entrenched in this category. Example languages include Russian, Georgian, Hungarian, Mokilese, and Margi (cf. note 146).

In fact, the Quechua data demonstrate that the derivational perfective category can provide an additional aspectual source for inflectional past tense. As indicated by the dotted arrow in the lower right of Figure 9.3, the path from derivational perfective to inflectional past tense is not mediated by the perfect category. Evidence for this path of development is presented above in Figure 9.1, where perfect meaning is conspicuously absent from the continuous chain of overlapping synchronic meanings of the set of directional markers. Further support comes from the synchronic reflexes of the former directional suffix *-rqu* 'out' in other Quechuan varieties, as summarized above in Table 9.3.[160]

Figure 9.3 reflects two additional modifications to the diagram presented by Bybee et al. First, I represented directional markers and 'finish' verbs as separate sources for completives because there is no instance of 'finish' becoming a derivational perfective, as far as I am aware. Second, the path from directional markers to perfects (via completives) does not seem warranted as there are no known instances of this development (1994:61).

The synchronic reconstruction methodology based on SCQ discourse data allowed us to sketch the overall path of development leading from directional meaning, to derivational completive and perfective aspect, and finally to inflectional past tense. In addition, a fine-grained examination of synchronic reflexes of *-rqu* 'out' in neighboring Quechuan varieties revealed a patterned sequence of "micro-stages," that is, small shifts in meaning and morphosyntactic structure along the trajectory leading from derivational to inflectional meaning. Finally, the Quechua findings were situated within a cross-linguistic framework for the development of perfectives and past tense.

The results of the investigation presented so far provide a good description of the sources and paths of development leading to perfective and past. Beyond identifying particular innovations, that is, *what happened*, we are especially interested in understanding *how these*

---

[160] We might wonder why past tense in SCQ developed from *-rqu* 'out' versus some other directional marker, e.g., *-yku* 'in', *-rku* 'up', or *-rpu* 'down'. For example, past in Margi (Chadic) appears to come from a directional marker meaning 'toward' (see Hoffman 1963:136 and note 152). In contrast, the Cheyenne (Algonquian) marker meaning 'toward the speaker' is identical to a marker that refers not to recent past but to remote past (Bybee et al. 1994:103, citing Leman 1980:147, 191). Recent past in other languages develops from directional verb plus case marker sequences, such as French *venir de* 'come from', and from the ablative *-inya* in Pitta-Pitta (Australian) (Heine and Kuteva 2002:33-4). In keeping with their derivational status, the selection of these particular directional markers appears to be purely idiosyncratic.

innovations happened in terms of the forces that motivated them. Mithun underscores the need for a more detailed examination of such interacting forces:

> A full understanding of the processes of grammaticization must involve not only a knowledge of the possible sources of grammatical markers and categories, but also of the factors that motivate their development, especially their potential *interaction with the grammatical systems in which they emerge*. Such interaction is bound to be complex, involving multiple factors and *varying degrees of motivation or hindrance*. Yet as we discover more about these interactions, we have much to gain in our overall understanding of the *forces that motivate grammatical systems* (1991:183, emphasis added).

The next section takes up this challenge by examining in detail how grammatical systems are shaped by forces that increase or diminish motivations for the movement of grammatical morphemes along paths of grammaticization.

9.7 Diachronic forces in the evolution of perfectives

Most current research in grammaticization seems to be based on an assumption that universal mechanisms of semantic change (e.g., metaphorical extension, semantic generalization, pragmatic inferencing) constitute a "PROPELLING FORCE" that drives grammatical markers along a trajectory of development. This notion is expressed, for example, by Bybee et al.:[161]

> Underlying these cross-linguistic patterns are the true universals which are the mechanisms of change that *propel* grams along these paths of development (1994:302, emphasis added).

While this one-force "PROPELLING" model accounts for many grammatical developments (e.g., directional to completive to perfective), it does not account for the conventional observation that a grammatical marker may stop at any point along a path of change. In other words, grammaticization is not inevitable. For example, in Quechua, Russian, and Mokilese (plus the handful of languages listed in note 146), directional markers have grammaticized into derivational perfectives. Why, though, did this process stop at derivational perfective in Russian and Mokilese, while in Quechua the relevant morpheme (the suffix *-ru*) continued along a path of development to inflectional past tense?[162]

---

[161] See also Heine, Claudi, and Hünnemeyer 1991, Haspelmath 1999, Fischer et al. 2000:319, Kuteva 2001:167, Shibatani 2007:42, Heine and Kuteva 2007:303-14, among others.

[162] There is intriguing evidence for this path of development in Margi. The directional suffix *-(ə)ri* meaning 'toward' appears to have grammaticized as a derivational perfective. In a later

I approach this issue by examining the assumptions that underlie our current model, in particular, the nature of the forces or "functional pressures" that motivate grammaticization. In addition to PROPELLING FORCE, I propose a holistic scenario that involves two additional force types: "ATTRACTING FORCE" and "OBSTRUCTING FORCE." The following discussion shows how PROPELLING FORCE and ATTRACTING FORCE work in concert to "move" perfective *-ru* along the path from derivational to inflectional meaning. It also suggests how OBSTRUCTING FORCE can diminish the motivation for similar grammatical developments in Russian and Mokilese. It is the interaction of these three force types, I suggest, which underlies the tension between diachronic change and diachronic stability (cf. Nichols 2003:283ff.).[163]

9.7.1   PROPELLING FORCE

A PROPELLING FORCE motivates the movement of a morpheme out of one category towards a more grammatical category, that is, one with more general or abstract semantics. Several mechanisms which have a propelling effect have been described throughout this chapter. For example, the entire set of former directional suffixes has taken on completive aspect early on. **Metaphorical extension** from one semantic domain (space) to another (aspect) is a propelling mechanism that tends to operate during early stages of grammatical development, but not through intermediate and later stages (Bybee et al. 1994:297).

While directional markers become completives in many languages, the resulting aspect markers subsequently become perfectives in only a few languages (see note 146). One mechanism that propels grammatical morphemes along this path from completive to perfective aspect is **semantic generalization**, whereby the meaning of the morpheme is extended to more and more situations via a gradual spread through the lexicon. Evidence for semantic generalization is seen in the synchronic distribution of the set of former directional markers in SCQ discourse. As detailed above in Figure 9.1, the meanings of these markers substantially overlap along a path of development in stages from directional to completive, then perfective, and finally inflectional past tense. In this account, derivational completives shade into perfective meaning, and derivational perfectives may generalize to a point at which one becomes a viable candidate for reanalysis as inflectional past tense.

Because semantic generalization is realized as an ongoing process, Bybee et al. (1994:290) question whether generalization itself may result from changes realized by means of another mechanism. The Quechua data support Schwenter's (1994:101) assertion that **pragmatic**

---

section labeled "Past conjugations," Hoffman discusses the suffix *-(ə)ri* which "indicates an action in the past" (1963:196-200). It is plausible that the derivational perfective *-(ə)ri* may have been reanalyzed as an inflectional past perfective, similar to the reanalysis of the SCQ derivational perfective *-ru* to inflectional past perfective.

[163] The interacting forces described here are compatible with the notion of "competing motivations" advanced by Du Bois (1985) and his view of "language as a complex adaptive system … in which some functional motivations come into conflict with others" (2010:1).

inferencing may be one such mechanism.[164] In §9.3 above we saw that perfective *-r(q)u* in some Quechuan varieties conveys 'completed past action'; in others this has generalized to 'recent completion'. This sense of immediacy is precisely the meaning we would anticipate as a precursor to recent past tense. As the inference of recent completion became routinized over time, this frequently-expressed distinction eventually became reified as recent past tense *-ru* in SCQ. From this perspective, pragmatic inferencing may be understood as a mechanism which drives semantic generalization (cf. Hopper and Traugott 2003:75ff.).

The three propelling mechanisms presented so far—metaphorical extension, semantic generalization, and pragmatic inferencing—are known to apply cross-linguistically. Naturally, other mechanisms may be evident in language-specific circumstances. I suggest that an additional propelling force motivating the movement of *-ru* to inflectional past tense in SCQ is **overpopulation** within the derivational perfective category. This grammatical class was occupied by at least the five suffixes *-rku, -yku, -ski, -ri,* and *-r(q)u.* Competition within the confines of this expanding perfective space led to the emergence of one member (*-ru*) as more highly grammaticized along the path to inflectional past tense.

This "overpopulation" scenario in SCQ presents an opportunity to refine the notion of specialization in which "the choice of grammatical forms becomes reduced as certain ones become generalized in meaning and use" (Hopper and Traugott 2003:113). We might refer to that process as *early-stage specialization* as it involves a "thinning out of the field of [lexical] candidates for grammaticalization" (ibid.:116). By contrast, the analogous process we have just examined in SCQ exemplifies *late-stage specialization*. Here, the remaining forms in the derivational perfective set do not "thin out" but rather, as entrenched grammatical morphemes, adapt to discourse pressures by taking on a fine gradation of semantic nuances which differentiate these perfective suffixes in the modal realm, as described in Chapter 6.

9.7.2   ATTRACTING FORCE

An ATTRACTING FORCE motivates the movement of a morpheme from a less grammatical to a more grammatical status along one among various potential trajectories. Neither PROPELLING FORCE nor ATTRACTING FORCE should be thought of as "coercive," but simply functional pressures or tendencies that may be present to a greater or lesser degree in the environment in which grammatical developments are observed to occur. Conceptually, the basis of attraction is semantic or structural congruence, that is, similarity between linguistic features of the developing morpheme with features of corresponding morphemes in a more grammatical category. The more grammatical category need not be located in the same language; as illustrated below, it may be a linguistic resource available to the speaker in a contact language or

---

[164] Schwenter (1994:101): "In the case of the Alicante PP [Present Perfect], I would argue that generalization is in fact the outcome of multiple implicatures/inferences which interlocutors have made as regards the use of the PP in discourse contexts."

dialect. Within this model, an ATTRACTING FORCE works together with PROPELLING FORCE along the same trajectory.[165]

The role of ATTRACTING FORCE can be illustrated by the movement of derivational perfective *-ru* (from *-rqu* 'out') to inflectional past tense in Quechuan varieties such as SCQ. First, in the domain of phonology, the Proto Quechua suffix *-rqu* has the canonical shape CCV, as in (270)a. As with other directional suffixes, the final vowel of *-rqu* is lowered to [*a*] when followed by a "trigger" suffix, such as cislocative *-mu* in (270)c.

(270) a. *-rqu*   CCV   'out'

     b. *puri-rqu-n*   'he walks'
        walk-OUT-3

     c. *puri-rqa-mu-n*   'he walks here'
        walk-OUT-FAR-3

The lowered allomorph of *-rqu* [*-rqa*] 'out' has precisely the same shape as the suffix *-rqa* 'past', illustrated in (271)a and (271)b.

(271) a. *-rqa*   CCV   'past'

     b. *puri-rqa-n*   'he walked'
        walk-PST-3

Rice (2005) hypothesizes that prosodic contours (CV sequences) play a role in shaping the order of morphemes in the Athapaskan verbal template. The Proto Quechua forms *-rqu* 'out' and *-rqa* 'past' share not only prosodic contour (CCV) but phonological segments of the form *-rqV*. As illustrated in (270) and (271), even the final vowel is identical in some morphological environments.

Heath observes a similar pattern in Uto-Aztecan languages (Cupan subgroup) in which certain innovations are "triggered crucially in each case by the fortuitous partial phonological similarity of the old independent stem and an old affix" (1998:730). The difference in SCQ is that the phonological similarity is between two affixes, one young (perfective *-r(q)u*), the other old (past *-r(q)a*).[166]

---

[165] Heine et al. allude to attracting force as distinct from propelling force: "... a new form tends to be recruited on the same conceptual pattern as the old one" (1991:246). Likewise, Hopper observes that grammar is continually shaped by phonological and contextual similarities "and other kinds of resonance" (1987:147).

[166] Heath rejects the notion of propelling force: "Nor are lexical items like 'go' and 'have' propelled by preprogrammed navigational paths into morphology" (1998:730). Instead, he argues for a "pull-chain model" of grammatical development: "The old and new formations may

Previous sections of the present chapter showed that synchronic reflexes of *-rqu* 'out' in modern Quechuan languages (e.g., Huallaga, Ambo-Pasco, Tarma, etc.) have acquired aspectual and past time reference functions similar to *-rqa* 'past'. In the model proposed here, the similarity of form and meaning between the former derivational perfective *-ru* and inflectional past *-ra* constitutes an ATTRACTING FORCE toward this particular trajectory from derivational to inflectional status.

ATTRACTING FORCE is also relevant in language contact situations. In the formation of auxiliaries within the native construction STEM–NOMINALIZER + $\boxed{\text{VERB}}$, for example, Hintz (2010) shows that Quechua-Spanish bilingual speakers recruit only those Spanish "light" verbs (similar semantics) which are easily accommodated to the canonical shape CVCV found in native verb roots (similar form). The borrowing of Spanish verbs—such as *pasar* 'pass' > *pasa-* 'completive aspect', *seguir* 'follow' > *si:gi-* 'continuative aspect' (cf. §11.2 and §11.3)—would not be understood in this model as driven by PROPELLING FORCE. Rather, this foreign lexical material is drawn toward the native (more grammatical) auxiliary category, motivated by the ATTRACTING FORCE of linguistic similarity in terms of both semantics and structure. Spanish verbs that do not conform to the CVCV pattern, and those with greater lexical specificity than "light" verbs, have considerably less motivation for incorporation into the pre-existing Quechua system of aspectual auxiliaries. We could think of such hindrances to grammatical development as motivated by OBSTRUCTING FORCE, the concept presented in the next section.

9.7.3 OBSTRUCTING FORCE

An OBSTRUCTING FORCE motivates diachronic stability, mitigating the predisposition for a particular grammatical development. As with PROPELLING FORCE and ATTRACTING FORCE, OBSTRUCTING FORCE should be understood as a functional pressure that may be present to a greater or lesser degree. For example, Mokilese does not have grammatical tense but expresses past time reference via the aspectual system, adverbs, and determiners with time nouns (Harrison 1976:85, 224-40). Thus, it comes as no surprise that derivational perfectives in Mokilese have not become inflectional past tense markers, given that the organization of the existing grammatical system diminishes the motivation for such a development.

Russian, on the other hand, does have grammatical past tense, but the forms in the perfective and past tense categories are not linguistically similar. They developed from very different sources, they have different morphological expression (prefix versus suffix), and they are not phonologically similar. Thus, ATTRACTING FORCE along the path from derivational perfective to

---

also be similar in formal structure. Then, as the old formation recedes and eventually vanishes, it pulls the new formation behind it" (1998:753). In contrast, I propose that both PROPELLING FORCE and ATTRACTING FORCE work together to motivate grammatical development. Competition between PROPELLING FORCE and ATTRACTING FORCE on the one hand, and OBSTRUCTING FORCE on the other, underlies the tension between diachronic change and diachronic stability (cf. Figure 9.4 and the relevant discussion below).

inflectional past tense is minimal in Russian, unlike the Quechua situation in which ATTRACTING FORCE is strong. Presumably, OBSTRUCTING FORCE which motivates diachronic stability in the Russian aspect system outweighs the combined effect of PROPELLING FORCE (e.g., the inference of recent completion which propels semantic generalization) and ATTRACTING FORCE (e.g., similarity in meaning and/or form which attracts derivational perfective to inflectional past tense).

Beyond the factors already cited, Bybee et al. note that the generalization of derivational to inflectional expression does not appear to be common (1994:61). In keeping with this observation, the fact that derivational perfectives do not attain inflectional status outside of a few Quechuan languages suggests a high level of resistance to change beyond the derivational perfective stage. But what is the cognitive basis for the reluctance of language users to reanalyze a derivational marker as inflectional?

Slobin suggests one way to get at the mental activity that goes on in speech production:

> ...study the contents of grammatical categories that seem especially resistant to historical change in a language or group of languages, on the assumption that these categories are exceptionally *deeply ingrained* as systems of thinking for speaking (1987:436; see also Slobin 1996:81-9).

While this idea of "deeply ingrained" categories is intuitively appealing, until now it has been difficult to operationalize. The notion of OBSTRUCTING FORCE, however, allows us to motivate these general observations of diachronic stability in terms of the functional load of the relevant grammatical morphemes.

Resistance to change can be illustrated by observing differences between the functional load of derivational perfectives in Quechua, on the one hand, and Russian, on the other. In Russian, the semantic opposition between perfective and imperfective is robust. The vast majority of verbs are formally specified as either perfective or imperfective, that is, the perfective category carries a high functional load in Russian discourse (e.g., Forsyth 1970:32). In contrast, less than half the verbs in Quechua discourse appear with either a derivational perfective or imperfective marker. In other words, these markers carry a low functional load. In this sense, derivational perfectives in Quechua would be less resistant to further grammatical development than their "deeply ingrained" Russian counterparts. The high functional load of derivational perfectives in Russian constitutes an OBSTRUCTING FORCE, reducing the motivation for further development along the trajectory from derivational to inflectional status. (A detailed comparison of aspect in SCQ and Russian is presented in §12.4.)

9.7.4 THE BOXCAR METAPHOR

One way to imagine the scenario of diachronic change versus diachronic stability expressed through multiple force types (PROPELLING, ATTRACTING, OBSTRUCTING) is through the metaphor in Figure 9.4. The boxcar represents a grammatical morpheme (GRAM) and the railroad track is an independently laid pathway of grammaticization. The grammatical morpheme is propelled along a path of grammatical development when a mechanism such as semantic generalization operates, much like a locomotive pushing a boxcar along a track.

Figure 9.4 *Boxcar metaphor for multiple force types in grammaticization*

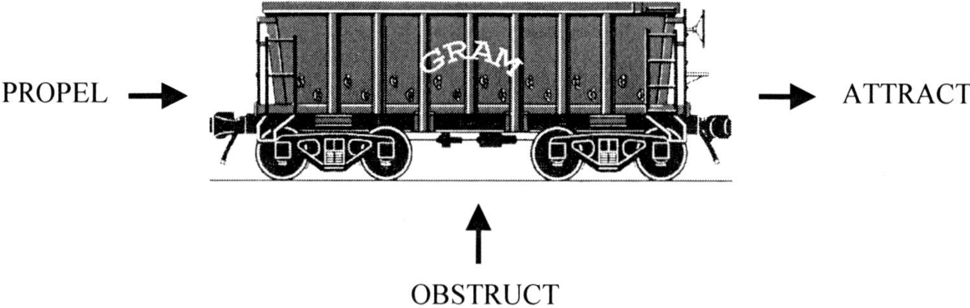

Within this scenario, other forces are potentially involved in the movement of the boxcar (grammatical morpheme). A locomotive attached to the right would produce an attracting force that "pulls" the boxcar toward a familiar destination, analogous to the pre-existence of a similar linguistic feature (or an entire category) further down the grammatical path, either in the history of the language (e.g., past tense *-ra* in SCQ) or in a language contact situation (e.g., auxiliaries recruited by Quechua-Spanish bilinguals). Just as a boxcar does not jump the track without calamity, so a grammatical expression tends to follow a track that was previously laid.

Resistance to movement along the track could be reduced by "greasing the wheels," as it were, via similarity among linguistic features. Conversely, just as a boxcar at rest is more resistant to movement when it is fully loaded or "ingrained," a grammatical morpheme encounters resistance to change when its functional load is high (e.g., derivational perfectives in Russian). Such movement would be less constrained when functional load is low (e.g., derivational perfectives in Quechua).

Extending the current one-force model of grammaticization to a more articulated model of PROPELLING, ATTRACTING, and OBSTRUCTING forces can help to explain not only developments that occur but also those that do not. Moreover, this enriched three-force model better reflects the relationship between language-internal and language-external processes than existing models, illuminating how grammatical systems are shaped by forces that move grammatical markers along cyclical, language-internal paths of change, and also by contact, that is, via the infusion of foreign grammatical patterns and forms into these paths of change.

9.8   Conclusion: The evolution of perfectives

The concern in the present chapter has been to examine in detail the historical development of perfective aspect in SCQ. Distinctive features of this loosely organized grammatical system, together with the strategic location of SCQ within the Central Quechua dialect continuum, present an especially fertile environment for investigating emergent properties of grammar as it is shaped by forces that move grammatical markers along pathways of evolutionary development.

The effects of lexicalization and grammaticization processes are clearly visible within the set of former directional markers (cf. Figure 9.1 above). Each suffix has fused with certain lexical verbs in which the literal directional meaning is still preserved (e.g., *-yku* 'in', *yayku-* 'enter'). At an early stage, these suffixes derived verb stems that would have expressed telic movements through space. Later, speakers increasingly employed these grammatical resources in non-spatial contexts. Each former directional suffix would have acquired completive meaning through strengthening of the inference of telicity. As the frequency and lexical diffusion of these derivational markers continues to increase over time, the completive sense further generalizes toward perfective aspect. At the same time, as discussed in Chapters 6 and 7, speakers exploit modal nuances that distinguish individual suffixes within the set of developing derivational perfectives.

One member of the original set of directional suffixes (*-rqu* 'out') is no longer a derivational perfective in SCQ but has traversed the path to inflectional past perfective/tense. This theoretically significant grammatical development has not been documented outside of Quechuan languages. A detailed study of the synchronic status of cognate markers in other Quechuan varieties reveals that the path from derivational to inflectional status involves a series of small semantic and morphosyntactic "micro-stages." The relevant suffix appears to have "migrated" rightward to the inflectional TAM slot I2 in the verbal template. In reality, the boundary between derivation and inflection most likely shifted to the left of the suffix, facilitated in part by the lack of phonological material (i.e., grammatical zeros) in the intervening slots.

I positioned these language-specific findings within the cross-linguistic framework proposed by Bybee et al. (1994:105) for the development of perfects, perfectives, and pasts. Within this scenario, perfects are the only aspectual category leading directly to past tense. Significantly, the Quechua data reveal that not only perfects but also derivational perfectives can continue on their respective paths of grammatical development, converging on the inflectional perfective and past tense categories (cf. Figure 9.3 above).

Finally, most current research on grammaticization assumes that underlying mechanisms move relevant morphemes along evolutionary pathways of development. On the one hand, driving mechanisms do appear to account for certain grammatical developments, such as directional to completive and completive to perfective. On the other hand, PROPELLING FORCE alone does not account for the fact that the process stopped at derivational perfective in Russian and Mokilese, while in Quechua the relevant morpheme continued along the trajectory to inflectional past tense. Extending the current one-force PROPELLING model of grammaticization with the addition of ATTRACTING and OBSTRUCTING force types provides a more natural and robust account of the synchronic situation in each of these languages. Encouraging more articulated models of grammaticization can lead to new discoveries about the interaction of forces that motivate diachronic change versus diachronic stability, resulting in a deeper understanding of the synchronic systems shaped by these forces.

10 THE EVOLUTION OF IMPERFECTIVES

In the previous chapter we examined the historical development of perfective aspect in SCQ. This chapter continues this line of inquiry in the realm of imperfective aspect. As presented in Chapter 3, imperfective aspect is expressed in SCQ through a set of eleven markers with specialized meanings that are more specific than "general imperfective." Speakers combine derivational elements with inflectional and periphrastic elements to convey a wide variety of imperfective distinctions.

Naturally, the pathways of grammaticization traversed over time by imperfective markers are distinct from those that give rise to perfectives. At the same time, the underlying mechanisms that move grammatical morphemes along those paths—e.g., pragmatic inferencing, semantic generalization, etc.—are essentially equivalent. Moreover, data from Quechuan languages in general confirm both the utility and the conceptual validity of this grammaticization model in which a small set of lexical (or less grammatical) sources traverse diachronic paths that converge on more grammatical categories.

In addition to the usual grammaticization processes, a pivotal development in the Quechua imperfective category is the emergence of grammatical zero in the inflectional TAM slot I2. Presumably, present imperfective zero was motivated by the rise of the inflectional past perfective category. Subsequent developments involving this zero marker further refine our understanding of diachronic forces that shape the grammatical system.

The chapter begins by introducing in §10.1 the emergence of present imperfective marked by grammatical zero. In §10.2 I examine the development of three distinct progressive markers across the language family and show how these markers narrowed the meaning of zero from present imperfective to present habitual. §10.3 summarizes the paths leading to and from imperfective.

In §10.4 I present paths of development traversed by the rich set of derivational imperfective markers that specify internal temporal structure through duration and recurrence. §10.5 shows how this diverse array of categories tends to converge on habitual meaning over time. In §10.6 I review the rise of imperfective markers restricted to the past. I conclude in §10.7 by assessing the grammatical status of imperfectives and the scenario for the ongoing development of aspectual contrasts in modern Quechuan languages.

10.1 The emergence of present imperfective zero

In the present study I have limited the discussion of contrasts between SCQ and other Quechuan varieties, for the most part, to those points which clarify particular features of the SCQ aspectual system. Beyond the comments germane to the analysis of SCQ, however, the expression of perfective and imperfective aspect varies a great deal across the spectrum of Quechuan languages.

Within this milieu of diverse aspectual forms and meanings, one shared inflectional feature appears to frame all other aspectual distinctions throughout the language family. Virtually all Quechuan languages have a synchronic reflex of **-rqa* 'past' which appears in paradigmatic contrast with grammatical zero in an inflectional slot far from the verb root (referred to throughout this book as TAM slot I2; cf. Figure 4.1). This zero marker (synchronically present habitual in SCQ) would have become conventionalized as a present imperfective when **-rqa* attained inflectional status as a past perfective.[167] As discussed in Chapter 3, the present imperfective category encompasses various aspectual functions, including habitual/generic as well as progressive. To the extent that present imperfective reports situations that include the present moment, it also expresses present tense.[168]

Certain characteristics of present imperfective zero (**-Ø*) distinguish it from other grammatical markers in Quechua. In particular, it did not arise through the usual grammaticization processes. For example, this zero does not have a lexical source and thus did not result from the fusion or reduction of phonetic material. Similarly, it did not pass through different stages of desemanticization and decategorialization on a grammaticization scale.

On the other hand, both **-rqa* and **-Ø* have been subject to the loss of functions through competition with younger developing markers. The rise of overt progressive-continuous and habitual markers has reduced the semantic territory covered by present imperfective zero substantially in Quechuan languages. In the next section I examine the development of progressives and related markers across the language family.

---

[167] A variety of other finite and nonfinite markers appear in the inflectional slot I2. Those markers tend to vary according to region (cf. note 10).

[168] Presumably, zero became a present imperfective in Quechua, and not a general imperfective, because the pre-existing grammatical system would have already included a past imperfective category. On the other hand, it is possible that past imperfectives, such as past habitual **-q* plus **ka*-PAST- and narrative past **-ña-q* plus **ka-*, were a later innovation. In that case, overt past imperfectives would have taken over part of the former general imperfective meaning of the zero morpheme.

10.2 The development of progressives across Quechuan languages

The reconstruction of early forms of progressive suffixes is relatively straightforward across the language family. After presenting reconstructions in this section, I address in subsequent sections (and in Chapter 11) the following research questions that illuminate the larger picture in the evolution of imperfectives:

- What are the pathways of grammaticization for the continuing development of progressives?
- What motivated three distinct progressive suffixes across the language family?
- What mechanisms of change operationalized their grammatical development?
- How can we account for the fact that these markers only partially fall along the lines of the traditional classification into two branches (e.g., Torero 1964)?
- How has the development of a progressive category affected the structure of the imperfective system as a whole?
- What source material gave rise to each progressive suffix?

The relevant synchronic progressives and related markers are presented in column 1 of Table 10.1. Four primary groups of forms exhibit a great deal of geographic coherence, with evidence of borrowing at the fringes of these areas (see column 3 and Map 10.1 on overleaf). We can identify three source suffixes *-yka:* (Central and N Peru), *-ch'ka:* (Southern, with the sound change **ch'* > *sh/s* _ C yielding *-sh(k)a* and other variants further south), and **-ku* (Northern). Most modern Quechuan languages have just one progressive suffix, though at least two (Huanca and Cajamarca) have two due to borrowing. As far as I am aware, each progressive suffix is compatible with any inflectional TAM marker, including past, present, and future tense, and also conditional and imperative moods. (Such studies have not been conducted in many of these languages.)

All progressive suffixes are positioned before the inflectional TAM markers. The position varies, however, with respect to the slot that marks the person of the object. Specifically, *-yka:* (Central Quechua) appears before an object suffix (closer to the verb root), but *-ch'ka:* and *-ku* appear after it (in the examples I have seen). Cajamarca is exceptional in that *-ch'ka* precedes the object slot, while *-yka* follows it (Quesada 1976:129).[169]

---

[169] In a large cross-linguistic sample, Bybee et al. (1994:174) find that progressives are usually expressed through periphrasis. As seen in Table 10.1, progressives in Quechuan languages are expressed primarily via suffixes. Most of these suffixes (though not **-ku*) are reduced from former periphrases. Surprisingly, periphrastic progressives are rarely reported in Quechua studies (see §11.2 and §11.3). It is probably not uncommon, in general, for progressives to be expressed via bound morphology in polysynthetic languages.

Table 10.1 *Progressives and related suffixes across Quechuan varieties*

SUFFIX FORM	QUECHUAN LANGUAGE	REGION	SOURCE
	Quechua I		
-yka:	SCQ	CENTRAL	Snow and Stark 1971:65
-yka:	Huallaga	CENTRAL	Weber 1989:145
-yka:	Corongo	CENTRAL	Hintz 2000:189
-yka:	Huamalíes	CENTRAL	Benson 1987:87
-yka:	Huaylas	CENTRAL	Parker 1976:128
-yka:, -yya, -ya:	Huanca	CENTRAL	Cerrón-Palomino 1976:211
-chka:	Huanca*	CENTRAL	ibid.:213
-ycha:	Oyón	CENTRAL	Fuqua 1987:77
-yya:	Yanahuanca	CENTRAL	Mark Bean, p.c.
-ya(:)	Tarma	CENTRAL	Adelaar 1977:124
	Quechua II		
-yka	San Martín	N PERU	Coombs et al. 1976:126
-yga	Chachapoyas	N PERU	Taylor 2000:75
-ya	Lambayeque	N PERU	Torero 1964:470
-yka	Cajamarca	N PERU	Quesada 1976:133
-ch'ka	Cajamarca	N PERU	ibid.
-chka	Ayacucho	SOUTHERN	Soto 1976a:111
-chka	N Bolivia	SOUTHERN	Stark 1985:532
-sha, -sya	Cuzco	SOUTHERN	Cusihuamán 1976a:182
-sha	Arequipa	SOUTHERN	Kindberg 1987:183
-sha, -sa, -sqa	Cochabamba	SOUTHERN	Lastra 1968:32
-shka	Santiago del Estero	SOUTHERN	Landerman 1991:84
-ku	Inga	NORTHERN	Levinsohn 1976:97
-hu	Imbabura	NORTHERN	Cole 1982:148
-u	Pastaza	NORTHERN	Nuckolls 1996:49

---

* Progressive *-chka:* in Huanca would be due to contact with Ayacucho/Huancavelica Quechua.

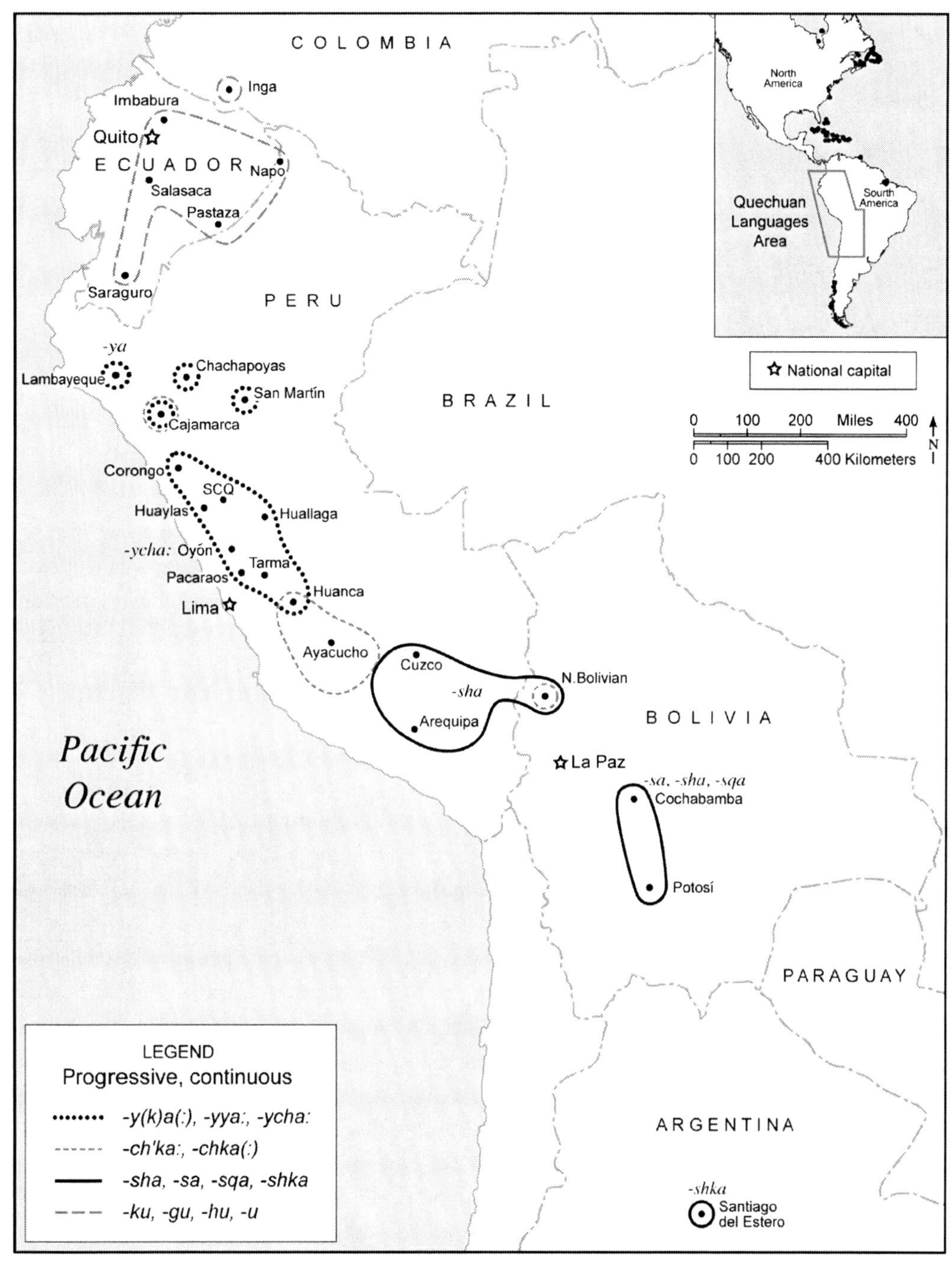

Map 10.1 PROGRESSIVE SUFFIXES ACROSS THE QUECHUA LANGUAGE FAMILY

The forms in Central Quechua allow us to surmise a Proto Central progressive form *-yka:*, as in (272). Synchronic reflexes of *-yka:* also appear in the area just north of Central Quechua (labeled "N PERU").[170]

(272)   *-yka:*   >   -yya(:)   >   -ya: >   -ya
                        -yka
                        -yga
                        -ycha:

The progressive forms along the border between Central and Southern Quechua suggest the reconstruction of the form *-ch'ka:*.[171] In Table 10.1 see Huanca (Central), Ayacucho and N Bolivia (Southern), as well as Cajamarca (N Peru).[172]

(273)   *-ch'ka:*   >   -chka: >   -chka

Above in §5.4 we observed that *-yka:* in Huamalíes (Central) is developing general imperfective functions on a path toward inflectional status. The form *-chka* appears to have evolved further along a similar trajectory in terms of semantics and also morphological position. First, the meaning is more general than progressive or continuous, as in the following Ayacucho examples in Soto (1976a:111).

---

[170] It is intriguing that the form *-yka* marks past habitual in Potosí, e.g., *puri-yka-ni* 'I used to walk' (Crapo and Aitken 1986:7), but progressive in Central Quechua and North Peruvian. Past habitual is expressed in most other Quechuan languages by *-q* plus the auxiliary *ka-* (see §5.3 and §10.6).

[171] The source of the retroflexed alveopalatal affricate in *-ch'ka:* remains enigmatic (Cerrón-Palomino 2003:146). One possibility would be the Central Quechua locative suffix *-ch'aw* (David Weber p.c.). Landerman (1991:220) points out that *-ch'aw* itself is probably derived from pre-Proto *xaw* 'middle, center'. Another possibility would be the progressive form *-ach* in the Kampan (Arawakan) languages located on the eastern fringe of the geographically contiguous areas in which Huanca and Ayacucho Quechua are currently spoken (see Payne 1982:332 on Ashéninca and Shaver 1996:79 on Nomatsiguenga). Unfortunately, serious research of contact effects through historical diffusion between languages in the Andes and languages in the adjacent Amazonian region remains in its infancy.

[172] The cognate form *-chka* in N Bolivia is attested in an area known to be colonized by Quechua speakers from southern Peru less than a century prior to the arrival of Europeans (Stark 1985:518). The form *-chka* is also reported by González Holguín ([1607] 1842:243) in Lengua General, a lingua franca which some modern scholars consider an amalgam of Southern Quechuan varieties (e.g., Durston 2004:150ff.).

(274) AYACUCHO QUECHUA
    *Binitu   Awqakusi-m   ka-**chka**-ni*
    Benito Aucacusi-DIR be-**PROG**-1

    'I **am** Benito Aucacusi.'

(275) AYACUCHO QUECHUA
    *iskay   wasi-y-mi   ka-pu-wa-**chka**-n*
    two   house-1-DIR   be-BEN-1OBJ-**PROG**-3

    'I **have** two houses.' (Lit., 'My two houses are for me.')

Second, in terms of morphological structure, *-yka:* in SCQ and other Central Quechuan varieties is positioned before the slot that marks the person of the object, e.g., *-ma* in (276).

(276) SCQ
    *taqay tuku-qa   may   ranya-**yka:**-ma-n-mi*
    that   owl-TOP   valid   portend.evil-**CONT**-1OBJ-3-DIR

    'That owl **is foreshadowing evil** against me.'

In contrast, *-chka* appears after the object slot, adjacent to the inflectional TAM position in Ayacucho examples (275) and (277) (1976a:96) and in Huanca example (278) (Cerrón-Palomino 1976:213).

(277) AYACUCHO QUECHUA
    *qawa-wa-**chka**-n*
    observe-1OBJ-**PROG**-3

    'S/he **is observing** me.'

(278) HUANCA QUECHUA
    *wik   iskina-kaq-ch'aw   alka-qla-ma-**chka**-nki*
    that   corner-DEF-LOC   wait.for-OUT-1OBJ-**PROG**-2

    'You **will be waiting for** me at that corner.'

Most Southern Quechuan varieties are characterized by a progressive form with an initial sibilant (*sh* or *s*). These sibilant-initial forms are cognate with the affricate-initial forms, an analysis advanced by Middendorf (1890).[173] **-ch'ka* would have become *-s(y)a/-sh(k)a* via the syllable-final sound changes **ch' > ch > sh~s / _ C*. Sample affected morphemes in Cuzco include **puch'ka- > puska-* 'spin thread' and **uch'pa > usp^{h}a* 'ash' (Cusihuamán 1976a:106, 157).

---

[173] Similar observations are found in comparative studies by Torero (1964:470), Landerman (1991:67), Cerrón-Palomino (2003:193, 214), among others.

(279) **-ch'ka*   >   *-chka*   >   *-shka*   >   *-sha*   >   *-sya*   >   *-sa*
                                                    -ska/-sqa

It is noteworthy that Aymara has a progressive-imperfective form *-ska* (Herminia Martín 1974:38; de Lucca 1983:685) which is almost identical to *-shka* in Santiago del Estero Quechua (Bravo 1965:155). (280) is from de Lucca and (281) is from Bravo. Since Aymara is spoken in areas bordering Southern Quechuan varieties, one might wonder whether the form *-ska* may be borrowed due to language contact. However, as Willem Adelaar (p.c.) points out, *-ska* in Aymara can be analyzed as two separable components, *-s(i)* ' reflexive' plus *-ka* 'incomplete or ongoing event'. Thus, borrowing is unlikely, though it cannot be ruled out since Hardman (1966 and 2000) does not report a progressive-imperfective form similar to *-ska* in Jaqaru (Aymaran).

(280) AYMARA
      lura-__ska__-ña
      work-__IPFV__-INF
      'to be __working (doing)__'

(281) SANTIAGO DEL ESTERO QUECHUA
      contesta-pu-sqa   ri-__shka__-sqa-n-ta   cerco-ta   rúa-j
      answer-BEN-PST3   go-__PROG__-NMLZ-3-OBJ   wall-OBJ   do-PRMT
      'He answered that he __was going__ to build a fence.'

Finally, the Proto Northern progressive form can be reconstructed as **-ku* 'middle voice'. This cross-linguistically unusual development from middle voice to progressive aspect is discussed in detail above in §8.6. Like the forms derived from **-ch'ka*, the progressive forms derived from **-ku* typically appear before the inflectional TAM slot, following the object marker. (See, e.g., Table 3-1 in Nuckolls 1996:43 for Pastaza).[174]

(282) **-ku*   >   *-hu*   >   *-u*

Sequences in the development of the three Quechua progressive suffix forms **-yka:*, **-ch'ka:*, and **-ku* are summarized in Table 10.2. Significantly, in each language area (column 1), a progressive suffix has taken over functions of the original present imperfective zero marker.

---

[174] According to Cole (1982:196-7), the Imbabura progressive *-ju* precedes the first person object *-wa* when there is an intervening suffix (*-ju-* ... *-wa*), but *-wa* precedes *-ju* when they are adjacent (*-wa-ju*).

Table 10.2 *Sequences of developments of progressive suffixes in Quechua areas*

QUECHUA AREA	PROTO FORM	REDUCED FORMS					
CENTRAL and N PERU	*-yka:	>	-yya(:) -yka -yga -ycha:	>	-ya:	>	-ya
SOUTHERN (Ayacucho vicinity)	*-ch'ka:	>	-chka:	>	-chka		
SOUTHERN (south of Ayacucho)	-chka > -shka	>	-sha -ska/-sqa	>	-sya	>	-sa
NORTHERN	*-ku	>	-hu	>	-u		

10.3 Paths leading to and from imperfective aspect

As observed in previous chapters, progressive-continuous -*yka:* is compatible with dynamic and stative predicates in SCQ. In neighboring Huamalíes, -*yka:* has generalized still further toward general imperfective status by taking on durative and present functions as well. This pathway of grammaticization is represented in (283).

(283) PROGRESSIVE   >   CONTINUOUS   >   IMPERFECTIVE

Bybee et al. (1994:139) initially propose the path in (283), but ultimately reject the intermediate "CONTINUOUS" stage because that meaning does not occur in their database. In a later study, Heine and Kuteva similarly propose the path "CONTINUOUS > HABITUAL" and conclude that "more research is required to establish the significance of this pathway" (2002:93).[175] In Central Quechua at least, continuous markers constitute an intermediate stage between progressive and imperfective. Further study is needed in other Quechuan languages to determine the extent to which the modern progressive suffixes descended from *-*yka:*, *-*ch'ka:*, and *-*ku* have developed continuous and habitual meanings.

The ongoing development of progressives as continuous and imperfective markers in Quechua encroaches on the semantic territory formerly occupied by the zero marker, originally a present imperfective but currently a present habitual in SCQ. This narrowing of the functions of zero, that is, a shift from more to less general meaning, is represented in (284). The acquisition of habitual meaning by progressive-continuous markers in Quechuan languages such as

---

[175] Languages in which a progressive has become an imperfective by acquiring habitual meaning are listed Chapter 5, note 104.

Huamalíes could lead to the eventual obsolescence of zero. (For more on this general diachronic process, see Bybee et al. 1994:151).[176]

(284) ... < HABITUAL < IMPERFECTIVE

In a manner of speaking, the semantic territory associated with zero is besieged by the other half of the imperfective domain as well, as a class of derivational durative and repetitive markers show evidence of grammaticizing as habitual markers. The elaboration and expansion of habitual aspect in Quechua is treated in the next section.

10.4 The elaboration of habitual aspect

The previous section sketched a path to habitual aspect via subtraction. That is, the former present imperfective zero marker (expressing present, habitual/generic, and progressive) lost part of its aspectual meaning through the corresponding development of overt progressive suffixes. As a result, this zero marker is now limited to present habitual meaning.

This section reviews categories with specific imperfective meanings and their synchronic locations along various paths that tend to converge on habitual meaning over time. In §3.1 we observed the rich set of distinctions in SCQ which further specify internal temporal structure through duration or recurrence over time, including duratives, continuatives, frequentatives, distributives, iteratives, and activities portrayed as customary.[177] The geographic distributions of many Quechua forms that express recurrence are shown in Maps 10.2 and 10.3.

---

[176] There is no credible evidence for a progressive suffix in Quechua when grammatical zero became a present imperfective in the inflectional TAM position (see §11.5). On the other hand, progressive meaning may have been expressed through periphrasis as is currently attested in some modern Quechuan languages, e.g., *-sh(pa)* plus *tiya-* in Chachapoyas (Taylor 2000:75) and in Santiago del Estero (Bravo 1965:43). The development of aspect suffixes from periphrastic constructions is discussed in Chapter 11.

[177] Unlike duratives, continuatives, etc., customary activities are not grammatical categories. Rather, markers associated with customary activities are discussed in this work because "early sources of habitual grams [grammatical markers] ... denote that the subject is accustomed to or disposed to perform a certain action" (Bybee et al. 1994:159).

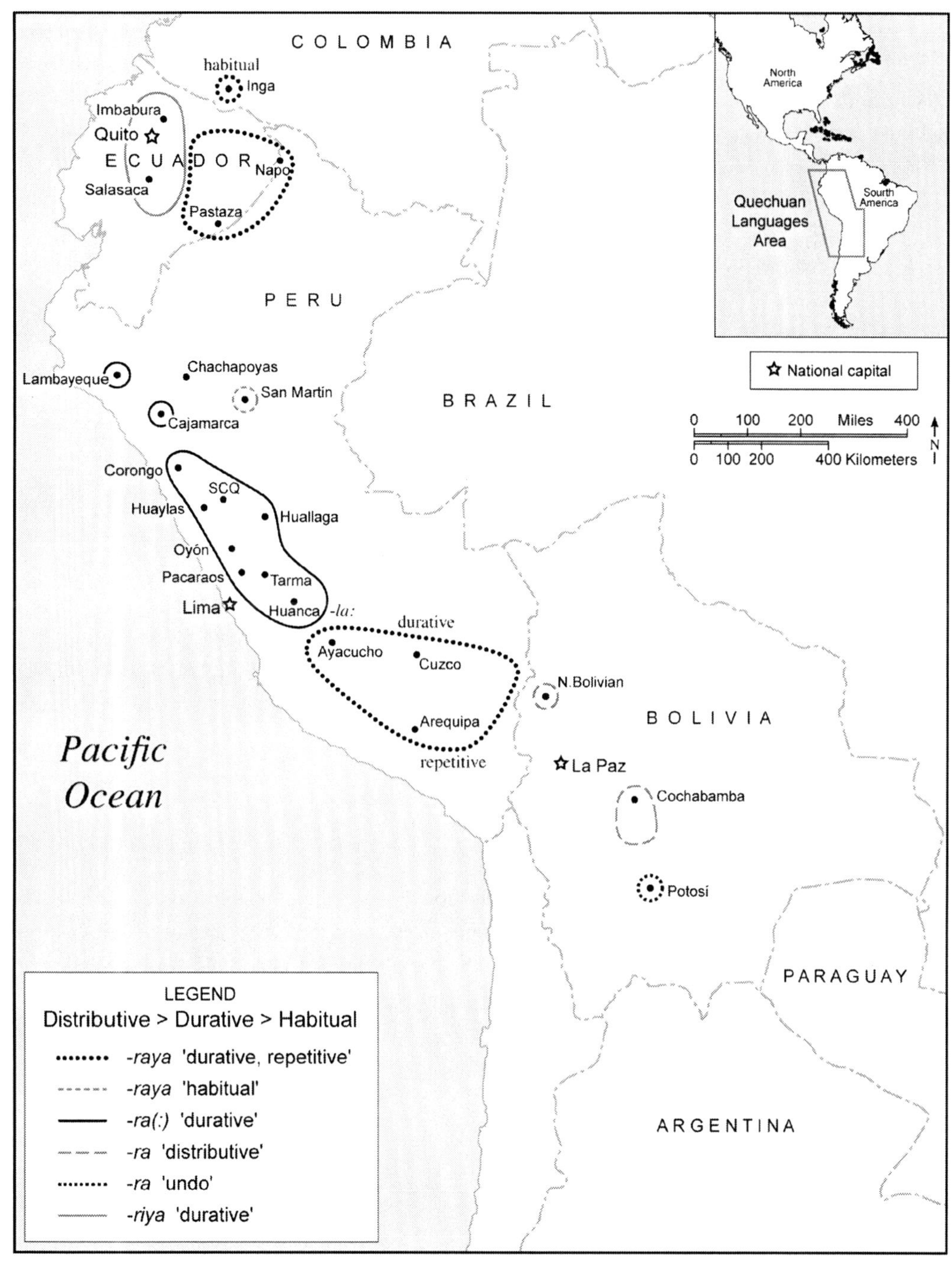

Map 10.2 DISTRIBUTIVES, DURATIVES, AND HABITUALS FROM *-raya

Durative *-ra:* in SCQ (reduced from **-raya*) presents a situation as temporally extended (§3.1.1). Cognate forms include distributive *-ra* in Cochabamba (Lastra 1968:30), durative *-raya* in Cuzco (Cusihuamán 1976a:198), durative-habitual *-raya* in Ayacucho (Soto 1976a:113), and habitual *-raya* in Inga (Levinsohn 1976:97) and in San Martín (Coombs, Coombs, and Weber 1976:126). Presumably, the path of development leads from distributive to durative aspect to habitual aspect.

(285) DISTRIBUTIVE   >   DURATIVE   >   HABITUAL

The suffix *-rayka:* in SCQ was derived historically through the amalgamation of durative *-ra:* plus continuous *-yka:*. With dynamic verbs *-rayka:* presents an event as repeated often (frequentative) or continually (continuative); cf. (66)-(71) in §3.1.3.

(286) SCQ
    ari watuka-__rayka__-nki, sino:-qa   llaki-ku-n   mas-cha:
    yes visit-__DUR.C__-2   or.else-TOP be.sad-MID-3 more-MUT
    'Yes, you __visit often__, or else she may become too sad.'

In situations that involve customary activities, *-rayka:* can take on a habitual reading. These noncompositional meanings are more than the sum of the original durative and continuous elements. (With stative verbs, by contrast, the meaning of *-rayka:* is compositional, often translated as 'remain' or 'be'.)

(287) DURATIVE +   >   FREQUENTATIVE/   >   HABITUAL
     CONTINUOUS   CONTINUATIVE

Distributive *-paku* in SCQ may have been formed through the amalgamation of benefactive *-pu* plus middle voice *-ku*, with the initial element *-pu* lowered to *-pa* by the form *-ku*, yielding *-paku* (§3.1.5). Ordinarily *-ku* does not trigger lowering, but Parker (1976:130) provides an example in neighboring Huaylas Quechua which supports this reconstruction. In (288) he shows that the lowering effect in Huaylas is variable synchronically. The implied plural object 'things' in (288) is compatible with the semantics of distributives.[178]

---

[178] Parker does not characterize the suffix combination *-pu* plus *-ku* as a distributive in Huaylas, but rather "the subject is the beneficiary of an action directed to other people ... as an index of a commercial or professional activity" (1976:119, my translation).

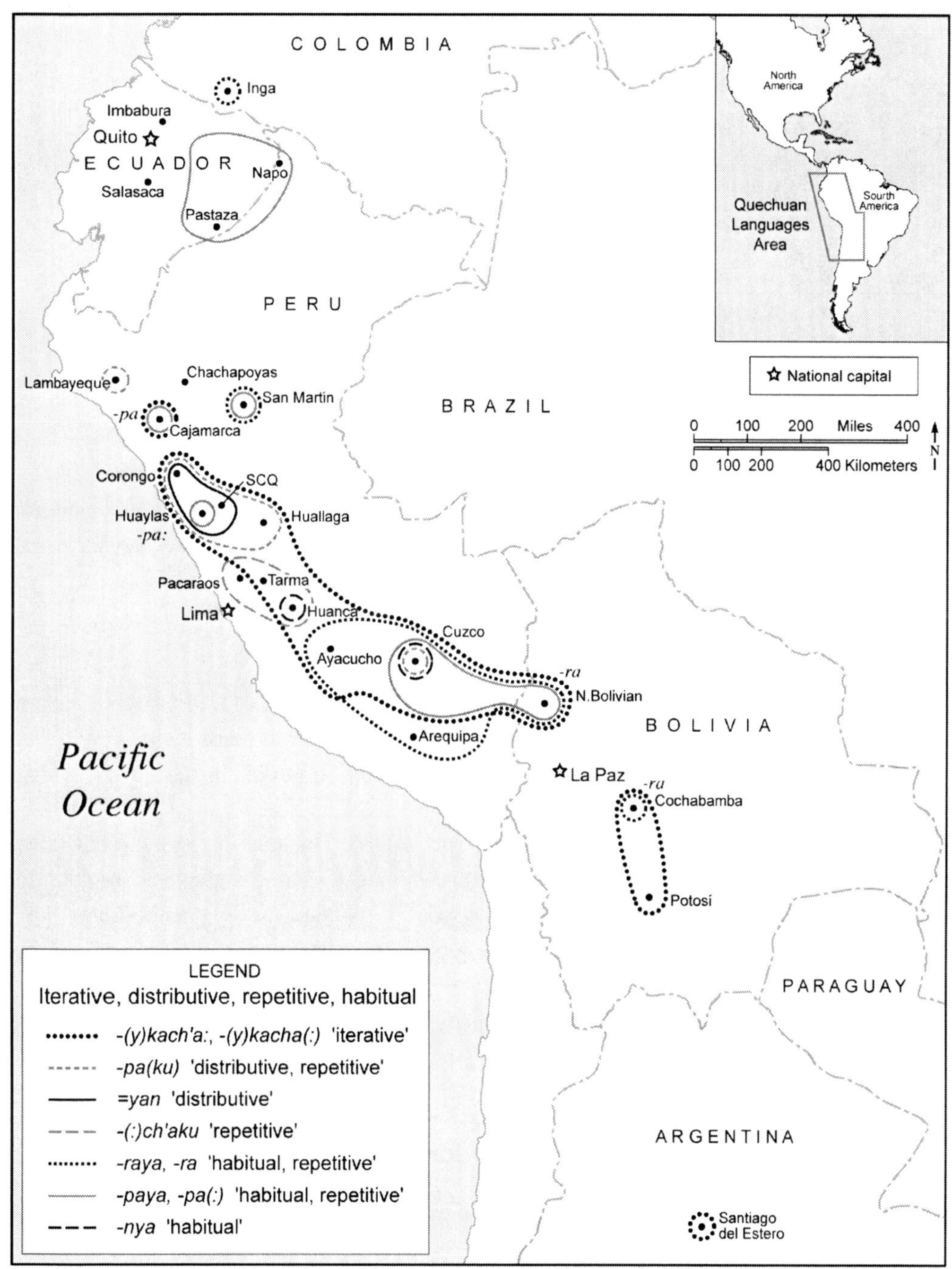

Map 10.3 QUECHUA DISTRIBUTIVES, REPETITIVES, AND HABITUALS *

---

* In addition to the Quechuan varieties indicated in Map 10.3, the form *-paku* is also reported in Tarma and Pacaraos, but not with distributive or repetitive meaning. Similarly, the form

(288) HUAYLAS QUECHUA
    *miku-**pu**-**ku**-nki*   ~   *miku-**pa**-**ku**-nki*
    eat-BEN-MID-2   eat-BEN-MID-2
    'You eat things for others.'

Only the lowered alternative *-paku* is valid in SCQ and most other Quechuan varieties with the non-compositional distributive meaning.

(289) SCQ
    *mika-**paku**-nki*
    eat-DISTR.S-2
    'You eat various of those things.'

The high vowel in the final element *ku* is lowered to *a* (allomorph *-paka*) when followed by a trigger suffix, as illustrated above in (86).

The cognate form *-pa(ku)* in Cuzco Quechua has a repetitive meaning (Cusihuamán 1976a:204). As in the paths represented in (285) and (287), distributives and repetitives can develop habitual meaning.

(290) DISTRIBUTIVE   >   REPETITIVE   >   HABITUAL

Distributive *=yan* presumably developed through the cliticization of a distributive numeral *yan* 'n each' (§3.1.6). This meaning later would have generalized to 'each entity', the current meaning of *=yan* with nonverbal elements. The distribution of entities in space (places) later extended to the distribution of events in time (occasions).

The enclitic *=yan* is found only in Ancash and western Huánuco in central Peru (Hintz 2000:189). The verbal plural suffix *-ya:* is attested in the same geographical region, and distributive *=yan* and plural *-ya:* do not co-occur. Cross-linguistically, distributives are a common source for plural markers through the grammaticization of the inference of multiple participants (Mithun 1999a:90). These facts suggest that distributive *=yan* and plural *-ya:* may be cognate. Similar facts suggest a shared etymology linking distributive *-paku* and plural *-pa:ku* (spoken east and south of SCQ).

(291)   DISTRIBUTIVE > DISTRIBUTIVE > DISTRIBUTIVE > PLURAL
      NUMERAL   (ENTITIES)   (OCCASIONS)   (PARTICIPANTS)

Iterative *-ykacha:* in SCQ (§3.1.4) generally presents a situation with multiple subactions which recur on a single occasion, as in (292).

-ch'aku/-chaku is reported in Corongo, Huaylas, SCQ, and Huallaga, but not as a repetitive. The cognate forms *-paya*, *-pa:*, and *-pa* are reported in Ayacucho, Huanca, Tarma, Pacaraos, Huallaga, SCQ, Corongo, and Imbabura, but not as habituals or repetitives.

(292) SCQ

> *tinyaq-kuna   allqu-ta   qati-__kacha__-yku-n*
> bee-PL.N   dog-OBJ   follow-__ITER__-PFV.O-3
>
> 'The bees __keep pursuing__ the dog.'

Cognate forms are spoken throughout Central and Southern Quechua, as well as in Cajamarca in North Peruvian Quechua (see Map 10.3 above). These forms include *-(y)kach'a(:)* in Huanca (Cerrón-Palomino 1976:213), Tarma (Adelaar 1977:142), and Corongo (Hintz 2000:180), *-kach'a* in Cajamarca (Quesada 1976:134), *-(y)kacha* in Cuzco (Cusihuamán 1976a:198), and *-kacha* in Santiago del Estero (Bravo 1965:38).

The etymology of iterative *-ykacha:* is uncertain due to several complicating factors. One plausible source, suggested by Santo Tomás ([1560] 1995:84), would be the infinitive suffix *-y* plus the verb **kach'a-* 'send (with an implied return)'. Cross-linguistic support for this hypothesis is found in Heine and Kuteva (2002:259). These authors mention only one lexical source for iteratives, the verb 'return'.

One difficulty with this hypothesis is that Proto Quechua lacked long vowels (Parker 1963:123). A proto form **-ykach'a* would not account for the final long vowel in SCQ (*-ykacha:*) and other modern Central Quechuan varieties. A clue to solving this puzzle may lie in the fact that Quechuan varieties throughout Ancash (SCQ, North Conchucos, Corongo, Sihuas, Chiquián, and parts of Huaylas) and western Huánuco (Huamalíes) have two related lexical items *kacha-/kach'a-* 'send' and *kacha:-/kach'a:-* 'untie, loosen'. The second form *kacha:-* suggests a motive for the final long vowel in Central Quechuan varieties, the hypothesis **-ykach'a > -ykach'a:* by analogy. (The sound change **ch' > ch* is well attested in many Quechuan varieties.)

Another plausible source for the final long vowel would be the suffix combination *-yku* plus *-ch'a:*, an alternative interpretation suggested by Adelaar (1986:45) for the Pacaraos stem *salta-yka-ch'a:-* 'jump-IN-REPETITIVE'. This analysis is based on the suffix form *-ch'a(:)* which means 'distributive' in Tarma and 'repetitive' in Pacaraos (ibid:40).

Regardless of the etymology of **-ykach'a(:)*, the path from iterative to habitual is well documented cross-linguistically (e.g., Bybee et al. 1994:170, Heine and Kuteva 2002:183-4).

(293) ITERATIVE > (FREQUENTATIVE) > HABITUAL

The aspectual functions associated with verbal reduplication in SCQ cluster into two groups, as shown in Table 10.3 (reproduced from Table 3.2 in §3.1.7). In the first group labeled REDUP₁ (Types 1 and 2), inflected verbs reduplicated in their entirety express continuative or frequentative meanings. These typically involve speech-act participants and correspond to situations with a high level of affect. In the second group labeled REDUP₂ (Types 3-6), only the verb root is reduplicated. These latter reduplication types express iterative, distributive, and durative meanings, and do not directly convey affect.

Table 10.3 *Aspect and verbal reduplication types in SCQ*

ASPECT **REDUPLICATION TYPE**	ITERA- TIVE	DISTRIBU- TIVE	DURA- TIVE	CONTIN- UATIVE	FREQUEN- TATIVE
	NEUTRAL AFFECT			*INTENSE AFFECT*	
REDUP₁					
1. INFLECTED FINITE VERB				✓	
2. INFLECTED NONFINITE VERB					✓
REDUP₂					
3. ROOT~ROOT + VERB MORPH.	✓	✓			
4. SOUND~SOUND + VERB MORPH.	✓				
5. ROOT~ROOT	✓				
6. ROOT-SS ROOT + VERB MORPH.			✓		

Cross-linguistically, repetition of a dynamic verb often signals repetition of the action specified by the verb. This iconic association suggests that a natural, early (or the earliest) aspectual meaning to arise from reduplication would be iterative (cf. Bybee et al. 1994:159). As shown in Table 10.3, this observation appears to hold for REDUP₂ in SCQ, but not for REDUP₁. Instead, Type 1 and Type 2 inflected verb reduplications would not represent former iteratives but rather the continuative and frequentative meanings appear to be motivated by the immediate context which involves intensive effort and affect. Similar meanings are seen in English reduplications, such as *she ate and ate (kept eating) but was never satisfied.*

Type 3-5 ROOT~ROOT (REDUP₂) reduplications are of a different sort. These encode iterative meaning, which can be interpreted as distributive when the repeated action involves multiple patients or is realized over a more extensive area during a longer period of time. SCQ verbal reduplication thus suggests an alternate distributive stage intervening between iterative and habitual. Finally, reduplication Type 6 ROOT-SS ROOT is a specialized construction which presents sustained effort, giving rise to durative aspect with habitual readings.

(294) ITERATIVE   >   (DISTRIBUTIVE)   >   DURATIVE   >   HABITUAL

The sense of 'sustained effort' conveyed by reduplication Type 6 is similar to that of the suffix *-chaku* 'concerted effort', a type of manner with incipient aspectual functions (§7.2.2). *-chaku* presumably results from the amalgamation of two suffixes. The second element would be middle voice *-ku*, but the identity of the first element is less certain because there is no productive suffix with the form *-cha* in SCQ. Cognate forms with suitable meanings elsewhere in Central Quechua include *-ch'a* 'distributive' in Tarma (Adelaar 1977:141), *-cha:* 'iterative' in Huallaga (Weber 1989:151), and *-ch'a:* 'repetitive' in Pacaraos (Adelaar 1986:40).

The combined form *-ch'aku* (or *-chaku*) appears in Tarma as a type of distributive (Adelaar 1977:147), in Huanca as 'repetitive' (Cerrón-Palomino 1976:186), and in Huallaga as 'concentratedly' (Weber 1989:172). In SCQ *-chaku* 'concerted effort' has durative readings in some contexts.

(295) DISTRIBUTIVE   >   REPETITIVE   >   CONCERTED   >   DURATIVE
                                                EFFORT

Total *-ka:ku* is derived historically from the amalgamation of passive *-ka:* plus middle voice *-ku*. We can account for this semantic contradiction by recognizing a two-step process in the historical development. Presumably, passive *-ka:* first became lexicalized or fused with certain verb roots (e.g., *mantsa-* 'fear', *mantsaka:-* 'be afraid'). These passive forms could then take the middle suffix *-ku* (e.g., *mantsaka:-ku-* 'be totally afraid'). The innovative meaning ('totally') was not attributed to *-ku* alone, but rather to the combination of final *-ka:* plus *-ku*, now reanalyzed as the grammatical suffix *-ka:ku*. Total *-ka:ku* can also report activities that recur customarily, yielding habitual readings (see §7.2.2).

(296) LEXICALIZED   >   PASSIVE+MIDDLE   >   CUSTOMARY   >   HABITUAL
      PASSIVE   VOICE

Finally, the Proto Quechua suffixes middle voice **-ku* and punctual **-ri* have undergone significant developments in modern Quechuan languages. As shown in Chapter 8 (see esp. Figure 8.1), these developments provide evidence for a pathway of grammaticization leading in stages from punctual (perfective aspect) to reflexive/middle voice (in Northern Quechua), and from middle voice to habitual (in Central Quechua) and progressive (in Northern Quechua).

(297) PUNCTUAL   >   REFLEXIVE   >   MIDDLE VOICE   >   HABITUAL   (Central)
                                                                PROGRESSIVE (Northern)

10.5 Summary of paths to habitual

The previous section presented several grammatical categories in Quechua with meanings which are much more specific than general imperfective. These categories may be viewed as intermediate stages along interconnected pathways of grammatical development that converge on habitual aspect. The historical relationships among the categories are summarized in Figure 10.1.[179]

---

[179] As mentioned above, the expression of imperfective aspect varies a great deal across the spectrum of Quechuan languages. I report many of these imperfective forms in this note to facilitate ongoing research. In addition to the forms presented in §10.4, others include *-nya* 'habitual' in Huanca (Cerrón-Palomino 1976:214), *-nya* 'continuative', reduplication 'habitual', and *-paya* 'frequentative' in Cuzco (Cusihuamán 1976a:87, 200-1), *-paya* 'habitual with purpose' in San Martín (Coombs et al. 1976:126), *-riya* 'durative' in Imbabura (Cole 1982:150), *-riri* 'iterative' in Cajamarca (David Coombs, p.c.), *-rqacha* 'iterative', *-tata* 'sudden iterative', and *-yka* 'past habitual' in Potosí, Bolivia (Crapo and Aitken 1986:3, 7), and *-tiya* 'repetitive' in

Figure 10.1 *Paths of grammaticization that converge on habitual aspect in Quechua*

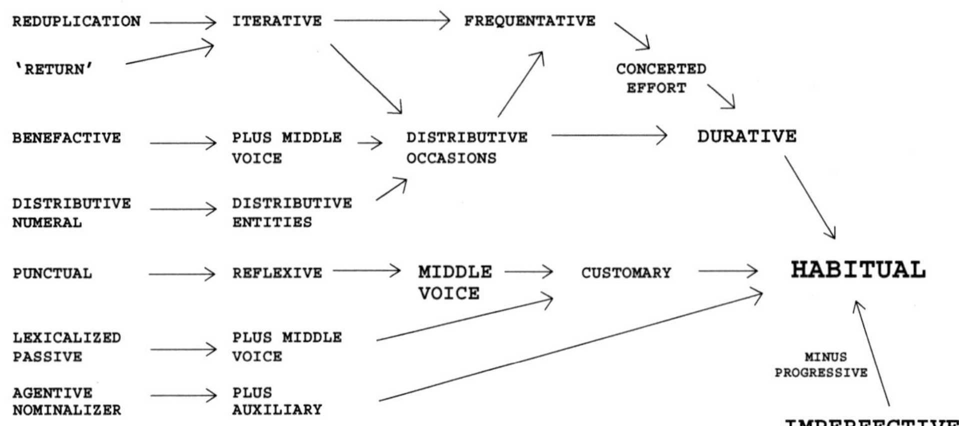

10.6 Imperfectives restricted to past time reference

In addition to grammatical zero and the various derivational imperfective markers presented above, SCQ has two inflectional imperfective markers that are restricted to the past. Historical developments involving narrative past *-na:* and past habitual *-q* are presented above in §5.2 and §5.3, respectively (see also Maps A.6 and A.7 in Appendix A). In short, both markers were formerly expressed by periphrastic constructions in which a deverbal suffix was followed by the copular auxiliary *ka-* (i.e., **-ña-q ka-* and **-q ka-*). In order to further specify habitual **-q* plus *ka-* for past situations, the copula was inflected with a past suffix, as currently attested in Huanca Quechua (Cerrón-Palomino 1976:176), Imbabura Quechua (Cole 1982:149), and Lambayeque Quechua (Shaver 1987:31). The past suffix no longer occurs in SCQ, but the past meaning was absorbed by the remaining phonological material, i.e., *-q/-q=ka.*

The periphrastic constructions from which these two imperfective markers originate illustrate one of the principal diachronic processes that gives rise to Quechua aspect suffixes. Aspectualizing constructions are discussed in Chapter 11.

10.7 Conclusion: The evolution of imperfectives

We have examined the grammatical development of imperfective aspect across the Quechua language family, focusing especially on the highly elaborated system of derivational and inflectional markers in SCQ. Just as diachronic forces move directional and perfect markers along pathways of grammaticization that converge on the more general perfective category

---

Ayacucho (Soto 1976a:113). Aspect expressed through analytic verbal constructions is treated in Chapter 11.

(Figure 9.3), specific markers of duration, continuity, and recurrence traverse paths that converge on the more general imperfective category (Figures 10.1 and 10.2).

In addition to these evolutionary processes, our investigation of the diachrony of aspect in Quechua also illuminates emergent properties of grammar. The rise of the inflectional perfective-imperfective distinction is a case in point. Synchronic reflexes of the past suffix *-rqa* and imperfective zero are found in virtually all modern Quechuan languages. *-rqa* would have developed via the usual processes of desemanticization, decategorialization, and phonetic reduction. When *-rqa* attained inflectional status, the lack of a marker in the TAM slot I2 was conventionalized (by contrast) as present imperfective, formally marked by grammatical zero. In other words, present imperfective zero did not originate as a less grammatical or lexical item that subsequently traversed evolutionary paths of grammaticization. Instead, the abstract grammatical meaning of zero emerged through contrast with inflectional perfectives.

While grammatical zero emerges without phonetic substance, the genesis of other imperfective markers involves, in each case, a less grammatical expression (and/or lexical material) pressed into service for more grammaticized functions. This is seen, for example, in the subsequent development of the four overt progressive suffixes *-yka:*, *-ch'ka:*, *-shqa*, and *-ku*, each corresponding to a geographic region. At least one progressive suffix has taken over functions of the original present imperfective zero marker in each modern Quechuan language.

An imperfective complement to progressives is habitual aspect, which is instantiated in Quechuan languages by a wide variety of markers with specific durative and repetitive functions. These markers were shown to traverse a complex network of paths that converge toward habitual aspect over time (see Figure 10.1 above).

As summarized in Figure 10.2, habituals and progressives tend to converge on a more general imperfective category. As noted above, present imperfective formally marked by zero does not traverse these paths, but rather emerges via contrast with inflectional perfectives. The subsequent loss of aspectual functions of this zero marker to developing progressives and habituals constitutes a shift from more to less general meaning as the competing forms encroach on the present imperfective domain.

Figure 10.2 *Paths of grammaticization that converge on imperfective (and habitual)*

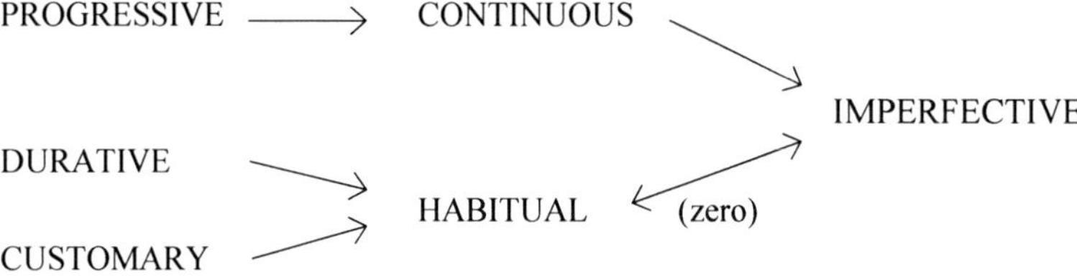

Finally, the evolution of imperfectives is inextricably linked to the evolution of perfectives and provides an intriguing scenario for the ongoing development of aspect in modern Quechuan languages. We have seen evidence for a wide variety of diachronic processes that shape the grammatical systems, including "standard" grammaticization as a product of gradual context-induced reinterpretations (*-*rqu* 'out' > -*ru* 'past perfective'), the emergence of present imperfective *-Ø via contrast with inflectional perfectives, the narrowing of the functions of older grammatical markers through competition with younger developing markers (*-Ø 'present imperfective' > 'present habitual'; *-*rqa* 'past' > 'remote past'), the amalgamation of existing suffixes (-*ra:* 'durative' plus -*yka:* 'continuous' > -*rayka:* 'habitual'), lexicalization with the final element subsequently split off in combination with another suffix (-*ka:ku* 'customary, total'), cliticization (=*yan* 'distributive'), and two types of reduplication.

We also have seen evidence for renewal through periphrastic constructions that combine lexical and grammatical elements (-*q* plus *ka-*, -*na:* plus *ka-*, -*shqa* plus *ka-*). The aspectual meanings expressed through a set of developing auxiliaries provide further synchronic evidence for the constructions from which the more grammatical aspect markers would have developed. In the next chapter, we will consider aspectualizing constructions expressed through periphrasis in greater detail.

11 ASPECTUALIZING CONSTRUCTIONS

In Chapters 9 and 10, we examined grammatical developments in the Quechua aspectual system and its organization into perfective and imperfective categories. Reconstructed Proto Quechua forms, primarily suffixes, served as points of origin for subsequent stages along evolutionary paths of development. The present chapter allows us to step back further in time, as it were, to investigate the gradual emergence and elaboration of aspectual categories from earlier sources, that is, from "lexical phrases and words which develop into auxiliaries or particles and then eventually into affixes" (Bybee et al. 1994:40).

Analytic verbal constructions in naturally-occurring speech in modern Quechuan languages, such as SCQ, offer one means to examine the prospective source material from which aspect suffixes would have emerged. Specifically, the aspectual meanings expressed through a set of developing auxiliaries and particles provide synchronic evidence for the lexical substance and phonological material employed in the ongoing grammaticization of aspect markers. The aim of the present chapter, then, is to investigate aspectual constructions, beginning with their genesis or "first emergence" in SCQ and across the Quechua language family. I especially focus on the development of auxiliary verbs which subsequently cliticize and give rise to aspect suffixes, a process described by Heine (1993:53-5), among others.

In §11.1 I discuss the auxiliation process and introduce the Quechua construction STEM–NOMINALIZER+AUXILIARY which has given rise to many aspect suffixes. §11.2 and §11.3 illustrate seventeen such auxiliaries attested in various Quechuan languages. §11.4 summarizes the observed nominalizer plus auxiliary combinations and, as applicable, the aspect suffixes that have resulted from these analytic configurations. §11.5 draws on Quechua-specific auxiliation patterns as well as cross-linguistic evidence to motivate the reconstruction of the Central Quechua progressive suffix *-yka:. §11.6 describes two additional sources for aspect suffixes that do not involve auxiliary verbs. Finally, in §11.7 I review various diachronic processes and "aspectualizing construction" types which elaborate aspectual systems in Quechua.

11.1 The aspectualizing construction STEM–NOMINALIZER+AUXILIARY

The analyses presented in this chapter employ the framework proposed by Heine in which auxiliaries are interpreted as "products of grammaticalization" that "involve at the same time more than one linguistic item" (1993:27,31). The auxiliation process is aptly summed up by Kuteva:

> What in the source construction is a free verb form followed [preceded] by a nominal or nominalized complement becomes, in the resulting auxiliary structure, a regularized grammatical marker followed [preceded] by a main verb form (2001:1, brackets added).

Auxiliation in Quechua is represented in schematic form in (298), where V_1 is a free verb form (often a "light" verb) and V_2 is the stem form of a nominalized complement. What happens, essentially, is that V_1 develops into an auxiliary verb, and the combination of the two linguistic items "NOMINALIZER AUXILIARY" comes to express a single grammatical concept through periphrasis.

(298) AUXILIATION IN QUECHUA

      V_2–NOMINALIZER V_1 > V–NOMINALIZER AUXILIARY

In SCQ and other Quechuan languages, such analytic verbal constructions typically express aspectual notions.[180] In most of these aspectualizing periphrases, inflectional TAM and subject person suffixes are obligatorily added to the auxiliary, but an object person suffix, if needed, is marked immediately prior to the erstwhile nominalizing suffix in the V (main verb) element. The V element is an open slot that can be filled by virtually any verb stem, that is, a lexical verb root that may carry additional suffixes. For this reason, I refer to this configuration as the STEM–NOMINALIZER+AUXILIARY construction.[181]

The aspectualizing construction STEM–NOMINALIZER+AUXILIARY appears to be very time stable in Quechua. As shown in the following sections, particular instantiations of this construction have given rise to many aspect suffixes via the cliticization of the auxiliary to the erstwhile nominalized complement. In fact, the auxiliation process continues to introduce aspectual contrasts in Quechua, exemplifying what has been referred to as the "renewal" stage of grammaticization; see Bybee et al. (1994:21-2), Hopper and Traugott (2003:121-3), among

---

[180] A small number of auxiliary constructions in SCQ express modal concepts; cf. note 186. Other auxiliaries express non-TAM concepts, e.g., *ima-* 'happen' in (120).

[181] In a study "mainly devoted to aspectual periphrases" in Romance languages, Squartini (1998:23-4) provides a detailed account of analytic constructions formed with a finite verb form plus a nominal or nonfinite form.

others.[182] Accordingly, constructions such as STEM–NOMINALIZER+AUXILIARY have been characterized as "processing units" that supply lexical substance for grammaticization:

> Grammaticalization occurs when a new construction or a *specific instance of an old construction* becomes a processing and storage unit (Bybee 1998:6, italics added).

While some auxiliaries are highly grammaticized and easily recognizable (e.g., copula *ka-*), others in the earliest stages of development have not been reported in the traditional Quechuanist literature (e.g., *usha-* 'finish, completely'). As Kuteva observes, "instances of incipient auxiliation often remain unrecognized" (2001:5). In general, emergent patterns of grammatical expression tend to be overlooked in studies that rely exclusively on elicitation or edited monologic data. By contrast, the corpus of naturally-occurring SCQ speech used in this work facilitates the discovery of emerging auxiliary constructions observable as high-frequency "nominalizer plus light verb" combinations that exhibit non-compositional interpretations.[183]

In what follows I present seventeen distinct auxiliary verbs that appear in combination with a variety of nominalizers and other nonfinite markers. Nine auxiliaries found in SCQ (and other Quechuan languages) are described and illustrated in §11.2. Eight additional auxiliaries do not occur in SCQ but are found in other Quechuan languages as illustrated in §11.3. Periphrastic constructions are presented from twenty-one Quechuan varieties, each indicated in Map 11.1 (overleaf). The aspectual meanings expressed by the specific verbal periphrases and derived forms presented here are placed in parentheses to the right of the relevant illustrations.

---

[182] Munro illustrates this renewal process by providing evidence for older and newly developing auxiliaries in Chickasaw (Muskogean), a language in which "auxiliarization begins at different times and occurs at different rates with different source constructions" (1984:334).

[183] As corpora of naturally-occurring speech become available for other Quechuan languages, we can anticipate that discourse-based methodologies, such as employed in this study, will reveal additional incipient auxiliary constructions.

Map 11.1 Quechuan varieties illustrated in §11.2 and §11.3 (auxiliaries)

11.2 Aspectual auxiliaries in SCQ (and other Quechuan languages)

Nine auxiliaries participate in verbal periphrases to express a wide array of aspectual distinctions in SCQ, as well as in other Quechuan languages. This section begins by introducing auxiliaries derived from copulas (*ka-*, *kawa-*), then phasal verbs (*usha-*, *qalla-*, *tuku-*), and finally verbs related to motion (*puri-*, *(h)aku*, *keda-*, *si:gi-*).

11.2.1 *ka-* 'be'

The principal copula in most Quechuan languages is a form descended from **ka-* 'be'. For example, the modern form is *ka-* in SCQ and *-a* in Pastaza Quechua of Ecuador (Nuckolls 1996:285).[184] The copula **ka-* must have been a very early development, given that its reflexes are found in virtually all Quechuan languages.[185]

(299) SCQ
    papa:-ne: **ka***-ra-n* *karpinte:ru-m*
    father-1   **be**-PST-3 carpenter-DIR
    'My father **was** a carpenter.'

(300) PASTAZA QUECHUA (ECUADOR)
    a*-w-ra-chu*
    be-DUR-PST-NEG
    '**Was** he there?'

Modern reflexes of the copula **ka-* also function as auxiliary verbs in various periphrastic constructions that express aspect, tense, and modality. Only constructions that express an aspectual function are illustrated here.[186] In (301), for example, a verb nominalized with the agentive suffix *-q* (glossed SUB) combines with the copular auxiliary *ka-* to yield a past habitual in Huallaga Quechua (Weber 1989:18).

---

[184] Pastaza Quechua (Ecuador) has an additional copula *ma-* illustrated in §11.3.

[185] Indeed, the form *ka-* is attested as a copula and also an auxiliary in Santo Tomás, the earliest reliable Colonial source, e.g., *ka-ni* 'yo soy [I am]', *miku-q ka-ni* 'yo como [I eat habitually]' ([1560] 1995:43, 94).

[186] Past conditional mood is expressed by the periphrasis of the finite conditional suffix *-man* plus the copula *ka-* inflected with a past tense suffix, e.g., *miku-nki-man ka-ra-n* eat-2-COND be-PST-3 'you should have eaten'. In another periphrastic construction, the irrealis nominalizer *-na* plus a possessive suffix combines with *ka-* to express deontic modality, e.g., *miku-na-yki ka-yka-n* eat-NMLZ.I-2 be-CONT-3 'you must eat'. An emerging class of English modal auxiliaries from erstwhile main verbs is discussed by Krug (2001).

(301) HUALLAGA QUECHUA   (PAST HABITUAL)
    *Pillku-man   aywa-**q   ka**-:*
    Pillcu-ALL   go-**SUB   be**-1
    'I **used to go** to Pillcu.'

In SCQ the adjoining elements *-q* plus the copula *ka-* are beginning to fuse together, forming a single grammatical bound morpheme. For example, in Huallaga and other Central Quechuan varieties the negative marker *-tsu* intervenes between *-q* and *ka-*, but in SCQ *-tsu* can follow both elements and the person marker, as in (302).[187]

(302) SCQ   (PAST HABITUAL)
    *riñon-wan   sufri-r   ... trabaha-y-ta   pwe:di-**q=ka-:-tsu***
    kidney-COM   suffer-SS   work-INF-OBJ   be.able-**PST.H-1-NEG**
    'During the time I was suffering with a kidney infection **I was not able to work**.'

In (303) the past participle *-sh(q)a* combines with *ka-* to yield a perfect in Huallaga (1989:18).

(303) HUALLAGA QUECHUA   (PERFECT)
    *Pillku-man   aywa-**sha   ka**-shaq*
    Pillcu-ALL   go-**PTCP   be**-1FUT
    'I **will have gone** to Pillcu.'

The periphrastic perfect construction has given rise to the past perfective third person suffix *-sh(a)* in SCQ. The use of *-sh(a)* in consecutive main clauses of narrative sequences, as in (304), demonstrates that it no longer functions as a perfect marker. Example (304) is extracted from the longer stretch of discourse illustrated above in (154).

(304) SCQ   (PAST PERFECTIVE)
    *tsay-na   aywa-**sh**   tsay-man,   ... tsa   papa:-nin-ta   willa-pti-n-qa.*
    that-NOW   go-**PST.R3**   that-ALL   then   father-3-OBJ   inform-DS-3-TOP

    *tsay Ernesto Garay-qa   aywa-**sh**   don Benito-man-qa   ari   ni-q-nin.*
    that Ernesto Garay-TOP   go-**PST.R3**   sir Benito-ALL-TOP   yes   say-PRMT-3

    'Then his dad **went** over there after (his son) told him. So Ernesto Garay **went** to Benito to talk to him.'

---

[187] According to Heine (1993:43), discontinuous grammatical markers are a widespread characteristic of verbal periphrases that involve auxiliaries.

In SCQ the narrative past (past imperfective in conversation) is formed through the periphrasis of the suffix *-na:* (from *-ña-q*) plus the auxiliary *ka-*.[188]

(305) SCQ   (PAST IMPERFECTIVE)
   ke:-no: baha:da-qa   kurba   kurba   kurba   kurba   tse:-no:-pa   dere:chu-n-pa
   this-SIM descent-TOP   curve   curve   curve   curve   that-SIM-GEN   straight-3-GEN

   pa:sa-ski-ya:-__na:=ka-__: *mana   kurba-ta   tuma-ypa*
   pass-PFV-PL.V-**PST.N=be**-1   no   curve-OBJ   turn-ADV

   'Though the path descended with many curves, we **were going straight** down without following the switchbacks.'

In Huanca Quechua the auxiliary *ka-* no longer appears in the narrative past construction. Instead, the subject person marker attaches directly to the reduced form *-ña* (Cerrón-Palomino 1976:174). *-ña* plus the first person suffix *-:* is seen in (306).

(306) HUANCA QUECHUA   (NARRATIVE PAST)
   paka-__ña-__:
   hide-**PST.N**-1
   '**I was hiding**.'

11.2.2 *kawa-* 'exist, be alive' (from **kawsa-*)

As mentioned above, the widespread reflexes of the copula **-ka* suggest that this form developed very early. Several copulas that developed more recently are reported in certain Quechuan languages, and these also participate in analytic verbal constructions.[189] In Chachapoyas Quechua, for example, *kawsa-* (from **kawsa-* 'be alive, exist') can function as a locative copula, similar in meaning to Spanish *estar* (Taylor 1979:81).[190]

(307) CHACHAPOYAS QUECHUA
   che-b   __kawsa__-n   plasa-k
   that-LOC   **be.at**-3   plaza-TOP
   'The plaza **is located** there.'

---

[188] **-ña-q* would have been a nominalizer in periphrasis with the copula *ka-*. Presumably, the final element *-q* was the agentive nominalizer.

[189] Additional copular auxiliaries are presented in §11.3, including *ma-* in Pastaza Quechua, and *tiya-* in several Northern and Southern Quechuan languages. These two forms do not function as copulas (nor as auxiliaries) in SCQ.

[190] A historical relationship between **kawsa-* and the copula **ka-* has not been shown, but such a connection would not be implausible.

Taylor (2000:73) also provides examples of a periphrastic construction in Chachapoyas in which the clause linker *-sh* (from **-shpa* 'same subject adverbializer') combines with the copular auxiliary *kawsa-* to express habitual aspect.

(308) CHACHAPOYAS QUECHUA   (HABITUAL)
  atux *ilh-k-__sh__* __*kawsa*__-*n*
  fox steal-MID-__SS__ __live__-3
  'The fox __lives stealing__.'

When combined with *-shpa*, the verb *kawsa-* can also function as a habitual auxiliary in Pastaza Quechua of Peru, as in the following example in Toedter, Waters, and Zahn (2002:114).

(309) PASTAZA QUECHUA (PERU)   (HABITUAL)
  pay-kuna-mi *karan* *upya-hu-shka-n-kuna-pi* *kaha-__shpa__* __*kawsa*__-*nahun*
  he-PL.N-DIR each drink-PROG-NMLZ-3-PL.N-LOC play.drum-__SS__ __live__-3PL
  'They __customarily play__ the drum whenever they drink (masato).'

The cognate form *kawa-* in SCQ (meaning 'exist, be alive') does not function as a copula, but this form does participate in similar aspectualizing constructions. For example, when *kawa-* is preceded by the past participle suffix *-sh* (from **-shqa*), the combination can yield a habitual interpretation. The meaning of the verbal construction in (310) is 'He always enjoyed his carefree life', and not 'He was alive enjoying his carefree life'.

(310) SCQ   (HABITUAL)
  felisida:-nin-ta *kushi-__sh__* __*kawa*__-*ku-na:*
  carefree-3-OBJ happy-__PTCP__ __live__-MID-PST.N

  fyesta-man *imayka-man* *aywa-r*
  fiesta-ALL all.kinds-ALL go-SS
  'He __always enjoyed__ (living) his carefree life, going to all kinds of fiestas.'

In (311) the combination of infinitive *-y* plus *kawa-* yields a durative interpretation.[191]

(311) SCQ   (DURATIVE)
  ku:ra-chu *yama-__y__* __*kawa*__-*ku-ya:-na:*
  priest-LOC be.well-__INF__ __live__-MID-PL.V-PST.N
  'He __continually got along well__ with the priest.'

---

[191] In §11.5 we will consider the role of **kawsa-* 'live, exist' in the earliest stages of development of the progressive suffixes *-yka:* and *-chka:* (presented above in §10.2).

Durativity is also associated with formulaic expressions in which infinitive *-y* is followed by *kawa-*. Examples such as *wiña-y kawa-y* 'eternal life' in (312) suggest that compounding may reinforce the association of a temporal sense with the sequence *-y* plus *kawa-*.

(312) SCQ   (DURATIVE)

  *wiña-**y**   **kawa**-y-ta-m   tari-sha:*
  grow-**INF**   **live**-INF-OBJ-DIR   find-1FUT

  'I will find **eternal life**.'

When not used in an analytic verbal construction, *kawa-* simply means 'exist' or 'be alive', as in (313). As Marchese observes for Kru languages, "when a verb takes on auxiliary characteristics, the verb from which it is derived does not cease to exist" (1986:96). This comment certainly applies to Quechuan languages and many others.

(313) SCQ

  *wawa-:-kuna,   huk-lle:lla   ollqu-q   **kawa**-n*
  child-1-PLUR   one-ONLY   male-HUMAN   **live**-3

  'Of all my children, only the male **is alive**.'

11.2.3 *usha-* 'finish'

In addition to copulas, certain phasal verbs also function as auxiliaries. When used in isolated clauses, the verb root *usha-* means 'end' or 'finish'. *usha-* is intransitive in (314) and transitive in (315).

(314) SCQ

  *tsay-no: kay kwentu **usha**-n*
  that-SIM   this story   **finish**-3

  'Like that this story **ends**.'

(315) SCQ

  *estudiu-yki-ta **usha**-r   profesyun-niki-man-ra: cha:-na-yki*
  studies-2-OBJ   **finish**-SS   profession-2-ALL-YET   arrive-NMLZ.I-2

  'After **finishing** your studies, you still must enter your profession.'

When *usha-* is preceded by the deverbal suffix *-r* (glossed SS for 'same subject'), however, the combination *-r* plus *usha-* expresses completive aspect. In (316), for example, the meaning of the verbal construction is 'I completely trampled', and not 'I finished trampling'. In other words, *usha-* functions as an auxiliary within this analytic construction, with the lexical meaning supplied by the stem that precedes *-r*. This periphrastically expressed completive is relatively frequent in the database, with nearly 30% of all instances of *usha-* preceded by *-r*. (The larger context for (316) is illustrated in Appendix F, Text 2 "Cows, oats, and guinea pigs," line 17.)

(316) SCQ   (COMPLETIVE)
      runa-pa   *abe:na-n-kuna-ta-si*   *qashu-tsi-**r***   **_usha_**-*ru-:*
      person-GEN oats-3-PL.V-OBJ-EVEN trample-CAUS-**SS** **finish**-PST.R-1
      'I **completely trampled** the owner's oat field.'

11.2.4   *qalla-* 'begin'

Another phasal verb in SCQ is *qalla-* 'begin', illustrated in (317).

(317) SCQ
      tsa   **_qalla_**-*n-na*   *re:su*
      then **begin**-3-NOW prayer
      'Then the prayer time **begins**.'

While *usha-* 'finish' is both transitive and intransitive, *qalla-* 'begin' is intransitive in that it cannot take a simple noun as a direct object. On the other hand, these two verbs can also function as complement-taking predicates. As is typical in SCQ, the complement takes the infinitive *-y* plus the object suffix *-ta*. In the next two examples, *usha-* and *qalla-* are syntactic main verbs interpreted as clause heads.

(318) SCQ
      i   *tsay-ta*   *palla-**y**-**ta***   **_usha_**-*ski-r-nin* *bolsiyu-n-man* *palla-shqa*
      and   that-OBJ gather-**INF**-**OBJ**   **finish**-PFV-SS-3 pouch-3-ALL   gather-PST.R3
      'After he **finished gathering** those (pears off the tree), he put them into his pouch.'

(319) SCQ
      tsay-lla-cho:-na   *shaka-**y**-**ta*** **_qalla_**-*ski-ya-n*
      that-DLM-LOC-NOW eat-**INF**-**OBJ** **begin**-PFV-PL.V-3
      'Right there now they **began to eat** them.'

In contrast, in the periphrastic construction *-r* plus *usha-* in (316), *usha-* 'finish' is interpreted semantically as a completive modifier rather than as a clause head. Similarly, in the construction *-r* plus *qalla-* in (320), *qalla-* 'begin' appears to function as an inceptive modifier. While *usha-* is clearly an auxiliary in (316), *qalla-* in (320) represents an earlier stage in the auxiliation process. Nearly 60% of all SCQ exemplars of *qalla-* participate in this periphrastic construction. Adverbial *-r* seems to be making substantial inroads into the terrain of infinitive *-y* in neighboring Huamalíes as well, but not in Huallaga (David Weber, p.c.).[192]

---

[192] The suffix *-ri* marks punctual aspect in SCQ, but inceptive aspect in many other Quechuan languages, e.g., Cuzco (Cusihuamán 1976a:210), Cochabamba (Lastra 1968:31), Pacaraos (Adelaar 1986:41), San Martín (Coombs et al. 1976:126), among others. In those languages the auxiliary *qalla-* appears to play a less significant role than in SCQ.

(320) SCQ   (INCEPTIVE)

      atoq-qa   *hirka-pa*   *su:bi-**r***   ***qalla**-na:*
      fox-TOP   mountain-GEN   go.up-**SS**   **begin**-PST.N

      'The fox **began climbing** up the mountain.'

In general, the SCQ suffix *-r* functions as an adverbial linker for clauses in which the subjects are coreferential. This function is seen in (310), (315), and (325). In contrast, *-r* has characteristics of an infinitive in the "*-r* plus *usha-*" and "*-r* plus *-qalla-*" aspectualizing constructions illustrated in (316) and (320).[193] Cole provides a similar illustration from Huaraz Quechua (due west of SCQ) to show that "the suffix *-r* is also used in certain infinitival constructions" (1983:14). Interestingly, the two elements in (321) appear in the opposite order, *qalla-* (plus inflection) followed by *-r*, presumably under the influence of Spanish (see Hintz 2009:192-3).

(321) HUARAZ QUECHUA   (INCEPTIVE)

      papa:-ni: ***qalla**-rqu-n*   *maqa-ma-**r***
      father-1   **begin**-PST.R-3   hit-1OBJ-**INF**

      'My father **began hitting** me.'

11.2.5 *tuku-* 'become, pretend, finish'

According to many grammars and dictionaries of Quechuan languages, the form **tuku-* 'become, pretend' is no longer an independent lexical item. In Pastaza Quechua (Ecuador), for example, *tuku-* functions as an auxiliary. Nuckolls (1996:54) refers to constructions that combine a nominalized verb form (e.g., using *-y* infinitive) with the auxiliary *tuku-* 'become' as "the passive completive."[194]

---

[193] Specifically, *-r* (or reflexes of **-shpa* in other varieties) functions as an infinitive in that it derives nonfinite forms which are not inflected to agree with a subject, and these forms almost never take TAM suffixes. Typically, adverbial clauses marked with *-r* can be strung together in succession. In contrast, when *-r* is used in one of these periphrastic constructions, only one such form is allowed.

[194] The verb *tuku-* can also mean 'finish' in Lengua General (González Holguín [1608] 1952:382). This meaning is also attested in modern Cuzco (Cusihuamán 1976b:147) and Ayacucho (Soto 1976b:109), making it a prime candidate for becoming a completive auxiliary in those languages.

(322) PASTAZA QUECHUA (ECUADOR)   (PASSIVE COMPLETIVE)
    *imanata   kara-**y**   **tuku**-ra-nchi   Ulpiano   urku-y*
    comp   give.food-**NOM** **become**-PAST-1PL   Ulpiano   hill-LOC
    'Do you remember how we **became fed** at Ulpiano hill?'

In other Quechuan languages, *tuku-* has become the second element of a suffix. In Huallaga Quechua, for example, the combination of nominalizer *-q* plus the auxiliary *tuku-* has given rise to the verbal suffix *-qtu* 'pretend' (Weber 1989:172).[195] Although the final vowel in **tuku-* apparently was not susceptible to lowering, in Huallaga "the /ku/ of *tuku-* has been reanalyzed as *-ku* ['middle'], and so undergoes morphophonemic lowering" (ibid.), as illustrated in (323).

(323) HUALLAGA QUECHUA   (PSEUDO-INCHOATIVE)
    *yanqa-lla   mutu-**qtu**-ka-ma-nki*
    in.vain-DLM   chop-**PRETEND**-MID-1OBJ-2
    '**Pretend** to chop me, but do so without force.'

In Margos-Yarowilca-Lauricocha Quechua the resulting suffix *-qtu* has attained the more general meaning 'less than complete' (Bean 1988:3). (*-qtu* in (324) was originally glossed 'PRETEND'.)

(324) MARGOS-YAROWILCA-LAURICOCHA QUECHUA   (LESS THAN COMPLETE)
    *usya-**qtu**-n-pa-chaq   ka-yka-n*
    clear.up-**PARTIAL**-3-ADV-EVID be-CONT-3
    'The sky is **less than completely** clear.'

The suffix *-qtu* expresses a similar meaning in SCQ.

(325) SCQ   (LESS THAN COMPLETE)
    *tsay-kuna-ta   rura-r-qa   musya-**qtu**-pa-yka-ya-nki-m*
    that-PL.N-OBJ   do-SS-TOP   know-**PARTIAL**-BEN-CONT-PL.V-2-DIR
    'When you do those things, you **only partially** know (the trouble you're causing).'

---

[195] As many authors point out, the suffix form *-tuku* can also be added to nouns. For example, in Huallaga Quechua *runa-tuku-n* (person-PRETEND-3) means to 'act in a proud or haughty manner' (Weber 1998:549). In SCQ *haqa-tuku-sh runa* (debt-PARTIAL-PTCP person) refers to 'a person in debt' (not completely solvent).

11.2.6 *puri-* 'walk'

A third class of verbs that function as auxiliaries in Quechua involve motion (or the explicit lack of motion). The verb *puri-* (from *puri- 'walk') sometimes retains its original literal meaning, as in (326).

(326) SCQ

> *tse: runa-qa   tse:-lla-pa   **puri**-n.   mana ka:rru-ta   utilisa-n-tsu.*
> that person-TOP   that-DLM-GEN   **walk**-3   no   vehicle-OBJ   use-3-NEG
>
> 'That man always **walks** there. He never goes in a vehicle.'

The verb *puri-* can also refer to a customary activity, as in (327).

(327) SCQ

> *komo ochenta tsay-no: katekista yayku-ya-sha-:-pita,*
> or.so eighty   that-SIM   catechist enter-PL.V-NMLZ.R-1-ABL
>
> *na:maski   kimsa-q-lla-m   **puri**-yka:-ya-:*
> no.more.than   three-HUMAN-DLM-DIR   **walk**-CONT-PL.V-1
>
> 'Of the eighty or so who became catechists, only three of us **are continuing** (that vocation).'

In keeping with this secondary meaning of *puri-* as 'customary', the combination of *-r* 'same subject' plus *puri-* yields a habitual interpretation of the preceding stem. In (328) and (329), for example, *puri-* functions as a habitual auxiliary with the stems *yarqu-* 'leave' and *puklla-* 'play', respectively. That is, the periphrasis *yarqu-r* plus *puri-* means 'go out on a regular basis' and not 'walk leaving'. Similarly, *puklla-r* plus *puri-* means 'spend time playing', not 'walk playing'.

(328) SCQ   (HABITUAL)

> *aparti,   mami:ta,   kay ofendi-yku-n.   yarqu-**r** **puri**-ku-n-man.*
> in.addition   dear.lady   this offend-PFV.O-3 leave-**SS** **walk**-MID-3-COND
>
> 'In addition, dear lady, (her grandmother=my mother-in-law) insults her. She (my daughter) should be allowed to **go out on a regular basis**.

(329) SCQ   (HABITUAL)

> *wata-n usya   witsan-na-m   yapay kuti-ya:-mu-nki   ishka-ntsik*
> year-3 clear.up season-NOW-DIR   again return-PL.V-FAR-2 two-1₁
>
> *puklla-**r** **puri**-na-pa:*
> play-**SS**   **walk**-NMLZ.I1₁-PURP
>
> 'Please return again next dry season so the two of us can **spend time playing**.'

This periphrastically expressed habitual is relatively infrequent, with only 10% of all instances of *puri-* combined with *-r*. Occasionally, the two verbal elements appear in the opposite order, as in (330), which means 'we always share' and not 'we walk sharing'.

(330) SCQ   (HABITUAL)
      kanan-qa ***puri**-ya-:*   *komparti-**r**-mi i   llapa-n-wan-pis*
      now-TOP   **walk**-PL.V-1   share-**SS**-DIR   and   all-3-COM-EVEN
      shumaq-mi   ka-ya-:
      beautiful-DIR   be-PL.V-1
      'Now, we **always share with others** and we live beautifully with everyone.'

Finally, many Quechuan languages have a construction referred to as "purpose-motion."
This construction combines a finite motion verb with a verb nominalized by the agentive suffix
-q. The literal meaning of the construction, illustrated in (331), is 'initiate movement toward
another location to perform the action expressed by the nominalized form'.[196]

(331) SCQ
      *Walla-m   tutay   qewa-ku-**q**   **apa**-ra-n*
      Walla-DIR   previous   grass-MID-**PRMT**   **take**-PST-3
      'Walla a previous day **took it** (the donkey) to **graze**.'

In SCQ the verb *puri-* does not participate in the purpose-motion construction, though it does
in some other Quechuan languages. As illustrated in (332), the combination of *-q* plus the
auxiliary *puri-* can express a prospective future in Arequipa Quechua (Kindberg 1987:208).

(332) AREQUIPA QUECHUA   (PROSPECTIVE)
      *chaqay llaqta-ta   tiya-**q**   **puri**-saq*
      that   town-OBJ   reside-**PRMT**   **walk**-FUT1
      '**I'm gonna live** over there in that town.'

11.2.7   *(h)aku-* 'let's go'

Cusihuamán refers to the defective verb *haku* in Cuzco Quechua as "an auxiliary that
accompanies the principal verb...to denote the immediate initiation of the action" (1976a:191).

(333) CUZCO QUECHUA   (PROSPECTIVE)
      *haku   llank'a-**sun**-chis*
      let's.go   work-**IMP1**-PL.V
      'Let**'s begin** to work.'

The cognate form *aku* in SCQ typically appears with a finite future or imperative, as in
Cuzco.

---

[196] For more on aspectual suffixes derived from the purpose-motion construction, see the
auxiliaries *ri-* and *aywa-* in §11.3.

(334) SCQ   (PROSPECTIVE)

> *aku   shoqa-ska-mu-__shun__-ra:.*
> let's.go   console-PFV-FAR-__IMP1__-YET
> '__Let's go__ cheer him up.'

aku can also appear as a main verb in SCQ, though it does not take inflectional markers and can only be interpreted as a first person inclusive.

(335) SCQ

> *kanan-qa   __aku__   Lisa-kaq-pa-na*
> now-TOP   __let's.go__   Lisa-DEF-GEN-NOW
> 'Now __let's go__ to where Lisa is.'

Unlike most other auxiliaries, *(h)aku* typically precedes the second element, whether a finite form as in Cuzco (333) and SCQ (334), or a nonfinite form as in San Martín Quechua. In San Martín *aku(-)* functions as an auxiliary in a variety of analytic periphrases, including the prospective construction in (336) and the purpose-motion construction in (337) (Coombs et al. 1976:129).

(336) SAN MARTÍN QUECHUA   (PROSPECTIVE)

> *__aku__   lluka-__y__-pa*
> __let's.go__   climb-__INF__-GEN
> '__Let's climb__ up there.'

(337) SAN MARTÍN QUECHUA

> *__aku__-na   apari-mu-__k__   sara-ta*
> __let's.go__-NOW   carry-FAR-__PRMT__   corn-OBJ
> '__Let's go bring__ the corn.'

In San Martín the form *aku(-)* can be inflected optionally for person and number, though only first person inclusive examples are provided.[197]

(338) SAN MARTÍN QUECHUA

> *__aku__-y-chi-na   chakra-man*
> __let's.go__-IMP-PL.V-NOW   field-ALL
> '__Let's go__ to the field.'

---

[197] According to Muysken (1977:53) the defective exhortative form *haku* can distinguish between 'few' and 'many' in Ecuador and in Cajamarca, e.g., *haku* 'let's go', *haku-ychik* 'let's all go'.

11.2.8 *keda-, ke:ra-* 'stay, remain'

Certain Spanish verb forms have been recruited to serve as auxiliaries in the native construction STEM–NOMINALIZER+AUXILIARY. For example, the SCQ verb *keda-* is borrowed from Spanish *quedar* 'stay' (339). When *keda-* is preceded by the past participle suffix *-sh*, the combination expresses durative aspect (340).

(339) SCQ
      mana-mi   **_keda_**-*ku-:-man-tsu*
      no-DIR   **stay**-MID-1-COND-NEG
      'I shouldn't **stay** with you.'

(340) SCQ   (DURATIVE)
      i   *tsa*   *ri:ku*   *kushi-***_sh_**   **_keda_**-*ku-na:*
      and then rich.one be.happy-**PTCP** **stay**-MID-PST.N
      'Then the rich man **was happy**.' (lived happily ever after)

In Huallaga Quechua, the Spanish verb *quedar* takes the form *ke:ra-* (Weber 1989:24,25). (341) illustrates its use as an auxiliary verb combined with the past participle *-sha*.

(341) HUALLAGA QUECHUA   (DURATIVE)
      taka-ka-sha-n   *hinan-chaw*   *ranka-ka-***_sha_**   **_ke:ra_**-*ku-ra-n*
      strike-PASS-SUB-3 precisely-LOC lodge-PASS-**PTCP** **stay**-MID-PST-3
      'It **stayed lodged** right where it had struck.'

11.2.9 *si:gi-* 'follow, continue'

Another Spanish verb that participates in the native construction STEM–NOMINALIZER+AUXILIARY is *si:gi-*, from *seguir* 'follow, continue' (342). When *si:gi-* is preceded by the deverbal suffix *-r* 'same subject', the combination expresses continuative aspect (343).

(342) SCQ
      syempri-m   **_si:gi_**-*yka:-ya-:*   *kawa-q-kaq*
      always-DIR   **continue**-CONT-PL.V-1 live-AG-DEF
      'Those of us who are alive are always **continuing**.'

(343) SCQ   (CONTINUATIVE)
      yaku-chu   *puklla-***_r_**   **_si:gi_**-*ya-n*
      water-LOC   play-**SS**   **continue**-PL.V-3
      'They **keep playing** in the water.'

11.3 Aspectual auxiliaries attested elsewhere in Quechua

The previous section illustrated nine auxiliary verbs that appear in combination with a number of nominalizers (and other nonfinite suffixes) to express aspectual notions in SCQ and other Quechuan languages. This section illustrates eight additional auxiliary verbs that do not occur in SCQ, but which are reported to participate in aspectualizing constructions in other Quechuan languages. These include auxiliaries derived from two additional copulas (*ma-*, *tiya-*), a cognition verb (*yacha-*), and five other motion verbs (*ri-*, *aywa-*, *shamu-*, *pasa-*, *kacha-*). The auxiliary structures reported here provide further evidence for the source material from which various aspect suffixes have emerged.

11.3.1 *ma-* 'be', *a-* 'be'

The widespread copular auxiliary **ka-* and the more recent copular auxiliary *kaw(s)a-* were introduced in §11.2. In Pastaza Quechua of Ecuador, Nuckolls (1996:285) reports the copula *a-* (from **ka-*) as well as an additional copula *ma-*. While *a-* describes temporary conditions, locations, non-intrinsic traits, and actions low in agentivity, *ma-* usually refers to "relatively agentive" activities or "relatively intrinsic" traits.[198]

Both *a-* and *ma-* also function as auxiliaries in periphrastic constructions. For example, in (344) a verb nominalized with the agentive suffix *-k* combines with the copular auxiliary *a-* to yield habitual meaning.

> (344) PASTAZA QUECHUA (ECUADOR) (HABITUAL)
> *ñuka   mana   kanta-k̲-chu   a̲-ni*
> I   no   sing-AG-NEG   be-1
> 'I'm not **in the habit of singing** (anymore).'

The past suffix *-ra* is added to the auxiliary *ma-* in (345) to form a past habitual. Recall that the periphrasis combining the agentive nominalizer *-q* with the copula *ka-* in SCQ and Huallaga Quechua has come to express past habitual meaning without the addition of a past suffix in the auxiliary, as illustrated above in (301) and (302).

> (345) PASTAZA QUECHUA (ECUADOR) (PAST HABITUAL)
> *ñuka yaya yapa puri-k̲   ma̲-ra   Marañon-gama*
> my   father   much   travel-AG   be-PAST   Marañón-UNTIL
> 'My father **used to travel** a lot, as far as the Marañón river.'

---

[198] An anonymous reviewer suggests that the copula *ma-* almost certainly derives historically from a contraction of the assertive (direct) evidential *-m(i)* and the copula *a-* (from **ka-*).

The combination of *-q* plus *ka-* has begun to fuse into a single morpheme *-q=ka* in SCQ. This fusion has not been reported in Pastaza, that is, bound forms such as *-k=ma*, *-kma*, and derivatives.

11.3.2   *tiya-* 'sit, reside, be (at), have'

Another verb that functions as a copular auxiliary derives from the verb **tiya-* 'sit, reside'.[199] In Salasaca Quechua (Ecuador), for example, *tiya-* functions as a locative copula in (346), and a more general copula in (347). These examples are from Waskosky (1992:67, 71). Examples from Inga Quechua are found in Levinsohn (1991:152).[200]

(346) SALASACA QUECHUA
    *cai auto-ucu-bi   ñuchi-sh   **tiya**-rga-nchi*
    this car-INSIDE-LOC we-EVEN   **exist**-PST-1$_I$
    'We too **were** (located) inside this car.'

(347) SALASACA QUECHUA
    chai-ga   yuri-ya-shca-bug-ca   asuha-sh   listu
    that-TOP   dawn-BEC-NOM.PL-POSS-TOP   corn.beer-EVEN   ready
    ***tiya**-shca   nin-ga   ubiya-na-lla   ña*
    exist-PTCP   rpt-TOP   imbibe-INF-DLM   now
    'Then at dawn the corn beer **was**, they say, now completely ready for drinking.'

In other Quechuan languages, the copula *tiya-* also functions as an auxiliary. In Chachapoyas (North Peruvian), for example, *tiya-* combines with the clause linker *-sh* (from **-shpa* 'same subject') to yield progressive meaning. According to Taylor, this periphrastic progressive construction is "much more frequent" than the progressive suffix *-yka* (2000:75). Taylor provides an example of *tiya-* as a separate auxiliary in *(348)*a, and also fused with *-sh* in *(348)*b.

---

[199] Parker (1969b:48) glosses **tiya-* as 'sit down'. This form possibly had acquired the meaning 'reside' by the Proto Quechua stage.

[200] The form *tiya-* exhibits other functions typical of copulas. For example, *tiya-* can express existential meaning in Salasaca and other Quechuan varieties, e.g., *mana tiya-n-chu* [no exist-3-NEG] 'there are none' (from a Saraguro Quechua text in Weber and Orr 1987:26). The verb *tiya-* can also express possession, similar to Spanish *haber* or *tener* 'have', in San Martín Quechua (Coombs et al. 1976:132) and in Chachapoyas Quechua (Taylor 1979:176), e.g., *ñuka-nch-pa tiya-n ishkay bestya* [I-1$_I$-GEN have-3 two horse] 'we have two horses'.

(348) CHACHAPOYAS QUECHUA   (PROGRESSIVE)
  a. *shamu-**sh***   ***tiya**-n*
     come-**SS**   **be.at**-3

  b. *shamu-**shtiya**-n*
     come-**PROG**-3

  'He **is coming**.'

This progressive construction formed with the copular auxiliary *tiya-* is also attested in Santiago del Estero Quechua (Argentina). The following two examples are found in Bravo (1965:31, 43). Although the suffix *-s* (and *-sh* in Chachapoyas) is glossed 'same subject', it does not function as an adverbial clause marker in this aspectual periphrasis (see note 193).

(349) SANTIAGO DEL ESTERO QUECHUA
     ashqo   *tulla*   ***tiya**-n*
     dog   thin   **be**-3
     'The dog **is thin**.'

(350) SANTIAGO DEL ESTERO QUECHUA   (PROGRESSIVE)
     pay-kuna   *puñu-**s***   ***tiya**-n-ku*
     he-PL.N   sleep-**SS**   **be**-3-PL.V
     'They **are sleeping**.'

The following Chachapoyas example shows that *-sh* plus *tiya-* can also express habitual meaning in the past. Given both a progressive and a habitual sense, this construction could be considered a more general imperfective marker. However, it is unclear whether the habitual interpretation occurs only in past contexts, as is common with progressives in other languages, including continuous *-yka:* in SCQ (as noted in §5.4).

(351) CHACHAPOYAS QUECHUA   (HABITUAL)
     kaxa-k-sh   *ño:pa-k*   *yak-ta-k*   *apari-**sh***   ***tiya**-sh-sab*
     drum-MID-SS   front-TOP   water-OBJ-TOP   carry-**SS**   **be.at**-PST-PL.V
     'Long ago they **would carry** water playing the drum.'

The suffix *-shti/-sti*, which is attested in many Quechuan languages, may have arisen through the fusion of **-sh* (the initial element in *-shqa* and *-shpa*) plus **tiya-*. (A less likely source for the second element would be the verb **ati-* 'be able'.) Among the meanings attributed to the suffix *-sti* in Cuzco Quechua is 'imminent' or 'prospective' (Cusihuamán 1976a:224).[201]

---

[201] Cusihuamán describes the suffix *-sti* in Cuzco Quechua as, "Consecutive sequence. A verbal root marked by this nominal [nominalizing-DJH] suffix indicates that the action referred to is realized immediately after the action of the principle verb ends, is realized in passing, or it

(352) CUZCO QUECHUA   (PROSPECTIVE)
      *para-ri-mu-**sti**-lla-n-ñan*   *ka-sha-sqa*
      rain-INCH-FAR-**IMMINENT**-3-NOW   be-PROG-PST.P
      'By now it was **about to start raining**.'

The suffix *-tya:/-titya:* is also attested with the meaning 'imminent' in Huanca Quechua (Cerrón-Palomino 1976:214). This suffix is cognate with the forms *-tiya* and *-tya:* which are attested in various Quechuan varieties spoken within a geographically contiguous area in southern Peru. Presumably, these forms either derive historically from a similar periphrasis with the auxiliary verb **tiya-* or through contact with Southern Quechua.[202]

(353) HUANCA QUECHUA   (PROSPECTIVE)
      *pasa-**tya**-qlu-n-ña-m*   *tamya-kaq*
      pass-**IMMINENT**-OUT-3-NOW-DIR   rain-DEF
      'The rain **is about to stop** now'

11.3.3 *yacha-* 'know'

The verb **yach'a-* 'know, know how' can also function as an auxiliary in a periphrastic construction that expresses habitual aspect.[203] In (354), for example, the combination of infinitive *-na* plus *yacha-* is translated 'customarily' in Saraguro Quechua (Ecuador) (Weber and Orr 1987:26).[204]

---

is *about to happen*" (1976a:224, my translation and italics). The suffix *-sti/-shti(n)* is also reported in Ayacucho (Weber and Phelps 1987:170) in Southern Quechua, in Cajamarca (Quesada 1976:121) in North Peruvian Quechua. and Huanca (Cerrón-Palomino 1976:178) and Tarma (Adelaar 1977:101) in Central Quechua. This suffix does not occur in SCQ, nor in most other Central Quechuan varieties.

[202] Cognate suffixes include *-tiya* 'short repeated intervals' in Ayacucho (Soto 1976a:113) and 'unusual manner' in Cuzco (Cusihuamán 1976a:203), and *-tya(:)* 'sudden interrupted action' in Tarma (Adelaar 1977:143) and Pacaraos (Adelaar 1982:43).

[203] A natural link between the cognition verb "know" and a habitual aspect is seen, for example, in Orr and Wrisley: "*yachana* 'saber, aprender' [know, learn]; *yacharina* 'acostumbrarse, habituarse' [get accustomed to, get used to]" (1981:91). In some Quechuan varieties, verbs derived from **yach'a-* have acquired the additional sense 'reside at', e.g., Huaylas (but not SCQ). For cross-linguistic support for the path from "know" to "habitual" see Heine and Kuteva (2002:186-8).

[204] In spoken varieties of Ecuadorian Spanish the verb *saber* 'know' has practically replaced *soler* 'be accustomed to, be in the habit of'. In a lexicon of Ecuadorian Spanish, for example, Estrella Santos includes the following entry: "**saber**. tr. Soler, ser frecuente. *Aquí sabía*

(354) SARAGURO QUECHUA   (HABITUAL)
     tukuy   laya   aycha-ta   apa-mu-__na__   __yacha__-rka
     all.kinds type meat-OBJ take-FAR-__INF__ __know__-PST3
     'He __customarily brought__ all kinds of meat.'

Levinsohn illustrates a similar habitual construction in the Santiago dialect of Inga Quechua (Colombia) (1991:152, 163). Unlike most other auxiliaries, *yachá* in (355) precedes the nonfinite element, similar to the auxiliary *(h)aku* in §11.2.

(355) INGA QUECHUA   (HABITUAL)
     __*yachá*__   *kapa-ri-ku-__nga__*
     __know__   cry-MID-CONT-__INF__
     'It __used to cry__.'

In SCQ and other Quechuan languages, by contrast, when *yacha-* appears in finite forms, the preceding infinitive is case-marked by *-ta* as a direct object complement. In (356), for example, the verb *parla-* 'speak' is marked by infinitive *-y* and accusative *-ta*. In terms of semantics, the resulting translation is 'she knows how to speak Quechua', not 'she customarily speaks Quechua'.

(356) SCQ
     tse: kechwa-ta-qa   po:ku   parla-__y-ta__   __yacha__-n
     that   quechua-OBJ-TOP little speak-__INF-OBJ__ __know__-3
     'She __knows how to speak__ Quechua only a little.'

At the same time, when *yacha-* appears in nonfinite forms, as in (357), the direct object suffix is typically omitted from the preceding infinitive. The combination of infinitive *-y* plus *yacha-* in nonfinite forms constitutes an ideal linguistic environment for the lexical component to be reanalyzed as part of a more abstract construction with a habitual interpretation. In other words, *yacha-* in SCQ appears to be in an early stage of auxiliation, whereas *yacha-* in Saraguro and Inga is more fully developed as an auxiliary.[205]

----

descansar Bolívar. [to be frequent. *Bolivar was accustomed to resting here.*]" (2007:681, my translation.) It is uncertain whether this innovation originated in Spanish, Quechua, or another substrate language.

[205] For Cuzco Quechua, Cusihuamán (1976b:167) lists *yachakuy* as '*acostumbrarse*' ('get accustomed to'), but doesn't provide an example.

(357) SCQ
*kechwa mana liyi-**y**   **yacha**-q   mana qellqa-**y**   **yacha**-q-qa*
quechua no   read-**INF** **know**-AG no   write-**INF** **know**-AG-TOP

mana-mi peruwa:nu-tsu aw?
no-DIR   peruvian-NEG   yes

'Anyone who doesn't **know how to read or write** Quechua isn't (a bona fide) Peruvian, right?'

11.3.4   *ri-* 'go'

Auxiliaries derived from motion-related verbs in SCQ were introduced in §11.2. These include *puri-* 'walk', *(h)aku* 'let's go', *keda-* 'stay', and *si:gi-* 'follow'. Additional motion verbs take on auxiliary functions in other Quechuan languages. For example, in North Peruvian Quechuan varieties prospective situations can be expressed through the combination of the nominalizer *-q* plus the auxiliary verb *ri-* 'go'. A situation expressed through periphrasis is usually more imminent than a situation marked with a future tense suffix. The following example is from Cajamarca Quechua (Quesada 1976:119).

(358) CAJAMARCA QUECHUA   (PROSPECTIVE)
*qayna   ranti-**q** **ri**-ni aycha-ta*
tomorrow buy-**AG** **go**-1 meat-OBJ
'Tomorrow **I'll buy** meat.'

As observed by Muysken (1977:107) and others the suffix *-gri*, common in Northern Quechuan varieties, arose through the fusion of *-*q* plus **ri-*. The resulting suffix *-gri* is sometimes glossed 'inchoative', as in (359).[206]

(359) NORTHERN QUECHUA   (INCHOATIVE)
*miku-**gri**-ni*
eat-**INCH**-1
'I am **going to eat**.'

Cole (1982:150) labels *-gri* in Imbabura Quechua with the similar term 'ingressive', an aspect that profiles the beginning of an event.

---

[206] Northern Quechuan varieties are characterized by the sound change **q* > *k*, resulting in a merger with **k* (Torero 1964:451). This suffix is traditionally represented as *-gri* because the velar occlusive assimilates voicing from the following *r*.

(360) IMBABURA QUECHUA   (INGRESSIVE)
       ruwana-ta   rura-__gri__-rka
       poncho-OBJ   make-__INGRESSIVE__-PST3
       'He **began making** a poncho.'

According to Waskosky (1992:27), *-gri* in Salasaca Quechua "indicates that an action is beginning or is about to take place." In other words, the action is imminent, a prospective aspect.

(361) SALASACA QUECHUA   (PROSPECTIVE)
       yacha-__gri__-ni
       know-__INCH__-1
       'I am **about to discover** something.'

In other Northern varieties, such as Pastaza Quechua (Ecuador), *-gri* appears to retain a spatial orientation as a translocative. According to Nuckolls, "Quechua speakers understand translocative verbs as...aspectually punctual" (1996:49, 88).

(362) PASTAZA QUECHUA (ECUADOR)   (PUNCTUAL)
       pi-ta   pay-ta   rima-__gri__-nga
       who-Q.C   he-OBJ   speak-__TRLOC__-FUT3
       'Who will **go and tell** him (that there's something to catch)?'

In similar fashion, Weber and Orr (1987:28) gloss *-gri* in Saraguro Quechua as 'punctual'. In examples such as (363), the situation appears to be prospective, similar to the periphrasis *-q* plus *ri-* in Cajamarca (358), and the suffix *-gri* in Salasaca (361).

(363) SARAGURO QUECHUA   (PROSPECTIVE)
       kunan-mari   kam-bak gente-kuna-wan   kawsa-__gri__-ngi chi   llakta-pi
       now-DIR.SUR you-GEN people-PL.N-COM live-__PUNC__-2   that town-LOC
       'Now you **can/will live** again with your people in town.'

The combination of *-q* plus *ri-* has an aspectual interpretation in some varieties of Southern Quechuan but not in others. The following Santiago del Estero Quechua example in Bravo (1965:42) reports an action about to take place, just as in Cajamarca Quechua (358) above.

(364) SANTIAGO DEL ESTERO QUECHUA   (PROSPECTIVE)
       noqa   puñu-__q__   __ri__-ni
       I   sleep-__AG__   __go__-1
       '**I'll be asleep**.'

In Cuzco Quechua, however, *-q* plus *ri-* appears to retain the more compositional meaning of the purpose-motion construction, as in the following example (Orconi 1987:219). In this verbal construction, the initial element marked by -*q* functions as a complement of the following motion verb which serves as a complement-taking predicate.

(365) CUZCO QUECHUA
      *Manuel-cha-qa   qhawa-**q**   **ri**-rqa-n*
      Manuel-DIM-TOP   see-**PRMT**   **go**-PST-3
      'Manuelito **went to see**.'

11.3.5 *aywa-* 'go'

In Central Quechuan varieties, the lexeme for 'go' is *aywa-*, and the combination of -*q* plus *aywa-* parallels the syntactic configurations of -*q* plus *ri-* 'go' described above for non-Central Quechua. For example, in SCQ the combination of -*q* plus *aywa-* expresses 'purpose-motion' in (366), the same meaning as -*q* plus *ri-* in the previous Cuzco example.[207]

(366) SCQ
      *hallqa-chu   u:sha-man   apa-**q**   **aywa**-r-nin rika-mu-ru-:   ari*
      high.grassland-LOC   sheep-ALL   take-**PRMT**   **go**-SS-3   see-FAR-PST.R-1   yes
      'Right, in the high grassland I saw it there while **going to take** the sheep.'

In Huallaga Quechua, the combination of -*q* plus *aywa-* has taken on a prospective function, just as -*q* plus -*ri* in Cajamarca (358). According to Weber, this periphrasis "is rapidly displacing the simple future tense as the most common way to express futurity" (1989:114).

(367) HUALLAGA QUECHUA   (PROSPECTIVE)
      *fista-ta   rura-**q**   **aywa**-:*
      fiesta-OBJ   make-**SUB   go**-1
      '**I'm going to put on** a party.'

As we saw in the previous section, the combination -*q* plus *ri-* has given rise to a suffix form -*gri* in some Northern Quechuan varieties. In Central Quechua as well there is evidence that the elements -*q* plus *aywa-* are developing into a suffix of the form -*qaywa*, although this grammaticization process is in a very early stage. In (368), for example, the object+subject person marking "spans it [-*q aywa-*] as though it were a single tense marker" (1989:114).

---

[207] For further illustrations of the purpose-motion construction in SCQ, see (21), (22), (23), (150), (155), (156), (162), (236), (304), and (331).

(368) HUALLAGA QUECHUA   (PROSPECTIVE)
     *tari-pa-ma-**q**   **aywa**-nchi*
     find-BEN-1OBJ-**SUB**   **go**-1₁
     'He **will catch up** to us.'

In Corongo Quechua, presumably under the influence of Spanish, the two elements of this periphrastic future have undergone syntactic reversal from the native order STEM–*q* plus *aywa-* to the Spanish order *aywa-* plus STEM–*q*. The following example is from Hintz (2000:197). We saw in §11.2 that foreign forms (e.g., *keda-* and *si:gi-*) can be recruited to participate in native constructions. Here, it is not a form that is borrowed, but rather the grammatical pattern itself (see Hintz 2009).

(369) CORONGO QUECHUA   (PROSPECTIVE)
     *ñoxa   **e:wa**-:   akshu-ta   iki-**x***
     I   **go**-1   potato-OBJ   slice-**AG**
     'I**'m gonna slice** the potatoes.'

11.3.6 *shamu-* 'come'

The following example from Inga Quechua (Colombia) shows the nominalizer -*g* followed by the suffix -*samu* (Levinsohn 1991:151). The form -*samu* is transparently derived from the independent verb **shamu-* 'come'. The -*g* plus *samu-* periphrasis is similar to the English aspectualizer *come to*, for example, *she came to realize*.

(370) INGA QUECHUA   (INCHOATIVE)
     unaypi, sug   iskay hura-pi-sina,
     later,   other two   hour-LOC-SIM,

     *rigchari-**g**-**samu**-rca,   piscu tucu-spa*
     wake.up-**NMLZ**-**COME**-PST3   bird   become-SS
     'About two hours later, he woke up [**became awake**], turned into a bird.'

Muysken (1977:108-9) observes that in certain varieties of Ecuadorian Quechua, cislocative meaning is expressed by the suffix -*mu* with motion verbs. With non-motion verbs cislocative meaning is expressed by a "periphrastic participial construction" involving the verb *shamu-* 'come'. (The suffix -*mu* has become fused as the final element of *shamu-*.) The use of *shamu-* as an auxiliary is illustrated in (371).

(371) CALDERÓN QUECHUA   (PARTICIPIAL)
     *randi-**shpa**   **shamu**-ni*
     buy-**SUB**   **come**-1
     'I **come** from having bought.'

Muysken further reports various "reductions of a stylistic nature" in which the phonetic material of -*shpa* erodes, leaving only the auxiliary *shamu*-. The pattern illustrated in (372), coupled with the rise of the inchoative suffix -*gri* from -*q* plus *ri*-, prompts the observation that "complex verbs which involve auxiliary constructions give way to [derivational] suffix combinations" (1977:107).

(372) a. *randi-shpa*   *shamu-ni*
       b. *randi-sha*   *shamu-ni*
       c. *randi-sh*   *shamu-ni*
       d. *randi*   *shamu-ni*

11.3.7 *pasa*- 'pass'

Nuckolls refers to a construction that combines a nominalized verb and the auxiliary *pasa*- 'pass' (from Spanish *pasar*) as "the periphrastic completive" in (373) and "the periphrastic resultative" in (374) (1996:53).

(373) PASTAZA QUECHUA (ECUADOR)   (COMPLETIVE)
       miku-y   ***pasa***-*ra-ngi-chu*
       eat-**NOM**   **pass**-PAST-2-NEG
       'Did you **finish eating**?'

(374) PASTAZA QUECHUA (ECUADOR)   (RESULTATIVE)
       *ña   ri   **pasa**-n*
       now   go   **pass**-3
       'He**'s** already **gone**.'

The initial infinitive suffix -*y* is required on the verb *miku*- 'eat' in (373), but does not appear on the verb *ri* 'go' in (374), perhaps due to the final *i*. The optionality of infinitive -*y* in the aspectualizing construction (-*y*) plus *pasa*- in Pastaza is reminiscent of the optionality of initial *y* in the iterative suffix -*(y)kacha:* in SCQ and other Quechuan languages (as presented in the next section).

11.3.8 *kacha*- 'send'

All previous illustrations of auxiliary structures in §11.2 and §11.3 are from modern Quechuan languages. The development of suffixes from periphrastic constructions is also reported, to some extent, in the Colonial literature. For example, Santo Tomás observes that the verb *kacha*- means 'send' (from **kach'a*-), but a "noun or verb [i.e., an infinitival form ending in -*y*] combined with *kacha*- means to go about doing the action of the noun" ([1560] 1995:84, my translation and bracketed comment). According to Torero (1964:451) and Parker (1969c:165) the Colonial Quechua variety described by Santo Tomás was probably spoken in the central coast of Peru.

(375) COLONIAL QUECHUA (PERU COAST)　　　　　　　　　　(ITERATIVE)
　　　 llulla-y-kacha-ni
　　　 lie-INF-SEND-1
　　　 'I **go about lying**.'

The combination of *-y* 'infinitive' plus *kach'a-* 'send' would have given rise to the widely attested iterative suffixes derived from *-ykach'a:*. The verb form *kacha-* does not function as an auxiliary in SCQ, but iterative *-ykacha:* is illustrated in (376). For more on the etymology of this suffix, see the discussion following (291) in §10.4. Its modern geographical distribution is shown in Map A.8 in Appendix A.

(376) SCQ　　　　　　　　　　　　　　　　　　　　　　　　(ITERATIVE)
　　　 kushi-ku-r　　　　 *tapri-ykacha-ma:-shun-mi*
　　　 be.happy-MID-SS　 knock.over-ITER-1OBJ-FUT1₁-DIR
　　　 'They will happily knock us down **at every opportunity**.'

11.4 Summary of aspect expressed via auxiliary structures

The development of suffixes from periphrastic auxiliary constructions has been recognized in Quechuanist studies since the Colonial era. In the modern era, grammarians have reported a small number of auxiliary structures in individual Quechuan languages. The present work extends our understanding of auxiliation in Quechua by assembling these scattered observations and by introducing emergent auxiliaries found in naturally-occurring speech in SCQ.

A total of seventeen auxiliary verbs appear in combination with a variety of nominalizers (and other nonfinite suffixes) to express a wide assortment of twenty-seven perfective and imperfective aspectual notions across the Quechua language family. Nine auxiliaries appear in SCQ, namely *ka-*, *kawa-*, *usha-*, *qalla-*, *tuku-*, *puri-*, *aku*, *keda-*, and *si:gi-* (§11.2). Eight additional auxiliaries appear only in other Quechuan languages, namely *ma-*, *tiya-*, *yacha-*, *ri-*, *aywa-*, *shamu-*, *pasa-*, and *kacha-* (§11.3). A handful of the auxiliaries are highly grammaticized (e.g., **ka-* 'be, exist', **ri-* 'go'), while others are found at the earliest stages of grammaticization (e.g., **puri-* 'walk', *keda-* 'remain').

As summarized in Table 11.1, Quechua auxiliaries derive from copulas, phasal verbs, motion verbs, and at least one cognition verb (column 1). Most auxiliaries are of native etymology, but Spanish loans are also appropriated to fill the auxiliary slot of the STEM–NOMINALIZER+AUXILIARY construction, viz., *keda-*, *si:gi-*, *pasa-* (column 2). Each auxiliary appears in combination with one or more nominalizers (column 4).

Table 11.1 *Auxiliary verb sources in Quechuan languages*

VERB TYPE	AUXILIARY	SOURCE MEANING	NOMINALIZER
COPULA	**ka-*	'be, exist'	*-q, -sh(qa)*
	ma-	'be, exist'	*-q*
	**kawsa-*	'be alive, be at, exist'	*-y, -sh(qa), -sh(pa)*
	**tiya-*	'sit, reside, be (at)'	*-sh(pa)*
PHASAL	**qalla-*	'begin'	*-r*
	**tuku-*	'become'	*-q, -y*
	**usha-*	'finish'	*-r*
MOTION	**aywa-*	'go'	*-q*
	**ri-*	'go'	*-q*
	**puri-*	'walk'	*-q, -r*
	**haku(-)*	'let's go'	*-q, -y*
	**sha(mu)-*	'come'	*-q, -sh(pa)*
	**kach'a-*	'send'	*-y*
	pasa- (Sp.)	'pass'	*-y*
	si:gi- (Sp.)	'follow'	*-r*
	keda- (Sp.)	'remain'	*-sh(qa)*
COGNITION	**yach'a-*	'know'	*-y, -na, -nqa*

The twenty-seven aspectualizing periphrases illustrated in §11.2 and §11.3 are summarized in the next two tables. In Table 11.2 the first element is one of six nominalizers (or nonfinite suffixes) of the form *-q, -sh(qa), -sh(pa), -y, -r,* or *-na* (column 1). In each instantiation, the second element is grammaticized to serve as an auxiliary or is currently developing that function (column 2). The more entrenched or routinized auxiliary-final constructions have given rise to aspectual suffixes or enclitics in modern Quechuan languages (column 5). The evidence for a specific nominalizer plus auxiliary combination as the source material for a given aspect suffix is particularly compelling when the longer periphrastic form is attested in one variety, and a semantically compatible reduced suffix form is attested in the same or a neighboring variety.

Table 11.2 *The Quechua aspectualizing construction* STEM–NOMINALIZER+AUXILIARY

| **1st Element** | **2nd Element** | | | |
NOMIN-ALIZER	**AUXILIARY**	**MEANING OF AUXILIARY**	**MEANING OF CONSTRUCTION**	**SUFFIX**
-q	*ka-*	'be, exist'	'habitual, past habitual'	*-q=ka, -na:*
-q	*ma-*	'be, exist'	'habitual'	…
-q	*tuku-*	'pretend'	'pretend, not complete'	*-qtu*
-q	*ri-*	'go'	'ingressive'	*-gri*
-q	*shamu-*	'come'	'inchoative'	*-samu*
-q	*aywa-*	'go'	'prospective'	…
-q	*puri-*	'walk'	'prospective'	…
-sh(qa)	*ka-*	'be, exist'	'perfect, past perfective'	*-sh(qa), -shka*
-sh(qa)	*kawa-*	'live, exist'	'habitual'	…
-sh(qa)	*keda-/ke:ra-*	'remain'	'durative'	…
-sh(pa)	*tiya-*	'sit, reside'	'progressive, habitual'	*-shti, -tya(:)*
-sh(pa)	*shamu-*	'come'	'participial'	*-shamu*
-sh(pa)	*kawsa-*	'live, exist'	'habitual'	…
-y	*kawa-*	'live, exist'	'durative, progressive'	*-y(k)a(:)*
-y	*kacha-*	'send'	'iterative'	*-ykacha(:)*
-y	*tuku-*	'pretend'	'passive completive'	…
-y	*yacha-*	'know'	'habitual'	…
-y	*pasa-*	'pass, happen'	'completive, resultative'	…
-r	*usha-*	'finish'	'completive'	…
-r	*qalla-*	'begin'	'inceptive'	…
-r	*puri-*	'walk'	'habitual'	…
-r	*si:gi-*	'follow'	'continuative'	…
-na	*yacha-*	'know'	'habitual'	…

Quechuan languages are usually described as verb-final, though variant orders conditioned by pragmatic factors are very frequent in connected speech (Weber 1989:15ff.; Diane Hintz 2003). In keeping with these word order facts, the auxiliary is usually the final constituent of a verbal periphrasis (as in Table 11.2) but it is occasionally initial (as in Table 11.3), in most cases due to contact with Spanish. An additional nominalizer *-nga* is attested in combination with the auxiliary *yacha-* 'know' in Inga Quechua (Colombia).

Table 11.3 *The Quechua aspectualizing construction AUXILIARY+STEM–NOMINALIZER*

| 1st Element | 2nd Element | | |
AUXILIARY	NOMIN-ALIZER	MEANING OF AUXILIARY	MEANING OF CONSTRUCTION
aywa-	*-q*	'go'	'prospective'
(h)aku(-)	*-q*	'let's go'	'prospective'
aku	*-y*	'let's go'	'prospective'
yacha(-)	*-nga*	'know'	'habitual'

We have seen that the STEM–NOMINALIZER+AUXILIARY construction provides a rich environment for the grammaticization of perfective and imperfective suffixes in Quechua. Some aspect suffixes are clearly derived from specific nominalizer plus auxiliary combinations, e.g., *-gri* in Northern Quechua (from *-q* plus *ri-*) and *-q=ka* in SCQ (from *-q* plus *ka-*). The sources for other aspect suffixes are less transparent due in part to the processes of desemanticization, decategorialization, and phonetic reduction. Linguistic material from the aspectualizing constructions presented above can provide additional clues for the earliest stages in the historical development of these suffixes. Based in part on this evidence, in §11.5 we will examine four proposals for the reconstruction of progressive *-yka:*.

11.5 The emergence of progressive *-yka:*

The reconstruction of the Proto Central Quechua progressive suffix *-yka:* is relatively straightforward, as shown above in §10.2. The relevant forms from Table 10.1 are reproduced here in Table 11.4 and stages of development are shown in (377). Reconstruction to a pre-Proto stage, however, presents a more interesting challenge, that is, recovery of the source material that gave rise to *-yka:*. (Note that all forms are from the Central and N Peru regions, and none are Southern. The significance of this geographical distribution is treated later in this section.)

Table 11.4 *Forms derived from *-yka: in Quechuan languages*

SUFFIX FORM	QUECHUAN LANGUAGE	REGION	SOURCE
-yka:	SCQ	CENTRAL	Snow and Stark 1971:65
-yka:	Huallaga	CENTRAL	Weber 1989:145
-yka:, -yya, -ya:	Huanca	CENTRAL	Cerrón-Palomino 1976:211
-ycha:	Oyón	CENTRAL	Fuqua 1987:77
-yya:	Yanahuanca	CENTRAL	Mark Bean, p.c.
-ya(:)	Tarma	CENTRAL	Adelaar 1977:124
-yka	San Martín	N PERU	Coombs et al. 1976:126
-yka	Cajamarca	N PERU	Quesada 1976:133
-yga	Chachapoyas	N PERU	Taylor 2000:75
-ya	Lambayeque	N PERU	Torero 1964:470

(377)   *-yka:* > *-yya(:)* > *-ya:* > *-ya*
         -yka
         -yga
         -ycha:

Many proposals for the grammaticization of *-yka:* have been set forth, some more speculative than others. Parker (1969a:138) was on the right track in suggesting that the form *-yka* (lacking vowel length) derives from a periphrastic construction. Specifically, he posits the infinitive *-y* plus the copula *ka-*. In a subsequent study, Parker (1973:31) recognizes vowel length in the second element of the hypothesized Proto Central form *-y-ka:*, but continues to associate *ka:* (long vowel) with the copula *ka-* (short vowel) without explaining the source of vowel length, a serious omission. Nor does he provide evidence for the sequence *-y* plus *ka:*- in any Quechuan variety, past or present. These unresolved issues leave this proposal inconclusive.

Cerrón-Palomino (2003:147) specifically addresses the long vowel issue, positing the sequence *-y-ka-ya*, in which the third element is a purported Proto Quechua progressive form *-ya*. In this scenario, the initial innovation would be the fusion of *-y* plus the copula *ka-* > *-yka* (short vowel), as in Parker's original formulation. Subsequently, Central Quechua would have added *-ya*, that is, *-yka-ya* > *-yka:* (long vowel). The advantage of this hypothesis is that it provides a plausible account for the long vowel via the well-attested reduction of the sequence *aya* > *a:* in Central Quechua (e.g., *-paya* > *-pa:* 'benefactive', *ch'aya-* > *ch'a:-* 'arrive', etc.).[208]

---

[208] Parker (1969a:137) observes that the form *ya* is the final element in the Proto Quechua suffixes *-paya* 'repetitive', *-raya* 'durative', and *-naya* 'desiderative'. On the basis of these three suffix forms, which are attested in most modern Quechuan languages, he postulates that

The main issue with the *-*y-ka-ya* hypothesis is that the case for a Proto Quechua progressive suffix *-*ya* is not convincing. The evidence essentially hinges on a sole example from the Colonial Quechua variety described by Santo Tomás.[209] Santo Tomás specifically describes -*ya* as "inchoative" (not durative/progressive), translating this suffix throughout his grammar as profiling the transition of a property to a state, e.g., "*macho* means 'old', *macho-ya-ni* means 'I become old' ... *chiri-ni* means 'I feel cold', *chiri-ya-ni* means 'I become cold'" ([1560] 1995:87-8, my translation).[210] Moreover, this suffix -*ya* does not appear with dynamic verbs, an essential characteristic of progressives. Torero sums up the situation well: "in Domingo de Santo Tomás we do not find the expression of durative [progressive]" (1964:470, my translation).

In one example in his section on inchoative -*ya*, however, Santo Tomás does provide a Spanish translation that includes a progressive or durative element, specifically, *cono-cu-ya-ni* 'voyme callentando [sic]' (English: 'I move about getting warm'). Duration here does not appear to correspond to -*ya*, but rather to the use of middle voice -*cu* (-*ku*) in this particular context, that is, the movement required for the subject to become warm. It is such contexts (involving duration) that would have provided fertile ground for the reanalysis of -*ku* as 'progressive' in Northern Quechua (cf. §8.6). The suffix -*ya* here is most likely 'inchoative', as Santo Tomás himself labels this section and all other examples of -*ya* in his grammar.[211]

---

*-*ya* was a pre-Proto Quechua suffix meaning 'intensive'. While the reconstruction of a suffix form *-*ya* seems plausible, no evidence is available to support the meaning 'intensive'.

[209] Cerrón-Palomino (2003:146) also cites an example from the Peruvian chronicler Garcilaso de la Vega ([1609] 1963:80), *páquir cayan* 'lo está quebrando' (English: 'He is breaking it'). Although Gracilaso's translation suggests a progressive meaning, there are good reasons to doubt this. 1) As Cerrón-Palomino observes, this is almost certainly one word (not two) with the suffix -*rqaya* (not -*ya*). 2) The grammarian González Holguín ([1607] 1842:252) provides several examples of -*rqaya* with more precise translations, including *paqui-rcaya-ni* 'break into many pieces' and *pitu-rcaya-rini* 'take care of many things together'. In modern terminology, -*rqaya* is a verbal collective (plural) action marker, i.e., "sets of events viewed collectively" (Mithun 1999a:92). In the words of González Holguín, "hacer mucho de lo que dice el verbo con gran multiplico o abundancia, no en la acción, sino en la cosa hecha." Thus, the examples *páquir cayan* (Garcilaso de la Vega) and *paquircayani* (González Holguín) do not support the hypothesis of a Proto Quechua progressive suffix *-*ya*.

[210] The "inchoative" suffix -*ya(:)* described by Santo Tomás is still attested in most modern Quechuan languages, e.g., the SCQ forms *ruku* 'old' versus *ruku-ya:-* 'become old'.

[211] Hypothetically speaking, even if -*ya* in the Santo Tomás example *cono-cu-ya-ni* were a progressive suffix, it would most likely represent the final stage of reduction in the historical sequence in (377) *-*yka:* > -*yka* > -*yya* > -*ya* suggested by the Yanahuanca, Tarma, and Lambayeque forms in Table 11.4. Note that: 1) progressive -*ya* is attested in Lambayeque, a modern variety located near the Peruvian coast, and 2) both Torero (1964:451) and Parker

Another issue with *-y-ka-ya* is the lack of evidence for the discourse construction in which the postulated sequence of morphemes would have occurred. (Neither Parker nor Cerrón-Palomino provide such evidence.) A related matter is the unspecified motivation for the routinization of the sequence of forms *-yka* plus *-ya*. We might imagine a state of affairs in which the first (clearly progressive) element *-yka* would have become lexicalized with certain verb roots, motivating the productive addition of *-ya* to such roots. Since there are no verb roots ending with *yka-*, however, that suggestion remains highly improbable. It thus appears that neither Parker's proposal of *-y-ka:* nor Cerrón-Palomino's proposal of *-y-ka-ya* provides a satisfactory account for the long vowel in *-yka:*.

Adelaar (1984) approaches the issue from another angle. He proposes that the proto form is simply *-yka* (short vowel). In this account, the allomorph *-yka:* (in those modern varieties which permit long vowels) would arise through a synchronic process of vowel lengthening in open syllables. This hypothesis is plausible, given that low vowels tend to have longer duration than high vowels. The downside of this proposal is its "ad hoc nature," as characterized by Landerman (1991:218). Vowel lengthening, as formulated, always applies to the small set of non-final verbal suffixes ending in /a/, yet rarely applies to the large open class of verb roots ending in /a/. This idiosyncratic behavior across morpheme boundaries—lengthen final /a/ in one open syllable but not in another—requires a convincing rationale.

Given the unresolved issues involved in the previous three proposals based on the infinitive *-y* plus copula *ka-* hypothesis, we might want to consider another alternative. As demonstrated above in §11.1-4 and summarized in Table 11.2, aspectualizing periphrases of the form STEM–NOMINALIZER+AUXILIARY often give rise to aspect suffixes. Accordingly, another approach to recovering the source material for progressive *-yka:* would be to examine the nominalizer/deverbal plus auxiliary combinations that are actually attested, beginning with those that lie within the semantic domain of imperfective.

One auxiliary verb that yields imperfective meanings in periphrasis with deverbal forms is *kawsa-* 'be alive, exist'. For example, the combination of the deverbal suffix *-sh* plus *kaw(s)a-* yields a habitual interpretation in Chachapoyas, Pastaza (Peru), and in SCQ, as illustrated above in (308)-(310). Similarly, the combination of infinitive *-y* plus *kawa-* in (311) and (312) has a durative interpretation in SCQ.

Consider the historical sequence proposed in (378) which begins with infinitive *-y* plus auxiliary *kawsa-* in Stage 1. These two forms cliticize in Stage 2. Stage 3 reflects the well-motivated Central Quechua (and Lambayeque) sound change *s > (h) > Ø. Although this innovation is considered relatively recent in lexical forms, that is not necessarily the case in grammatical forms, such as auxiliaries. As the two original forms (*-y* plus *kawsa-*) come to express a single grammatical meaning through periphrasis, the increased frequency of the grammaticizing construction would increase potential for the erosion of phonetic material [s],

---

(1969c:165) consider the Colonial Quechua variety described by Santo Tomás to be coastal. (Coastal waters and plains facilitate people movement and contact.)

yielding *-y=kawa* (cf. Bybee 2001:11; Hopper and Traugott 2003:145; among others).[212] The subsequent reduction of **awa* to *a:* would account for the long vowel in Stage 4. (The sound change **awa* > a: is attested in SCQ forms, such as *pa:ri-* 'fly' from **pawari-*.) By Stage 5 *-yka:* would have become a full-fledged verbal suffix.

(378)   PROPOSED STAGES LEADING TO PROTO CENTRAL QUECHUA **-yka:* 'progressive'

1. (auxiliary)		2. (enclitic)		3.		4.		5. (suffix)
**-y* plus **kawsa-*	>	*-y=kawsa*	>	*-y=kawa*	>	*-y=ka:*	>	*-yka:*

The independent lexical item *kawsa-* would have continued unchanged long after the grammatical developments involving the auxiliary *kawsa-*. The coexistence of a reduced auxiliary and the verb from which it is derived has been documented for a large number of languages, e.g., English *I've seen it* versus *I have it*; see also Marchese (1986:96) on Kru. In a more recent innovation, the lexical verb *kawsa-* has followed a similar trajectory **s* > (h) > Ø. It is currently attested as *kawa-* in most Central Quechuan varieties, but elsewhere continues in its original form *kawsa-*.

Cross-linguistic evidence lends support to the hypothesis of **-y* plus **kawsa-* 'be alive, exist' as a possible source for Proto Central Quechua **-yka:*. Heine and Kuteva (2002:127) illustrate progressive-continuous morphemes that derive from verbs meaning 'exist' in Kongo (Bantu), Yagaria (Trans-New Guinea), and Ghanaian Pidgin English. Bybee et al. (1994:129) cite the sequence of a verb meaning 'be, live, exist' plus a 'participle' which yields progressive in Kui (Dravidian). They also find that progressive auxiliaries may derive from verbs that express the notion 'live' or 'reside', another meaning associated with *kaw(s)a-*.

We have seen that in Chachapoyas and other Quechuan languages, *kaw(s)a-* has taken on an additional locative copula function, as illustrated above in (307). Bybee et al. find that progressives often develop from a locative element, as in the English historical sequence 'be at work' > 'be aworking' > 'be working'. Similarly, Heine and Kuteva report verbs meaning 'live' as a principal lexical source for locative copulas in Basque, English, German, and Tunica (Gulf), with the caveat that "more examples are required to substantiate this pathway" (2002:198). In turn, locative copulas can generalize as progressives and equative copulas (ibid.:97-9). The locative and aspectual auxiliary functions of the form *kaw(s)a-* in Central and North Peruvian (N Peru) Quechua reported above in §11.2 and the progressive forms in Table 11.4 support these proposed grammaticization paths.

A possible "weak link" in the **-y* plus **kawsa-* hypothesis in (378) is that Stage 3 (**s* > (h) > Ø) is a more recent innovation than Stage 4 (**awa* > a:) with respect to lexical forms. Whether Stage 3 predates Stage 4 in developing grammatical forms, such as **-yka:*, remains an open question. The sound change **s* > (h) > Ø is limited to the Central Quechua region (where

---

[212] Bybee (2001:11): "Phonetic change often progresses more quickly in items with high token frequency. This effect is particularly noticeable in grammaticizing elements or phrases."

-yka: presumably originated), but is also found in Lambayeque (N Peru). It is especially variable in Ancash (see map and discussion in Hintz 2000:50-6).

Returning our attention to Table 11.4 above, we see that forms derived from progressive *-yka:* are attested throughout Central Quechua and N Peru Quechua, but not Southern Quechua where progressive forms derive from *-ch'ka:*. This geographical distribution has led to the assumption that *-yka:* dates back to Proto Quechua in Central Peru.[213] At a later stage, observes Parker, "The durative function of earlier *-yka* is taken over by a new Proto Southern suffix *-ch-ka*" (1969:171). This hypothesis is not without controversy. First, we lack direct evidence for an original progressive form *-yka* in Southern Quechua (lexicalized forms, grammatical residue, etc.). Second, no motivation has been offered for the presumed "replacement" of *-yka* by *-chka*. Third, the source for the initial element ch'/ch is considered "mysterious" (Parker 1973:33) and "enigmatic" (Cerrón-Palomino 2003:146); cf. note 171 in Chapter 10.

The possibility that *-yka:* may **not** date back to Proto Quechua warrants reconsideration. If Quechua spread from the central Peru homeland southward without progressive *-yka:*, a form which later developed in Central Quechua, that would account for the lack of evidence for forms derived from *-yka:* in Southern Quechua.[214] The Proto Southern progressive *-ch'ka* would have come about later, presumably based on the same discourse construction as *-yka:*, but with a different grammatical element (such as locative *-ch'aw > ch'*) in the initial slot.[215]

If indeed *-yka:* developed in Central Quechua after the Proto Quechua stage, we are left with two competing scenarios for N Peru Quechua. Either 1) Quechua spread from Central Peru to N Peru after the development of *-yka:* in Central, or 2) N Peru borrowed *-yka:* (native to Proto Central) due to language contact. In what follows, I present evidence for contact between N Peru and northern varieties of Central Quechua.[216]

The existence of an ancient route (later fortified during the Incan era) connecting Cajamarca (N Peru) with Corongo (Central) is documented in the autobiography of the explorer Franck (1917:271-95). Thus, it should come as no surprise that several linguistic features are shared

---

[213] There is broad consensus among linguists of the modern era that Quechua originated in Central Peru, later spreading southward and northward, e.g., Parker (1963), Torero (1964), Landerman (1991), Cerrón-Palomino (2003), among others.

[214] The development of *-yka:* in Central Quechua after the Proto Quechua stage would also concord with the more recent independent development of progressive *-ku* and variants (from middle voice *-ku*) in the Northern Quechuan varieties of Ecuador and Colombia, as described above in §8.6.

[215] David Weber (p.c.) suggests locative *-ch'aw* as a possible source for /ch'/ in Southern Quechua *-ch'ka*.

[216] These data do not contradict the hypothesis of linguistic expansion from Central Peru to N Peru subsequent to the Southern expansion.

between N Peru (QII) and the northernmost Central (QI) varieties, features which are not shared with Southern (QII) nor with most other Central (QI) varieties. The following are relevant:[217]

- Quechua speakers in San Martín and Chachapoyas (N Peru) refer to their native language as *llakwash* just as Corongo and Sihuas speakers (Central) refer to their language as *llaqwash*, a language name restricted to this area of Peru (Coombs et al. 1976:25; Taylor 1979:102; Hintz 2000:24).

- Cajamarca (N Peru) and Corongo, Sihuas, and North Conchucos (Central) allow the topic enclitic (from *-qa*) to be followed by an evidential in the same word, e.g., *kanan-qa-m*. No other Quechuan language allows this enclitic stacking, that I am aware (Quesada 1976:157; Hintz 2000:31).

- San Martín (N Peru) and Corongo and Sihuas (Central) have an evidential enclitic *-ma* in paradigmatic contrast with the evidential enclitic *-mi*. This *-ma* versus *-mi* distinction has not been attested in other Quechuan varieties (Coombs et al. 1976:161; Hintz 2000:186-7).

- Lambayeque (N Peru) uses the same subject adverbializer *-r*, first person verbal object *-ma*, and an aspect suffix *-ski*. All three of these forms are attested in the northernmost Central Quechuan varieties (Torero 1968:297-8).

- Lambayeque (N Peru) and Northern Ancash (Central) have undergone *s > (h) > Ø (Shaver 1987; Hintz 2000:50-6).

- Cajamarca and Chachapoyas (N Peru) and Corongo and Sihuas (Central) retain the retroflexed alveopalatal affricate *ch'. All other varieties in Ancash and Huánuco (except Ambo-Pasco) have undergone *ch' > ch. Similarly, all N Peru varieties retain the proto affricate *ch, as does Sihuas (Central) (Landerman 1991:94ff.).

- Cajamarca and Lambayeque (N Peru) and Corongo, Sihuas, and North Conchucos (Central) use the lexeme *rupay/rupe:* 'sun'. All other Quechuan varieties (except Canta, Lima) use the form *inti* (Torero 1968:305).

- Chachapoyas (N Peru) and Corongo, Sihuas, and North Conchucos (Central) use the lexeme *wañuchi-/wañutsi-* 'kill' with the additional sense 'blow out candle, turn off light', a sense not found in the rest of Ancash which uses the form *upitsi-* (Taylor 1979:195-6; Hintz 2000:221).

---

[217] The now extinct Culli language was spoken into the 20th century in the geographic region separating the N Peru Quechua and northern Central Quechua areas (Solís 1986:1). Of course contact effects between Culli and Quechua are also in evidence, but those observations are beyond the scope of the immediate discussion.

- Cajamarca and Lambayeque (N Peru) and Corongo (Central) use the lexeme *akshu* 'potato', whereas most other Quechuan varieties (with notable exceptions) use the form *papa* (Torero:304).

Given the evidence of linguistic features shared exclusively, or nearly so, between N Peru Quechua and northern Central Quechua, we cannot rule out the possibility that the Proto Central progressive suffix *-yka:* may have spread to its N Peru cousins via contact.

A final matter is that Huanca (at the Central-Southern border) and Cajamarca (at the Central-N Peru border) each have two progressive suffixes, one derived from *-yka:* and the other from *-ch'ka:* (see Map 10.1 in Chapter 10). In each language, the two progressives are distinguished by semantic nuances (Cerrón-Palomino 1976:211-2; Quesada 1976:133). Huanca (Central) would have borrowed *-chka* from neighboring Ayacucho (Southern). It is plausible that Cajamarca could have borrowed *-ch'ka* due to Incan (Southern) occupation forces and extended residence by the royal entourage at Los Baños del Inca.[218]

To conclude, each of the four proposals discussed here concerning the source material for progressive *-yka:* presents certain advantages but also disadvantages. The proposals and major issues are summarized in Table 11.5:

Table 11.5 *Summary of four proposals for the sources of *-yka:*

PROPOSAL	ISSUES
1. *-yka: < *-y+*ka:-	vowel length on *ka:- not explained no evidence for discourse construction
2. *-yka: < *-ykaya < *-y+*ka-+*-ya	progressive *-ya not convincing no evidence for discourse construction
3. *-yka < *-y+*ka-	lengthening rule idiosyncrasies not explained
4. *-yka: < *-ykawa < *-y+*kawsa-	*awa > a: predates *s > Ø in lexical forms (but *s > Ø is natural in grammaticizing forms)

Throughout this chapter I have characterized auxiliation in Quechua as involving particular instantiations of the discourse construction STEM–NOMINALIZER+AUXILIARY. In the case of *-yka:*, the deverbal element was probably infinitive *-y (as in all four proposals), and the auxiliary would have been *ka- 'be' (or a variant) or *kawsa- 'be alive, exist'. Hopefully,

---

[218] Cajamarca was a major city on the Andean route linking Cuzco and Quito. It was during one of these "royal visits" that the Inca (emperor) Atahualpa was murdered by Francisco Pizarro's troops in 1532.

continuing research will help clarify the larger historical picture. Unfortunately, unresolved issues force us to conclude that the source of final vowel length in *-yka:* remains uncertain.

11.6 Other aspectualizing constructions

In addition to auxiliary structures, some Quechua aspect suffixes derive from other sources. One source discussed in previous chapters is the STEM–SUFFIX₁-SUFFIX₂ construction, that is, the amalgamation or fusion of co-occurring derivational suffixes to yield new aspectual categories. Mithun and Ali refer to amalgamation as "a less well known but flourishing mechanism by which aspectual systems may be elaborated" (1996:127).

In SCQ, for example, the combination of durative *-ra:* plus continuous *-yka:* has grammaticized as *-rayka:*, a suffix that expresses habitual meaning with dynamic predicates (§3.1.3). Amalgamation may also add a modal sense to perfective suffixes. For example, the combination of punctual *-ri* plus perfective *-yku* yields *-ri:ku*, a perfective suffix with the modal nuance of 'forcefulness' (§2.1.6).[219]

A third source for aspect suffixes is the STEM–NOMINALIZER+PARTICLE construction. Instead of an auxiliary verb in the final position of the lexical phrase, this construction has a particle, that is, a free monomorphemic element with no synchronic internal structure (as the term is used in the Americanist tradition). The final element eventually cliticizes and the combination of the two linguistic items "NOMINALIZER PARTICLE" becomes a single aspect suffix. Heine refers to stages in this process "loosely [as] the ADPOSITION-to-TAM chain" (1993:77).

An excellent illustration of this process is seen in the development of the Proto Quechua suffix *-rqa* 'past (perfective/tense)'. Weber (1987a; 1987b:60) argues on the basis of internal reconstruction that the final element **qa* in *-rqa* (as well as in **-shqa* 'past participle') was a pre-Proto demonstrative. Similar space to time/tense developments are reported in many other languages; see Hymes (1975), Traugott (1978), Gildea (1993), among others. More recent evidence for **qa* as a demonstrative is seen in the recurrence cross-linguistically of developments from demonstrative to focus marker (Heine and Kuteva 2002:111). The focus marker *-qa* is found throughout the Quechua language family.

Weber does not comment on the initial element **-r* in *-rqa*. Parker (1969a:140) suggests that **-r* was an "obscure aspect suffix," but no evidence is presented for this meaning, nor for the discourse construction in which **-r* and **-qa* would have appeared together. Instead, **-r* was more likely an infinitive or other deverbal marker. As noted above in §11.2, the modern 'same subject' suffix *-r* is often characterized synchronically as an adverbial linker for clauses in which the subjects are coreferential. In aspectualizing auxiliary constructions, however, *-r* has characteristics of an infinitive (see also note 193 above and Cole 1983:14). In addition, *-r* can

---

[219] Suffix reduplication would constitute a special case of amalgamation in which SUFFIX₁ and SUFFIX₂ refer to the same morpheme. For example, middle voice *-ku* includes a modal sense of volition. The reduplicated form *-kuku* indicates a heightened sense of volition (cf. §8.4.2).

appear with person markers from the possessive set, but not from the verbal set, suggesting that *-r* may have been a nominalizer at a very early stage of development.[220]

The pre-Proto deverbal suffix *-r* in *-rqa* 'past (perfective/tense)' may also be the initial element in the directional suffixes *-rku* 'up', *-rpu* 'down', and *-rqu* 'out'. These three directional suffixes subsequently developed perfective meanings, though not restricted to the past like perfective *-rqa*. The modern reflex of *-rqu* in SCQ became even more similar to *-rqa* as it developed inflectional past perfective/tense meaning via the path of grammaticization detailed in Chapter 9.

Unfortunately, there is insufficient evidence to reconstruct the second elements of *-rku*, *-rpu* , and *-rqu* (i.e., *ku*, *pu*, *qu*) with certainty. In particular, we lack support for the discourse constructions in which *-r* would have combined with *ku*, *pu*, or *qu*. The amalgamation of *-ri* plus *-ku* would be one plausible source for *-rku*, but no definitive evidence is available on this point (cf. notes 22 and 30 in Chapter 2).[221]

Seven nominalizer plus particle combinations are presented in Table 11.6. The first element is one of three nominalizers (or nonfinite suffixes) of the form *-r*, *-y*, or *-sh* (column 1). The identity of the second element is not always recoverable, but it tends to be a demonstrative, another particle, or some other linguistic constituent (column 2). Each combination has given rise to a proto suffix (column 3) that eventually takes on a perfective meaning in SCQ (column 4).

---

[220] Other adverbial clause markers, like same subject *-r*, appear to have developed in the context of nominalized complements. As shown in §11.2, the modern suffix *-shti* may derive from *-sh(pa)* plus *tiya-*. Similarly, 'different subject' *-pti* and *-qti* would have derived from nominal phrases involving the genitive forms *-p(a)* and *-q*, respectively. For more on the development of adverbial clause markers in Quechua, see Hintz (2003).

[221] For more on the grammatical status and *-CCV* shape of the proto directional suffixes, see note 151 in Chapter 9.

Table 11.6 *The Quechua aspectualizing construction* STEM–NOMINALIZER+PARTICLE

1ˢᵀ ELEMENT (NOMINALIZER)	2ᴺᴰ ELEMENT	PROTO SUFFIX	MEANING OF CONSTRUCTION	
-r	*qa*	*-rqa*	'past'	> 'past perfective/tense'
-r	*qu*	*-rqu*	'out'	> 'past perfective/tense'
-r	*ku*	*-rku*	'up'	> 'perfective'
-r	*pu*	*-rpu*	'down'	> 'perfective'
-y	*ku*	*-yku*	'in'	> 'perfective'
-sh	*ki*	*-shki, *-ski*	'to'	> 'perfective'
-sh	*qa*	*-shqa*	'past participle'	> 'past perfective/tense'

11.7 Conclusion: Aspectualizing constructions

We have investigated the genesis and elaboration of aspectual categories throughout the Quechua language family. The main focus was auxiliation, but we also examined the cliticization of independent nonverbal elements and the amalgamation of suffixes. Developing aspectual structures were shown to supply the lexical substance and phonological material for the ongoing grammaticization of aspect suffixes.

Aspectual notions expressed through verbal periphrases involve semantically general verbs that develop into auxiliaries. Quechua auxiliaries derive from copulas, phasal verbs, motion verbs, and cognition verbs (cf. Table 11.1). Most are of native etymology, but Spanish loans are also recruited to fill the auxiliary slot in the native construction STEM–NOMINALIZER+AUXILIARY. In addition to the borrowing of Spanish "light" verbs, native constituents of analytic verbal constructions have been reordered in some Quechuan languages, replicating the Spanish model. This replication process and its typological consequences are elaborated by Hintz (2009).

Seventeen auxiliary verbs—illustrated here in twenty-one Quechuan varieties—appear in combination with seven different nominalizers to express a wide array of perfective and imperfective notions (cf. Tables 11.2 and 11.3). While some auxiliaries are highly grammaticized (e.g., the copula *ka-*), others are best characterized as emergent auxiliaries, that is, general verbs in the earliest stages of auxiliation.

Interestingly, it is not always possible to determine whether a particular auxiliary in this emerging set results exclusively from language-internal motivations. On the one hand, for example, one might assume that the auxiliary derived from the native verb *usha-* 'finish' (cf. §11.2) is strictly a product of internal processes because comparable sources for completive aspect are widely attested cross-linguistically (Bybee et al. 1994:105). On the other hand, the set of developing auxiliaries is attested only recently and in areas where Spanish influence has been intense. As Matras and Sakel (2007:848) have shown, multilingual speakers draw upon their full repertoire of linguistic resources to express themselves in a given communicative situation. Thus, it is plausible that Quechua-Spanish bilinguals would appropriate native forms to fill the auxiliary slot in the native construction, based on Spanish patterns, e.g., *terminar de comer* 'finish eating'. The interaction of language-internal and -external motivations for auxiliation in Quechua is examined by Hintz (2010).

In addition to auxiliary structures, some Quechua aspect suffixes derive from the STEM–NOMINALIZER+PARTICLE construction. Instead of an auxiliary verb in the lexical phrase, this construction has a nonverbal final element which combines with the preceding nominalizer to form a single aspect suffix. The pre-Proto Quechua source for *-rqa* 'past (perfective/tense)', for example, would be the verbal periphrasis of *-r* 'nominalizer' plus *qa* (shown by Weber 1987a to be a demonstrative). The cliticization of nonverbal elements gives rise to perfectives but apparently not imperfectives (cf. Table 11.6).

A third mechanism contributing to the enrichment of the aspectual system is the amalgamation or fusion of co-occurring derivational suffixes to yield new aspectual categories. As with auxiliation, amalgamation gives rise to both perfective and imperfective suffixes.[222]

Table 11.7 *Quechua aspectualizing construction patterns and associated mechanisms*

ASPECTUALIZING CONSTRUCTION	MECHANISM
1. STEM–NOMINALIZER+AUXILIARY	Auxiliation
2. STEM–NOMINALIZER+PARTICLE	Cliticization of a nonverbal element
3. STEM–SUFFIX$_1$-SUFFIX$_2$	Amalgamation

Table 11.7 summarizes the three general patterns of aspectualizing constructions in Quechua, along with the relevant diachronic mechanisms. As noted above, the first two are analytic verbal constructions. Over time, the routinized combination of the developing auxiliary or particle with the erstwhile nominalized complement can merge into a single grammatical aspect suffix. The third construction represents the amalgamation of adjacent word-internal derivational suffixes. Specific instances of these three construction types, illustrated throughout this chapter, constitute the earliest stages in the elaboration of aspectual categories in Quechua. The evolutionary developments detailed in Chapters 9 and 10 represent subsequent stages in the grammaticization of perfectives and imperfectives.

---

[222] Amalgamation is discussed in §2.1.2 (note 22), §3.1.3 (note 52), §8.7, §10.4, as well as §11.6 in the present chapter.

PART V – CONCLUSION

12 THE EMERGENCE OF GRAMMATICAL SYSTEMS

12.1 Overview

I have presented a comprehensive account of the grammatical expression of aspect and related semantic domains in SCQ. The analyses are based on a corpus of naturally-occurring speech, including some 9,600 clauses in over five hours of recordings with 37 speakers. The approach applied here integrates the description of the synchronic system with an investigation of cognitive and communicative forces of semantic change that have shaped over time the grammatical system in SCQ and related structures across the Quechua family as a whole.

We observed in PART II that aspect in SCQ does not constitute a neatly organized system of maximal contrasts. Instead, the aspectual system comprises a network of twenty productive grammatical markers characterized by subtle semantic distinctions and considerable overlap within the perfective and imperfective categories (Chapters 2-4). The grammatical expression of aspect is further enriched by the distribution of individual elements diffused through interdependent layers of morphology. While some aspect markers are clearly derivational, others have attained full inflectional status. In addition, several ambiguous cases are located "in between," that is, they retain certain features of derivational expression and satisfy some but not all of the criteria for inflection (Appendix B).

Maintaining a clear conceptual distinction between semantic domains, such as aspect and tense, represents an essential component in the linguist's arsenal of analytic tools. At the same time, as demonstrated in PART III, one and the same SCQ aspect marker typically encodes elements of more than one domain. In other words, the aspectual system is not a separately delineated grammatical category. Instead, as in many languages, aspect in SCQ is tightly interwoven with tense and with modality (Chapters 5 and 6). Quechuan languages offer the additional opportunity to examine the less explored grammatical interfaces linking aspect with manner and with middle voice (Chapters 7 and 8).[223]

---

[223] The study of naturally-occurring speech in Central Quechuan varieties adjacent to SCQ (e.g., Huaylas, North Conchucos, Huamalíes, etc.) reveals that the aspectual systems are similarly organized. At the same time, differences in the formal status of cognates and the use of non-cognate aspect markers are among the factors which impede full mutual intelligibility

Aspect in Quechua and its grammatical interfaces with tense, modality, manner, and middle voice provide an ideal environment in which to investigate emergent properties of grammar. In PART IV we examined how grammatical meaning and expression are attained through a variety of mechanisms that move individual morphemes along evolutionary pathways of development (Chapters 9 and 10). Aspectual auxiliaries and particles in the earliest stages of development allow us to explore the gradual emergence and elaboration of aspectual categories from prior sources, that is, the lexical substance and phonological material employed in the ongoing grammaticization of aspect markers (Chapter 11).

Beyond identifying *what* innovations happened, we focused throughout on *how* these innovations happened in terms of the competing motivations and diachronic processes that fashioned them. The empirical investigation reveals that the grammatical expression of aspect is shaped by discourse in an ongoing process. Yet a defining feature of aspect in Quechua, evident in the extensive inventory of markers and combinations that speakers actually use, is lack of convergence on the classic "binary-opposition" types described in §4.2. Instead, the aspectual system could be characterized as "a continual movement toward structure" (Hopper 1987:142). In sum, by examining the larger context of constructions in connected SCQ speech, complemented by patterns and structures across the language family, we have observed a grammatical system in the making.

12.2 Diachronic processes

A key to understanding grammatical systems lies in discovering how they take shape over time through the interaction of language-internal and -external processes. I have examined such processes in detail throughout the present study of aspect and aspectual interfaces in Quechua. Language-internal processes are summarized in the first column of Table 12.1. The second column provides brief illustrations together with section numbers in which the relevant process is treated in detail. Each of these fourteen diachronic processes yields grammatical aspect markers, with the exception of LEXICALIZATION (line 12), which imparts aspectual meanings to lexical items. The REDUPLICATION processes (lines 13 and 14) refer to the historical patterns that gave rise to this mode of expression, not the synchronic instantiations.

---

among these varieties. In more distant Quechuan languages—e.g., Ecuadorian Pastaza (Nuckolls 1996) and Cuzco (Cusihuamán 1976a)—the grammatical expression of aspect appears to vary a great deal from the SCQ system described here (cf. Chapter 11 and the maps in Appendix A).

Table 12.1 *Language-internal processes in the development of aspect in Quechua*

DIACHRONIC PROCESS	SECTION AND EXAMPLE	
1 FUNCTIONAL GENERALIZATION + Increasing distribution of a gram	9.2	*-rqu* 'out' > -*ru* 'past perfective' derivation > inflection
2 ANALYTIC VERBAL CONSTRUCTION I Nonfinite gram + Auxiliary	9.5	*-shqa* 'PTCP' + *ka-* 'be' > 'perfect' > -*sha* 'past perfective'
3 ANALYTIC VERBAL CONSTRUCTION II Nonfinite gram + Particle	11.6	*-r* + *qa* 'demonstrative' > *-rqa* 'past'
4 AMALGAMATION I 2 or more different grams	11.6	-*ra:* 'durative' + -*yka:* 'continuous' > -*rayka:* 'continuous-durative, habitual'
5 AMALGAMATION II Reduplicate gram	8.4.2	-*ku* 'middle' + -*ku* 'middle' > -*kuku* 'heightened volition'
6 EMERGENCE OF GRAMMATICAL ZERO Via contrast with an overt inflectional category	10.1	Ø 'present imperfective' vs. 'inflectional past'
7 FUNCTIONAL NARROWING Older gram	5.4 10.3	Ø 'present imperfective' > 'present habitual' (due to development of continuous -*yka:*)
8 COPULA FORMATION Lexeme to locative and/or existential copula	11.2 11.3	*kawsa-* 'live, exist' > locative copula (e.g., Chachapoyas) *tiya-* 'sit' > general copula (e.g., Salasaca, Santiago del Estero)
9 PHONOLOGICAL REDUCTION	9.3 11.5	*-rqu* 'out' > -*ru* 'past perfective *-y* 'infinitive' + *kawsa-* 'be alive, exist' > -*yka:* 'continuous'
10 CLITICIZATION Nonbound nominal form	3.1.6 10.4	*yan* 'n each' > =*yan* 'distributive'
11 LEXICALIZATION + AMALGAMATION New suffix via 2-step process	7.2.2	Step 1. ROOT + -*ka:* 'passive' > ROOT-*ka:-* Step 2. ROOT-*ka:-*+-*ku* 'middle' > -*ka:ku* 'total'
12 LEXICALIZATION New verb roots	4.5.3	*cha-* + -*ri* 'punctual' > *tsari-* 'grab' *cha-* + -*ra:* 'durative' > *tsara:-* 'hold'
13 REDUPLICATION I Fully inflected verb	3.1.7 10.4	*ashi-ya-:* *ashi-ya-:* search-PL.V-1 search-PL.V-1 'We keep on searching.' ('continuative')
14 REDUPLICATION II Bare verb root	3.1.7 10.4	*tikra-tikra-yku-r-ra:* turn-turn-PFV.O-SS-YET 'Turning around individually.' ('iterative')

In addition to internally-motivated processes, we also have observed contact-induced developments, that is, the infusion of foreign grammatical patterns and forms into native pathways of grammaticization. Language-external processes are summarized in the first column of Table 12.2, with relevant section numbers and glossed examples provided in column 2. Lines 1 and 2 involve the replication of foreign grammatical structures. Lines 3 and 4 involve the replication of foreign linguistic material. Line 5 involves the replication of both foreign syntax and foreign lexical material. Note in lines 1, 4 and 5 that the meanings of the replicated structures are not necessarily more grammatical than the meanings of the model structures. For example, in line 1 *qalla-rqa-n maqa-ma-r* (with constituent order modeled on Spanish verbal periphrasis) is not more grammatical than *maqa-ma-r qalla-rqa-n* (the native Quechua order). In contrast, each language-internal process in Table 12.1 does yield a more grammatical meaning.[224]

---

[224] Table 12.2 summarizes contact-induced phenomena resulting in developments to aspectual systems in Quechua. In addition, grammatical patterns and forms in Quechua have given rise to notable changes in neighboring languages, especially local varieties of Spanish. Such developments are reported, for example, by Godenzzi (1987), Bustamante (1991), Klee and Ocampo (1995), Escobar (1997), Calvo (2001), Sánchez (2004), and Diane Hintz (2007a).

Table 12.2 *Language-external (contact) processes in the development of aspect in Quechua*

DIACHRONIC PROCESS	SECTION AND EXAMPLE
1 REPLICATION I: SYNTACTIC REORDERING Native complex predicate constituents in Spanish order (AUX initial) (Result is NOT more grammatical)	11.2 *qalla-rqa-n maqa-ma-r* begin-PST-3 hit-1OBJ-SS 'He began hitting me.' 11.3 *e:wa-: akshu-ta iki-x* go-1 potato-OBJ slice-PRMT 'I'm gonna slice the potato.'
2 REPLICATION II: GRAMMATICIZATION OF NATIVE FORM IN NATIVE CONSTRUCTION BASED ON FOREIGN PATTERN Newly developing Quechua auxiliaries (Result is more grammatical)	11.2 *qashu-tsi-r usha-ru-:* trample-CAUS-SS finish-PST.R-1 'I completely trampled it.' 11.3 *aycha-ta apa-mu-na yacha-rka* meat-OBJ take-FAR-INF know-PST3 'He customarily brought meat.'
3 REPLICATION III: BORROWED LEXEME Recruitment of foreign lexical form to native construction, e.g., Spanish "light" verb to Quechua auxiliary slot (Result is more grammatical)	11.2 *ranka-ka-sha ke:ra-ku-ra-n* lodge-PASS-PTCP remain-MID-PST-3 'It stayed lodged.' 11.2 *puklla-r si:gi-ya-n* play-SS follow-PL.V-1 'They keep playing.'
4 REPLICATION IV: BORROWED GRAM Recruitment of foreign affix, e.g., Spanish participle to Inga Quechua, San Martín Quechua, and others ('progressive' in Aymara and Quechua is suggestive, but questionable) (Result is NOT more grammatical)	*wañu-du* (Levinsohn 2008:30) die-PRTC (Park et al. 1976:103) 10.2 *ri-shka-n* (Quechua, Argentina) go-PROG-3 'He is going.' 10.2 *lura-ska-ña* (Aymara) work-PROG-INF (or -*s-ka* REFL-INCP) 'To be working'
5 REPLICATION V: LEXICAL REINFORCEMENT Doubling of native gram with borrowed (Spanish) adverb (Result is NOT more grammatical)	3.1.6 *maña-ku-ru-ntsik=yan syempri* pray-MID-PST.R-1ᵢ=DIST always 'We always prayed on each occasion.' 8.2 *ama:las keda-yku-ya-:* obligatory remain-PFV.O-PL.V-1 'We obligated him to stay.'

12.3 Areal tendencies

An additional language contact phenomenon can be seen in the diffusion of grammatical features across a considerable geographic area. Aspect systems elaborated in large part through derivational morphology, especially suffixes, are observable not only in Quechuan languages but in a wide array of genetically unrelated language families native to the Andean region and adjacent Amazonian lowlands. A representative sample includes Aymaran (Hardman 1966:48ff.), Araucanian (Smeets 2007:17, 177), Arawakan (Wise 2005), Jivaroan (Fast, Fast, and Fast 1996:47-8), and Panoan (Valenzuela 2003:279ff.). Casting the net still further, the expression of aspect through derivational suffixes characterizes much of the Amazonian linguistic area (e.g., Dixon and Aikhenvald 1999:8-10). Presumably, given the extreme improbability of independent evolution, this extensive group of geographically contiguous languages has undergone similar grammaticization processes as a result of language contact.

Much remains to be discovered about the areal tendencies of derivational aspect and the extent to which it is elaborated cross-linguistically. As Dahl observes, "derivational processes, by their nature, lend themselves less easily to systematization than inflectional categories" (1999:31). Derivational aspect appears to be well developed in many languages in North America (Mithun 1999a:165ff plus language family descriptions) as well as Eastern Europe (Dahl and Velupillai 2005:267). In addition to these two familiar areas, as I suggest above, the derivational expression of aspect can be considered an areal feature of languages native to western and northern South America.

12.4 Cross-linguistic perspective

Throughout this work I compared aspectual properties in Quechuan languages with those found in other languages of the world (see Index of languages and language families). Aspect system types widely attested cross-linguistically were reviewed in Chapter 4 and the SCQ aspect system was positioned within this typological framework. We observed many recurrent tendencies in aspectual features, as anticipated, but also discovered properties unique to Quechua. At the highest level, aspect in SCQ is organized through interdependent layers of derivational and inflectional morphology. These layers are comparable to a Slavic-type derivational system, on the one hand, and a tripartite inflectional system, on the other. At the same time, particular features of aspect in SCQ distinguish it from both of these general system types. For example, a present-past tense distinction is not relevant at the level of "general imperfective" (as in a typical tripartite system) but in the habitual category, one level down.

Perfectives in Quechuan languages have been likened to their Russian counterparts.[225] To facilitate the comparison of these two aspectual systems, and because the perfective-imperfective

---

[225] "The use of the perfective aspect in southern Quechua I is reminiscent of the use of perfective verbs in Slavic languages such as Russian" (Adelaar and Muysken 2004:231). "Their

distinction in Russian is sometimes viewed as "the paradigm example of an aspectual category" (Dahl 1985:27; also Hopper 1982:9), I have summarized in Table 12.3 (overleaf) similarities and contrasts between these two languages.

Perfectives in Russian and Quechua share a similar meaning (1) and origin (2), and semantic extensions into the domain of manner (3) ("procedurals" in the terminology of Forsyth 1970:21ff.). These points of similarity are offset by a number of contrasting features. For example, perfective aspect is expressed solely through derivational morphology in Russian, whereas in SCQ it can be expressed both derivationally and inflectionally (4). Perfectives in Russian tend to depend heavily on the meaning of the verb (Bybee and Dahl 1989:86). In contrast, their SCQ counterparts are very productive and tend to occur with all verbs (5). Perfective-imperfective "aspectual pairs" are pervasive in Russian but rare in SCQ (6). Russian has relatively few markers, whereas SCQ has many (7). Aspect is formally marked in nearly all Russian verbs but typically optional in SCQ (8). Derivational aspect and tense are formally independent categories in both languages (9), but only in SCQ has a derivational perfective attained inflectional status as a past perfective (10). Future tense in Russian is formed through periphrasis with imperfectives, but via a separate set of future suffixes in SCQ (11). Perfectives in SCQ further distinguish modal nuances, such as obligation versus mutual consent (12).

---

function and properties are not unlike the verbal prefixes of Latin or Russian" (Landerman 1991:60).

Table 12.3 *Comparison of aspect between Russian and South Conchucos Quechua*

	RUSSIAN (SLAVIC)	SOUTH CONCHUCOS (QUECHUA)
1 DERIVATIONAL PERFECTIVE MEANING	Complete telic situation	Complete telic situation
2 ORIGIN OF PERFECTIVES	Directionals (bounders)	Directionals (bounders)
3 ASPECT AND MANNER (PROCEDURALS)	Yes	Yes
4 MODE OF EXPRESSION	Derivational	Derivational and inflectional layers
5 PRODUCTIVITY	Strong tendency for perfectives to be restricted to telic verbs; the choice of form is largely unpredictable	Tendency for perfectives to occur with all verbs; the derivational and inflectional layers are very productive
6 ASPECTUAL PAIRS	Pervasive	Rare
7 INDIVIDUAL MARKERS	Relatively few	9 perfectives, 11 imperfectives
8 FORMAL MARKING	Nearly all verbs formally marked	<u>Derivational</u>: Optional <u>Inflectional</u>: Shares slot with mood and deverbal markers
9 ASPECT AND TENSE	Aspect and tense formally independent categories	<u>Derivational</u>: Aspect independent from tense <u>Inflectional</u>: Past perfectives, present habitual, past habitual, past imperfective
10 PATH FROM DERIVATION TO INFLECTION	No	Yes
11 MORPHOLOGICAL FUTURE	No, periphrasis formed from imperfectives	Yes, independent from aspect
12 ASPECT AND MODALITY	Perfectives do not distinguish obligation vs. mutual consent	Perfectives distinguish obligation vs. mutual consent
13 PERFECTIVITY AND TRANSITIVITY	Correlation with direct objects	Correlation with high agency and individuation, but not with direct objects

Finally, Russian perfective forms have a propensity to take direct objects (e.g., Bybee and Dahl 1989:89), which supports the link between aspect and transitivity postulated by Hopper and Thompson (1980:251ff.). Interestingly, in contrast, perfective and imperfective forms take direct objects with comparable frequency in the SCQ corpus (13). On the other hand, in keeping with the attributes of high agency and high individuation (among Hopper and Thompson's transitive properties), named individuals appear in many sentences with perfective markers (cf. examples in Chapter 2), whereas named individuals are rare in sentences with imperfective markers (cf. examples throughout Chapter 3).

12.5 On emergence and self-organization

Aspect and aspectual interfaces in Quechua provide an exceptionally clear illustration of emergent properties of grammar. Quechua speakers have not followed a "master plan" for introducing new distinctions into their grammatical systems, e.g., by shifting the meaning of **-rqu* 'out' to perfective aspect and ultimately past tense. Rather, the grammatical expression of semantic oppositions, such as perfective-imperfective aspect and past-present tense, represents a set of "structures which are produced by human beings who do not intend or even notice them, as if they were 'led by an invisible hand'" (Keller 1994:68).

Many linguists support the notion that grammar emerges over time through the routinization of patterns of thought and speech frequently expressed in discourse (e.g., Givón 1979, Du Bois 1985, Hopper 1987, Mithun 1991, Bybee et al. 1994, Haiman 1994, Helasvuo 2001, Chafe 2005, and many others). Scholars outside the field of linguistics who research emergent phenomena in complex systems have long recognized that interacting subunits may acquire qualitatively new properties through a process known as "self-organization." This idea is expressed in biology, for example, by Camazine et al.:

> *Self-organization* is a process in which pattern at the global level of a system emerges solely from numerous interactions among the lower-level components of the system...The pattern is an *emergent property* of the system, rather than a property imposed on the system by an external ordering influence (2001:8, emphasis added).

In this specialized sense, the grammatical expression of aspect in Quechua can be viewed as a self-organizing, emergent system. Even though recurring discourse patterns crystallize over time into relatively stable linguistic structures, aspect suffixes continue to evolve, occasionally across semantic domains (namely, tense, modality, manner, and middle voice). In addition, foreign patterns and forms exert an influence, and new aspectualizers develop in the form of analytic verbal constructions. Ongoing innovations in these aspectual elements introduce shifting patterns of internal organization within the grammatical system. As the present study has shown, more significant than the autonomous meaning of each individual aspect marker is the interaction of the elements within the system as a whole.

Andrew Wedel, in an interview with Harrison (see Harrison 2005), illustrates self-organization and emergent properties of language structure by analogy with phenomena in the natural environment:

> Sand dunes in the desert or ripples at the bottom of a streambed come about from the air or water flowing over them and the way individual grains of sand happen to bounce against one another. No individual sand grain knows that it is part of a sand dune or streambed. It is these repeated, small-scale interactions that, over time, result in this big, global structure that has a lot of order but isn't preprogrammed into the sand grains in any direct sense.

> Some parts of language structure may be the dunes and the individual sand grains may be the countless conversations carried on between people and parents teaching their children for millennia. All of this cycling is a prerequisite for self-organization.

Discovering patterns in the grammatical expression of aspect and related semantic domains in Quechua can help to explain diachronic stability and diachronic change. I hope that the findings presented in this book result in a deeper understanding of processes that shape natural language.

APPENDIX A. Maps of aspect markers across the Quechua language family

The nine maps presented below highlight the most common Quechua aspect markers and their geographic distributions across the language family. Each map extends from Colombia (north) to Argentina (south). Aspectual features of eighteen Quechuan varieties are represented in all nine maps. These are indicated by * in the middle column of Table A.1. An additional seven varieties are represented in a subset of the nine maps, based on the relevant published data. The data for all maps are provided by the researchers listed in the final column. Scientific illustrators Dottie McLaren and Roberta Bloom assisted with the production of the maps.

Table A.1 *Primary sources for the Quechua data represented in Maps A.1-9*

	QUECHUAN VARIETY	SOURCE
NORTHERN QUECHUA	* Inga	Levinsohn 1976
	* Imbabura	Cole 1982
	* Salasaca	Waskosky 1992
	* Napo	Leonardi 1966, Waters 1996
	* Pastaza	Nuckolls 1996, Toedter et al. 2002
	Saraguro	Weber and Orr 1987
NORTH PERUVIAN QUECHUA	Lambayeque	Torero 1968, Shaver 1987
	* Cajamarca	Quesada 1976
	* Chachapoyas	Taylor 2000
	* San Martín	Coombs et al. 1976
CENTRAL QUECHUA	* Corongo	Hintz 2000
	* Huaylas	Swisshelm 1974, Parker 1976
	* SCQ	Hintz field notes, SCQ corpus
	* Huallaga	Weber 1989
	Oyón	Fuqua 1987
	* Pacaraos	Adelaar 1986
	* Tarma	Adelaar 1977
	* Huanca	Cerrón-Palomino 1976
SOUTHERN QUECHUA	* Ayacucho	Soto 1976a
	* Cuzco	Cusihuamán 1976a
	Arequipa	Kindberg 1987
	North Bolivian	Gómez 2000
	* Cochabamba	Lastra 1968
	Potosí	Crapo and Aitken 1986
	Santiago del Estero	Bravo 1965, 1967

Quechuan languages are represented in the maps by a black dot and label. In order to highlight the spread of an aspectual form or meaning, varieties that are in relatively close proximity may be enclosed within a single boundary line. For example, Quechuan varieties in

Ecuador are grouped together in Map A.2. Although unrelated languages, such as Waorani, may lie within the enclosed area incidentally, the boundary lines designate only that the relevant aspect form is found in the indicated Quechuan varieties.

While some forms mark aspectual meanings in one or more varieties (or dialect clusters), cognates in other varieties may have non-aspectual meanings. In most cases, only aspectual or closely related meanings are represented in the maps. For example, derivatives of *-ch'aku* are listed in Map A.8 for Huanca, Tarma, and Pacaraos with the meaning 'iterative' or 'repetitive'. Cognate forms in other Central Quechuan varieties are not listed in the map because the meaning 'concerted effort' does not lie within the domain of aspect but within manner. The evolving meanings of cognates are treated in various chapters of this work.

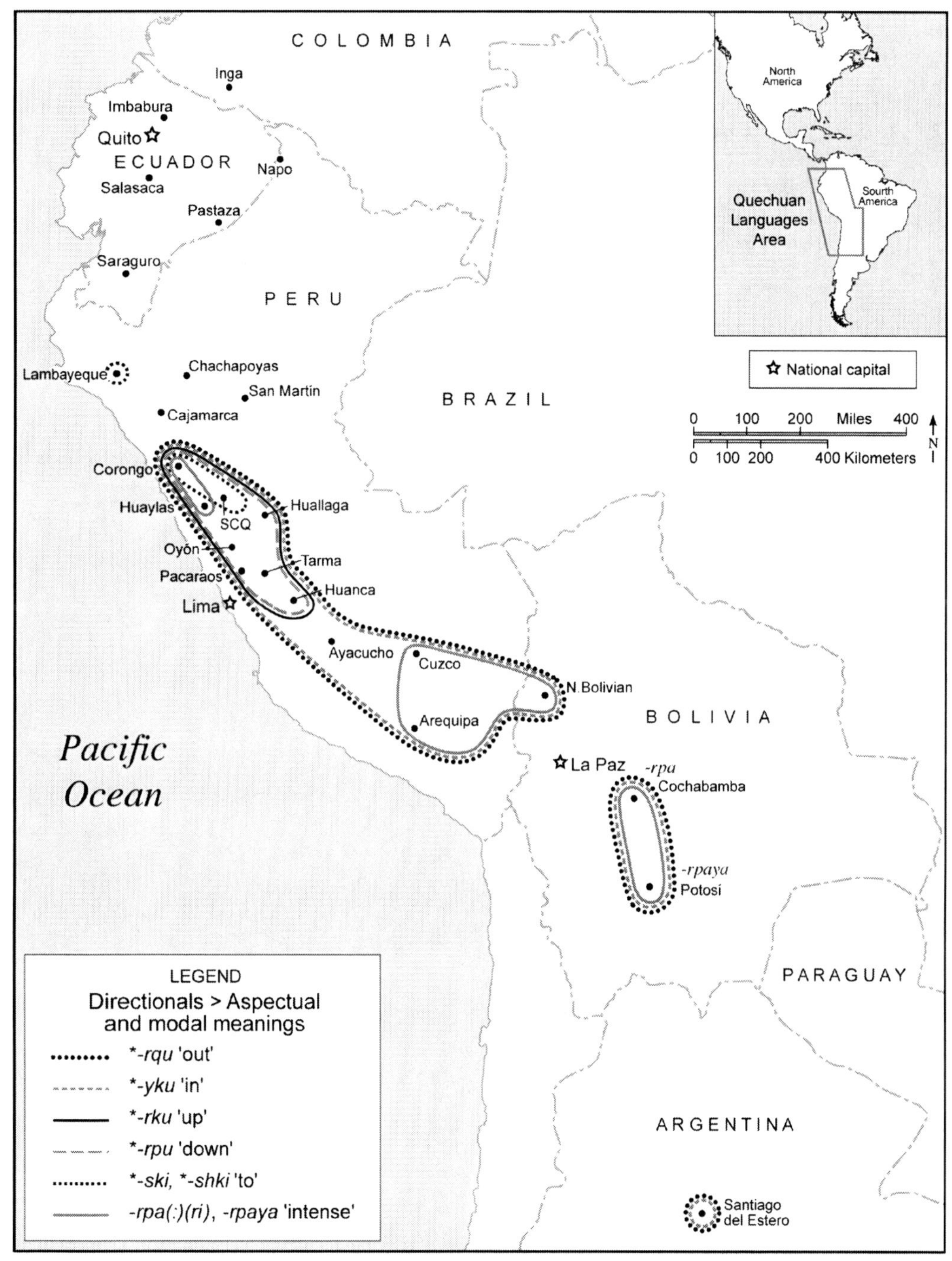

Map A.1 DIRECTIONAL SUFFIXES > ASPECTUAL AND MODAL MEANINGS

Map A.2 PERFECT > PERFECTIVE (FROM *-*shqa* 'PAST PARTICIPLE' PLUS COPULA **ka-*)

Note: The past suffix -*sqa* in Southern Quechua probably derives from **-shqa*. It is described in most sources as a narrative, historic, or reportative past, and thus is shown in Map A.7.

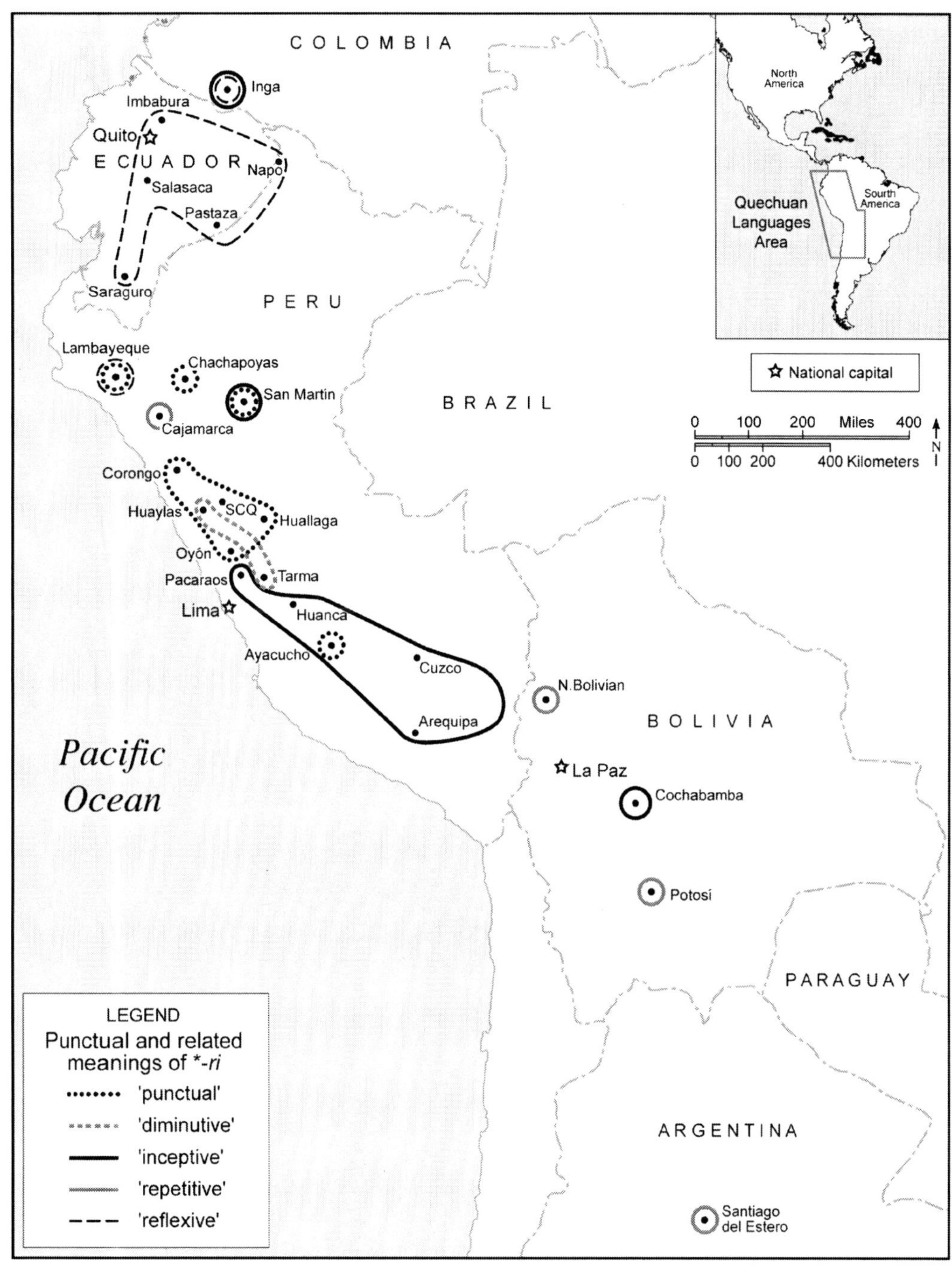

Map A.3 PUNCTUAL AND RELATED MEANINGS FROM *-ri

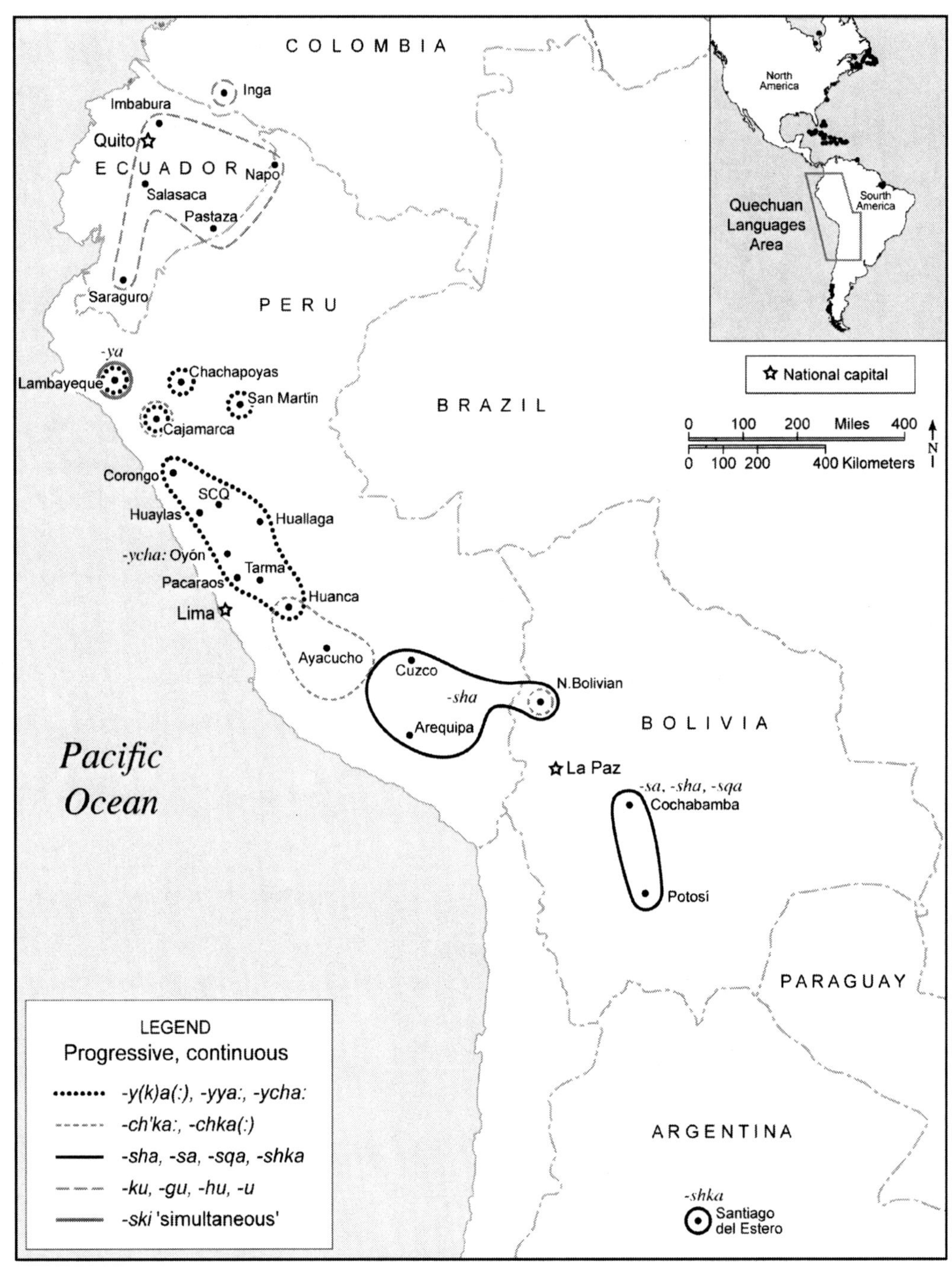

Map A.4 PROGRESSIVE SUFFIXES

Map A.5 DISTRIBUTIVES, DURATIVES, AND HABITUALS FROM *-raya*

Note: In San Martín, -raya reportedly means 'habitual without purpose', whereas -paya means 'habitual with purpose' (Coombs et al. 1976:126).

Map A.6 PAST HABITUALS

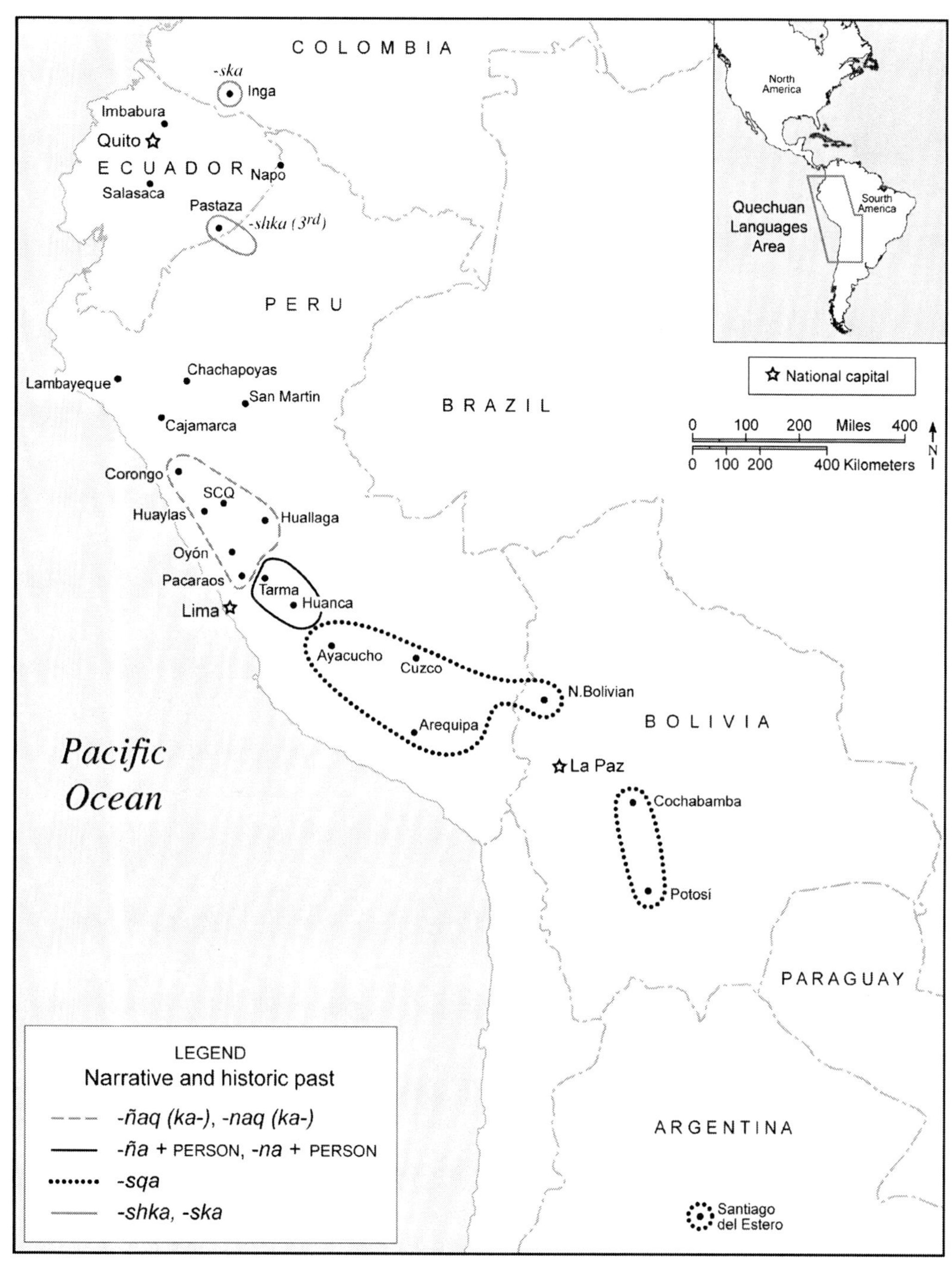

Map A.7 Narrative and reportative pasts

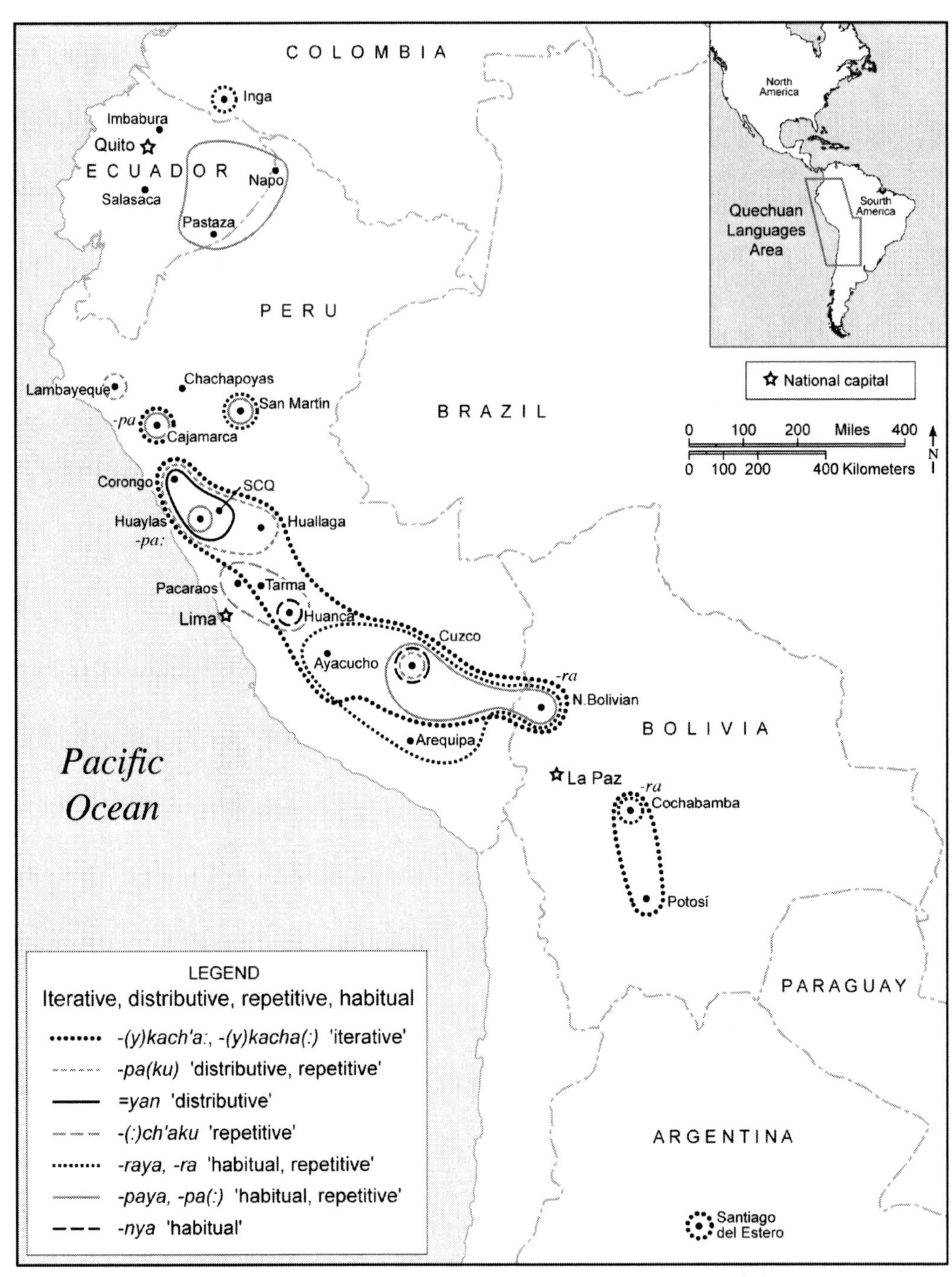

Map A.8 DISTRIBUTIVES, REPETITIVES, AND HABITUALS

<u>Notes:</u>

The cognate forms *-paya*, *-pa:*, and *-pa* are reported in Ayacucho, Huanca, Tarma, Pacaraos, Huallaga, SCQ, Corongo, and Imbabura, but not as habituals or repetitives.

The form *-paku* is reported in Tarma and Pacaraos but not as a distributive or a repetitive.

The form *-ch'aku/-chaku* is reported in Corongo, Huaylas, SCQ, and Huallaga as 'concerted effort'.

Repetitives not shown in Map A.8 include *-ri* (Cajamarca), *-cha:* (Huallaga), *-ch'a:(ri)* (Tarma), *-r(q)ari* (Cuzco), *-rqacha* (Potosí), *-tata* (Potosí), and *-tiya* (Ayacucho).

Map A.9 PROSPECTIVE, IMMINENT

Note: In Cuzco, Ayacucho, Tarma, and Pacaraos the forms -*tiya* and -*tya*: (presumably cognate) do not report an imminent situation.

APPENDIX B. SCQ aspect and the derivation-inflection continuum

A traditional approach to morphological description often involves the implicit or explicit assumption of a discrete division between derivational and inflectional expression. A growing number of recent works, on the other hand, recognize that for many languages a clear-cut boundary between derivation and inflection cannot be substantiated. For instance:

> "This chapter considers the derivation/inflection distinction as a continuous scale, rather than a discrete division of expression types" (Bybee 1985:109).

> "No clear dividing line can be found between derivational and inflectional morphology. ... Thus, the difference between inflectional and derivational morphology is not clear-cut, but rather one of degree" (Corbett 1987:329).

> "The inflection/derivation distinction is not absolute but allows for gradience and fuzzy boundaries. As Stephany (1982), Bybee (1985), Corbett (1987) and especially Plank (1994) have demonstrated, we are dealing with a continuum from clear inflection to clear derivation, with ambiguous cases in between" (Haspelmath 1996:47).

> "Markers may apparently slide along the continuum between derivation and inflection" (Mithun 1999b:41).

Similar accounts of derivation-inflection as a gradient phenomenon are reported by Dressler (1989:6), Naumann and Vogel (2000:929), Plungian (2000:188), Haspelmath (2002:71), Hay and Baayen (2005:342), among others.

I summarize here in Appendix B the findings of an analysis of the formal morphological status of aspect markers in SCQ. The following question is central to this line of inquiry: ***How can we operationalize a fine-grained analysis of derivational versus inflectional expression?*** An appropriate starting point, I suggest, entails a set of essentially non-controversial formal criteria widely accepted by linguists from functional and formal persuasions. Proposals advanced by Bybee (1985:81ff.), Anderson (1992:75ff.), Stump (1998:14ff.), and Haspelmath (2002:71) are summarized as the nine criteria for inflection listed in Table B.1.

Table B.1 *Formal criteria for inflection*

1.	OBLIGATORY SLOT
2.	NON-OCCURRENCE DENOTES MEANINGFUL Ø
3.	FAR FROM VERB ROOT
4.	CLOSED TO FURTHER DERIVATION
5.	ONE MARKER/SLOT
6.	REGULAR MEANING
7.	HIGH FREQUENCY
8.	UNLIMITED APPLICABILITY
9.	RELATIVELY ABSTRACT MEANING

The formal status of each SCQ aspect marker was evaluated in terms of these nine criteria for inflection. The results are presented in Figures B.1 and B.2 below. The patterns suggest that individual SCQ aspect markers can be placed along a cline ranging from prototypical derivation (on the left) to prototypical inflection (on the right), and what Haspelmath refers to as "ambiguous cases in between" (1996:47).

First, Figure B.1 presents several imperfective suffixes in SCQ. The suffixes to the left satisfy fewer of the inflectional criteria, while those to the right progressively satisfy additional criteria. Each has a RELATIVELY ABSTRACT MEANING (#9). The least inflectional are the duratives *-ra:* and *-rayka:*. Durative *-ra:* shows just one additional characteristic of inflection—REGULAR MEANING (#6)—in that it consistently expresses a longer-than-normal duration of time. On the other hand, *-ra:* is infrequent and is generally restricted to dynamic verb roots that do not involve motion or cognition; nor does it occur with stative verbs, but can derive a stative from a nonstative telic verb (cf. §3.1.1).

Midway along the scale are middle voice *-ku* and continuous *-yka:*. (Middle *-ku* is included in the table because it has a habitual reading in the context of customary activities; cf. §8.5.) These two suffixes satisfy more criteria than the duratives but fewer than the inflectional present and past habituals. Specifically, middle *-ku* and continuous *-yka:* are very HIGH FREQUENCY (#7) and have REGULAR MEANINGS (#6), but do not satisfy most of the other criteria for inflectional status. The Cajamarca Quechua cognate of *-yka:* (*-yka*) occurs after the object marker, and thus satisfies the additional criteria (#3) and (#4) (cf. §10.2).

The most inflectional imperfectives are present habitual *-Ø* and past habitual *-q* which satisfy all but one of the criteria for inflection. The anomalous low frequency of *-q* shows that not all of the criteria are equally relevant in the analysis of a particular grammatical marker. The low frequency of *-q* simply reflects the fact that speakers do not often have occasion to refer to past habitual situations.

Figure B.1   *The formal status of imperfectives in SCQ*

| | DERIVATIONAL | | | | INFLECTIONAL | |
| **CRITERIA FOR INFLECTION** | *-ra:* | *-rayka:* | *-ku* | *-yka:* | *-Ø* | *-q* |
	DUR	DUR.C	MID	CONT	PRS	PST.H
1. OBLIGATORY SLOT	–	–	–	–	✓	✓
2. NON-OCCURRENCE DENOTES Ø	–	–	–	–	✓	✓
3. FAR FROM VERB ROOT	–	–	–	–	✓	✓
4. CLOSED TO FURTHER DERIVATION	–	–	–	–	✓	✓
5. ONE MARKER/SLOT	–	–	–	✓	✓	✓
6. REGULAR MEANING	✓	–	✓	✓	✓	✓
7. HIGH FREQUENCY [*]	– 13	– 31	✓ 132	✓ 169	✓ 488	– 22
8. UNLIMITED APPLICABILITY	–	–	✓	✓	✓	✓
9. RELATIVELY ABSTRACT MEANING	✓	✓	✓	✓	✓	✓

Figure B.2 shows a similar analysis of perfective suffixes. The least inflectional is *-rpu*. This suffix reports downward direction in the context of spatial motion, but in situations that do not involve motion it expresses completive aspect (cf. §2.1.1). Based on the relevant criteria, *-rpu* is clearly derivational.

Midway along the scale from derivation to inflection are the perfectives *-yku* and *-ski*, and punctual *-ri*. These three suffixes satisfy more of the criteria for inflection than *-rpu* and *-rku*, but fewer than the past perfectives *-ru* , *-sha*, and *-ra*. Specifically, these markers have relatively HIGH FREQUENCIES (#7), UNLIMITED APPLICABILITY (#8), and REGULAR, ABSTRACT MEANINGS (#6, #9). These findings correspond with the subtle semantic distinctions and considerable overlap expressed by these and other markers within the perfective domain (cf. Figure 2.2 in §2.3).

The most inflectional suffixes in Figure B.2 are the past perfectives *-ru, -sha*, and *-ra*. These three satisfy all the criteria for inflection. The frequency of *-ru* is lower than might otherwise be expected because it shares past tense function with both *-sha* and *-ra*. In addition, *-ru* is restricted to speech-act participants, whereas *-sha* is a portmanteau suffix that combines past perfective with third person subject.

---

[*] To facilitate consistent comparisons, frequencies from the coded data of 1,452 verbs (cf. §1.3.2) are used for HIGH FREQUENCY (criterion #7) in Figures B.1 and B.2.

Figure B.2 *The formal status of perfectives in SCQ*

	DERIVATIONAL					INFLECTIONAL		
CRITERIA FOR INFLECTION	*-rpu*	*-rku*	*-yku*	*-ski*	*-ri*	*-ru*	*-sha*	*-ra*
	COMPL	PFV.M	PFV.O	PFV	PUNC	PST.R	PST.R3	PST
1. OBLIGATORY SLOT	–	–	–	–	–	✓	✓	✓
2. NON-OCCURRENCE DENOTES Ø	–	–	–	–	–	✓	✓	✓
3. FAR FROM VERB ROOT	–	–	–	–	–	✓	✓	✓
4. CLOSED TO FURTHER DERIVATION	–	–	–	–	–	✓	✓	✓
5. ONE MARKER/SLOT	–	✓	✓	✓	✓	✓	✓	✓
6. REGULAR MEANING	–	–	✓	✓	✓	✓	✓	✓
7. HIGH FREQUENCY	–21	–24	✓–48	✓79	✓64	✓–45	✓174	✓78
8. UNLIMITED APPLICABILITY	–	–	✓	✓	✓	✓	✓	✓
9. RELATIVELY ABSTRACT MEANING	–	✓	✓	✓	✓	✓	✓	✓

Summarizing, a set of nine formal criteria for inflection (Table B.1) facilitated a fine-grained analysis of the morphological status of aspect markers in SCQ. The evaluation of each marker based on these criteria shows that they do not all fit into a neat division between derivation and inflection. Instead, the derivation-inflection distinction allows for gradience, suggesting a continuum between prototypical derivation and prototypical inflection, with ambiguous cases in the territory between. These findings align with those of the various studies cited at the beginning of this appendix.

The analysis I have sketched here is not meant to tell the entire story. Adelaar, for example, suggests an approach to Tarma Quechua in which the foremost criterion for distinguishing an inflectional suffix from a derivational one is absence from "co-lexicalized" combinations (2006:127). This hypothesis suggests that non-final verbal suffixes that do not bond with any given verb root form a separately delineated block of inflectional suffixes in between "clear derivation" and "clear inflection." Unfortunately, this approach is untenable for SCQ because virtually every non-final verbal suffix (except for plural and object suffixes) can co-lexicalize with at least one verb root. A fruitful direction for furthering our understanding of modes of expression in Quechua morphology, I suggest, would be to integrate elements of an "in between" structural approach, such as proposed by Adelaar (1988; 2006) or by Booij (1996), with the insights of the usage-based gradient approach sketched here in Appendix B. For now, the latter analysis provides a better fit with the SCQ data.

APPENDIX C. Suffixes and enclitics in the SCQ verb

Table C.1 (overleaf) details SCQ verb structure and the relative order of 83 verbal suffixes and enclitics. SET D suffixes occur in the six non-obligatory positions closest to the verb root. These suffixes range in meaning from specific types of imperfectives and perfectives, to various expressions of modality and manner, to valence changes and other grammatical distinctions. Suffixes in SET D appear in a relatively prescribed order, with the exception of causative *-tsi* and delimitative *-lla:*. Those in the rightward slots D4-D6 are located midway along a scale from derivation to inflection (cf. Appendix B).

SET I suffixes occur in paradigmatic contrast in four obligatory positions located farther from the verb root. The order of these suffixes is invariant. Tense-aspect-mood suffixes and various deverbal suffixes occur in SLOT I2. They are preceded by the object (when relevant) in SLOT I1, and followed by the subject in SLOT I3. Many of the suffixes in SLOT I2 yield finite verbs, including various past perfectives and imperfectives, present habitual, a set of futures, along with imperative and conditional moods. The futures and imperatives are portmanteau suffixes that also encode the person of the subject. Other SLOT I2 suffixes yield nonfinite verbs, including an assortment of nominalizers, adverbializers, and participials. Nonfinite verbs take only nonverbal suffixes following SLOT I2. Conditional *-man* in SLOT I4 must be preceded by a subject suffix in SLOT I3, and must *not* be preceded by any SLOT I2 suffix. The future modal suffix *-pa:* in SLOT I4, which tends to occur only in conversations, must be preceded by a future tense suffix in SLOT I2.

The cislocative suffix *-mu* is listed in SLOT I1 because it follows plural *-ya:* (SLOT D6) and does not co-occur with the object suffixes *-ma:* and *-shu* in the next consecutive position. On the other hand, *-mu* lacks some features normally associated with inflection. For example, its non-occurrence does not imply a specific contrastive meaning. Instead, the verb is simply not specified for cislocative meaning. Landerman (1991:222) suggests that *-ma:* derives historically from the combination of **-mu* 'cislocative' plus **-wa* 'first person object'. Both forms are currently attested outside of Central Quechuan varieties.

Finally, optional suffixes and enclitics may appear in the INDEPENDENT positions of SET E (1-2) in the far right of Table C.1. Most of these markers can occur with either verbal or nonverbal elements. They range in meaning from evidentials to negatives and other discourse markers. The scope typically reaches beyond the immediate clause. The formal status of some of these SET E markers (enclitic versus suffix) is not entirely transparent. Like the SET D suffixes, many of the SET E markers can combine, and sometimes give rise to a qualitatively new meaning. The verbal template may be properly understood as comprising three INDEPENDENT slots, but I have simplified Table C.1 to two primary slots because the analysis of aspect in SCQ does not depend on a fine-grained morphological account of these markers. They are written with a hyphen in Table C.1, following the practice of grammarians in the Quechuanist tradition.

Table C.1 *83 suffixes and enclitics in the SCQ verb arranged by position and function*

◄— MORE DERIVATIONAL | MORE INFLECTIONAL —► | INDEPENDENT

VERB ROOT	SLOT SET D						SLOT SET I				SLOT SET E	
ROOT	1	2	3	4	5	6	1	2	3	4	1	2
IMPERFECTIVE REDUP₁ REDUP₂	*-ra:* DUR	*-paku* DISTR.S	*-ykacha:* ITER	*-yka:* CONT *-rayka:* DUR.C				*-Ø* PRS *-q* PST.H (*-na:* PST.N)			*-yan* DISTR.T	
PERFECTIVE			*-ri* PUNC	*-rpu* COMPL *-rku* PFV.M *-yku* PFV.O *-ski* PFV *-ri:ku* PFV.F				*-r(q)u* PST.R *-sha* PST.R1 *-r(q)a* PST				
INCIPIENT ASPECT		*-chaku* EFFORT *-ka:ku* TOTAL *-ku* MID *-kuku* MID.R										
NON-ASPECTUAL		*-ka:* PASS *-na:* DES *-pa:* BEN *-ya:* INCH	*-naku* RECP *-:shi* HELP *-tsa* CAUS.BE		*-pu* BEN	*-ya:* PL.V *-:ri* PL.DIR	*-ma:* 1OBJ *-shu* 2OBJ *-mu* FAR	*-sha:* FUT1 *-shun* FUT1$_1$ *-shayki* FUT1>2 *-nqa* FUT3 *-y* IMP2 *-tsun* IMP3 *-shwan* COND1$_1$ *-nqa* NMLZ.R *-sh(q)a* NMLZ.R *-na* NMLZ.I$_1$ *-q* AG *-y* INF *-r* SS *-pti* DS *-ypa* ADV *-sh(q)a* PTCP *-:ni* UNDONE *-qtu* PARTIAL *-q* PRMT	*-:* 1 *-nki* 2 *-yki* 2_P *-n* 3 *-ntsik* 1_1	*-man* COND *-pa:* FUT.M	*-ra:* YET *-na* NOW *-pis/-si* EVEN *-ku* Q.P *-kush* Q.T *-ta:* Q.C *-ta:ku* NEG.EMPH *-ra:ku* NEG.APP *-tsu* NEG *-tsura:* DUB	*-mi* DIR *-chi* CNJ *-cha:* MUT *-chir* APP *-shi* RPT *-ran* DIR.YET *-qa* TOP *-ri* SURE

The derivational suffixes *-tsi* CAUS and *-lla:* DLM do not occur in a single fixed position.

APPENDIX D. Quechua suffixes with the shape C.CV

An examination of the SCQ verbal suffixes in Table C.1 on the previous page reveals nine phonological patterns. These nine suffix patterns are displayed in Table D.1 along with the type frequency and an example of each canonical shape. Approximately 40% of the 82 verbal suffixes in Table C.1 have the shape CV (line 1). An additional 23% have the shape C.CV (line 2), including suffixes that begin with compensatory lengthening of the preceding vowel (e.g., *-:ri* 'PL.DIR'). Note that the first C forms the coda of the preceding syllable and the second C forms the onset of the next syllable. The nine type frequencies in Table D.1 total 100%.

Table D.1 *Canonical shapes and frequencies of SCQ verbal suffixes*

	CANONICAL SHAPE	TYPE FREQUENCY	EXAMPLE SUFFIX	
1.	CV	40%	*-ri*	'PUNC'
2.	**C.CV**	**23%**	***-yku***	**'PFV.O'**
3.	CV.CV	12%	*-paku*	'DISTR.S'
4.	CVC	10%	*-yan*	'DISTR.T'
5.	C	7%	*-q*	'AG'
6.	C.CVC	3%	*-shwan*	'COND1$_1$'
7.	CVC.CV	3%	*-rayka:*	'DUR.C'
8.	C.CV.CV	1%	*-ykacha:*	'ITER'
9.	Ø (zero)	1%	*-Ø*	'PRS'

Significantly, nearly 50% of the C.CV verbal suffixes in SCQ (line 2) have aspectual meanings. In addition, some aspect suffixes with the synchronic shape CV have reduced from a proto suffix of the form *-C.CV (e.g., *-ru* 'PST.R' from *-rqu* 'out'). The propensity for aspect suffixes of the shape C.CV is not a coincidence. As discussed throughout Chapter 11, C.CV suffixes typically are comprised of two historical elements. The initial element (C) often derives from a deverbal suffix composed of a single C such as *-y* 'INF', *-r* 'SS', or *-q* 'AG' (cf. Tables 11.2, 11.3, and 11.5). The second element (CV) can develop from an auxiliary verb or a nonverbal form, such as a particle. For example, *-yka:* 'CONT' would have derived from the combination *-y* 'INF' plus either 1) a lengthened version of the copula *ka-* or 2) the reduction in stages of the auxiliary *kawsa-* 'exist, be alive' to *kawa*, and then to *ka:* (cf. §11.2 and §11.5).

A wide array of suffixes with the canonical shape C.CV are reported across the Quechua language family. While some of the C.CV suffixes presented in Table D.2 (below) are widely attested, others are specific to a particular variety or geographic area. The table is arranged with "1st Elements" (C) in eight rows and "2nd Elements" (CV) in twenty columns. The resulting 8x20 "sparse matrix" shows that forty-nine C.CV combinations are attested, while many others are not.

The C.CV suffixes in Table D.2 exhibit synchronic and diachronic patterns similar to those found in SCQ. For instance, 35% (17 of 49) express an aspectual meaning (see shaded cells). In addition, several of the "1ˢᵗ Elements" (C) are former deverbal suffixes and many of the "2ⁿᵈ Elements" (CV) derive from auxiliaries or nonverbal units. For example, *-gri* 'INCH' is a product of auxiliation, arising from the combination **-q* 'AG' plus the auxiliary **ri-* 'go' (Muysken 1977:107). Similarly, *-rqa* 'past' develops from the combination **-r* plus the demonstrative **qa* (Weber 1987a). The data in Table D.2 suggest fruitful directions for further research on the formation of Quechua suffixes and the diachronic stability of polysynthesis in this language family.

Table D.2 *49 suffixes with the shape C.CV across the Quechua language family*
(shading indicates aspect suffix)

1st ELEMENT (C)	cha:	chik/q/s	ka(:)	ki	ku	lla:	naq	ni(n)	pa(:)(ri)	pi	pu	qa	qu(n)	ri	sha	shi	ta(:)	ti(n)	tu	ya(:)
-y INF	ycha:		yka(:)	yki	yku	ylla:	yna(q)	yni(n)	ypa(ri)				yqu(n)			yshi	yta(:)		ytu	yya(:)
-r SS			rka(:)		rku				rpa(:)(ri)		rpu	rqa	rqu							
-q AG			q=ka			qlla				qpi				gri	q=sha		qta(:)	qti	qtu	qya
-sh PTCP			ska	ski					shpa			shqa					shta	shti	stu	sya
-n ?		nchi(k)		nki	nku		nna(q)	nni(n)			npu	nqa					nta	nti		nya(:)
-p(a) GEN																		pti		
-ch LOC? loan?			chka(:)																	
-ti(ya) 'sit'																				tya(:)

APPENDIX E. Perfective *-ski* as a former directional suffix

Many of the perfective suffixes in SCQ expressed directional meanings at a prior stage of grammatical development. Specifically, the proto directional suffixes **-rpu* 'down', **-rku* 'up', **-yku* 'in', and **-rqu* 'out' gave rise to completive *-rpu*, derivational perfectives *-rku* and *-yku*, and inflectional past perfective/tense *-ru*, respectively. In contrast, the etymology of perfective *-ski* is less than transparent. Stewart (1984:76) alludes to the possibility that it may be a former directional marker, but no evidence has been available on this point prior to the present study (cf. Hintz, forthcoming). Evidence is presented here to show that *-ski* almost certainly was a directional suffix with the form **-ski* or **-shki*. A plausible meaning would have been 'toward deictic center'.

The geographic territory of *-ski* is indicated by the shaded region in Map E.1. As the map shows, *-ski* is attested in a contiguous area beginning in Corongo and Sihuas in the north of Ancash Department, continuing southeast through Pomabamba (North Conchucos) and Huari (South Conchucos) and extending across the Marañón River into Huamalíes and Dos de Mayo in western Huánuco Department. Notably, *-ski* is not attested in the neighboring Quechuan varieties spoken in Huaraz (Huaylas) and Chiquián in Ancash, nor in Huallaga, Pachitea, and Margos-Yarowilca-Lauricocha in Huánuco, nor in the departments of Lima, Cerro de Pasco, and Junín.

Characteristics of suffixes derived from the set of proto directionals are illustrated throughout this book, especially in Chapters 2 and 5-7. We observed that their meanings have shifted over time from directional concepts to temporal and modal concepts. Based on these and other findings, we will consider whether perfective *-ski* was also a directional suffix during a prior stage of development. First, I present four types of evidence internal to the Quechuan varieties in which *-ski* is attested: morphology, phonology, semantics, and discourse patterns. Then I assess the distribution of directional suffixes across the language family. The observations are numbered consecutively (1-17) in the following discussion.

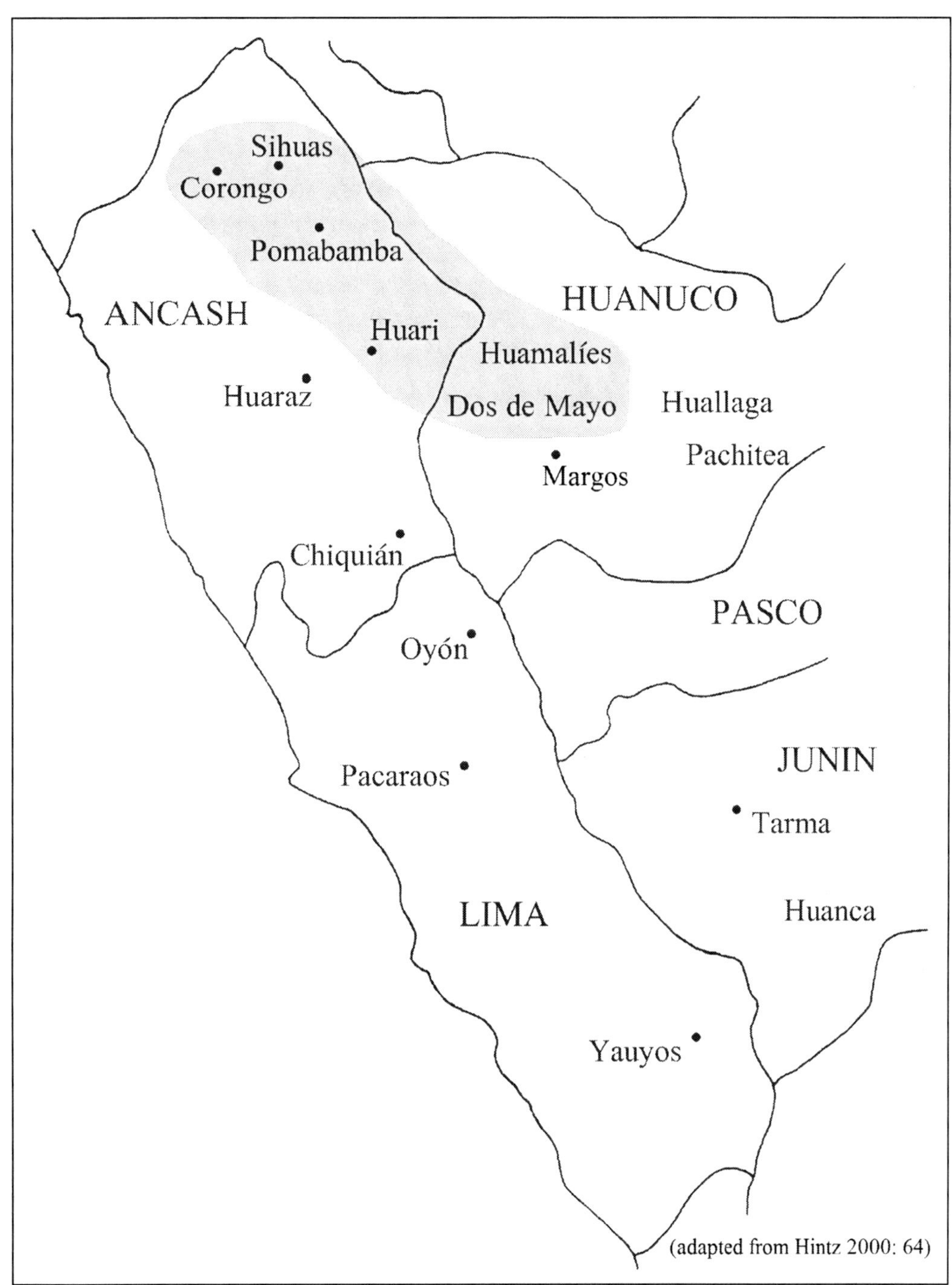

Map E.1   THE GEOGRAPHIC RANGE OF *-ski* IN CENTRAL PERU

Morphology

(1)   Each of the former directional suffixes has developed completive and perfective meanings expressed through derivational morphology. The suffix *-ski* in SCQ is also a derivational perfective (cf. §2.1.4).

(2)   The directional suffixes do not productively co-occur with other directional suffixes in the same word. Likewise, *-ski* does not co-occur with the directional suffixes.

(3)   Another formal characteristic shared by *-rpu*, *-rku*, and *-yku* is that each occurs in the derivational slot D4 close to the verb root. *-ski* occurs in the same non-obligatory slot as these well-known former directional suffixes, preceding the obligatory inflectional slot I2 located further from the verb root.

(4)   Like the directional suffixes, *-ski* can be followed by other derivational suffixes prior to the inflectional person, tense, and mood suffixes.

(5)   In most central Quechuan varieties, the suffix *-ru* (from **-rqu* 'out') occurs in an optional slot before the inflectional object slot. In Ancash Quechua *-r(q)u* has undergone further grammatical development and now occurs farther from the verb root in an inflectional (obligatory) position after the object slot. The meaning has become 'past tense, perfective aspect'. It is probably not a coincidence that *-ski* is attested only in the Quechuan varieties in which **-rqu* has attained this past perfective meaning.[226]

(6)   The general plural suffix in South Conchucos has the form *-ya:*, whether for subjects or objects. The less common plural suffix *-:ri* 'all, every' occurs only with the former directional suffixes, with middle voice *-ku* (the probable final element in **-rku* 'up' and **-yku* 'in'), and with the suffix *-ski*. As illustrated in (379), plural *-:ri* triggers morphophonemic lowering with the directionals and also with *-ski* (lowered allomorph *-ska*). In Central Quechuan varieties east and south of Ancash, *-:ri* is the only plural suffix used with directionals and middle *-ku*.

(379)	*hita-rpu-n*	'he throws it down'		*ishki-ski-n*	'he falls down'
	hita-rpu-ya-n	'he throws them down'		*ishki-ski-ya-n*	'they fall down'
	hita-rpa-:ri-n	'he throws them all down'		*ishki-ska-:ri-n*	'they all fall down'

Phonology

(7)   Each Proto Central directional suffix has the canonical shape CCV. Specifically, the first consonant is a non-nasal sonorant, the second is a voiceless plosive, and the vowel is high (**-rpu* 'down', **-rku* 'up', **-yku* 'in', **-rqu* 'out'). *-ski* is the only other SCQ suffix with exactly these phonological characteristics. One feature difference is voicing of the initial consonant. (For more on CCV suffixes, see Appendix D.)

---

[226] *-ski* does not occur in Huaylas, where *-rqu* is restricted to recent events.

(8)   The high final vowel in each directional suffix lowers to [*a*] when followed by certain trigger suffixes, such as cislocative *-mu*, causative *-tsi*, or plural *-:ri* (illustrated above in (379)). *-ski* becomes *-ska* in exactly this morphological environment, e.g., *qeshpi-ski-n* 'it escapes' versus *qeshpi-ska-mu-n* 'it escapes and returns here'.

(9)   Simultaneous events are marked in some Southern, Central, and North Peruvian Quechuan languages by the adverbial clause marker *-shti/-sti*, presumably from *-shti. *sh* is also the initial element in the suffixes *-shpa/-spa* 'same subject adverbializer' and *-shqa/-sha* 'past participle'. The proto phoneme *s* rarely appears as the initial element in reconstructed Proto Quechua forms (Parker 1969b:128). These forms suggest that the initial element of modern day *-ski* may have been *sh*, that is, *-shki*, although we cannot rule out *-ski*.

<u>Semantics</u>
(10)   The former directional suffixes *-rku* and *-yku* express not only perfective aspect, but also the modal senses 'mutual consent' and 'obligation', respectively. Likewise, *-ski* expresses perfective aspect plus the modal sense 'mirative'.

(11)   The continuous subset of meanings in Figure 9.1 (in Chapter 9) suggests that *-ski* would have had a directional meaning during a prior stage.

(12)   The directional suffixes have fused with certain verb roots (cf. Table 4.9). *-ski* also appears to have fused with certain verb roots, e.g., *chaski-* 'receive', *muski-* 'sniff', and *alle:ski-* 'heal, return to normal'. The exact meaning of *-ski* is uncertain, but based on these and other lexicalized forms, we mght posit the directional meaning 'toward deictic center'. The arguments presented here for *-ski* as a former directional suffix do not depend on the reconstruction of a specific directional meaning.

<u>Discourse patterns</u>
(13)   The frequency and distribution of *-ski* in naturally-occurring SCQ speech is very similar to that of perfective *-yku* (from *-yku 'in'), and is comparable to that of other former directionals. These discourse patterns are presented in detail in §4.4 to §4.6 in terms of aspect marker combinations and the distribution of aspect markers with non-aspectual linguistic elements.

<u>Distribution across the language family</u>
(14)   Central Quechua has a propensity for more directional suffixes than other areas of the language family. Counting *-ski* as a former directional, SCQ and its closest neighbors would have five. Most other Central Quechuan varieties have four, Southern Quechua has two (*-yku* and *-rqu*), and Northern Quechua has none (see Map A.1 in Appendix A).

(15)   The derivational suffix *-ski* occurs only in a contiguous area in the departments of Ancash and Huánuco (see Map E.1 above). The form *-ski* does not occur elsewhere in the language family, with the exception of Lambayeque (North Peruvian) (see Map A.4).

(16)   The form *-ski* is one of several affinities between Lambayeque and Central Quechuan varieties. In Lambayeque, the form *-ski* is very infrequent (Shaver and Shaver 1992:200). It

marks progressive aspect (a subtype of imperfective), with the further implication that the action is simultaneous with some other action (Torero 1968:297). This imperfective meaning contrasts with the perfective meaning of *-ski* in SCQ.

Cross-linguistic support for a semantic split

(17) Bifurcation between imperfective and perfective meaning has been attested in other languages. For instance, in an article on progressive forms in Japanese, Mandarin Chinese, and Korean, Shirai (1998:680) expands on the observation made by Kindaichi (1950) and others that progressives can also serve resultative functions. For example, the progressive function of the combination *-te* plus *i-* in (380) (glossed ASP for 'aspect') focuses on the action performed by the subject. In contrast, the resultative function of the same form *-te* plus *i-* in (381) focuses on a change of state (1998:661).

(380)   MODERN JAPANESE   (PROGRESSIVE)
        *Ken-ga   utat-**te** **i**-ru*
        Ken-NOM   sing-**ASP**-NON.PAST
        'Ken is singing.'

(381)   MODERN JAPANESE   (RESULTATIVE)
        *mado-ga   ai-**te** **i**-ru*
        window-NOM   open-**ASP**-NON.PAST
        'The window is open.'

Let us assume, for the sake of argument, that *-ski* in Central Quechua and *-ski* in Lambayeque Quechua are cognate. We have already seen above in §5.4 that progressives can generalize to become imperfectives by taking on habitual meaning (Bybee et al. 1994:139). We are also familiar with the path of development from resultatives to perfects to past perfectives (see Figure 9.3 above). If we apply the observations on Japanese to the form *-ski* in Quechua, it is plausible that a single proto suffix (*-*ski* or *-*shki*) could have undergone a semantic split, functioning as a *progressive* in dynamic durative situations (as in Lambayeque), and as a *perfective* in non-dynamic durative situations (as in Central Quechua).

The sound recordings associated with the two transcriptions below are available at www.ucpress.edu/9780520098855. The end of each line of transcription corresponds to the end of an intonation unit. Multiple intonation units on a single line are separated by the symbol "‖". Brackets "[ ]" enclose overlapping speech; left brackets are vertically aligned. "@" represents a single laugh pulse or laughter during a word. Derivational and inflectional aspect markers are underlined and appear in boldface. In addition, derivational aspect markers are shaded.

1. Lost donkey

	SPEAKER	GENDER	AGE	COMMUNITY	RELATIONSHIPS
PARTICIPANTS:	Rita (R)	female	20s	Huaripampa	youngest sister of Guillermo
	Guillermo (G)	male	20s	Huaripampa	older brother of Rita

BACKGROUND: The following SCQ conversation was recorded August 20, 1993 in Huaraz, Peru. Rita and her brother Guillermo talk about events of the previous week. Rita had participated in the annual *Tayta Pancho* (San Francisco) fiesta in Huaripampa (elevation 10,500 feet) and Guillermo had missed those events due to an obligation in Huaraz. This one-minute conversation segment is taken from a 21 minute recording.

1   R: *A:ha-m, alba-ku-ya-__ra__-:*   *pay-wan*
          yes-DIR   first.night-MID-PL.V-__PST__-1   he-COM
          'Yes, we spent the opening night with him,

2   *"Keda-ku-shun   keda-ku-shun"   ni-r*
          stay-MID-FUT₁   stay-MID-FUT₁   say-SS   __REDUP__ (INFLECTED VERB)
          by repeatedly saying "Let's stay together, let's stay together,"

3   *ama:las keda-__yku__-ya-__Ø__-:.*
          forced   quedarse-__PFV.O__-PL.V-__PRS__-1
          we obligated him to stay.

4   *Tsay   alba   tsakay, ‖ tsay-kaq-ta-ra: willa-__yku__-shayki-qa,*
          that   first.night   night   that-DEF-OBJ-YET   inform-__PFV.O__-FUT1>2-TOP
          That opening night, I will tell you about that.

5   *Este=   ...   tsay kampyuna:tu-ta organisa-ya-__rqa__-n,*
          um   that tournament-OBJ organize-PL.V-__PST__-3
          They organized that tournament.'

6   G: *Eskwela.*
          school
          'The school.'

7   R: ... *mhm,*
              mhm
          'mhm,'

8   G: *uh   huh,*
          uh   huh
          'uh huh,'

9   R: ...*Tsay   o:ra-qa-m,* || ...*Ninfi:tu   ari   bu:rru-ntsi:-qa,*
              that   hour-TOP-DIR   Ninfa   yes   donkey-1₁-TOP
          'At that time, Ninfa, our donkey,

10   *pi   pri:ma-ntsi: Dina-pa   ka-q   wayi-n-kaq-chu   ka-**yka:**-mu-**rqa**-n.*
         who   cousin-1₁   Dina-GEN   be-AG   house-3-DEF-LOC   be-**CONT**-FAR-**PST**-3
         was over by our cousin Dina's house.'

11   G: *uh   huh,*
          un   huh
          'uh huh,'

12   R: ...*I=   Negra-wan   Kapcha-qa   kay-la:-pa-na*
               and   Blacky-COM   Capcha-TOP   this-SIDE-GEN-NOW

          *sha-mu-sh   ka-**ra**-n   wayi-kaq-pa-na.*
          come-FAR-PTCP   be-**PST**-3   house-DEF-GEN-NOW
          'And Blacky and Capcha had already come over to this side of the house.'

13   G: *uh   huh,*
          uh   huh
          'uh huh,'

14   R: ...*I=   las   kwatru   sinku-na-chir   ka-**ra**-n-qa.*
               and   o'clock   four   five-NOW-APP   be-**PST**-3-TOP
          'And it was about four or five o'clock.

15   ... *I=   noqa-pis   mana   qayku-**ski**-**∅**-:-pis-tsu,*
              and   I-EVEN   no   enclose-**PFV**-**PRS**-1-EVEN-NEG
          And I don't even shut them in,

16   *"Tempra:nu-lla-ra:-cha:"* *ni-r,*
    early-DLM-YET-MUT   say-SS
    "It's still early" saying,

17   *oqra-**yku**-ya-**Ø**-:*   *tsakay* *bu:rru-ta-qa.*
    lose-**PFV.O**-PL.V-**PRS**-1 night donkey-OBJ-TOP
    we lose the donkey in the night.'

18 G: *uh huh,*
    uh huh
    'uh huh,'

19 R: *Llapa-:-kuna, ||* *Niko,*
    all-1-PL.N   Niko
    'All of us, Niko,

20   *llapa-:-kuna tsakay ashi-ya-**Ø**-:* *ashi-ya-**Ø**-:*
    all-1-PL.N night seek-PL.V-**PRS**-1 seek-PL.V-**PRS**-1   REDUP (INFLECTED VERB)
    all of us keep searching in the night

    bu:rru-ta-qa,
    donkey-OBJ-TOP
    for the donkey.

21   .. *Mana-na tari-**yku**-[ya-**Ø**-:-na-tsu].*   @ @
    no-NOW find-**PFV.O**-PL.V-**PRS**-1-NOW-NEG
    We don't find it.'

22 G: *[#-tsu]*
           -NEG
    (unintelligible)

23 G: *[Peru,]*
    but
    'But,

24 R: *[@ @]*

25 G: ... *kostumbri-m tse:. **Ø***
    custom-DIR that **PRS**
    that's typical.

26 R: @ @

27   G: *Wata   wata   tsa: [fyesta-cho:-qa]   oqra-ka-__Ø__-n   [₂burriku-qa,]*
         year   year   then   fiesta-LOC-TOP   lose-PASS-__PRS__-3   donkey-TOP
         Year after year during the time of the fiesta the donkey is lost.

28   R: *[@   @]*   *[₂@]*

29   G: *Illa-ka-__ski__-__Ø__-n,*
         be.absent-PASS-__PFV__-__PRS__-3
         It disappears,

30   R: @

31   G: *Wamra-pis   ka:su-__Ø__-n-tsu*
         child-EVEN   pay.attention -__PRS__-3-NEG
         The children don't pay attention,

32   *ni   noqa-ntsik-pis   yarpa-__ski__-__Ø__-ntsik-tsu,*
         nor   I-1₁-EVEN   think-__PFV__-__PRS__-1₁-NEG
         and we ourselves don't even think about it.'

33   R: *Tsa: tsay   o:ra-lla-na   ari   arpa-kuna-pis   @[cha:-ya:-mu-__ra__-n,]*
         then   that   hour-DLM-NOW   yes   harp-PL.N-EVEN   arrive-PL.V-FAR-__PST__-3
         'At just that time the band arrived too.

34   G: *[@   @]*

35   R: *Tsay-chu   [₂pas   kushi-sh   __ka-ku__-ya-sha-:-yaq]*
         that-LOC   very   be.happy-PTCP   __be-MID__-PL.V-NMLZ.R-1-LIM
         During the time that we were happily occupied there (at the fiesta),

36   G: *[₂@   @@ @]*

37   R: *@oqra-ka-__ski__-__na:__.   [₃@@@]*
         lose-PASS-__PFV__-__PST.N__
         it got lost (wandered off).

38   G: *[₃@]*

39   *...Ay   kara:.*
         what.a.deal   gosh
         'What a deal, gosh.'

2. Cows, oats, and guinea pigs

	SPEAKER	GENDER	AGE	COMMUNITY	RELATIONSHIPS
PARTICIPANTS:	Lita (L)	female	59	Huari	mother of Eli
	Felipe (F)	male	13	Chawpi Loma	friend of Lita's family
	Eli (E)	male	25	Huari	son of Lita

BACKGROUND: This spontaneous SCQ conversation was recorded July 7, 2002 in the home of Lita, a resident of the municipality of Huari (pop. *circa* 2500, elevation 10,000 feet) in central Peru. Felipe lives nearby in Chawpi Loma, a close-knit community of five families located in the *puna* (high mountain grasslands) at 13,000 feet. Lita was raised in Chawpi Loma. Felipe, Lita, and her son Eli discuss cows and crops in this one-minute segment of a much longer conversation.

1   F: *Tsay-pita-na-m   kuti-tsi-ya:-mu-__ru__-:-si,*
     that-ABL-NOW-DIR   return-CAUS-PL.V-FAR-__PST.R__-1-EVEN
     'Then I made them (the cows) return.

2   *"Tsay-qa aywa-ku-__Ø__-n-na-chir"   ni-__Ø__-n-mi.*
     that-TOP   go-MID-__PRS__-3-NOW-APP   say-__PRS__-3-DIR
     "Those return by habit" he (my father) said.'

3   L: ... *Tsay-ta.*
        that-OBJ
        'That.'

4   F: ... *Ni-pti-n   aywa-ku-__sha__-tsu-qa   otru.*
        say-DS-3   go-MID-__PST.R3__-NEG-TOP   another
        'Although he said that, one did not go.

5   ... *Ta:yanqocha-la:-pa   ari,*
        tayanqocha-SIDE-GEN   yes
     To Tayancocha Lake, that is,

6   *qeshpi-pa:-ma-__sha__-qa   Huamparan-pita Kachitsinan-la:-pa.*
     escape-BEN-1OBJ-__PST.R3__-TOP   Huamparán-ABL   Kachitsinan-SIDE-GEN
     it escaped from me near Huamparán heading also for Kachitsinan (place of salt).

7   ... *Tsay-la:-chu:-na-sh   punta-ta-si   tari-ya:-__na:__.*
        that-SIDE-LOC-NOW-RPT   first-OBJ-EVEN   find-PL.V-__PST.N__
        In that area (Kachitsinan) we found them on a previous occasion.'

8   L: ... *"Tsay=-pa   kuti-sha:, ‖   aywa-shun" ni-__Ø__-n-chir,*
        that-GEN   return-FUT1   go-FUT₁   say-__PRS__-3-APP
        '"I'll return to that place, let's go" he (the cow) probably said.

9   *"Tsay-pa-m   reqi-__Ø__-:-qa"*   @   *ni-__Ø__-n*   @@@
        that-GEN-DIR   be.familiar-__PRS__-1-TOP   say-__PRS__-3
        "I know that place" he said.'

10   F: *I   ..[ko:rri   ko:]rri   ko:rri,*
        and   running   running   running   __REDUP__ (BARE VERB ROOT)
        'And running running running,

11   L: *[Ura-pa-m],*
                down-GEN-DIR
        'Downward.'

12   F: *punta cha:-mu-sh   na:ni-ta   ichik   yaqa-q-ta*
        first   arrive-FAR-PST.R3 road-OBJ   small   fork-AG-OBJ

        witsa-ypa   tari-__ski__-r-qa,
        climb-ADV   find-__PFV__-SS-TOP
        the first ones arrived, finding a path, a little side path going up.

13   *defrenti   aywa-__ski__-__Ø__-n, ‖   wakin-kaq   hikpa-chu   ke:da-__ski__-__Ø__-n.*
        straight   go-__PFV__-__PRS__-3   other-DEF   behind-LOC   remain-__PFV__-__PRS__-3
        They went straight (immediately) on that path, but the others remained behind.'

14   L: *Kuti-__yka__-__Ø__-n-na   tsay-kaq-qa.*
        return-__CONT__-__PRS__-3-NOW   that-DEF-TOP
        'Those (that remained behind) were returning by then.'

15   F: *Tsay-kaq   kuti-__yka__-__Ø__-n-na,*
        that-DEF   return-__CONT__-__PRS__-3-NOW
        'Those were returning by then.'

16   L: ... *mmm,*
             mmm
        'Mmm.'

17　F:　... *Runa-pa*　　*abe:na-n-kuna-ta-si,* ||　*qashu-tsi-**r***　　　@***usha-ru**-:.*
　　　　　person-GEN　　oats-3-PL.N-OBJ-EVEN　　trample-CAUS-SS　　**finish**-**PST.R**-1
　　　　'I **completely trampled** the owner's oat field.' (*usha-* as a **completive auxiliary**)

18　L:　*We:ra,*
　　　　interjection
　　　　'How awful!'

19　E:　... *Mana-ku Llalli rika-ya:-shu-**ru**-yki?*
　　　　　no-Q.P　　Llalli　see-PL.V-2OBJ-**PST.R**-2ₚ
　　　　'Didn't Llalli see you?'

20　F:　*Mana.*
　　　　no
　　　　'No.'

21　L:　... *Tsay　witsay-pa,* ||　*abe:na-qa　aw,* ||　*mana-m　qarpa-ya-**Ø**-n-tsu?*
　　　　　that　segment-GEN　oats-TOP　yes　　no-DIR　irrigate-PL.V-**PRS**-3-NEG
　　　　'In that area is it true they don't irrigate oats?'

22　F:　*Mana-m　qarpa-ya-**Ø**-n-[tsu　　　ari].*
　　　　no-DIR　irrigate-PL.V-**PRS**-3-NEG　yes
　　　　'No, they don't irrigate.'

23　L:　　　　　　　　　　　　　　*[Tsa=y]-mer,* ||　*haka-ta-qa　　　wanu-tsi-**Ø**-n,*
　　　　　　　　　　　　　　　that-DIR　　　guinea.pig-OBJ-TOP　die-CAUS-**PRS**-3
　　　　'That's why it kills guinea pigs,

24　　　　*tsay　ima-r.*
　　　　that　do.what-SS
　　　　or causes other harm.

25　　　　... *Wamra-:-pa　ha=tun　haka-n　　　pe,*
　　　　　child-1-GEN　big　　guinea.pig-3　so
　　　　My child's big guinea pig,

26　　　　*abe:na-ta　ranti-pa-**yka**-mu-nqa-n,* ||　　　*..wanu-**sh**.*
　　　　oats-OBJ　buy-BEN-**PFV.O**-FAR-NMLZ.R-3　die-**PST.R3**
　　　　—because of the oats he bought for it—it died.'

27　F:　... *Imay-ra:　qarpa-ya-**Ø**-n-na=-si,*
　　　　　when-YET　irrigate-PL.V-**PRS**-3-NOW-EVEN
　　　　'I have no idea when they irrigated.

28   *kanan-kuna-qa,   shikshi-Ø-n shikshi-Ø-n pe,*
           now-PL.V-TOP   spike-**PRS**-3 spike-**PRS**-3 so   **REDUP** (INFLECTED VERB)
           The current ones are in the process of forming spikes (heads).

29   *..Llullu-kaq-ta-na-cha*   *pe*   *qarpa-yka:-ya-Ø-n.*
           baby-DEF-OBJ-NOW-MUT   so   irrigate-**CONT**-PL.V-**PRS**-3
           Now they are watering the tender plants.'

Bibliography

Adelaar, Willem F. H.
- 1977   *Tarma Quechua: Grammar, Texts, Dictionary*. Lisse: Peter de Ridder.
- 1982   Características del quechua de Pacaraos. In R. Cerrón-Palomino, ed., *Aula quechua*, 19-33. Lima: Signo.
- 1986   *Morfología del quechua de Pacaraos*. [CILA Documento de Trabajo 53]. Lima.
- 1988   Categorías de aspecto en el quechua del Perú central. *Amerindia: Revue d'Ethnolinguistique Amerindienne* 13.15-41.
- 2006   The vicissitudes of directional affixes in Tarma (Northern Junín) Quechua. In G.I. Rowicka and E.B. Carlin, eds., *What's in a verb. Studies in the verbal morphology of the languages of the Americas*, 121-41. Utrecht: LOT.

Adelaar, Willem F. H. with Pieter Muysken
- 2004   *The languages of the Andes*. Cambridge: Cambridge University Press.

Aikhenvald, Alexandra Y.
- 2004   *Evidentiality*. Oxford: Oxford University Press.

Anderson, Stephen R.
- 1992   *A-Morphous morphology*. Cambridge: Cambridge University Press.

Axelrod, Melissa
- 1993   *The semantics of time: Aspectual categorization in Koyukon Athabaskan*. Lincoln: University of Nebraska Press.

Berentsen, Adrian and Youri Poupynin, eds.
- 2001   *Functional grammar: Aspect and aspectuality, tense and temporality*. Munich: Lincom Europa.

Bean, Mark
- 1988   *-qtu* less than complete. Ms.
- 1990   *-riyku* y otros sufijos de aspecto en el quechua de Dos de Mayo, Huánuco. In R. Cerrón-Palomino and G. Solís F., eds., *Temas de lingüística amerindia*, 39-56. Lima: Consejo Nacional de Ciencia y Tecnología.

Benson, Bruce
- 1987   Juan U:su. In D.J. Weber, ed., *Juan del Oso*, 87-101.

Benson, Janice
- 1996   El aspecto perfectivo en la narrativa del quechua de Huamalíes. In S. Parker, ed., *Estudios etno-lingüísticos III*, 5-26. [Documento de Trabajo 31].

Berman, Ruth A. and Dan Isaac Slobin
- 1994   *Relating events in narrative: A cross-linguistic developmental study*. Hove, UK: Erlbaum.

Binnick, Robert I.
- 1991   *Time and the verb: A guide to tense and aspect*. Oxford: Oxford University Press.

Booij, Geert
    1996   Inherent versus contextual inflection and the split morphology hypothesis. In G. Booij and J. van Marle, eds., 1-16.

Booij, Geert and Jaap van Marle, eds.
    1996   *Yearbook of Morphology 1995*. Dordrecht: Kluwer.

Bravo, Domingo A.
    1965   *Estado actual del quichua santiagueño*. Tucumán, Argentina: Universidad Nacional de Tucumán.
    1967   *Diccionario quichua santiagueño-castellano*. Buenos Aires: Instituto Amigos del Libro Argentino.

Brown, Penelope and Steven C. Levinson
    1987   *Politeness: Some universals in language usage*. Cambridge: Cambridge University Press.

Bustamante, Isabel
    1991   El presente perfecto o pretérito perfecto compuesto en el español quiteño. *Lexis* 15.2.195-230.

Bybee, Joan L.
    1985   *Morphology*. Amsterdam: Benjamins.
    1994   The grammaticization of zero: Asymmetries in tense and aspect systems. In W. Pagliuca, ed., *Perspectives on grammaticalization*, 235-54. Amsterdam: Benjamins.
    1998   The emergent lexicon. *Chicago Linguistic Society* 34, 421-35.
    2001   *Phonology and language use*. Cambridge: Cambridge University Press.

Bybee, Joan and Östen Dahl
    1989   The creation of tense and aspect systems in the languages of the world. *Studies in Language* 13.1.51-103.

Bybee, Joan L. and Paul J. Hopper, eds.
    2001   *Frequency and the emergence of linguistic structure*. Amsterdam: Benjamins.

Bybee, Joan, Revere Perkins and William Pagliuca
    1994   *The evolution of grammar: Tense, aspect, and modality in the languages of the world*. Chicago: University of Chicago Press.

Calvo, Julio
    1993   *Pragmática y gramática del quechua cuzqueño*. Cuzco, Peru: Centro de Estudios Regionales Andinos "Bartolomé de las Casas."
    2001   Caracterización general del verbo en el castellano andino y la influencia de la lengua quechua. In T. Fernández, A. Palacios and E. Pato, eds., *El indigenismo americano*, 111-30. Madrid: Universidad Autónoma de Madrid.

Camazine, Scott, Jean-Louis Deneubourg, Nigel R. Franks, James Sneyd, Guy Theraulaz and Eric Bonabeau
    2001   *Self-organization in biological systems*. Princeton: Princeton University Press.

Cerrón-Palomino, Rodolfo

1976   *Gramática quechua: Junín-Huanca*. Lima: Ministerio de Educación and Instituto de Estudios Peruanos.

2003   *Lingüística quechua* (Second edition). Cuzco, Peru: Centro de Estudios Rurales Andinos "Bartolomé de las Casas."

Chafe, Wallace

1970   *Meaning and the structure of language*. Chicago: University of Chicago Press.

1980   *The pear story*. Online version: www.linguistics.ucsb.edu/faculty/chafe/pearfilm.htm.

2005   The relation of grammar to thought. In C. Butler et al., eds., *The dynamics of language use: Functional and contrastive perspectives*, 55-75. Amsterdam and Philadelphia: Benjamins.

Chung, Sandra and Alan Timberlake

1985   Tense, aspect, and mood. In T. Shopen, ed., *Language typology and syntactic description*, Vol. 3, 202-58. Cambridge: Cambridge University Press.

Cole, Peter

1982   *Imbabura Quechua*. Amsterdam: North-Holland.

1983   Switch reference in two Quechua languages. In J. Haiman and P. Munro, eds., *Switch reference and universal grammar*, 1-15. Amsterdam: Benjamins.

Comrie, Bernard

1976   *Aspect: An introduction to the study of verbal aspect and related problems*. Cambridge: Cambridge University Press.

1985   *Tense*. Cambridge: Cambridge University Press.

1995   Tense and aspect. In J. Jacobs, A. von Skehow et al., eds., *Syntax: An international handbook of contemporary research*, Vol. 2, 1244-52. Berlin: Walter de Gruyter.

2001   Some thoughts on the relation between aspect and Aktionsart. In A. Barentsen and Y. Poupynin, eds., *Functional grammar: Aspect and aspectuality, tense and temporality*, 43-50.

Coombs, David, Heidi Coombs and Robert Weber

1976   *Gramática quechua: San Martín*. Lima: Ministerio de Educación and Instituto de Estudios Peruanos.

Corbett, Grevelle

1987   The morphology/syntax interface: evidence from possessive adjectives in Slavonic. *Language* 63.2.299-345.

Crapo, Richley H. and Percy Aitken

1986   *Bolivian Quechua Reader and Grammar-Dictionary*. Ann Arbor: Karoma.

Cusihuamán, Antonio

1976a   *Gramática quechua: Cuzco-Collao*. Lima: Ministerio de Educación and Instituto de Estudios Peruanos.

1976b   *Diccionario quechua: Cuzco-Collao*. Lima: Ministerio de Educación and Instituto de Estudios Peruanos.

Dahl, Östen

    1985   *Tense and aspect systems*. Oxford: Blackwell.

    1999   Aspect: Basic principles. In K. Brown and J. Miller, eds., *Concise encyclopedia of grammatical categories*, 30-6. Amsterdam: Elsevier.

Dahl, Östen and Viveka Velupillai

    2005   Tense and aspect. In M. Haspelmath, M. Dryer, D. Gil and B. Comrie, eds., *The world atlas of language structures*, 266-81. Oxford: Oxford University Press.

DeLancey, Scott

    1997   Mirativity: The grammatical marking of unexpected information. *Linguistic Typology* 1.33-52.

Dixon, R.M.W. and Alexandra Y. Aikhenvald, eds.

    1999   *The Amazonian languages*. Cambridge: Cambridge University Press.

Dowty, David R.

    1979   *Word Meaning and Montague Grammar*. Dordrecht: Reidel.

Dressler, Wolfgang U.

    1989   Prototypical differences between inflection and derivation. *Zeitschrift für Phonetik, Sprachwissenschaft und Kommunikationsforschung* 42, 3-10.

Durston, Alan

    2004   *Pastoral Quechua: The history and Christian translation in Peru: 1550-1650*. Vol. 1, Ph.D. dissertation, University of Chicago.

Du Bois, John W.

    1985   Competing motivations. In J. Haiman, ed., *Iconicity in syntax*, 343-65. Amsterdam: Benjamins.

    2007   The stance triangle. In R. Englebretson, ed., *Stancetaking in discourse: Subjectivity, evaluation, interaction*, 139-82. Amsterdam: Benjamins.

    2010   Competing to cooperate: Motivating the grammaticization of complexity. Paper presented at the Conference on Competing Motivations, Max Planck Institute for Evolutionary Anthropology, Leipzig.

Escobar, Anna Maria

    1997   Contrastive and innovative uses of the present perfect and the preterite in Spanish in contact with Quechua. *Hispania*, 859-70.

Escribens, Augusto and Paul Proulx

    1970   *Gramática del quechua de Huaylas*. Lima: Universidad Nacional Mayor de San Marcos.

Estrella Santos, Ana Teresa

    2007   *Estudio del léxico del Ecuador*. Ph.D. dissertation, Universidad Nacional de Educación a Distancia, Madrid.

Fast, Gerhard, Ruby Warkentin de Fast and Daniel Fast

    1996   *Diccionario Achuar-Shiwiar—Castellano*, Serie Lingüística Peruana 36. Lima: Instituto Lingüístico de Verano.

Fischer, Olga, Ans van Kemenade, Willem Koopman and Wim van der Wurff
2000   *The syntax of early English.* Cambridge: Cambridge University Press.
Fleischman, Suzanne
1989   Temporal distance: A basic linguistic metaphor. *Studies in Language* 13.1.1-50.
1995   Imperfective and irrealis. In J. Bybee and S. Fleischman, eds., *Modality in grammar and discourse*, 519-51. Amsterdam: Benjamins.
Floyd, Rick
1996   Sufijos direccionales/aspectuales del quechua. In S. Parker, ed., *Estudios etno-lingüísticos III,* 27-44. [Documento de Trabajo 31].
1999   *The structure of evidential categories in Wanka Quechua.* Dallas: Summer Institute of Linguistics and University of Texas, Arlington.
Forsyth J.
1970   *A grammar of aspect: Usage and meaning in the Russian verb* [Studies in Modern Languages]. Cambridge: Cambridge University Press.
Franck, Harry A.
1917   *Vagabonding down the Andes.* New York: The Century Co.
Fuqua, Deborah
1987   Juan Osito. In D.J. Weber, ed., *Juan del Oso*, 77-85.
Garcilaso de la Vega, Inca
[1609] 1963 *Comentarios reales de los Incas.* Biblioteca de Autores Españoles. Madrid: Atlas.
Garr, W. Randall
1991   Affectedness, aspect, and biblical *'et. Zeitschrift für Althebraistik* 4.119-34.
Geniušienė, E. and V.P. Nedjalkov
2001   Towards a typology of the polysemy of reciprocal markers. In A. Barentsen and Y. Poupynin, eds., *Functional grammar: Aspect and aspectuality, tense and temporality*, 51-65.
Gildea, Spike
1993   The development of tense markers from demonstrative pronouns in Panare (Cariban). *Studies in Language* 17.1.53-73.
Givón, Talmy, ed.
1979   *Discourse and syntax* [Syntax and semantics 12]. New York: Academic.
Gómez, Donato
2000   *Manual de gramática quechua.* La Paz: Ichtus.
Godenzzi, Juan Carlos
1987   Variantes etno-sociales del castellano en Puno. *Allpanchis* 29/30.133-50.
González Holguín, Diego
[1607] 1842 *Gramática y arte nueva de la lengua general de todo el Peru llamada lengua qquichua o lengua del Inca.* Lima: Francisco del Canto (1842 edition, Genoa: Pagano).

[1608] 1952 *Vocabvlario de la lengva general de todo el Perv llamada lengva qquichua o del Inca*. Lima: Francisco del Canto. (1952 edition by Raúl Porras Barrenechea, Lima: Imprenta Santa María; 1989 reprint, Lima: Universidad Nacional Mayor de San Marcos).

Haddington, Pentti
    2005   *The Intersubjectivity of Stance Taking in Talk-in-Interaction*. Ph.D. dissertation, University of Oulu.

Haiman, John
    1994   Ritualization and the development of language. In W. Pagliuca ed., *Perspectives on grammaticalization*, 3-28. Amsterdam: Benjamins.

Hardman, M.J.
    1966   *Jaqaru: Outline of phonological and morphological structure*. The Hague: Mouton.
    2000   *Jaqaru*. Munich: Lincom Europa.

Harrison, Jeff
    2005   *Linguistics research moving in new direction*. An interview of Andrew Wedel. Office of University communications, University of Arizona. Online version: http://uanews.org/node/10823.

Harrison, Sheldon P.
    1976   *Mokilese reference grammar*. Honolulu: University of Hawaii Press.

Haspelmath, Martin
    1996   Word-class-changing inflection. In G. Booij and J. van Marle, eds., *Yearbook of Morphology 1995*, 43-66.
    1999   Why is grammaticalization irreversible? *Linguistics* 37.6.1043-68.
    2002   *Understanding morphology*. London: Oxford University Press.

Hay, Jennifer B and R. Harald Baayen
    2005   Shifting paradigms: Gradient structure in morphology. *Trends in Cognitive Sciences* 9.7.342-8.

Heath, Jeffrey
    1998   Hermit crabs: Formal renewal of morphology by phonologically mediated affix substitution. *Language* 74.4.728-59.

Heine, Bernd
    1993   *Auxiliaries: Cognitive forces and grammaticalization*. Oxford: Oxford University Press.

Heine, Bernd, Ulrike Claudi and Friederike Hünnemeyer
    1991   *Grammaticalization: A conceptual framework*. Chicago: University of Chicago Press.

Heine, Bernd and Tania Kuteva
    2002   *World lexicon of grammaticalization*. Cambridge: Cambridge University Press.
    2007   *The genesis of grammar: a reconstruction*. Oxford: Oxford University Press.

Helasvuo, Marja-Liisa
    2001   Syntax in the making: The emergence of syntactic units in Finnish conversation.
            Amsterdam: Benjamins.
Herminia Martín, Eusebia
    1974   *Bosquejo de estructura de la lengua aimara*. Lima: Universidad Nacional Mayor
            de San Marcos.
Hickey, Raymond
    2005   *Dublin English: Evolution and change*. Amsterdam: Benjamins.
Hintz, Daniel J.
    1992   Pasado y ablativo en el quechua de Corongo. In S. Parker, ed., *Estudios etno-
            lingüísticos III,* 136-46. [Documento de Trabajo 31].
    2000   *Características distintivas del Quechua de Corongo*. Serie Lingüística Peruana
            50. Yarinacocha, Peru: Instituto Lingüístico de Verano.
    2003   The emergence of adverbial clauses in Quechua. Paper presented at the annual
            meeting of the Society for the Study of the Indigenous Languages of the
            Americas, Atlanta, GA.
    2005a   Imperfectivity in Quechua: The status of *-yka:*. Paper presented at the 8th
            Workshop on American Indigenous Languages, Santa Barbara, CA.
    2005b   From directionals to past tense in Quechua. Paper presented at the biennial
            meeting of the International Conference on Historical Linguistics, Madison, WI.
    2006a   Derivational aspect in Quechua. Paper presented at the annual meeting of the
            Society for the Study of the Indigenous Languages of the Americas,
            Albuquerque, NM.
    2006b   La evidencialidad y la co-construcción del conocimiento en el quechua del sur de
            Conchucos. Paper presented at the 52nd International Congress of Americanists,
            Seville, Spain.
    2007   De aspecto a modalidad en quechua: Las categorías gramaticales de 'común
            acuerdo' versus 'obligación'. *Proceedings from the V Congreso Nacional de
            Investigaciones Lingüístico-Filológicas* [CD: Syntax section], 1-11.
    2008   Achkë. In D.J. Weber and E. Meier, eds., *Achkay: Mito vigente en el mundo
            quechua*, 71-8.
    2009   Reordenamiento sintáctico en construcciones verbales analíticas del quechua por
            el contacto con el castellano. *Lingüística* 22.187-201.
    2010   Auxiliation in Quechua: The role of contact within evolution. Paper presented at
            the annual meeting of the Society for the Study of the Indigenous Languages of
            the Americas, Baltimore, MD.
    forth. La historia de *-ski* del quechua: desde espacio hasta tiempo y más allá. In F. Julca
            and G. Solís, eds., *Tras las huellas de la lengua en Ancash*, Serie Lingüística
            Quechua. Lima: CILA, Universidad Nacional Mayor de San Marcos.

Hintz, Diane M.

2003   *Word order in South Conchucos Quechua*. M.A. thesis, University of California, Santa Barbara.

2007a   Duplicación de patrones discursivos: Empleo del perfecto en el castellano que está en contacto con el quechua. *Proceedings from the V Congreso Nacional de Investigaciones Lingüístico-Filológicas* [CD: Language Contact section], 1-10.

2007b   *Past tense forms and their functions in South Conchucos Quechua: time, evidentiality, discourse structure, and affect*. Ph.D. dissertation, University of California, Santa Barbara.

Hoffmann, Carl

1963   *A grammar of the Margi language*. London: Oxford University Press.

Hooper, Robin

2002   Deixis and aspect: The Tokelauan directional particles *mai* and *atu*. *Studies in Language* 26.2.283-313.

Hopper, Paul J.

1979   Aspect and foregrounding in discourse. In T. Givón, ed., *Discourse and syntax*, 213-41. [Syntax and semantics 12].

1982   Aspect between discourse and grammar: An introductory essay for the volume. In P.J. Hopper, ed., *Tense-aspect: Between semantics and pragmatics*, 3-18. Amsterdam: Benjamins.

1987   Emergent grammar. *Berkeley Linguistics Society* 13, 139-57.

2001   Hendiadys and auxiliation in English. In J. Bybee and M. Noonan, eds., *Complex sentences in grammar and discourse*, 145-74. Amsterdam: Benjamins.

Hopper, Paul J. and Sandra A. Thompson

1980   Transitivity in grammar and discourse. *Language* 56.251-300.

Hopper, Paul J. and Elizabeth Closs Traugott

2003   *Grammaticalization* (Second edition). Cambridge: Cambridge University Press.

Howard, Rosaleen

2002   The Tragedia del fin de Atahuallpa as evidence of the colonisation of knowledge in the Andes. In H. Stobart and R. Howard, eds., *Knowledge and learning in the Andes: Ethnographic perspectives*, 17-39. Liverpool, Liverpool University Press.

Howard-Malverde, Rosaleen

1990   *The speaking of history: 'Willapaakushayki' or Quechua ways of telling the past*. London: Institute of Latin American Studies.

Huerta, Alonzo de

[1616] 1993 *Arte de la lengva qvechua general de los Yndios de este Reyno del Piru* (Facsimilar edition), R. Moya and E. Villacís, eds. Quito: Proyecto Educación Bilingüe Intercultural and Corporación Editora Nacional.

Hymes, Dell

1975   From space to time in tenses in Kiksht. *International Journal of American Linguistics* 41.313-29.

Izard, Carroll E.

1977   *Human emotions.* New York: Plenum.

Keller, Rudi

1994   *On language change: The invisible hand in language.* London: Routledge.

Kemmer, Suzanne

1993   *The middle voice.* Amsterdam: Benjamins.

Kindaichi, Haruhiko

1950   Kokugo dooshi no ichibunrui [A Classification of Japanese Verbs]. *Kokugo Kenkyuu,* 15, 48-65.

Kindberg, Eric

1987   Juan el Oso. In D.J. Weber, ed., *Juan del Oso,* 181-209.

Klee, Carol A. and Alicia M. Ocampo

1995   The expression of past reference in Spanish narratives of Spanish-Quechua bilingual speakers. In C. Silva-Corvalán, ed., *Spanish in four continents: Studies in language contact and bilingualism,* Washington, D.C.: Georgetown University Press, 52-70.

Krug, Manfred G.

2001   Frequency, iconicity, and categorization: Evidence from emerging modals. In J. Bybee and P. Hopper, eds., *Frequency and the emergence of linguistic structure,* Amsterdam: Benjamins, 309-36.

Kuryłowicz, Jerzy

1965   The evolution of grammatical categories. *Diogenes* 51, 55-71.

Kuteva, Tania

2001   *Auxiliation: An enquiry into the nature of grammaticalization.* Oxford: Oxford University Press.

Landerman, Peter Nelson

1991   *Quechua dialects and their classification.* Ph.D. dissertation, University of California, Los Angeles.

Larsen, Helen

1976   Los sufijos derivacionales del verbo en el quechua de Ancash. [Datos Etno-Lingüísticos 43]. Instituto Lingüístico de Verano and Ministerio de Educación.

Lastra, Yolanda

1968   *Cochabamba Quechua syntax.* The Hague: Mouton.

Leman, Wayne

1980   *A reference grammar of the Cheyenne language* (Occasional Publications in Anthropology, Linguistic series no. 5). Greeley: University of Northern Colorado Museum of Anthropology.

Leonardi F., José
  1966   *Lengua quichua (Dialecto del Napo): Gramática y diccionario.* Quito: Fénix.
Levinsohn, Stephen H.
  1976   *The Inga language.* The Hague: Mouton.
  1991   Variations in tense-aspect markers among Inga (Quechuan) dialects. In M. Ritchie Key, ed., *Language change in South American Indian languages,* 145-65. Philadelphia: University of Pennsylvania Press.
  2008   Iskay wagchu. In D.J. Weber and E. Meier, eds., *Achkay: Mito vigente en el mundo quechua,* 21-36.
Lewis, M. Paul, ed.
  2009   *Ethnologue: Languages of the World* (Sixteenth edition). Dallas: SIL International. Online version: http://www.ethnologue.com/.
Li, Charles N.
  1991   The aspectual system of Hmong. *Studies in Language* 15.1.25-8.
Lucca, Manuel de
  1983   *Diccionario Aymara-Castellano, Castellano-Aymara.* La Paz: Comisión de Alfabetización y Literatura en Aymara.
Lyons, John
  1969   *Introduction to theoretical linguistics* (Second edition). Cambridge: Cambridge University Press.
  1977   *Semantics,* Vol. 2. Cambridge: Cambridge University Press.
Maldonado, Ricardo
  1999   *A media voz: Problemas conceptuales del clítico se.* Mexico, D.F.: Instituto de Investigaciones Filológicas.
Mannheim, Bruce
  1991   *The language of the Inka since the European invasion.* Austin: University of Texas Press.
Macaulay, R. K. S.
  1978   Review of Comrie (1976) and Friedrich (1974). *Language* 54.416-20.
Marchese, Lynell
  1986   *Tense/aspect and the development of auxiliaries in Kru languages.* Dallas: Summer Institute of Linguistics and University of Texas, Arlington.
Matras, Yaron and Jeanette Sakel
  2007   Investigating the mechanisms of pattern replication in language convergence. *Studies in Language* 31.4.829-65.
Mayer, Mercer
  1969   *Frog where are you?* New York: Dial.
Middendorf, Ernst W.
  1890   *Die einheimischen Sprachen Perus,* Vol. 1: *Das Runa Simi oder die Keshva-Sprache wie sie gegenwärtig in der Provinz Cuzco geschprochen wird.* Leipzig: Brockhaus.

Mithun, Marianne

1990   The role of lexicalization in shaping aspectual systems. In J. Redden, ed., *Proceedings of the 1990 Hokan-Penutian Languages Workshop*, 62-74. [Occasional Papers in Linguistics 15].

1991   The role of motivation in the emergence of grammatical categories: The grammaticization of subjects. In E. Traugott and B. Heine, *Approaches to grammaticalization*, Vol. 2, 159-84. Amsterdam: Benjamins.

1998   The codification of time on the North American Pacific Rim. In Y. Nagano, ed., *Time, Language, and Cognition*, 251-80. Osaka: National Museum of Ethnology.

1999a *The languages of native North America* [Cambridge Language Surveys]. Cambridge: Cambridge University Press.

1999b The status of tense within inflection. In G. Booij and J. van Marle, eds., *Yearbook of Morphology 1998*, 23-44.

2000   The legacy of recycled aspect. In R. Hogg, J.C. Smith, L. van Bergen and D. Bentley, eds., *Historical Linguistics 1995*, 261-77. Amsterdam: Benjamins.

2005   Iroquoian languages. In K. Brown, ed., *Encyclopedia of Language and Linguistics* (Second edition), 6.31-4. Oxford: Elsevier.

2006   Voice without subjects, objects or obliques. In R.M.W. Dixon and A.Y. Aikhenvald, eds., *Changing valency*, 213-36. Cambridge: Cambridge University Press.

Mithun, Marianne and Elizabeth Ali

1996   The elaboration of aspectual categories: Central Alaskan Yup'ik. *Folia Linguistica Europaea* 30.1.2.111-27.

Munro, Pamela

1984   Auxiliaries and auxiliarization in Western Muskogean. In J. Fisiak, ed., *Historical syntax,* 333-62. [Trends in linguistics. Studies and Monographs 23]. Berlin: Walter de Gruyter.

Muysken, Pieter

1977   *Syntactic developments in the verb phrase of Ecuadorian Quechua.* Lisse: de Ridder.

Naumann, Bernd and Petra M. Vogel

2000   Derivation. In G. Booij, C. Lehmann and J. Mugdan, eds., *Morphology*, 929-42. Berlin: Mouton de Gruyter.

Nichols, Johanna

2003   Diversity and stability in language. In B.D. Joseph and R.D. Janda, eds., *The handbook of historical linguistics,* 283-310. Oxford: Blackwell.

Nuckolls, Janis B.

1993   The semantics of certainty in Quechua and its implications for a cultural epistemology. *Language in Society* 22.235-55.

1996   *Sounds like life: Sound-symbolic grammar, performance, and cognition in Pastaza Quechua.* Oxford: Oxford University Press.

Ochs, Elinor and Bambi B. Schieffelin
  1989   Language has a heart. *Text* 9.7-25.
Orconi, Eugenio
  1987   Manuelito, El Oso. In D.J. Weber, ed., *Juan del Oso*, 211-37.
Orr, Carolyn and Betsy Wrisley
  1981   *Vocabulario de Quichua del Oriente.* Quito: Instituto Lingüístico de Verano.
Palmer, F.R.
  2001   *Mood and modality* (Second edition). Cambridge: Cambridge University Press.
Pantoja, Santiago, José Ripkens and Germán Swisshelm
  1974   *Cuentos y relatos en el quechua de Huaraz.* Huaraz, Peru: Estudios Culturales
           Benedictinos.
Park, Marinell, Nancy Weber and Víctor Cenepo
  1976   *Diccionario quechua: San Martín.* Lima: Ministerio de Educación and Instituto de
           Estudios Peruanos.
Parker, Gary J.
  1963   La clasificación genética de los dialectos quechuas. *Revista del Museo Nacional*
           32.241-52.
  1969a   Comparative quechua phonology and grammar II: Proto-Quechua phonology and
           morphology. *Working Papers in Linguistics* 1.1.123-47. Honolulu: University of
           Hawaii.
  1969b   Comparative quechua phonology and grammar III: Proto-Quechua lexicon.
           Working Papers in Linguistics 1.4.1-161. Honolulu: University of Hawaii.
  1969c   Comparative quechua phonology and grammar IV: The evolution of Quechua A.
           Working Papers in Linguistics 1.9.149-204. Honolulu: University of Hawaii.
  1969d   *Ayacucho Quechua grammar and dictionary.* The Hague: Mouton.
  1971   Comparative Quechua phonology and grammar V: The evolution of Quechua B.
           Working Papers in Linguistics 3.3.45-109. Honolulu: University of Hawaii.
  1973   *Derivación verbal en el quechua de Ancash.* [CILA Documento de Trabajo 25].
           Lima.
  1976   *Gramática quechua: Ancash-Huailas.* Lima: Ministerio de Educación and
           Instituto de Estudios Peruanos.
Parker, Stephen, ed.
  1992   *Estudios etno-lingüísticos II.* [Documento de Trabajo 23]. Yarinacocha, Peru:
           Ministerio de Educación and Instituto Lingüístico de Verano.
  1996   *Estudios etno-lingüísticos III.* [Documento de Trabajo 31]. Yarinacocha, Peru:
           Ministerio de Educación and Instituto Lingüístico de Verano.
Payne, Judith
  1982   Directionals as time referents in Asheninca. *Anthropological linguistics*
           24.3.325-37.

Payne, Thomas E.
  1997   *Describing morphosyntax: A guide for field linguistics*. Cambridge: Cambridge
          University Press.
Plank, Frans
  1994   Inflection and derivation. In R.E. Asher, ed., *Encyclopedia of Language and
          Linguistics* 3, 1671-8. Oxford: Pergamon.
Plungian, Vladimir
  2000   Agentive nouns in Dogon: Neither derivation nor inflection? In W. Dressler et al.,
          eds., *Morphological analysis in comparison*, 179-90. Amsterdam: Benjamins.
Quesada, Félix
  1976   *Gramática quechua: Cajamarca-Cañaris*. Lima: Ministerio de Educación and
          Instituto de Estudios Peruanos.
Rice, Keren
  2005   The role of prosody in constraining language change: Word formation in the
          Athapaskan verb. Plenary presented at the biennial meeting of the International
          Conference on Historical Linguistics, Madison, WI.
Sánchez, Liliana
  2004   Functional convergence in the tense, evidentiality and aspectual systems of
          Quechua Spanish bilinguals. *Bilingualism: Language and Cognition* 7.2.147-62.
Santo Tomás, Domingo de
  [1560] 1995 Grammatica o arte de la lengua general de los Indios de los Reynos del Peru.
          Valladolid. [facsim. ed. 1951]. Lima: Santa María.
Sasse, Hans-Jürgen
  2002   Recent activity in the theory of aspect: Accomplishments, achievements, or just
          non-progressive state? *Linguistic Typology* 6.2.199-271.
Schwenter, Scott A.
  1994   The grammaticalization of an anterior in progress: Evidence from a peninsular
          Spanish dialect. *Studies in Language* 18.1.71-111.
Shaver, Dwight
  1987   Juan del Oso. In D.J. Weber, ed., *Juan del Oso*, 29-35.
Shaver, Dwight and Gwynne Shaver
  1992   Diferencias lingüísticas entre el quechua de Lambayeque y Cajamarca. In S.
          Parker, ed., *Estudios etno-lingüísticos III,* 195-214. [Documento de Trabajo 31].
Shaver, Harold
  1996   *Diccionario   nomatsiguenga-castellano,   castellano-nomatsiguenga*.   Lima:
          Ministerio de Educación and Instituto Lingüístico de Verano.
Shibatani, Masayoshi
  2007   Grammaticalization of converb constructions: The case of Japanese *-te*
          conjunctive constructions. In J. Rehbein, C. Hohenstein and L. Pietsch, eds.,
          Connectivity in grammar and discourse, 21-50. Amsterdam: Benjamins.

Shirai, Yasuhiro
    1998   Where the progressive and the resultative meet: Imperfective aspect in Japanese, Chinese, Korean, and English. *Studies in Language* 22.3.661-92.
Shopen, Timothy, ed.
    1985   *Language typology and syntactic description* [Vols. 1-3]. Cambridge: Cambridge University Press.
Slobin, Dan
    1987   Thinking for speaking. *Berkeley Linguistics Society* 13.435-44.
    1996   From 'thought and language' to 'thinking for speaking'. In J.J. Gumperz and S.C. Levinson, eds., *Rethinking linguistic relativity*, 70-96. Cambridge: Cambridge University Press.
Smeets, Ineke
    2007   *A grammar of Mapuche*. Berlin: Mouton de Gruyter.
Smith, Carlota S.
    1997   *The parameter of aspect* (Second edition). Dordrecht: Kluwer.
Snow, Charles T.
    1972   The modal suffix *-skI* in Ancash Quechua. *Papers in Andean Linguistics* 1.1.17-27.
Snow, Charles T. and Louisa R. Stark
    1971   *Ancash Quechua*. Madison: University of Wisconsin.
Solá, Donald
    1958   *Huánuco Guechua* [sic]*: The grammar of words and phrases*. Ph.D. dissertation, Cornell University.
Solís Fonseca, Gustavo
    1986   La lengua culli revisitada. Paper presented at the Séptimo Congreso Peruano del Hombre y la Cultura Andina, Universidad Nacional Santiago Antúñez de Mayolo, Huaraz.
Soto, Clodoaldo
    1976a   *Gramática quechua: Ayacucho-Chanca*. Lima: Ministerio de Educación and Instituto de Estudios Peruanos.
    1976b   *Diccionario quechua: Ayacucho-Chanca*. Lima: Ministerio de Educación and Instituto de Estudios Peruanos.
Squartini, Mario
    1998   *Verbal periphrases in Romance. Aspect, actionality, and grammaticalization* [Empirical Approaches to Language Typology 21]. Berlin: Mouton de Gruyter.
Stark, Louisa
    1985   The Quechua language in Bolivia. In H.E. Klein and L.R. Stark, eds., *South American Indian Languages: Retrospect and Prospect*, 516-45. Austin, University of Texas Press.
Stephany, Ursula
    1982   Inflectional and lexical morphology: A linguistic continuum. *Glossologia* 1.27-55.

Stewart, Anne M.
 1984   Why *-skï*?: A study of verbal aspect in Conchucos Quechua. *Ohio State Working Papers in Linguistics* 29.70-104.

Streitberg, Wilhelm
 1891   Perfective und imperfective actionsart [sic] im Germanischen. *Beiträge zur Geschichte der deutschen Sprache und Literatur* 15.70-177.

Stump, Gregory T.
 1998   Inflection. In A. Spencer and A.M. Zwicky, eds., *The handbook of morphology*, 13-43. Oxford: Basil Blackwell.

Sturtevant, Edward H.
 1917   *Linguistic change*. Chicago: University of Chicago Press.

Swisshelm, Germán
 1974   Apéndice I: Los sufijos de derivación verbal en el quechua de Huaraz. In S. Pantoja et al., *Cuentos y relatos en el quechua de Huaraz*, 471-577. Huaraz, Peru: Estudios Culturales Benedictinos.

Taylor, Gerald
 1979   *Diccionario normalizado y comparativo quechua: Chachapoyas-Lamas*. Paris: Harmattan.
 2000   *Estudios lingüísticos sobre Chachapoyas*. Lima: Instituto Francés de Estudios Andinos.

Thelin, Nils B., ed.
 1990   *Verbal aspect in discourse: Contributions to the semantics of time and temporal perspective in Slavic and non-Slavic languages*. Amsterdam: Benjamins.

Toedter, Christa, William Waters and Charlotte Zahn
 2002   *Shimikunata asirtachik killka: Inka-castellanu* [Diccionario inga-castellano]. Serie Lingüística Peruana 52. Lima: Instituto Lingüístico de Verano.

Torero, Alfredo
 1964   Los dialectos quechuas. *Anales Científicos de la Universidad Agraria* 2.446-78.
 1968   Procedencia geográfica de los dialectos quechuas de Ferreñafe y Cajamarca. *Anales Científicos de la Universidad Agraria* 3.4.291-316.
 2002   *Idiomas de los Andes: Lingüística e historia*. Lima: Instituto Francés de Estudios Andinos.

Traugott, Elizabeth Closs
 1978   On the expression of spatio-temporal relations in language. In J. Greenberg et al., eds., *Universals of Human Language*, Vol. 3. Stanford: Stanford University Press, 369-400.

Underhill, Robert
 1976   *Turkish grammar*. Cambridge, MA: MIT.

Valenzuela, Pilar M.
 2003   *Transitivity in Shipibo-Konibo grammar*. Ph.D. dissertation, University of Oregon.

Vendler, Zeno
  1967   Verbs and times. In Z. Vendler, ed., *Linguistics in philosophy*, 97-121. Ithaca: Cornell University Press. Reprinted from Philosophical Review 1957.
Verkuyl, Henk J.
  1993   *A theory of aspectuality*. Cambridge: Cambridge University Press.
Vlach, Frank
  1981   The semantics of the progressive. In P.J. Tedeschi and A. Zaenen, eds., *Tense and aspect*, 271-92. [Syntax and semantics 14]. New York: Academic Press.
Wang, William S-Y
  1969   Competing changes as a cause of residue. *Language* 45.9-25.
Waskosky, Kristine E.
  1992   *Affixes of Salasaca Quichua: With special attention to derivational affixes which attach to verbs*. M.A. thesis, University of North Dakota.
Waters, William
  1996   Una breve comparación entre los rasgos gramaticales del quichua ecuatoriano del Napo y el quechua peruano del Pastaza. In S. Parker, ed., *Estudios etno-lingüísticos III,* 166-72. [Documento de Trabajo 31].
Weber, David J.
  1987a   El /qa/ del pre-protoquechua. In D.J. Weber, *Estudios quechua: Planificación, historia y gramática*, 35-48. Serie Lingüística Peruana 27. Yarinacocha, Peru: Ministerio de Educación and Instituto Lingüístico de Verano.
  1987b   Regularización de la flexión con los sufijos de tiempo en el Quechua I. In D.J. Weber, *Estudios quechua: Planificación, historia y gramática*, 49-75. Serie Lingüística Peruana 27. Yarinacocha, Peru: Ministerio de Educación and Instituto Lingüístico de Verano.
  1989   *A Grammar of Huallaga (Huánuco) Quechua*. University of California Publications in Linguistics, Vol. 112. Berkeley: University of California Press.
Weber, David J., ed.
  1987   *Juan del Oso*. Serie Lingüística Peruana No. 26. Yarinacocha, Peru: Instituto Lingüístico de Verano.
Weber, David J., Félix Cayco Z., Teodoro Cayco V. and Marlene Ballena D.
  1998   *Rimaycuna: Quechua de Huánuco: Diccionario del quechua del Huallaga con índices castellano e inglés*. Serie Lingüística Peruana 48. Yarinacocha, Peru: Instituto Lingüístico de Verano.
Weber, David and Elke Meier, eds.
  2008   *Achkay: Mito vigente en el mundo quechua*. Serie Lingüística Peruana 54. Lima: Instituto Lingüístico de Verano.
Weber, David and Carolyn Orr
  1987   Juan Ositomanta. In D.J. Weber, ed., *Juan del Oso*, 25-8.
Weber, David and Conrad Phelps
  1987   Okumaripa Watuchin. In D.J. Weber, ed., *Juan del Oso*, 169-80.

Wise, Mary Ruth
   2005   Evolution de raíces verbales en sufijos direccionales y de tiempo-aspecto en lenguas arawakas. *Revista Latinoamericana de Estudios Etnolingüísticos* 10.219-38.
Xiao, Richard and Tony McEnery
   2004   *Aspect in Mandarin Chinese: A corpus-based study*. Amsterdam: Benjamins.
Zagona, Karen
   2002   *The syntax of Spanish*. Cambridge: Cambridge University Press.
Ziegeler, Deborah
   2006   *Interfaces with English aspect: Diachronic and empirical studies*. Amsterdam: Benjamins.
Zoomers, Annelies
   2006   Pro-indigenous reforms in Bolivia: Is there an Andean way to escape poverty? *Development and Change* 37.5.1023-46.

Index of languages and language families

Index of Quechuan languages

Subject index

CPSIA information can be obtained at www.ICGtesting.com
Printed in the USA
BVOW080120161111

276223BV00008B/7/P